BEYOND THE STATE AND POLITICS

Capitalism for the New Millennium

Antony P. Mueller

BEYOND THE STATE AND POLITICS. CAPITALISM FOR THE NEW MILLENNIUM
Copyright © 2018 by Antony P. Mueller. All Rights Reserved.
ISBN-9781717773760
Also available as e-book

All rights reserved. No part of this book may be reproduced in any form or by any electronic or mechanical means including information storage and retrieval systems, without permission in writing from the author. The only exception is by a reviewer and by academics, who may quote short excerpts in a review.
Printed in the United States of America

First Printing: April 2018
Amazon KDP
New edition July 2018

CONTENTS

The Problem
Foreword
Introduction

Chapter I
Beyond the state and politics
Economy and society - State capitalism - Backgrounder: the origins of modern state capitalism – Institutional change – Democracy and capitalism – Projects of transformation – At the crossroads – Outlook

Chapter II
Capitalism
Capitalism in perspective - Backgrounder: Capital - Development stages of capitalism - Capitalism and the state – Backgrounder: Building blocks of modern capitalism - What are capitalists good for? – The stock market without puzzles – Backgrounder: US stock market - Commerce – Monetary economy – Equality is not justice – Origins of Western capitalism – Market process and competition – Backgrounder: Utility, value, and price – Prices and competition – Mass production – Freedom and capitalism – Summary

Chapter III
Wealth creation
The meaning of economic growth – Growth traps - Backgrounder: The rise and fall of parasitic economies - Economics of wealth creation - Backgrounder: time preference - Backgrounder: Interest, consumption, and savings - Value creation and capital structure - The state as an enemy of growth - Creative destruction - Obstacles to innovation - Free trade - Summary

Chapter IV
Socialism
A deadly utopia - Command economy - Backgrounder: Friedrich Hayek on central planning and totalitarianism - Economic calculation - Planned chaos - Marxist errors –

*Backgrounder: Marx theory of the collapse of capitalism – A dream becomes a nightmare
Systemic Misery - Summary*

Chapter V
Interventionism

Fascist roots of interventionism - Origins of modern state capitalism – Rational irrationality - Legacy of interventionism - Backgrounder: Effects of price interventionism - Interventionism and the market process - Employment – Power and economic law – Welfare: more costs than benefits – Healthcare costs – Cost explosion in education - Social policy – Backgrounder: origins of social policy - Missing standards – The chimera of social justice – Backgrounder: concepts of justice - Perpetual financial crisis – Backgrounder: the economics of the public debt - Backgrounder: where does the money comes from? - Capital, savings, and entrepreneurship - Summary

Chapter VI
Economic stabilization

The myth of crisis capitalism – Backgrounder: Stagflation - Backgrounder: Say's Law - Monetary policy - How small crises become big crises – A menu of models – Backgrounder: Survey of business cycle models – No crisis without a preceding boom - What happened in the Great Depression? - Lessons yet to learn - Backgrounder: Misery Index - Backgrounder: the economics of inflation and deflation – The sorrows of central banking – Inflation-targeting – Bailouts and stimuli – The pitfalls of policy-making – The value of money - End the Fed – The crisis of 2008 - Summary

Chapter VII
Anarcho-capitalism

The State and its minions - Voluntary servitude - The age of the individual - What is anarchism? - Concepts - Is Anarcho-capitalism possible? - The struggle for liberty - Death of the gatekeepers - Toward the new world of freedom- Sortition(demarchy) -Agenda - Outlook

Appendix

Anarcho-individualist order - basic concepts
Main types of government failures
Ten fundamental indictments against the State
Principles of economic governance
Principles of anarcho-capitalism
Principles of anarchist individualism

Bibliographical References

Annotated bibliography of anarcho-capitalism (by Hans-Hermann Hoppe)

About the author

LIST OF TABLES AND FIGURES

I. BEYOND THE STATE
Principles of anarcho-capitalism
The position of libertarianism in the political spectrum
Main steps to an anarcho-capitalist order

II. CAPITALISM
Stages of modern capitalism
Types of capitalism
Structural elements of capitalism
Main forces of economic progress
Barter
Monetary exchange
Foundational factors Preference ranking
Determinants of value
Chain of value determination
Chain of determinants of remuneration of modern capitalism
Market process
Cost spiral
Determinants of price
Competitive process
Features of modern capitalism

III. WEALTH CREATION
Savings components
Poverty trap
Determinants of the market interest rate
Cycle of welfare spending and economic stagnation
Main barriers to innovation
Return Matrix of Venture Capital Projects
Dimensions of economic knowledge
Geographical market dimensions
Effects of free trade

IV. SOCIALISM
State Murders by Socialist Regimes 1917-1979
Democides by the Soviet regime
Organizational structure of the centrally planned economy
Command and information chain of a centrally planned economy
Arrow of production
Arrow of valuation
Design defects of socialism

V. INTERVENTIONISM

Characteristics of market knowledge
Lags of policy measures
Types of government intervention
Classical unemployment model
Healthcare spending and life expectancy
Selected consumer goods and wages compared to general price level, 1997-2017
Selectivity of institution and income by study area
Government spending in percent of gross domestic product since 1880
Concepts of justice
Coefficients of public debt
Determinants of the debt coefficient
Central bank balance
Commercial bank balance sheet
Main monetary aggregates

VI. ECONOMIC STABILIZATION

U.S. economic growth since 1870
Deflationary and inflationary gap in Keynesian perspective
Stagflation
Structural deficiencies of the Keynesian economic model
Price-wage-price spiral
Keynesian, monetarist, and neoclassical sequences
Structural defects of monetarism
Velocity of central bank money, 1928-2016
Idealized public debt cycle
Ratchet effect of public deficits and debt
Typology of business cycle models
The Marxist model
Keynesianism
Post-Keynesianism
New Keynesians
Schumpeter's business cycle model
Real Business Cycle Theory
Neo-classical crisis model
Monetarism
Austrian Business Cycle Theory
Capital-based business cycle
Bad policy cycles
New Deal Policies
International Financial Obligations after WWI
International Financial System under Dawes and Young Plan

Kindleberger spiral
Contraction of world trade, 1929-1933
The German economy - economic growth and inflation, 1926-1939
Dimension of the Great Depression
United States. Great Depression – Data 1929-1940
Rothbard's 'Do's and 'Don'ts' in a depression
Components of the misery index
Purchasing Power of the U.S.-dollar, 1913-2017
Global money creation by central banks, 2008-2017
United States. Labor and capital productivity, 1899-1937
Main objectives of macroeconomic policy
Main instruments of macroeconomic policy

VII. ANARCHO-CAPITALLISM

Historical Development Stages of the State
Types of egoism
Time-line of anarchism
Types of anarchism
Dimensions of freedom
Total State
Anarcho-Republic
Rule of the res publica
Institutional structure
Anarchistic individualism
Structure of governance
Sortition in the system of governance
Sortition structure

THE PROBLEM

Over the past two hundred years, technology has transformed human existence more than in the thousands of years before. Now, innovations will change the world more than happened in the past one hundred years.

What took place with manufacturing and basic services will encompass sophisticated workplaces. Job security is a thing of the past. A college degree serves no longer as an insurance policy against unemployment.

The policy agenda of the modern democracy asserts that government could prevent and cure unemployment, economic crises, recessions, depressions, inflation, deflation, and inequality and that the state could provide education, healthcare, and social security for all. The promises of rising incomes and employment dominate the political campaigns. Yet politics has never attained these assertions. In the time to come, the system of party politics will even less so fulfill its claims.

This book shows why the traditional policies have not worked and why they will even less so function in the new millennium. As the author explains, the answer is not more of the old, but that we must eliminate politics and the state. We must do away with the conventional economic and social policies. Not more welfare state and government intervention are the answer but less state and more free capitalism.

The new technologies contain the solution of the problems they present. While technological progress destroys occupations, innovations make the economy more productive. Not growth and jobs are the key to the future but higher productivity.

New tools will make the political apparatus obsolete and allow to privatize the functions of government and of public administration. With the end of party politics and of the monopolistic state dominance, a colossal financial burden falls from the shoulders of the population. Imagine a world where the cost of living is only a fraction of today, and taxes and contributions require only a negligible part of income. With productivity so high that the purchasing power of the salaries would exceed that of today, the anxieties that afflict people nowadays about job security would dissipate.

In contrast to a system of free capitalism and of a stateless society, the contemporary social-democratic, 'liberal' system of governance marches on to more government spending, more public debt, and more regulation. The inner workings of the present system lead to higher taxes and more contributions. Public debt will continue to rise. The endpoint of the existing system of party democracy, social welfare, and state capitalism is not stability, wealth, and liberty but state bankruptcy, misery, and suppression. Without a change to a libertarian order of a stateless society, the road leads to a system where the new technologies will become the deadly instruments of comprehensive state control in the hands of a totalitarian regime.

In order to avoid a new totalitarianism, the answer is more capitalism and fewer politics. Such a libertarian order would do away with party politics through a system called 'demarchy' or 'sortition', which has the legislative body selected by lottery. A political system free of party politics together with introducing a market-based monetary order and the private provision of law and security would minimize and finally abolish the state as a monopolistic organization of dominance. An anarcho-capitalist order would open the way for the new technologies to do away with the avalanche of public policies and regulations and thus eliminate the present system, which is so inefficient, corrupt, unjust, and which is in its essence also undemocratic.

"Capitalism Beyond the State and Politics" highlights in the first chapter the exigencies of a political and economic order beyond the current system of state capitalism, political party politics, and government intervention. The second chapter explains how free capitalism works. The third chapter treats wealth creation, while the next chapters expose wealth destruction through socialism, interventionism, and economic policies. The seventh chapter discusses the structure of governance in a libertarian order and the details of a process of composition of the legislative body by random selection among the members of the constituency. In the appendix, the author provides ten fundamental laws of economics as the guidelines of creating an anarcho-capitalist economic and political order.

"Capitalism Beyond the State and Politics" is an advocacy for free markets. Free capitalism together with the drastic reduction of the state and the abolishment of politics would do away with the financial burdens that afflict the modern citizen. Not state intervention in economic life leads to prosperity. The path to affluence is the withdrawal of the state and the end of politics.

The new millennium will belong to those societies that discard the administrative state and move towards a capitalism that is free of the state and of politics.

The goal of this book is to promote this insight.

The individual chapters reveal the defects of socialism, interventionism, and the futile attempt of managing the economy. The book examines the determinants of wealth creation and the forces that lead to the destruction of prosperity.

The final chapter treats how to do away with the state and with politics and how to establish a private law society.

Each chapter exhibits the shortcomings of the present political structure to live up the challenges.

INTRODUCTION

This book explains that a free capitalism embedded in a minimum state and a free social order is the appropriate economic system for the new millennium. Capitalism does not become better if it becomes more like socialism. In order to gain prosperity, capitalism must become more capitalistic. There is no rational alternative to free capitalism. Those nations that reject the libertarian order of a free capitalism will first stagnate, then decline and wither away into destitution and bondage, while those communities that welcome and foster free capitalism will enjoy prosperity in liberty.

The State has become a burden on the economy. Contrary to the claims, economic policy does not promote stability and economic growth. Interventionism hampers productivity gains and weakens the fulcrum of prosperity.

No complex economy can prosper under the constraints of tribal moral rules. Guided by obsolete principles – such as social justice – the economy becomes fragile and less productive. Yet instead of changing the current economic system towards more capitalism, the reverse has been taking place. Capitalism has become more administrative. We are marching towards socialism, and the price we must pay for this error is growing.

The modern administrative state is active in all sectors of the economy and society. Money is in the hands of the state. As such, the state takes part in each monetary transaction. The public sector is present in the form of taxation, and government plays the role of an economic agent with spending, particularly in areas such as the military, health, pension, and education.

The interventionist state has taken hold of the economy. Yet the government's economic policies themselves provoke many of the evils that they allegedly heal. Instead of smoothing the economic cycle to stabilize the economy and to strengthen the factors that bring about economic growth, the impact of the monetary and fiscal policy weakens and destabilizes the economy. Economic policymakers ignore that fluctuations of the economic activities are natural and indispensable since they show to the entrepreneurs that there are distortions of the capital structure and that business management must, therefore, alter faulty allocations. Economic stimulus policies suppress the crisis signals. Yet these indications - such as the interest rate - are important to inform about how the economy runs and are necessary to incentivize companies to change inadequate projects in due course. When prices, wages, and interest rates do no longer serve as reliable economic indicators, the market mechanisms of adjustment become distorted and the economic operators continue to commit mistakes. Distortions spread throughout the economy and the longer and the more intensive the state intervention has worked, the more difficult it becomes to amend the production structure. The artificial boom which governments instigated, becomes the prelude to the next bust.

A hyperactive policy has prolonged and deepened the crisis during the Great Depression of the 1930s. Massive fiscal and monetary stimuli have not pulled out Japan from its stagnation, which has afflicted this country since the 1990s. After the outbreak of the 2008 crisis, governments and central banks in the United States and Europe have been working to 'boost' their economies. Governments and central bankers claim that expanding government expenditure and by hyper-low interest rates, they averted a new depression. Yet the promised great economic recovery that has not become a reality. With about ten years into the 'recovery', the next deep slump is already waiting.

Guided by the false ideas that the media disseminate, and which form part of the syllabi at schools and universities, the government has become a suppressor of wealth creation. The public discussion of economic growth is full of myths, which excite the public as 'limits of growth'. Yet the growth of the market economy differs from the growth in nature. Economic growth does not mean more of the same goods but signifies new goods, an expanded variety of products, and less expensive goods. We eat, when we become more prosperous, not double portions but the variety of food and the practicability of preparing food improves as we become wealthier. The essence of wealth creation under capitalism is technological progress. The production of books and journals does no longer require the felling of trees but because of the technological progress we can carry whole libraries with us in a pen drive. Technological progress makes not only things cheaper, it comes also along with less use of resources.

It is time to abandon the myths about the state, politics and the economy. The modern political party system is neither democratic nor beneficial to the people. Parliaments are not representative of the people. The current international monetary system does not promote prosperity. To get out of these conundrums, more state and more politics will not help. We need a free society and a free economy. A decisive step to accomplish this goal is doing away with political elections. Modern technology allows the choice of representatives by random selection. A legislative Assembly whose members come into office by lot, even if larger than present parliaments, would cost less than an electoral system, be more representative, and in this sense would be much more democratic. With the length of service limited, the representatives would return to their civil life and their law-making would be free of the evils that come with the present political party system and its politicians whose main aim is the careerism.

***

Politics is an obstacle to wealth creation. Under the political system of the modern party-democracy, only a falsified kind of capitalism exists. The rule of the party democracy undermines the free market economy. In order to arrive at an unrestrained capitalism and to bring about an authentic market economy, there is a need to abolish politics. The less space there is for politics and the less there is government action, the faster a free capitalism will emerge. Such a change has become a necessity because we need an economic system of the highest productivity.

A step on the way to a free society would be, first, to establish a truly representative democracy by randomly selecting the people's delegates. Such an 'aleatory democracy', also called 'sortition', would set the conditions for a new legislation beyond the special interests that dominate a democracy based on elections. A body of randomly selected non-political law-makers would represent the people. Using public money to buy votes and to serve special interest groups to promote political careers would vanish. While the logic of the present system of political elections endorses government spending and more public debt and taxes, a randomly selected parliament would end the use of public money for buying votes. The role of the state would diminish along with the role of politics.

A further step toward free capitalism would be to end the central bank and to do away with the state monetary monopoly. A private monetary system would restrict the latitude of the state to spend. Doing away with a central bank and establishing a free money system would curtail the growth of public debt. The system of governance by political parties allows the deception according to which each citizen could live by the generosity of the state if only the right party would gain the election. A monetary system would unmask this fraud. Under free banking, the state loses its monopoly over the currency. The role of the national currency as the only 'legal tender' would disappear.

The libertarian revolution does not consist in a violent upheaval but comes through insight. Such a revolution requires an experimental approach. The victory of libertarianism does not requisite martyrs. A free capitalism will emerge as the economic system with the highest productivity when the shackles of the modern state will fall.

To some, the turning point to a true capitalism may seem utopian. However, this objection has been valid for all political innovations. The ancient Greeks were talking about democracy, but they could not imagine a society without slavery. The Romans thought it impossible to rule without capital punishment. The monarchy was sacred to the people of the Middle Ages. Just as these beliefs of the past have vanished, today's political creeds that a society needs political parties, state money, state administration, and a public monopoly over the application of force to guarantee justice and security will also disappear.

***

We are at a crossroads. Like the decades of before and after 1800, when the industrial revolution took off, those nations that did not recognize the signs of the time fell behind. The countries, which delayed or missed the industrialization, have suffered the loss of prosperity until our present days. Today, the world faces a similar challenge. Again, we must choose and take a decision. This time it is about more or less capitalism. Less capitalism will lead to socialism - whether or not one would want it - and thus to the misery associated with such a regime. The right way for the 21st century is the choice in favor of free capitalism. The future belongs to those countries that choose capitalism free from the state and from politics as their system of governance.

The triumph of real capitalism entails self-liberation according to which the individual finds himself, becomes his own, and delivers himself from the false dependencies and deceptive duties. Such a new order can only arise through voluntary action from which it derives its legitimation.

I.

BEYOND THE STATE AND POLITICS

> *Finally, one can say it with certainty, the distrust of all rulers, the insight into the useless and wearisome nature of these short-lived struggles, must push people to a completely new conclusion: the abolition of the concept of the state, the abolition of the opposition 'private and public.' Step by step private companies take over the affairs of state: even the toughest remainder left over from the old work of government (the activity, for example, which is to secure the private against the private), will finally be provided by private entrepreneurs."*
> Friedrich Nietzsche: Human: All too human.
> Chapter 10. Item Eight "A Look at the State" (1878)

- *Economy and society* -
- *State capitalism* -
- *Backgrounder: the origins of modern state capitalism* –
- *Institutional change* –
- *Democracy and capitalism* –
- *Projects of transformation* –
- *At the crossroads* –
- *Outlook*

All existing political systems have their anchor in violence. This is also the case with democracy in a state that claims the monopoly over the use of force. Genuine capitalism, in contrast, requires a system of universal freedom and non-violence.

'Anarcho-capitalism' is the name of a governance that has property, freedom, and non-aggression as its first principles. In the political spectrum, libertarianism differs from the classical liberalism and is distinct from the American usage of the word 'liberalism'.

Classical liberalism put the property into the center of its system of governance. Yet the classical liberals were not strict enough in holding up the barrier against the erosion of the property rights. A political order of freedom requires a society with a minimum of state.

Freedom requires uncompromising adherence to the property rights and to voluntary exchange relations. As much market as possible - as little state as necessary refers only to the way. Ultimately, the ideal of anarcho-capitalism is to minimize and to abolish the state as the bearer of the monopoly of violence.

Yet anarchism in the sense of no authoritative force does not mean that order would not exist.

According to the ideal of the liberal order, there will be a legal and a social order in place - only that it will be private. Anarcho-capitalism demands private institutions that take care of internal and external security. Anarcho-capitalism does not promote anarchy but the transform of the state as a public institution into a private legal order.

Economy and Society

An economic order and society neither arise nor do they pass away independent of each other. The question is, which social system and which political order harmonizes best with a productive economic system. A free capitalism cannot develop within a political system dominated by violence. In the past, all political order grew out of violence and came from the systematic application of force. None of the existing systems of governance has produced a free capitalism. There has been no period in history when people could enjoy the full potential of a productive economic system.

Neither the French Revolution nor the American independence movement was peaceful. The Soviets took the government by force. Later, the Soviet Union instituted its vassal governments in Eastern Europe by force. West German democracy emerged from the ashes of the Second World War. The foundation of the Federal Republic of Germany took place as an occupied country under the weapons of the Allied armed forces. The Allies themselves had force as the source of their legitimacy because - be it the American, French, Russian or, as with England, the 'glorious' revolution – each one of these had violence as its springboard.

It has not been possible for a free society to assert itself since there have always been violent movements that have suppressed freedom. A libertarian economic and social order stands at the end of history. It is a seminal change because beginning with the formation of political communities, the motor of societal evolution has been violence. It was only step by step that violence has been brought under control and put aside by the economy as the driving force of development. Under anarcho-capitalism, this process would come to its fruition rejecting aggression in favor of the enthronement of voluntary economic exchange relations. Different from all other forms of governance, the legitimation of a libertarian order and its institutionalization comes from insight and not force.

Not the present 'liberal democracy' marks the end of history, but anarcho-capitalism means the end of the State.

In contrast to other political systems, anarcho-capitalism rests on the strict observance of the principle of non-aggression. Therefore, a libertarian system of governance cannot come into existence through force. In this sense, the libertarian social order stands at the end of the historical political development. It is the political system by default. Libertarianism marks the end of the political evolution after the alternatives have all failed.

The libertarian social order comes into being after it has become manifest that the previous political systems (democracy, monarchy, nobility, fascism, interventionism, communism, military dictatorship, etc.) have failed and will also fail in the future whatever their modifications.

Anarcho-capitalism works as a private contract society.

The principle of personal self-ownership means that all social rules must accord to this principle, and therefore no other instance is legitimate (including the so-called 'right' of the majority) to rule over the individual.

Private ownership determines the right of the individual to use his property, including the goods of production.

An anarcho-capitalist order requires the demise of the state and the de-politicization of society.

Foundational principles of anarcho-capitalism

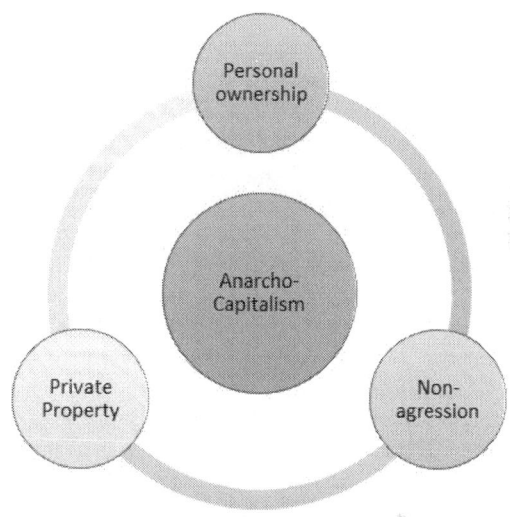

***

An anarcho-capitalist order becomes possible if the alternatives based on violence have lost their legitimacy. Libertarianism demands insight. No longer will be compulsion the way of political action, but political power itself will be subject to reason.

It is up to evolution whether the functions of the state continue as institutions, which are like the known state, and thus the state becomes smaller (the liberal order as a minimum state) - or if new forms of a state-free order will emerge. In principle, there can be free capitalism and a genuine 'rule of, by and for the people' only within an anarcho-capitalist order in which the monopoly of force of the state has disappeared and the political parties have vanished.

Antony P. Mueller

State Capitalism

In the political order of modern democracy, it is the majority vote with the principle 'one man, one vote', which distinguishes this system from the authoritarian forms of government of the earlier times. This political system, however, is a charade, because in democracy, too, the state apparatus prevails in an authoritarian and dictatorial manner. Democracy is not the rule of the majority but a tyranny of minorities. In the exercise of their tyranny, the democratic rulers, apparently legitimized by the majority vote, act as the proprietors of the state not much different from the manners of those who have come into power through violence, inheritance, tradition or charisma. The more the political parties and their leaders usurp the state, the less is the space for free capitalism. Not the people are in power in a democracy, but the leaders of the political parties and the representatives of special interest groups that direct the show behind the curtain.

The recent history of England - as the cradle of modern democracy - demonstrates how classical liberalism has failed. The liberalism of the nineteenth century has perished by the onslaught of party-democracy. As soon as the voting rights comprised persons without property, the days of the liberal order were over. However, England understood to delay this process of erosion. In the United Kingdom, during the 19th century, voting rights broadened to the less wealthy strata of the population. The rule 'one man - one voice' became valid after the third election reform of 1884, and until 1911, the Upper House, as the assembly of the Lords, could still veto the legislation of the Parliament (Lower House), while the suffrage of women in the United Kingdom began in 1928. So long as extending democracy to the masses was at bay, Great Britain flourished. The more the mass democracy took hold, the more the United Kingdom moved toward the slippery slope of economic decline. This fall was not because of the people. The broader the electorate became, the more prominent became party politics, and professional - mostly corrupt - politicians dominated the political game.

The economic systems that prevail in the world of today, even when called a 'market economy', is in the hands of a monopolistic state. In the modern state, there is no place for authentic capitalism and a true market economy. The economic systems of modern democracies are 'corporative capitalism' or 'state capitalism' with plutocratic and populist twists and turns.

Marxists call the present capitalism 'late' and designate the present time as 'post-capitalism' in contrast to the 'early capitalism' of the days of the industrial revolution. However, it is more appropriate to speak of the current system as 'pre-capitalism'. We are still at a stage before high capitalism, which is waiting to emerge.

Capitalist Evolution

After the early capitalism of the 19th century and the state capitalism of the 20th century, free capitalism is about to emerge in the 21st century.

Historical Stages of Capitalism

Early Capitalism (Take-off Capitalism)
- Mobilization of the factors of production capital and labor
- Savings and investment
- Capital accumulation
- Industrial Revolution
- Imperial expansion
- England
- 19th century

State Capitalism
- Systematic organization of production and distribution
- Discipline and control
- Strong link between state and the economy
- USA - Germany - Japan
- Economic nationalism
- 20th century

Full Capitalism
- Entrepreneurial innovation
- Connectivity and spontaneity
- Creative uncontrollability
- Separation of state and the economy
- Production clusters
- 'Digital cities'
- 21st century

***

Unlike state capitalism with its close interdependence between the state and the economy, entrepreneurial capitalism is independent of the state.

As a result, there is a de-politicization of society. Instead of nation and state, local – largely autonomous - production clusters are the centerpieces of the economy.

While capitalism of the nineteenth century aimed at mobilizing the factors of production and national capitalism, the hope for new millennium is that entrepreneurial capitalism will characterize the new epoch.

The creative uncontrollability of anarcho-capitalism will undermine the state's power in a natural way.

The capitalism of the nineteenth-century became global as imperialism and turned into the economic nationalism in the first part of the twentieth century to morph into the globalism of the nation-states in the second part of the 20th century. Now, '*glocalism*' (combining local and global) is emerging in the form of autonomous local units that are world-wide connected. The role of the nation-state makes way to *glocalization* and anarcho-capitalism. Like in the past, these great shifts do not happen without conflicts and setbacks.

'Glocalized anarcho-capitalism' is the socio-economic and political system of the future in contrast to the 'state capitalism' of the past.

Capitalist evolution

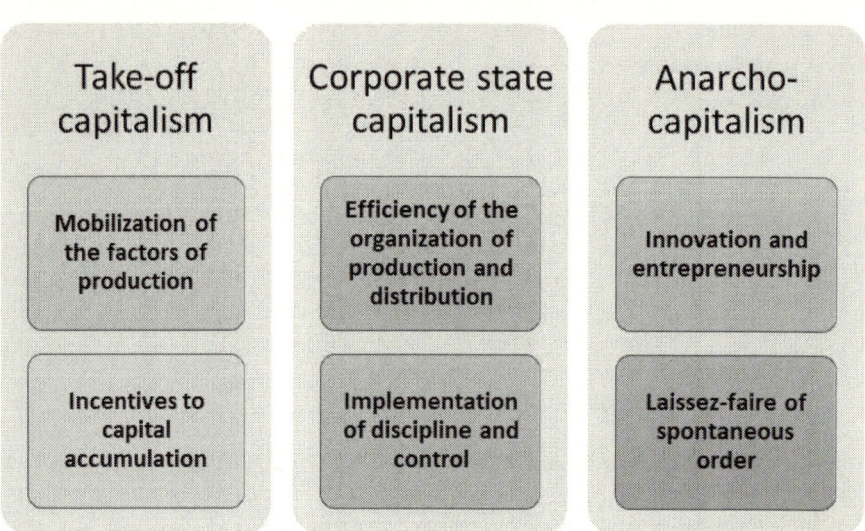

***

The principle anarcho-capitalism asserts that the activities of the state are superfluous and harmful. It is true that the private sector cannot produce best results everywhere and all the time. Yet, the deficiencies of the private economy will not go away with state intervention. On the contrary. The belief that the state could do better than the market is the great illusion of our time. State intervention exacerbates the problems instead of solving them.

There are areas of production, which suffer from economic inefficiencies due to their special characteristics of demand and supply. Yet state intervention does not make supply more efficient nor does it solve the ethical conflicts.

The great illusion that the state could do away with social problems rests on a misconception of the nature of the human problems. Most economic and social problems do not have solutions but only trade-offs. Coping with these problems requires individual valuation and judgment. The state intervention does not resolve these problems but makes them worse. A collective cannot assess trade-offs. Only individuals can evaluate.

That the state still enjoys legitimacy, has three roots:

First, all non-libertarian systems came to power through force. The state as a repressive apparatus appears natural to most people. The uncoordinated and chaotic use of violence which is typical for conquering state-power gives way to the organized system of force under the state. This monopoly of violence of the state should protect against criminals within society, but in fact, it serves to control the behavior of all of its own citizens. The state does not stop with taxation but interferes with the private ways in many forms. Most people accept the authority and follow blindly. Only small groups liberate themselves from the state ideology. Constant propaganda about how necessary and important the state is keeps the thoughts and actions of most people captive in bondage.

Second, authoritarianism and dictatorship are as old as the state. Traditions continue to exist because any alternative does not come to mind as it is 'unthinkable'. Albeit many people recognize the absurdity of the rule of the state and the political madness that surrounds it, they perceive this insanity as normal, because they deem it unavoidable.

Third, special interests mark day-to-day politics and the election process. Many voters are victims of the political propaganda and confound their own interests with the privileges of other groups.

Few people recognize that there is an alternative to state capitalism, democracy, communism, socialism, fascism, and the modern welfare-warfare state. Libertarianism as a new enlightenment changes the public opinion so that the infantile attitude to turn to the state as the universal problem solver will end. Getting rid of politics and the state must disavow the naïve attitude, which assumes as a principle without further ado, that the state can and should and must act as a problem-solver when in fact politics and the state are major sources of our troubles.

Backgrounder:
The origins of the modern state capitalism

State capitalism is a regime where the state exerts direct control over a large part of the economy. It is the preferred system of authoritarian and dictatorial regimes because it facilitates to keep the ruler in power. Yet state capitalism is also compatible with the oligarchical political system of party democracy.

Whatever was left of liberal capitalism vanished in the ashes of World War I in the years from 1914 on. The war economy became the great inspiration for central planning and government control of the economy. In as much as World War I was the womb to give birth to Soviet Communism and Nazism, it is also the cradle of the interventionist welfare-warfare state. In the 20th century, state capitalism with its multitude of variants has become the dominant socio-economic and political system. This system is now in crisis.

The principle of state capitalism is bribery; it is a system which bribes itself to power and keeps itself at the power through corruption. The beneficiaries of corruption range from corporations to trade unions and to the general bureaucracy and to specific state sectors such as the military or the education establishment. State capitalism expands as the welfare-warfare state whereby one or the other tendency may preponderate. Among the varieties of state capitalism, there is the authoritarian and the populist variant, the welfare type and the warfare type, the plutocratic, corporatist and kleptocratic variants and the respective number of combinations.

The American state capitalism concentrates on warfare, welfare, and corporatism, for example, while Switzerland is plutocratic but not biased towards warfare. State capitalism is organized in 'complexes', such as the 'industrial-military complex', the 'pharmaceutical-health complex' and the 'research and higher education complex' among others such as, for Germany, for example, the 'automobile industry complex'.

What differentiates the countries in their economic performance is the degree to which they are competitive or protectionist. Countries such as Denmark and Switzerland share with the US a competitive and open economic system different from Brazil, for example. Brazil has a kleptocratic state capitalism that lacks a competitive economic system and favors protectionism, which moves it closer to Russia or Nigeria in terms of economic performance.

Because it is based on bribery, the system of state capitalism is in permanent financial need. State authorities are desperate to promote economic growth and employment as the sources of state power. Tax receipts are never large enough to finance all the desired public spending. Modern state capitalism must resort to debt financing, which, in turn, makes this system biased towards inflation. State capitalism cannot survive. The great topic of the 21st century will be which socio-economic and political system should replace state capitalism. It is not capitalism that is in crisis, but it is state capitalism that is moribund. In as much as state capitalism has become the dominant system of governance during the past one hundred years, the death struggle of state capitalism marks the great battle of transition to the new libertarian system of free capitalism.

The pivotal event to launch modern state capitalism was World War I. This conflict experienced mass conscription and an outbreak of national fanaticism. It created the 'war is the health of the state' syndrome. World War I was the launching pad for Fascism, Communism, National Socialism, state interventionism, and all other kinds of ideological totalitarianism. World War I and II eliminated the difference between the military and the civil population when governments promoted the total war with the state as the organizer of genocide and democide.

The organizational root of state capitalism is fascism. The "Fascist Manifesto" proclaimed in 1919 by Alceste De Ambris and Filippo Tommaso Marienetti demanded universal suffrage and proportional regional representation of the electorate. The authors called for establishing a corporatist system of 'National Councils' formed by experts who were to be elected by their professional organizations and who should hold legislative power in their respective areas. The Manifesto called for an eight-hour work day and a minimum wage; it demanded worker representation in industrial management and equal standing of trade unions, industrial executives, and public servants. The authors of the Fascist Manifesto called for progressive taxation, invalidity insurance, and other types of social insurance, along with reducing the retirement age, the confiscation of the property of all religious institutions, and nationalizing the armament industry.

The Fascist Program
according to the Fascist Manifesto of 1919
("Il manifesto dei fasci di combattimento")

We demand:

a) Universal suffrage polled on a regional basis, with proportional representation and voting and electoral office eligibility for women.

b) A minimum age for the voting electorate of 18 years; that for the office holders at 25 years.

c) The abolition of the Senate.

d) The convocation of a National Assembly for a three-years duration, for which its primary responsibility will be to form a constitution of the State.

e) The formation of a National Council of experts for labor, for industry, for transportation, for the public health, for communications, etc. Selections to be made from the collective professionals or of tradesmen with legislative powers and elected directly to a General Commission with ministerial powers.

For the social problems: We demand:

a) The quick enactment of a law of the State that sanctions an eight-hour workday for all workers.

b) A minimum wage.

c) The participation of workers' representatives in the functions of industry commissions.

d) To show the same confidence in the labor unions (that prove to be technically and morally worthy) as is given to industry executives or public servants.

e) The rapid and complete systemization of the railways and of all the transport industries.

f) A necessary modification of the insurance laws to invalidate the minimum retirement age; we propose to lower it from 65 to 55 years of age.

For the military problem: We demand:

a) The institution of a national militia with a short period of service for training and exclusively defensive responsibilities.

b) The nationalization of all the arms and explosives factories.

c) A national policy intended to peacefully further the Italian national culture in the world.

For the financial problem: We demand:

a) A strong progressive tax on capital that will truly expropriate a portion of all wealth.

b) The seizure of all the possessions of the religious congregations and the abolition of all the bishoprics, which constitute an enormous liability on the Nation and on the privileges of the poor.

c) The revision of all military contracts and the seizure of 85 percent of the profits therein.

Source: Conservapedia

***

Since its inception, fascism was the main rival of communism with the question open which creed offered the better or rather the worse kind of socialism.

In 1922, Benito Mussolini came to power in Italy and put into practice most of the fascist program that he proclaimed. Adolf Hitler came into government in Germany in 1933 and installed a more radical version of the fascist program which included also a genocidal agenda. In the developing world, Brazilian President Getúlio Vargas (President from 1930 to 1945 and from 1951 to 1954) was inspired by both Mussolini and Hitler and introduced a vast arrangement of protective labor laws which gained him the support of the labor unions and the working class. Vargas established the Brazilian version of fascism.

Argentina adopted a kind of personalized fascism in the form of Peronism after World War II. Juan Domingo Peron became president in 1946 and set Argentina on the path of what can be called 'populist fascism'. General Francisco Franco established a fascist state in Spain in 1939 after winning the civil war (1936-1939), and Antônio de Oliveira Salazar established an authoritarian regime with strong fascist tendencies in 1933. Japan established a fascist regime in 1931, and China under Chiang Kai-shek in 1932.

By the early 1930s, fascism had become a global movement. Hitler succeeded with his economic program in doing away with mass unemployment. While the depression ravaged on in the United States, unemployment fell in half by 1935 in Germany and the country approached full employment by 1936, the year when John Maynard Keynes published his theory on how to overcome depressions. Government programs to stimulate the economy was the trademark of the Hitler regime. All he had to do for that purpose was to implement the plans in the drawers of the state bureaucracy of the governments before him. These plans were not put into practice because of the depression. Hitler's ploy was to launch the government programs combined with price and wage controls. This way the inflationary consequences of Hitler's economic policy remained hidden. In the United States, state capitalism experienced a heyday when president Richard Nixon implemented price and wage controls in 1971. This time, the policy's name was 'incomes policy' and received its blessing from Keynesian economic theory

Compared to the times of relative laissez-faire during the 19th century, the 20th century up to the present has been the era of national-socialism and international socialism and its manifold variations.

Modern state capitalism received its characteristic shape and contents in its fascist period. One might even say fascism has never ended but instead transmogrified into its present subtle forms. Yet in terms of its interventionist, anti-liberal character, modern state capitalism is not much different from its predecessor. In the modern state capitalism, the social claims of fascism are obvious although its nationalist and xenophobic strains were tamed and re-channeled into less deadly endeavors, such as international sports events.

After World War II, an expanding state capitalism has gone hand in hand with the spread of social democracy, which has become the dominant political ideology of the modern state. Social democracy or what is called 'liberalism' in America, is the soft mixture of both Communism and fascism. Almost each major political party, even if they do not have 'social' or 'democratic' in their name, profess the values of social democracy. Social democracy (or 'liberalism' as in the United States) is the unifying band across the mainstream political parties. It makes often only a minor difference whether the more 'right' or the more 'left' party forms the government.

In hindsight, fascism and Communism appear as the radical variants of the social democratic mainstream. It is, therefore, no surprise that both extremes still lurk behind the veil of tamed social liberalism - always ready to move into prominence.

Once it became accepted that the *raison d'être* of 'the state' would be to provide 'social justice' and 'social security', the classical liberal notion that government activity has limits had to make room for unbound state activity because different from hunger and shelter, for example, 'social justice' does not have a natural saturation point. While in the 19th century, it was the defense of liberty that served as the norm to limit state activity, this criterion has disappeared in favor of comprehensive 'rights'.

The 20th century experienced the rise of the social democracy as that political movement whose major plank is the claim of distributional rights, such as the right to work, the right to holidays, the right to social security, the right to free education, and so on with the expanding social rights agenda for so-called minorities. Equality is the battle cry of this movement.

Major steps in the project to establish the interventionist welfare state and state capitalism came with the rise of international organizations after World War II such as the United Nations, the International Monetary Fund, and the World Bank. Regional advances were made by creating the European Economic Community in 1957 and launching a common European currency in 1999. The warfare side of post-war state capitalism experienced a major advance with NATO and the Warsaw Pact during the Cold War. By these steps, state capitalism has become international and more efficient – both in its military and economic prowess. In as much as capitalism has become more productive after the end of World War II, national and global institutions have grown to control capitalism and shape it in a way that optimizes its capacity to serve as a host for the parasitic state activity.

Yet one cannot ignore the signs that the social democratic age including its two radical manifestations of fascism and communism is ending. Free capitalism and a libertarian political order now is the natural way to go. It is only due to tradition and lack of imagination that holds the people back. Rather than moving forward to the new system, some groups even favor one or the other of the radical variants of social democracy although no one with a sane mind could be in favor of either fascism or communism.

Institutional Change

The course of history follows not a pre-determined path but depends on the decisions we make. However, the presence is connected with the past because the current circumstances are the result of past decisions and events. The past is gone yet relevant insofar as it has determined our present situation. Beyond that, we must take new decisions at every moment. While the presence results from the past, the future is the effect of our present decisions. That the presence follows from past does not mean that the past determines the decisions we shall take today. This also holds for political institutions.

It is true that the current situation is the outcome of what has been decided before under the circumstances that then prevailed. While, of course, one cannot change the past, it is not so that the past would determine the future. Although we are free to choose institutions, we are not free from the consequences that follow from our decisions. Because history could have been different as it was, so our present situation and our future can be different as well.

In politics and society, there is freedom to choose specific institutions, yet each decision has its proper consequences. Each institution unfolds its own dynamics. A society may be free what institution it chooses but once an institution is in place, it becomes 'a fact' in social life. Institutions differ from 'culture'. What distinguishes North Korea from South Korea is not its culture but the institutions in North and South Korea.

No individual and no society are bound by 'culture' or 'tradition' but only by the belief in culture or tradition.

Each state constitutes itself as a monopolistic enterprise to apply force. The state as such, as we know it, suffers from the evils that come with a single provider. A monopoly, be it a private company or the state, is inefficient, resistant to innovation, and released from constraints to care for its customers. With the state, it is worse because the state has the monopoly of violence. The state, as the holder of the 'legitimate' physical force, is an attraction to psychopaths of all kind and to all those who seek power to satisfy their craving for dominance over other people's lives. What is political history but the story how bizarre men and women have conquered and abused their powers?

State supremacy, which exists as a monopoly in domestic politics, also drives their holders to extend their sphere of dominance to other countries. Throughout history, peaceful times and good rulers have been only short breaks in an ongoing tragedy, in which one wretched creature after the other at first tries to dictate over his countrymen and then strives to rule the world. The 'grip on the world power' comes to every political leader. Only resistance from other groups can keep these power-hungry madmen at bay. If this resistance fails, the monopolistic state goes berserk. With the state apparatus at his hand, the leader receives the arsenal of the public propaganda tools. The ruler of a country can manipulate the popular opinion and incite one nation to go to war against another without rational cause. International politics exceeds the madness of domestic politics.

The theorists who study parliamentary democracy say that the competition among political parties and the division of powers could keep state violence in check and hold its abuse under control. Yet there is abundant evidence that modern democracy offers no solution to the conundrum of the monopoly of the power of the state.

One can imagine how a free social order will work. With all the other systems of governance, it is the opposite. These ideologues do not know how their plans will work in reality but they are keen to install it anyhow. The Communists, for example, did not know how socialism could ever function, but they were resolute in their desire to get there - and be it by brutal force. The difficult task for the libertarians is to find out how to establish a non-aggression order when force is out of the question. The anarcho-capitalist worldview differs from the other political ideologies that the libertarians follow the principle non-aggression.

Different from libertarianism, the radical parties of the right or the left and even those of the center, can always opt for violence to establish and preserve their favored order. While the non-libertarian political movements want to seize power to exercise it, anarcho-capitalism wants to minimize the role of force and supremacy in society.

Democracy and Capitalism

The political election campaigns in the popular democracies consist in a competition among political parties about which party will promise the best to specific groups. An election in a democracy is about slogans and half-truths. There is a competition between parties, but the persons who represent these parties form a kind of band of their own. The modern politicians are apart from the people – not much different as it once was the case with the aristocracy. This separation comes with the use of force. The authority over violence sets the rulers apart from the ordinary people.

Modern democracy suffers from the contradiction that while most citizens mistrust the politicians and the state, and want fewer taxes and less state control, each voter is eager to use his vote in such a way as to get the largest piece of the cake. Such a system is neither democratic nor capitalist; it is corrupt as it produces a political game in which each voter tries to cheat all the other voters. The principle of modern democracy is that while the voters try to cheat one another in getting a free lunch, the political establishment cheats all of the voters.

The dominant system in the industrialized countries of today is neither capitalist nor democratic but the rule is 'state capitalism'. It has surfaced in the beginning of the 20th century and over the century it has transformed from authoritarian to democratic fascism. No longer prevails an authoritarian one-party system but in the modern democracy, people are in power who form a network which, although they take part in a competitive game with each other, do so together as a group. This democracy operates like a one-party system with various factions.

The results of an election about who forms the government gets decided at the margin, which means the great bulk of the leading members of the party that lost an election will not leave politics but stay on as the opposition and continue in the power play. Different from a bankrupt company which vanishes from the market, in politics, the losers of an election remain in the game and continue their activity – be it as members of the opposition or as coalition partners for the party that has 'won' the elections. Other than their role in the game, nothing has changed.

Under the conditions of the ruling fiduciary monetary system and the existing majority voting right, the current system does not move towards a free market economy even if most people should want so. Instead of an anarcho-capitalist order, there is a tendency to an interplay between left- and right-wing populism, between short pauses of peace and the return of terror and violence. In this sense, all modern parties in a democracy are social-fascist parties and the modern state is a democratic social- fascist state.

Libertarianism in the political spectrum

The political left, as well as the political right, recognize the authoritarian state power. In contrast to libertarianism, personal freedom of the individual is not their focus on the political value scale, but the state.

While 'The Left' refers to 'society' for legitimacy, 'The Right' reclaims as their legitimation basis 'the nation'.

The position of libertarianism in the political spectrum

"The Left"	Libertarianism	"The Right"
• Authoritarian state power • Society • Universal welfare state • International socialism	• Personal liberty • Individual • Economic freedom • Decentralization	• Auhoritarian state power • Nation • National welfare state • National socialism

In contrast to these two positions, the individual is at the center of political values for fundamental liberalism.

The leftist movements strive for a universal welfare state while right-wing political parties advocate a social state of a national character.

Libertarianism, in contrast, rests on economic freedom.

International socialism is the ultimate organizational aim of the left while the right is striving for National Socialism.

The political organizational ideal of libertarianism is the city-state or the regional minority, in contrast to the national greatness of the right and the internationalism of the left.

In order to arrive at a libertarian governance without violence, public opinion must change. Libertarianism has to offer visions and models to explain what is going on and can transform the public opinion in favor of a libertarian future. For this purpose, radical anarchist models are inappropriate. It is necessary to convince the public about the practical feasibility of libertarianism and to show that anarcho-capitalism is not only a theory, but practical and just. Beyond that one cannot and must not plan the transition to libertarianism. Its institutions must come about as a spontaneous order. A libertarian order is conceivable, and one can describe and explain how it does work, but the way to its realization must be evolutionary and spontaneous. Different from other political concepts, public opinion must not follow the lead, but for libertarianism, public opinion itself must be the leadership. Not violence and grand plans provide the path to a libertarian order, but a series of practical steps that provide the basis for a free society to unfold.

Antony P. Mueller

Projects of Transformation

Not for their establishment, but for their preservation, the political system needs the approval of public opinion. Power never exists as a crude force alone. State power dominates and falls with its legitimacy, which comes from the approval of public opinion. The great dictatorships of the twentieth century received their position of power from the belief in certain ideologies. Not the brutal violence made their rule possible, but the consent of the masses allowed the governments to use brutal force. Today, the belief in democracy as majority rule dominates the mindset of the population and forms the basis of legitimacy of this system. Yet democracy in the form of the majority voting system leads to interventionism, and from there, socialism is only a step away. Democracy does not protect against folly or tyranny.

How can one redesign the political system towards more freedom? In the first step, one must deprive the existing system of 'liberal' democracy of its false legitimacy and to show the alternative.

A false legitimation relates, first, to money. Habit and lack of knowledge are the reasons that for many people there is no alternative to the present system although there is a lot of uneasiness with the monetary order. In the modern economy, the state has the monopoly over money. Yet why this is so, there is no rational answer. With the national central bank, the state has a central command body over the financial system. This monetary system rests on centralism and monopolism. Central banking stands in opposition to the free capitalism.

The members of the central bank are among the most important holders of power. They come into these positions on intricate and opaque paths. Like the Constitutional Court, the members of the Central Bank are appointed. In the same way, as the supreme judges act as masters of the Constitution by pretending to protect them, the members of the central bank are the masters of the money system and claim to preserve the value of money. Not different from the 'protectors of the Constitution' as masters of constitutional transformation, the central bankers - as proclaimed 'guardians of our currency' - are the main culprits of the monetary havoc and the financial crises that have afflicted capitalism. In monetary matters, central bankers rule over the economy like a Soviet central committee. How these members of the uppermost power elite come into the respective positions remains hidden, and what they do is frightening.

The failure of the central bankers is no less apparent than the problem with the disgraceful verdicts of the supreme judges. The central bankers are responsible for the big economic catastrophes of the twentieth century: the hyperinflation of the 1920s in Germany and the Great Depression of the 1930s in the USA. The stagflation of the seventies is the produce of the mismanagement of central bankers as well as the financial crisis of 2008. Over the next ten years, the combined efforts of the central banks of the US, Japan, and Europe have instigated the largest speculative bubble the world has ever seen. By implanting interest rates that are below any reasonable level, central bankers have fueled a global speculative frenzy of gigantic proportions. Nevertheless, the media put the blame on 'capitalism', and praise central bankers and finance minister as the 'saviors' of the system. The public gets deceived by the pundits in academia and the media who praise the wolves as the guardians of the sheep.

The task is to reform the monetary system and to curb the national debt and to get to a real democracy. The existing monetary regime is a state-political instrument for the exercise of power, which allows the unrestrained expansion of the welfare state, war-making, and to accumulate public debt. A new monetary order is a decisive step towards the new economic order. The change of the system can come within the framework of the prevalent legal basis. Abolishing the state monopoly on money and to recognize private money as a means of payment is the way to start the reform of the monetary system. The point is to give back to the citizens the freedom of monetary choice over which currency to use. Economic actors should be free to decide which money they would like to have for their transactions.

As a first step, one must eliminate the prime position of the central bank as a central planning body. This can be done by imposing a limit on the quantity of the central bank money. If the central bank no longer has access to manipulating the money supply, it can no more manipulate the basic rate of interest. After that, it should be easy to phase out the central bank as a public institution by sending the officeholders into retirement. This measure would eliminate the main source of cyclical turmoil. Freezing the quantity of central bank money will put a brake on the government to accumulate debt and thus also help to neutralize the role of governmental interventionism as the other main source of creating economic havoc besides central banking.

***

As a second step, the plan comes into play of reforming the electoral system and to do away with the political class. Ending the current electoral system of majority vote in favor a a lottery for selecting the representatives of the people, would eliminate party politics and the professional politicians. With the modern means of communication, it is possible to select a representative body of the population by random sampling. According to this model of the political lottery, the members of this group would form the Legislative Assembly. Such an Assembly would be participatory and representative. Selecting the people's representative by lot would be also cheaper than the election campaigns and to maintain parliaments and congresses in their present forms. This Assembly would then hire private government management companies - to exert the function of government under the strict supervision of the Assembly.

In the United States, the Freedom Movement could push for this election model in individual states and from there the movement could spread across the country until after a phase of experimentation it could serve for the election of the members of Congress. In Europe, one could start with the city councils of the metropolitan areas. As a transitory method, one could also consider forming a kind of 'Upper House' or 'Senate' by the random selection of its members. This House would oversee the actions of the members of Congress and be the ultimate body of the approval of the laws. This assembly should have full veto power over new laws. The assembly would be composed of members who are selected by a rolling lottery with each member serving for two years has many advantages over the present system.

Private government management companies would emerge on competitive markets and offer their services first at the municipal and the state level and from there comprise larger entities up to the level of a country or a union of states. Private government management companies would be in the business to earn a profit and as such they must satisfy the demands of their client (which is the people represented by the Assembly) at the lowest cost.

Such a system would lead to the following consequences (for more detail see the last chapter on 'anarcho-capitalism':

First, serious policymaking in favor of the best for the population would replace the current political game plays that serves special interest groups.

Second, the random selection system would bring a wide range of expertise to the political system.

Third, the members of such an Assembly would not be power-hungry psychopaths and political careerists because, after their short period of life in politics, these persons would return to their private life.

Finally, such legislative procedures would give priority to cut government spending and to lower the tax burden because the members of the Assembly will be the ones who must pay for them.

One may expect that with 'demarchy', government spending will fall, taxes will be lower, and bureaucracy will be less.

The third project treats the legal and the security system. At present, the judicial order is contradictory since the judiciary itself is part of the political system about which it decides. To speak of the 'independence' of the courts is as unrealistic as to claim that the central banks are independent. The state-jurists praise the division of power, yet their existence proves otherwise and underlines that to realize the principle is impossible and exists only as a myth.

De-politicization, de-bureaucratization, and the private organization of justice, as well as internal and external security, are the mainstays on the way to establish a libertarian economic and social order.

Doing away with the professional politician, and of party politics, comes with the electoral reform that stipulates the selection of the legislative assembly by the principle of chance.

***

Main steps to an anarcho-capitalist order

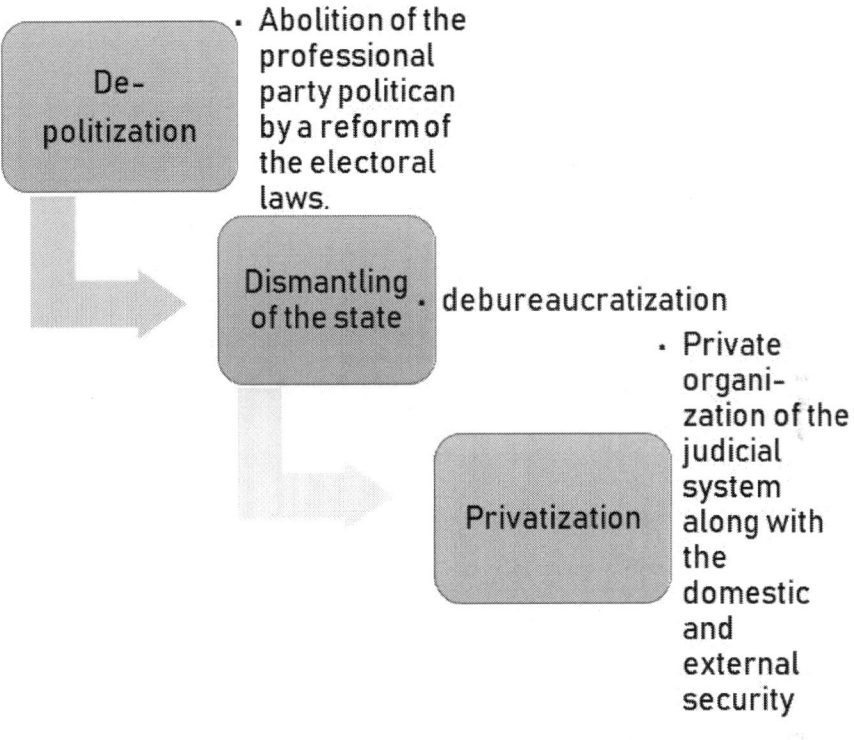

***

The legislative body will promote the de-bureaucratization of the state. Finally, the private organization of justice and internal and external security comes into existence.

In the modern political state, the division of powers is a fallacy, for the political parties are not only present in the legislative body but are also in government as well as they appoint the judges, including the members of the Constitutional Court. A state legal system is not independent as it exists in close ties to the prevailing power structure. All moral aberrations of the Zeitgeist sneak into the jurisprudence: from the local jurisdiction to the constitutional courts. There has been no perversity on this earth which was not legal at some time and with which the courts did not collaborate.

Not only the United States suffers from the discrepancy between the value system prevalent at the courts and that of the population. The loss of trust in the law has become as severe as the loss of confidence in politics.

A private system of jurisprudence would end with the exercise of the authority of the public judiciary over the people. A private legal system would cost less, be more effective and it would be more just. Artificial intelligence would come to its full potential under a private legal system and cut expenses for legal services to a small fraction of what it costs now.

At the Crossroads

Populist interventionism is the most widespread economic system. The countries differ by whether they are more active or less active in interventionism. Money is under the control of the state. The state mingles in the economic transactions through taxation. While some sectors are more under state control than others, the visible consequence is that these sectors where crises persist – such as the internal and external security, healthcare, old-age provision, education, money, and finance – are those, which are under the most intensive governmental control. A huge apparatus of subsidies sustains at huge costs the defense industry, the automobile sector, pharmaceuticals companies, large parts of the agricultural, and educational institutions.

***

Although the great debate no longer takes on the alternative between socialism and capitalism, the central question remains: whether society should move more to state intervention or more to a market economy. This way, the traditional question of socialism or capitalism is still on the table.

History does not have an inevitable path of development, but there are economic laws. The decision for this or that version of the economic system is free, but the consequences are not free to choose. Freedom refers to the choice of institutions, not to their consequences.

In this sense, there is a power of ideas, and at the same time, there is the impotence of ideas in the face of facts. There are situations where, as they say, that one cannot change the things anymore. Before one made the wrong decision, the options were open as they laid on the table. A different choice could have avoided the problems that have surfaced now as consequence of the wrong decision and the course of history would have gone in another direction.

As in the 1930s, socialist ideas can conquer the United States again as they did get hold of Europe since the beginning of the 20th century.

There is a tendency to choose socialism without considering what consequences will come with this choice. Emotions and prejudices are behind why socialism remains attractive. Despite its evocations of science, socialism is a fairy-tale for adults. Following their creed, the socialists dream of a society where righteousness and prosperity rule together with equality of all.

The infantile socialization of the upbringing reinforces the biological disposition for socialism because children and adolescents live under the socialist systems of the family, the schools, and the university until they are grown-up and often remain under the socialist spell for the rest of their lives.

It is through the efforts of the reason it becomes possible to free oneself from the socialist faith. The first step to deliverance from the socialist creed is the insight that not redistribution helps the poor, but rather economic growth and a free capitalism, which increases productivity and income.

Ironically, it was the success of capitalism that created the socialist expectation of a world without scarcity. The capitalist experience showed that a prosperous world was no longer a utopian fantasy.

The early socialists were convinced that socialism would increase the productivity of capitalism not despite but because of the equality of distribution. In the socialist paradise, one could have a greater material abundance than under capitalism along with the eradication of all kinds of injustices and discriminations. Socialism arises from the desire for the kingdom of Cockaigne. The driving motif of the early socialist movement was idealism. Today, this utopian system promises to the gullible that the smartphone comes free of charge, along with a free public transportation system and the purchase of a generous citizen's pension, as well as, of course, a guaranteed minimum income and free education and healthcare of the highest standards for all.

Some in the socialist movements find their way to socialism out of a personal need for social justice or based on religious motives. Among the wealthy and the rich heirs, there are socialists because of a bad conscience about their wealth. Yet the dream of a fair distribution is a great illusion.

First, the amount to distribute would be less than many socialists believe. For example, if the billionaires in the Forbes list would share all their wealth with the rest of the world's population, every single person on earth would receive no more than the single payment of an amount of the size of a moderate monthly salary of the workmen in the rich countries.

Second, even if the current billionaires would agree to this plan, they could not do so because their wealth does not consist in money but in shares and other business interests and in real estate. To distribute the money, the owners would have to sell these assets. Yet if they sell, who will buy?

Third, if one should want to apply a more drastic measure in the name of social justice and one would distribute by force the wealth of the world equally, it would take a short time, and a new uneven distribution would soon come back into existence, with the additional consequence that the overall poverty in the world would have become greater in the process.

If the redistribution in capitalism does not work, so some seem to ponder, only to impose full socialism will solve the problem of 'injustice'. In doing so, these socialists believe that they are good-hearted when they advocate socialism, yet they do not know that they speak in favor of an inhuman regime whose first victims by all probability would be themselves.

The great ideological battle continues in waves, although millions of people fell victim when the socialist terror regimes dominated the conflicts of the 20th century. History has shown that socialism in its international Soviet variant and in its national-socialist form can only exist through as tyranny. With the decision for interventionism and socialism, economic stagnation comes with this choice. In contrast, with the decision for a free market economy, the choice leads to economic progress. Theories and history show that socialism brings a compulsory economy and leads to stagnation, suppression, and poverty while capitalism is more productive the freer it is.

The 21st century will belong to those nations that choose the path to free capitalism while those countries that opt for socialism and interventionism will suffer economic stagnation and decline.

The alternatives are clear. On the one hand, free capitalism as an economic order that brings with it personal liberty and overall prosperity, and, on the other hand, the socialist command economy, leading to poverty and imprisonment.

A look at the experiences with the Communist rule in Eastern Europe and Asia and in other parts of the world makes the diagnosis unambiguous. Yet, instigated by insistent propaganda, popular discontent runs against the capitalist economic order. The media create the illusion that one could have both the wealth of capitalism and the supposed socialist equality and justice.

Socialism of the twentieth century is no longer the dominant ideology of our time, but anti-capitalism is still virulent, and this ideology is all over in the media, the schools, and the universities. The great error of the socialist is to believe that that poverty originates from capitalism and not from the interventionism that they themselves preach and practice. It should be obvious to everyone that socialism in all its variants is not a solution but a highway to hell. Communism has abdicated, but it has impregnated a powerful backstage in the form of poisonous anti-capitalism. Socialist desires are still virulent. It is dormant in many heads and often benign in its present forms, yet the socialist monster and Communist suppression can rise again at any moment.

This time, the regimes of terror would have a gigantic arsenal of modern technology at their disposal. Future dictatorships would be able to cement their power in a degree which was unheard of from the past. In this sense, the option for anarcho-capitalism is a choice for life over death.

Outlook

It would be a misunderstanding to characterize the libertarian order as 'anarchistic' in the sense of chaos and disorder. On the contrary. Anarcho-capitalism is the opposite of anarchy, mayhem, and lawlessness. Anarchy, chaos, and disorder characterize the present system. Free capitalism carries the social order within itself, as a system of governance that is free from the state. The road to a libertarian order is a revolution that is not disruptive. Libertarianism is an evolutionary system, not one that could or should be imposed from above or from the outside.

The vision and the models of an anarcho-capitalist order are clear. What is necessary for this transformation to succeed is a majority for an electoral reform, which would introduce the random selection principle of representatives. After the accomplishment and benefits of the anarcho-capitalist order become visible, libertarianism would spread by imitation. It takes only a few communities to adopt the principles of anarcho-capitalism and over time the libertarian order would find followers in other communities and countries.

II.

CAPITALISM

> "That much more knowledge of facts enters the market economy than any single person or any organization can know, is the decisive reason that the market economy is able to perform better than any other form of the economy."
> Friedrich August von Hayek: "Economy, Science and Politics" - Inaugural Lecture on 18 June1962 at the Albert-Ludwigs-University of Freiburg i. B.
> (Freiburger Studien, Tübingen 1969, p. 11

- *Capitalism in perspective* -
- *Backgrounder: Capital* -
- *Development stages of capitalism* -
- *Capitalism and the state* –
- *Building blocks of modern capitalism* -
- *What are capitalists good for?* –
- *The stock market without puzzles* –
- *Commerce* –
- *Monetary economy* –
- *Equality is not justice* –
- *Origins of Western capitalism* –
- *Market process and competition* –
- *Backgrounder: Utility, value, and price* –
- *Prices and competition* –
- *Mass production* –
- *Freedom and capitalism* –
- *Summary*

People are anti-capitalists not because of insight but out of ignorance. The term 'capitalism' emerged in the 19th century as a polemical concept. The negative connotations continue to stick until our time. Yet capitalism is as old as humanity itself if one understands capitalist production as the use of tools for manufacturing goods. At the turn of the 18th to the 19th century, modern capitalism arose as a system of production based on the private ownership of the means of production. The prominent feature of modern capitalism is that specialized firms operate with the goal of earning a profit. Since earning profits in competitive markets depends on productivity, the modern capitalist system compels the firms to maintain cost control and to strive for innovation.

Entrepreneurial competitive capitalism is an innovative economic system. Because productivity means wealth, capitalism is the economic system with the highest wealth creation. At all places where modern capitalism has taken hold, even in its diluted fashion, production and incomes have risen, particularly the earnings of the masses.

Modern capitalism as a monetary enterprise system distinguishes itself from the other economic forms of production by its feature to first ease and then abolish mass poverty. In capitalism, the customer and thus the end-user of the goods is the pivotal point of the system. In a market economy, the de facto owners of a business are not the legal owners in the formal sense. The customers of the firm determine whether the company can expand or must shut down. In a market economy, the economic owners of a business are its customers.

In a capitalist economy, not the state hierarchy determines the allocation of resources, but the preferences of the clients. The existential question of 'to be or not to be' in capitalism is 'to buy or not to buy' on the side of the customer which translates into profit or loss at the firm.

Different from socialism where the rule is to obey or to die, a capitalist economy is a consumer economy. Those companies, which resist the wishes of the consumers and pass them by, do not survive. The failed firms make way for those companies that meet the customer's requirements faster, better, and at a lower price. Competitive capitalism eliminates less productive companies and fosters the productive enterprises. This way, the overall productivity rises as the competitive process lifts incomes.

Capitalism in Perspective

'Capitalism' is a term that refers to a specific form of production that consists in the systematic use of capital and technology under the guidance of entrepreneurs. This system emerged around 1800 after a long period of incubation and has since then spread around the world. Capitalist production has led to a manifold increase in output per capita.

The final purpose of production is consumption. Production is the use of the factors of production – such as nature, labor, capital, technology, and entrepreneurship – to obtain the goods for human use. The pre-capitalist production process applied mainly nature and labor as the factors of production. The most primitive production process earns the fruits of nature without tools or with only a few instruments. Gaining one's living by nature and labor characterized the production process for most of history. Until the 19th century, slaves served as 'human machines'. The abolishment of slavery came with the industrial revolution. Machines substituted labor. This process has not yet ended. At first, machines substituted slaves, then the machines substituted most of the labor in agriculture. The 20th century saw the automation and robotization of manufacturing while the 21st century will experience the same in the service sector.

Only step by step did humans devise the systematic use of tools in production. Social cooperation and the division of labor has lifted output. But the increase of population and production went hand in hand. Nature worked as the limiting factor so that the production per capita did not rise throughout history until the capitalist revolution, which applied capital and technology to improve production in entrepreneurial firms.

Before the capitalist revolution - whose first manifestation was the industrial revolution – a group of people could improve its relative position concerning the access of consumption goods by extracting the goods and services from the labor force either of the subgroup within their own social body or by the conquest of an outside social group. The typical course of events was first to conquer and then to succumb the defeated people to slavery. A societal division occurred between the slaves and the ruling class with a small group of functionaries – such as the priests and the state officials - in between.

Production as a process changed with the capitalist revolution. It is no coincidence that modern capitalism took off during the same period when slavery ended. Capital substituted human labor, and the machines replaced the slaves. In due course, capitalism abolished not only slavery but liberated also the women.

The transition from mass poverty to prosperity came with the industrial revolution. The United Kingdom was the first country to get a higher income followed by the United States, which soon overtook England. Laggards are Latin America and Asia. China and India have freed their economies only recently.

Japan was the first Asian country to adopt capitalist production followed by South Korea and many other countries thereafter, including China. Nevertheless, the recent newcomers have still a lot ahead in order to avoid remaining stuck at the middle-income level and catch-up to US-level with stands at roughly 50,000 international dollars per capita.

Backgrounder: Capital

The term 'capital' is a generic concept used in different meanings. Principle distinctions refer to 'physical', 'financial', 'human', and 'social' capital.

'Physical capital' exists in tools, machines, and the physical infrastructure. Physical capital is visible and tangible. It comprises heterogeneous pieces of goods that have 'multiple specificities' for the production process so that capital goods can be re-switched to a certain degree but are not full substitutes. One can, for example, use a hammer for different tasks. It has a 'multiple specificity' of limited range. The 'capital structure' exists as a complex of complementary goods whose unifying principle is not physical but exists in the mind of the entrepreneur.

Physical capital exists in the form of capital goods that are identifiable, yet which link the individual capital goods to each other as one can observe with the machines in a factory or the connections of a bridge with the roads.

Ludwig Lachmann explains: *"The generic concept of capital without which economists cannot do their work has no measurable counterpart among material objects; it reflects the entrepreneurial appraisal of such objects. Beer barrels and blast furnaces, harbour installations and hotel-room furniture are capital not by virtue of their physical properties but by virtue of their economic functions. Something is capital because the market, the consensus of entrepreneurial minds, regards it as capable of yielding an income. This does not mean that the phenomena of capital cannot be comprehended by clear and unambiguous concepts. The stock of capital used by society does not present a picture of chaos. Its arrangement is not arbitrary. There is some order in it."* (Ludwig Lachmann: "Capital and Its Structure", 1956)

'Financial capital' is a concept that refers to the financial expression of assets. Financial capital exists as an accounting tool be it for a private or public enterprise or for a person or a family. The precondition of financial capital is money and accounting. Financial capital is a mental instrument of business management and serves for calculating one's assets in a homogeneous form.

'Human capital' is embodied in the individual person and exists in a person's skills, knowledge, and traits as they contribute to the production process. Different from physical capital, which suffers from depreciation over time, human capital tends to improve with its use.

'Social capital' - also called 'cultural capital' – represents the quality of the interrelation and interaction among the members of a society. 'Social capital' denotes the degrees and types of mutual trust (reciprocity) and societal cohesion as the precondition of market transactions.

Around 1800, capitalist production took off. The capitalist production consists in the systematic use of capital and technology to widen and to improve the output.

Capitalist production has led to a manifold increase of production per capita and has lifted the income to levels that exceeds any historical standards. The capitalist production marks a new era in the development of humankind and this period differs from all previous periods.

In as much as the modern economies have abolished slavery, they have become capitalist economies. Abandoning the capitalist form of production would imply the collapse of the production level. It would come along not only with mass poverty but also with mass starvation.

Development stages of capitalism

Not all countries take part in the history of capitalism.

In the period of 'take-off capitalism' led by England, most countries outside of Northern Europe and North America did not join and only when it showed how far they had fallen back did a reversal set it and these countries tried to catch-up. This holds also for parts of Southern and Eastern Europe. In Asia, Japan was the pioneer nation to adopt capitalism, while it took up to the 1990s of the 20th century for China to open its economy to markets. Take-off capitalism means mobilizing the factors of production, at first labor and capital.

Stages of modern capitalism

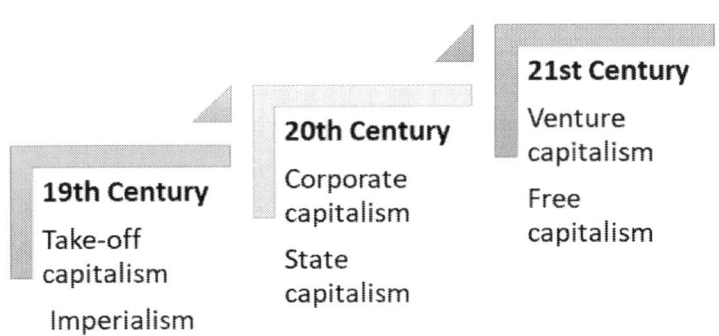

19th Century
Take-off capitalism
Imperialism

20th Century
Corporate capitalism
State capitalism

21st Century
Venture capitalism
Free capitalism

'Corporate capitalism' characterized the 20th century. It denotes the second stage after mobilizing the factors of production. Corporate capitalism concentrates on the efficiency of the use of the factors of production. The United States, Japan, and Germany are the most prominent members. These countries gained high rates of productivity in the organization of production and distribution by discipline and control. The Soviet Union, too, tried to achieve high productivity through discipline and control, yet failed because the Communists eliminated private property, profit, and market prices as the prime coordination mechanism and thus destroyed the tools of economic calculation.

'Venture capitalism' is the new stage of the capitalist development. Innovation dominates the emerging new forms of production. As the state recedes, entrepreneurship is on the rise. Connectivity substitutes organization and control and makes way for the spontaneous order that emerges on a local scale.

Not all countries will take part in the new stage. Not much different from at the time of 'take-off capitalism', certain societies reject creative destruction that comes with innovation and the new forms of doing business. The decline of the role of the nation-state will make way for local units to emerge with their proper kind of sovereignty and an individualistic political structure. The success of these new forms of production will invite imitation.

The alternative between socialism and capitalism as generic concepts does not exist. Socialism is a subcategory of capitalism. The point is whether more state or less state. Socialism is the strongest form of state capitalism while free capitalism is an economic system with least state and politics. It is also wrong to ask which system promises to offer more welfare and social security because the real point is productivity. The supposed difference between 'continental' and 'Anglo-Saxon' capitalism is also irrelevant as both are forms of capitalism typical of the 20th century's 'corporate capitalism'.

Types of capitalism

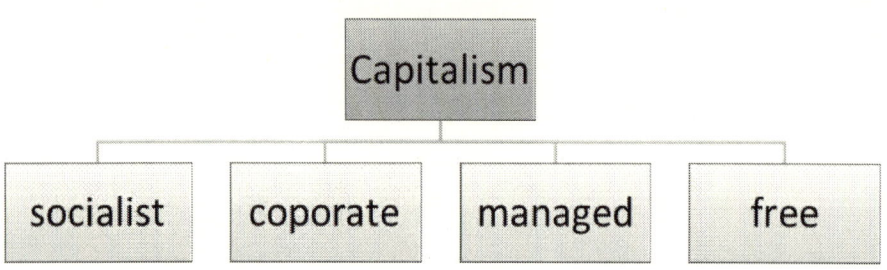

***

The historical movement goes on not without setbacks. Throughout history until the industrial revolution, the dominant system was socialist capitalism, and the socialism of the 20th century was tentative to restore the old system. Nostalgic feelings of a 'paradise lost' mark the socialists until our days. Outside of the socialist camp, the dominant system is 'corporate capitalism' in its many forms – including the welfare state. 'Managed capitalism' represents an advancement over interventionist capitalism as it tries to substitute general rules for discretionary policies as it is the case with monetary and fiscal policy rules. 'Ordo-liberalism' is such a tentative along with certain postulates that come under the label of 'neoliberalism'. Both these attempts must fail under the conditions of the modern system of democracy as a political party competition. 'Laissez-faire' capitalism is free capitalism. Its characteristic is the minimization and abolishment of the state and politics. This form of production requires 'demarchy' as a political system.

Emergence of a capitalist economy

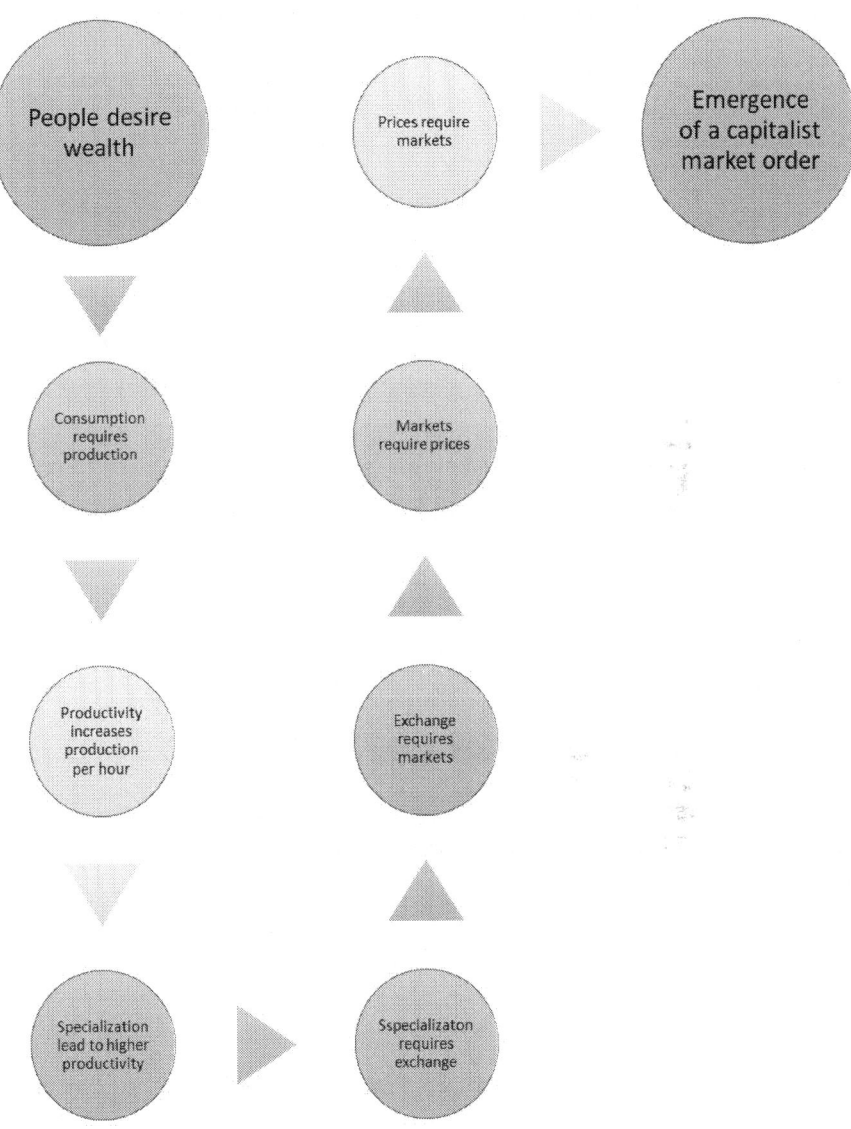

A capitalist free market order emerges naturally under laissez-faire conditions. Starting with the simple fact that consumption requires production, and that productivity means an increase of production, people will search for the most productive system of production. Working in groups enhances productivity because it enables division of labor and thus makes specialization possible, which is the key to productivity. Division of labor requires exchange, and exchange needs markets, which in turn need prices and money to work. A capitalist economy thus is the natural outgrowth of the search for higher productivity in order to gain prosperity.

Capitalism and the State

The theoretical justification of the modern state, as elaborated by Thomas Hobbes (1588-1679) in his "Leviathan" (1651), postulates that people voluntarily succumb to the power of the state. In this model, the fear of anarchy drives people into submission. Yet Hobbes ignores that people want not only security but also seek prosperity and freedom. The more the state dominates our lives, the less is there a space for a free capitalism and thus for freedom and prosperity. Hobbes' state is not sustainable without the permanent use of force. Instead of establishing peace, the Hobbesian state brings violence, disunity, rebellion, and war. The Hobbesian state is a warfare state.

Between the extremes of a state, which forbids private ownership of the means of production and where the state holds the authority to manage the entire economy and free capitalism without state interventions, there exist many mixed forms. The more socialist an economic system becomes the more people suffer not only material deprivation, but they lose also individual freedom. The more capitalist an economy, the more this society will enjoy freedom and prosperity.

Until the eighteenth century, the authorities almost everywhere in the world suppressed capitalism. Even today, political power is a constant threat to a free capitalism. The modern so-called 'mixed economy' exists as 'state capitalism' or as 'corporate capitalism'. In most countries, government tolerates capitalism only so far as it serves to enhance the power of the state. When modern capitalism manifested its productive capacity in the industrial revolution, the power of the state merged into a new system forming the dominant form of capitalism as state capitalism. Free capitalism will come to fruition not before the role of the state and of politics becomes minimal or vanishes altogether.

True capitalism is free capitalism. Free capitalism is a project of the future. Some countries are farther away from the capitalist ideal while other countries are closer to its pure form, but no country lives up to the ideal. Neither dictatorship nor democracy will automatically drive to free capitalism. Capitalism is still instrumental to the state. States use this form of production to promote the state's power. In the current system, the economy is subject to politics and the state. Most governments recognize that the more intense the competition in price-driven markets becomes, and the more there are entrepreneurial freedom and secure property rights, the wealthier this country will be. This is the path of the historical evolution. What has hitherto been the case will even be more valid in the future: the more a country approaches pure capitalism, the more prosperous it gets. Yet to achieve this goal, the state must give in and vanish.

Modern capitalism rests on private ownership of the means of production. 'Capital' in this sense is the core of capitalism. Property rights are a necessary condition for capitalism to function, yet property alone is not sufficient for a proper working of a market economy. The working of a capitalist system requires that price-driven competitive markets accompany private ownership, and that there is a wide space for the private initiative.

The more secure private property, the more price-driven the competitive markets, and the more there is freedom for the private initiative, the more productive the economy gets.

Pillars of capitalism

```
        Private property of
         the means of
           production

  Competitive              Private initiative
    markets
```

***

Liberal capitalism opposes communism and socialism and is not compatible with Nazism either. A motto, such as that of the National Socialist Workers' Party (NSDAP), 'public interest before self-interest' or the motto of the Hitler Youth (HJ): 'You are nothing, your nation is everything' runs against the spirit of a free economy. A free economy and the personal self-determination result when the individual can pursue his own interests. This not the case with totalitarianism. The credo as exposed by the Italian fascist leader Benito Mussolini (1883-1945): 'All within the state, nothing outside the state, nothing against the state 'is the opposite of the libertarian position. The most powerful institutions in the socialist countries - whether they are national-socialist or international-socialist - are the respective unitary party and the military. Other social institutions, up to the family, are subject to the dictates of the system. The Third Reich was just as much a military state as the Soviet Union.

The driving force behind the capitalist system is the private initiative. The historical experience demonstrates that where there are free markets that provide space for the individual initiative, where the property rights are safe, and the tax burden is low, prosperity thrives. When, however, the state restricts the individual rights, and when the state' bureaucracy suppress the private initiative, there is economic, social and cultural decline.

Economic stagnation results when business is losing its freedom to act because of excessive regulations and high taxes. New companies will not arise under these restrictions. Then the production becomes more expensive, the entrepreneurial spirit weakens, and investment and innovation wane. The economy stagnates, and the society impoverishes.

What are Capitalists Good For?

In the market economy, a vote takes place with every purchase. By deciding to buy this specific product and not another one, the consumers elect those companies that manufacture this good to go on with their production. By this vote, the consumers chose these companies and entrepreneurs to lead the production process. The ballot in capitalism consists in money, the vote is the purchase. The capitalists are the legal owners of the production resources such as gas stations, restaurants, and shopping malls, yet they only earn a yield on their capital stock by making their property available to the use by the customers. By purchasing the product, the customers determine the value of the capital, which serves to produce this good. Like consumer goods, production goods, too, have no intrinsic value. The price of capital goods reflects their capacity to produce goods, which customers want and will pay for.

The capitalists must maintain and improve the capital stock in order to earn a profit. Stores require maintenance; airplanes need checks and services; machines need repairs. Capitalists must bear the costs of preserving and adapting the capital structure. For this maintenance of keeping the capital structure intact, capitalists make advance payments. They assume the risk as to the uncertainties surrounding the future yield. While the workers receive their salaries right away, the capitalist get their compensation not before the good reaches the final consumer and gets paid. While the workers receive their remuneration during the production process before the goods reach the consumers, the capitalists bear both the initial costs and the risks of whether the capital goods will bring income in the end. The yield comes only when the end user pays for the goods. Whether an investment will have an economic value depends on the extent to which it contributes to producing goods that consumers want and will buy.

The customer expects that shops will provide a rich offer from which to choose. Hardly anyone wonders who keeps the store in operation and who makes sure that a variety of goods is available. Few customers spend a thought how much capital the capitalists put at the service for the customers before a buyer pays. If the government and its bureaucracy substitute capitalism or regulate, harass and confiscate the capitalists, it does not take long, and the capital structure will disintegrate. All it takes is to diminish the profit expectations of the capitalists and the capital structure crumbles.

Large wealth exists in company stocks or in other forms of participation in companies. Wealth comes from investments, and investments come from savings. More savings mean consumption. The wealth of the owners of a supermarket chain are their stores. The stockholders are the owners. Yet who are the actual beneficiaries of the stores? Those people who shop in these stores and enjoy the products offered.

A considerable number of the super-rich people pursue a modest lifestyle. Part of the financial success of these persons comes because of being thrifty and not to waste but to save and invest. Even a great fortune cannot last long when it gets into the hands of a hedonistic spendthrift. Wealth abhors high time-preference and stays with those who know how to economize.

The market itself takes care that wealth accumulation will not go on forever and accumulate in one or only a few hands. The profitability of a company is under constant threat from innovation. From the wealth of the railway barons at the end of the nineteenth century there is little left today. The Ford, Rockefeller, and Vanderbilt families, and the inheritors of the wealth of the other tycoons of the past have vanished from the top list of the wealthy. While Wal Mart seemed well established only a short time ago, it now faces a challenge from online shopping.

There will always be a group of super rich people, yet under capitalism, the composition among those who make up the high-wealth people, changes. In capitalism, innovation does away with old wealth. As such, capitalism differs from the economic systems of the past. Historically, to own land was the foundation of wealth. Before the industrial revolution, the main source of wealth was ownership in land, which formed the basis for inheritance. The titles on the property came along with the title of nobility and other social rank distinctions. In pre-capitalist times, the rich were the same families for long periods, and almost all those who were born poor were to remain poor.

If one compares the list of the super-rich, which the magazine Forbes publishes annually, few names – if any - show up over a longer period. The people of wealth change with the lines of business. Until the 1980s, there were no super-rich people from the software, electronics and computer sectors on the list, as they are now the broadest group because these production areas were only just at the beginning of their triumph. Now, names from this area dominate the list as in earlier times the owners of railway or oil companies made up the list a hundred years ago.

***

FORBES List of Top 10 Billionaires
First FORBES List of Top 10 Billionaires (1987)
Taikichiro Mori/property development
Yoshiaki Tsutsumi/transport, hotels
Yohachiro Iwasaki/logging, property
Shigeru Kobayashi/real estate
Haruhiko Yoshimoto/real estate
Brenninkmeyer family/retailing
Hans and Gad Rausing/liquid packaging
Albert, Paul, Ralph Reichmann/real estate
Kenneth Roy Thomson/media, petroleum

Eitaro Itoyama/property
2017 FORBES List of Top 10 billionaires
Bill Gates/software
Warren Buffett/investment
Jeff Bezos/online retailing
Amancio Ortega/retailing
Mark Zuckerberg/social media
Carlos Slim/cell phone
Larry Ellison/computer
David Koch/industrial conglomerate
Michael Bloomberg/financial information
Forbes' first list of 1987 was dominated by Japanese real estate tycoons, a group that has vanished from the 2017 list.
Source: https://www.forbes.com/billionaires/#5b3b1c97251c

***

Modern capitalism is an entrepreneurial capitalism. Its motor is innovation. Innovation brings with it ongoing structural change so that exceptional wealth eminence does not last long. Companies emerge and disappear, and the wealth of individuals and families grows and goes with them.

Today's wealth is ownership of stocks. How stocks perform, determine the wealth of the owners. Equity markets evaluate companies and thus determine the individual wealth of the owners of these companies. Becoming part of the club of the capitalists is open to everyone. One can buy individual stocks or investment funds. Start-ups go public and may offer opportunities for the investors willing to take higher risks. Modern capitalism is popular capitalism. It is a capitalism by the people and for the people. Modern capitalism realizes the socialist dream that the workers themselves become proprietors. This happens under capitalism through the stock market.

The Stock Market Without Puzzles

The stock exchange is a central institution of modern capitalism. Stock markets emerge with modern monetary capitalism. They had their first flourishing in Amsterdam and later in London. Today, New York is the center of the global stock trading. A stock market is a trading place. As to which types of assets and goods are the object of the trade, there exist commodity, foreign exchange, bond market markets, and the stock exchange. Exchanges are markets where supply meets demand and where the price formation takes place. It is wrong to take the price of a security as its value. A specific stock market price indicates that at a certain point in time and space, purchases and sales took place at this definite price. The so-called 'stock market value' of a company does not represent the 'value' of this company. As a price, the stock market valuation of an asset fluctuates with the trades at the stock exchange.

Of the total existing stocks, bonds, and commodities, only a small part trades in a session. It is therefore misleading to take the stock market quotation at face value to determine the 'value' of the entire company, as it is done, for example, when one calculates the so-called 'capitalization' of companies. This inappropriate approach is already obsolete at when the results get published. Stock market quotations are changing even if nothing spectacular happens to the company that the share represents because some people sell and buy.

The intense observation of the price quotations is useful when one wants to buy or to sell and is on the look-out for a good timing. The momentary quotations are important for the market professionals, yet for the investor, the short-term quotations are of little significance. What counts is being in the market and to earn the dividend in the long run. The dividends of stocks and the interest payments of bonds are the sources of the income for the capitalist - different from the speculator who wants to profit from the price changes and the market professionals who live from the trades.

There is a debate in finance about the determinants of the stock market prices. The dispute rages between representatives of the efficient market hypothesis (EMH) and the behavioral theorists.

The adherents of the efficient market hypothesis claim that the stock price itself is the best expression of the present value as it reflects the state of the obtainable information. Only new information changes the price. Therefore, stock market prices move in a random way as the information comes in. As an argument against the efficiency hypothesis, one can hold that the market is not perfect since people are not perfect, and markets are no more and no less 'information-efficient' than human beings can be information efficient. It is not 'the information' that makes the price, but the human decision to buy or to sell according to the individual evaluation of the information.

At the other extreme, the behavioral theory of asset markets is wrong because it tries to explain human action in the light of a psychology of irrationality. Yet what may seem irrational to the observer does not have to be irrational for the actor himself. Extreme fluctuations of the prices are not irrational, for example, when the market is narrow and when the participants change their views about how to assess the future profitability of a company. The efficient market hypothesis underestimates the costs of getting information.

The stock exchange has an anchor with the company profits. In order to distribute dividends, the company must generate profits. The main determinant of the price of a company's stock is its profit position relative to that of alternative investments and the respective expectations. Therefore, the current price of a share depends not only on the individual company but also on the profit situation and the profits of other companies and on the potential income and risks of alternative investments. The individual stock price is connected to the local stock and to the national markets and to all potential investments around the world and their respective currencies.

The price of an individual share, as well as the status of the securities market represented in its index, results from the valuations of all potential investments in the financial markets and their embeddedness in the national and global environment. Therefore, it is impossible to predict the movements of individual shares or the stock market index consistently. Yet such forecasts are also unnecessary because the main advantage of investing in stocks is to participate in the growth of the economy and to maintain at the same time high liquidity. Unlike real estate, for example, one can convert stocks into cash fast and also in small or in large quantities on the stock exchange. In this respect, the stock market investment is unique and provides advantages that no other kind of investment can offer.

The daily stock trading represents the so-called 'secondary market' in contrast to the market for new emissions in the form of initial public offerings (IPO) or the issue of new stocks by an established company to increase its capital base. Secondary market means that only a part of the investment holdings is available for trade. Depending on which side - whether demand or supply - there is more urgency, the prices will rise or fall. If the supply is tight, and the demand increases, the prices will rise. When demand falls and supply increases, prices drop. Sometimes the market is 'thin' because only light trading is going on. Under such a condition, the urgent need of liquidity by some market participants can provoke strong price cuts. This day-to-day trading is unpredictable and does not violate the principle of the theory - neither that of the efficient market hypothesis nor that of the behavioral financial economics. It is impossible to predict an individual event with certainty.

Long periods of a bull market (rising prices) or a bear market (falling prices) come about depending on whether more money flows into the stock market or more money leaves the market. This inflow and outflow reflect the tides of the amount of money that circulates in the economy and of the investment alternatives and their returns and their risks.

Booms of the stock market with the tendency of a bubble occur when the central bank floods the economy with money at a time when the real economy offers few attractive alternative investments. A bear market happens when liquidity shrinks or when many new investment opportunities arise in the real economy. Then there is a general lack of money or money remains outside of the stock exchange to finance business transactions. If securities owners want to sell with urgency in such a situation, they can do so only at low prices. Such a constellation offers opportunities for the buyer of stocks. The time to make a fortune is in the bear market.

The price movement of stocks is paradoxical because it often runs contrary to the tendency in the real economy. In the long run, however, stock prices depend on the growth of the real economy, since the purpose of holding securities is to earn dividends and the dividend payments depend on corporate profits.

As an owner of shares, the investor is at the origin of the wealth creation of the capitalist economy. Other forms of income depend on the wealth that the corporate world creates. Employment and income arise from and through the profits of companies. For the banks to pay interest on savings, they must generate income by granting loans to companies and consumers. For the state to pay interest on its bonds, the government must earn tax receipts that depend on profits, wages, and sales. In order to be able to employ workers, companies must make profitable deals. Before the government can spend, they need to tax. Government expenditure depends on the profits and the incomes in the private sector.

Since the 1980s, there has been a large increase in the financial sector of the economy. This growth of finance is evident in the USA. The growth of the financial sector coincides with the increase of the money supply and the rise of government debt. What some call 'casino capitalism' has its basis in the growth of the public debt and in monetary inflation. When the growth of government debt and of the money supply reach their limits, the share of the financial sector will decline, and the price levels of the securities will normalize.

Investment Strategies

The table below highlights the performance of various assets under different macroeconomic constellations. Overall, stocks perform well not only in an environment of low stable but also in periods of expansionary deflation and expansionary inflation. Bonds do well in an expansionary disinflation and a deflationary contraction while gold protects against global stagflation. The best time for commodities are in periods of expansionary inflation while real estate performs well when there is a low and stable inflation and in times of expansionary inflation.

Although real estate prices do not always decline and rise parallel to the stock market, they are not separate from the economic performance of the national economy. Unlike stocks and real estate, however, bonds and monetary savings suffer from inflation. Although the investment in gold protects against inflation, gold brings no current returns. One must sell gold to earn a yield on this investment.

As a general rule, one can say that the enemies of the stock market are the same as those of a prosperous economy. Besides the outright enemies such as socialization and nationalization, the hidden enemies comprise a higher price inflation, rising interest rates, and a growing public debt.

Macroeconomic constellation and asset type performance

	Stocks	*Bonds*	*Real Estate*	*Gold*	*Commodities*
Low Stable Inflation	+	0	+	0	0
Expansionary Disinflation	+	+	0	0	0
Deflationary Contraction	-	+	0	0	-
Global Stagflation	-	-	-	+	-
Local Stagflation	-	-	-	-	-
Expansionary Inflation	+	-	+	0	+

There is no such thing as a safe investment. Those investors who fear stock market crashes and panics and buy real estate or bonds instead cannot avoid losses when the political and social environment falls into chaos. Ultimately, the return on economic investments depends on how profitable the companies are. When these fail, everything else also falls to pieces.

Through the ownership of shares, the investor takes part in business and is at the place where the national wealth comes from. The yield of other investments - be it bonds, real estate or art - depends on the overall economic performance, i.e. the profit situation of the companies. This also applies to the public systems of old-age pensions. What counts is the extent to which the economy produces the goods and services that the pensioner needs in retirement.

The US stock market exhibits a long bull market period from 1870 to the First World War, a strong recovery towards the end of the 1920s and the long bear market of the Great Depression. It took over two decades for the stocks to return to the level before the Great Depression began. After the long postwar period, a bear market happened again during the stagflation in the 1970s. Since 1982, there has been a mega bull market, which experienced a slight interruption in the years from 2000 to 2008 only to re-surge again since then.

In the case of bear market periods, one must consider that when stock prices are low, equities have a low price-earnings ratio (P/E). Price-earnings ratios of less than ten, for example, say that those shares will recover their price in ten years through profits and the dividends they distribute. Stock market crashes do not imply that the investors go empty.

Commerce

To increase prosperity, one needs, first, accumulation of capital, more and better tools; second, human capital: the skills of the people to produce goods and services; third, innovation: to apply ideas on how to make the things people want and need; and four, commerce: the exchange of goods to enable the specialization of capital and labor. When these factors occur together, economic progress happens. The effectiveness of each of these factors depends on commerce, on freedom that exists in the realm of the exchange of goods and services in the markets. As commerce requires a free market economy, prosperity requires a free market system.

Main forces of economic progress

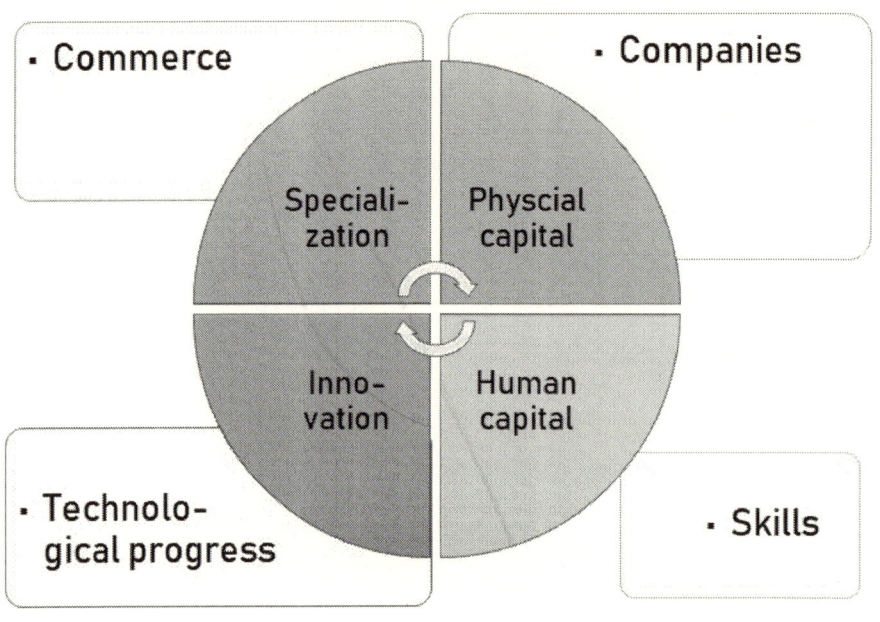

***

More prosperity comes from higher productivity. Specialization of labor and capital requires commerce. Firms are places of specialization of labor and capital. Companies provide capital while the workers and employees contribute their knowledge in the form of human capital. Technological progress means to realize new business ideas. These ideas will become profitable through entrepreneurial innovations.

All four factors are interrelated.

The more intensive the trade, the more accumulation of capital is possible.

The more capital is available, the more effective is the knowledge.

The larger the stock of physical and human capital, the more innovation comes.

With technical progress, productivity grows, and prosperity increases.

The more intensive the commerce, the more specialization is possible. The potential of specialization grows with the size of the market. What begins at the level of a simple exchange within the family and the local market continues at the regional and national levels, to embrace the whole globe.

For a market to expand beyond the neighborhood, the exchange of goods requires money. Money is productive because it facilitates the exchange of goods and services. Without money, the exchange possibilities would be limited and thus also the specialization and the productivity.

Without money, barter requires a 'double coincidence of wants', since the vendor must not only find someone who wants to buy his goods, but the purchaser must at the same time be someone who offers the good, which the seller wants to buy.

Barter

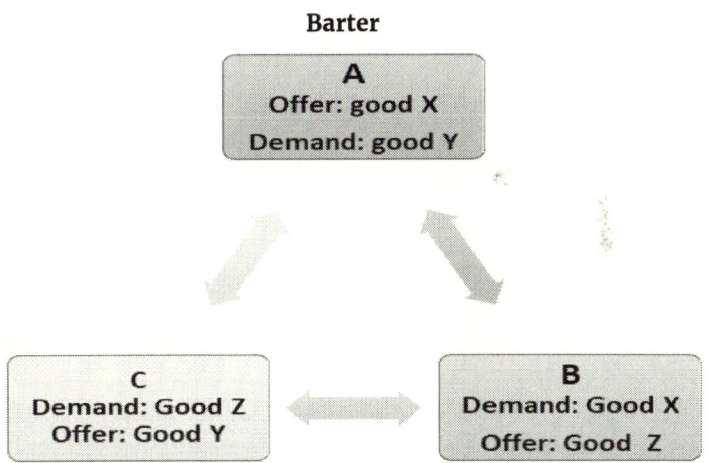

Without money, there is no exchange of goods between A, B, and C. Although A offers the good X, which B asks, B does not have the good Y, which A asks for exchange. Likewise, C has the good Y, which A wants, but not the good X that B wants.

After introducing money as a general means of exchange, the problem of the so-called 'double coincidence of wants' finds its solution. Person A sells the good X to B who pays with money. Person A demands the good Y, which person C has to offer, and C can acquire the good Z from B.

By using money as a general means of exchange and payment, this limitation of the double coincidence of wants disappears. In a monetary economy, the respective producer exchanges his goods for money and thus gains freedom of choice as to the suppliers of the goods he wants. Money is a means of facilitating the exchange of goods, which in turn enables specialization and thereby provides the foundation of productivity.

Monetary exchange

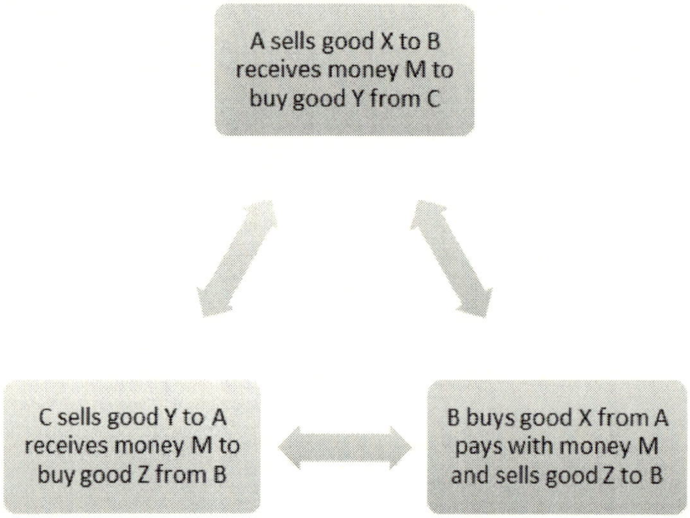

A sells good X to B receives money M to buy good Y from C

C sells good Y to A receives money M to buy good Z from B

B buys good X from A pays with money M and sells good Z to B

Money is productive. It allows and facilitates the exchange of goods. Pure barter limits the size of the market. Exchange through money comes with markets, and market transactions create the monetary prices.

The larger the market, the greater the potential for specialization. Money thus promotes productivity and prosperity.

***

Money is not sterile because it is a precondition for the division of labor and of specialization. Money is an instrument of rational economic calculation. When production exceeds its simple forms, the calculation in terms of natural goods is no longer sufficient. One cannot add up cheese, wine, and horse-carts and the whole plethora of other economic goods in a meaningful sense, but one can add, subtract, divide and multiply their respective monetary sums.

While money is instrumental to the division of labor and for calculation, it cannot serve as a 'storage of value' because all future consumption depends on future production. The economy as a whole cannot save today's production and conserve it for the years or decades to come. Buildings disintegrate, machines rust, food spoils. Most services - be it a medical treatment or a haircut - require that production takes place simultaneously with consumption. The future level of consumption depends on the future circumstances of the production. Money cannot fulfill the function of a storage of value because money flows through the banking system and borrowers spend the money that the lender saves. Money hoarders cannot know whether their notes will still be legal tender in the future or whether to own gold is still legal. Many countries have experienced monetary reforms with the old currency losing most of its purchasing power and sometimes losing all its value. In the United States, the Roosevelt government confiscated by Executive Order 6102 all private gold on April 5, 1933. There is only one sure way to 'save for the future' and this is to take care that the dark time will not come, and that free capitalism will prosper.

An economy can reach a higher output mobilizing the labor force - for example by integrating women. While the increase in the workforce does not lift productivity in terms of output per worker or per hour, it would nevertheless lead to an increase in the national income per capita. The output per worker and the hourly productivity depend on specialization. Specialization of the labor force goes hand in hand with the specialization of the capital. With a high degree of specialization and intensive division of labor, the use of special machines and thus the specialization of the capital is also intensive.

Companies are places of specialization. The more specialized a company is, the more it is worthwhile for this company to use special tools and to employ technical and administrative specialists. The key to prosperity is productivity. All differences in race, gender, and geographic location disappear regarding time. For everyone, the number of hours per day is the same. No human being can permanently work over eight or ten hours each day. More wealth by more work has a natural limit. Unlimited wealth creation comes through rising productivity.

Productivity grows with specialization, and specialization of both capital and labor takes place in companies.

Productivity increases prosperity. Money is productive in the sense that it allows specialization and price calculation.

Interventions, which disrupt the functioning of the markets and affect the monetary system, are harmful because they affect the specialization and thus reduce productivity and lead to loss of prosperity.

Antony P. Mueller

Monetary Economy

Modern capitalism is an entrepreneurial capitalism. The cradle of modern capitalism were the factories and workshops run by entrepreneurs as the place to combine capital, labor, and knowledge. Firms are the source of productivity and prosperity. The prevalence of modern capitalism, as it has developed since the industrial revolution, is the spread of private firms around the world. The obvious characteristic of our time compared to the situation of two hundred years ago is the number, size, and importance of business companies.

If one wants to give the term 'capitalism' a specific meaning, then it is about a wide network of profit-seeking firms. In modern capitalism, there are not only large companies active but even more so also medium, small, and micro-enterprises. The Marxists were wrong with their prediction that capitalism would bring with it a growing class of proletarians and a shrinking class of capitalists. A broad middle class is the hallmark of modern capitalism. If the middle class is small or shrinking, this is a sign that something is wrong with the economic system of this country.

The market competition takes place within a network of cooperation. A characteristic feature of the modern entrepreneurial economy is that the markets coordinate both competition and cooperation. The modern economy is a network of specialized units. The more complex and denser the network, the higher is the degree of possible specialization and the higher is the level of productivity.

The individual companies compete to produce the best products as cost-effectively as possible so that a company can make a profit. A firm attains this goal by way of cooperation with other companies as it embeds itself in the web of specialization and the exchange of goods. Capitalism is as much cooperation as it is competition. Cooperation happens within the company through the collaboration of the workforce and extends to the cooperation among different companies. An economy exists as a network of firms. The more a company specializes, the more it depends on suppliers. Cooperation does not exclude the competition but forms part of it. This cooperation, of course, can make it difficult for anti-monopolistic competition policy to single out market and price collusion. The supervisors will raise false accusations when they ignore that cooperation is an inherent feature of competition. The best policy against cartelization is an open market access and technological change and not an arbitrary policy intervention in the name of 'anti-cartelization' and 'competition' policy.

Companies can achieve extraordinary profits through innovation. This way, there is a continuous incentive to improve the offer of new and better goods and services. If these conditions prevail, monopolies are not only harmless but they also play an important role in the economic progress as the pioneers of innovation. The more open the market access, the less 'competition policy' is necessary.

The modern economy is a monetary economy. Modern capitalism is an 'entrepreneurial capitalism' that takes place in a monetary economy. Entrepreneurship is fundamental not only because of the role of companies as an economic unit of economic activity but also as the driving force behind economic growth, which is to accumulate capital and to realize innovation.

Entrepreneurship has redesigned the world. Prosperity has become universal. The beneficiaries of modern capitalism have been the ordinary people. In advanced industrial societies, the standard of living of a family with an average income surpasses the level of the living standard of the royal families of the past. The ordinary worker enjoys better living conditions than the nobility of the past. Electricity, refrigerator, washing machine, television, telephone, and an automobile have become common utensils in almost any household in the industrialized countries.

Progress, however, affects not only material things but also leisure. In the past, leisure time was not only rare but also not much exciting because there were few things to enjoy in the spare time other than to rest or get drunk. The time of youth was short, the adulthood full of hard work, and the old age burdened with frailty and boredom. Today, a considerable part of the economic output of an advanced economy consists in producing leisure goods. Capitalism creates not only material prosperity. By reducing the working hours, vast new possibilities have emerged for the productive enjoyment of the leisure time.

Equality Is Not Justice

Modern happiness research shows that the greatest effect on the increase of well-being due to rising income happens when moving up from the low to the middle-income strata. When incomes rise above the levels of the upper middle class, further income increases are no longer associated with significant gains of personal happiness. While satisfaction continues to rise, the marginal increases in happiness diminish the higher one climbs up on the wealth ladder.

The material progress from no bed to one bed is much more valuable than to own a house with several bedrooms to choose from as a place to sleep. To escape hunger has a much greater individual benefit than being able to afford double or triple portions. The marginal benefit of the second TV or the third car to the well-being of the family is much lower than the benefit that came with the first TV set and the first automobile. The rate of the increase in happiness, therefore, decreases per unit of money as the material wealth grows. The millionaire or billionaire is not a million-fold or a billion-fold happier than the average wage earner.

According to the results of Jason Schnittker's research on the economics of happiness (Diagnosing our national disease: Trends in income and happiness, 1973 to 2004, American Sociological Association), the marginal effect of income decreases for all categories of 'well-being'.

This result is most visible in the categories 'marital happiness' and 'self-clarified state of health'.

The diminishing marginal rate for 'satisfaction with the financial situation' and the assessment of the relative income is less pronounced.

Further research shows that America's super-rich people are only marginally, and by no means all, more satisfied than the average well-to-do American.

That more money does not contribute to a sharp increase in happiness from an income, which corresponds to the upper middle class, but serves for other motives such as self-expression or self-realization, for example, means that one should not attach too much importance to inequality. In a capitalist economic system, the poor are better-off, and that the country has a strong middle class.

***

The discussion about equality and inequality of wealth and income has turned into an ideological battlefield. Most of the debate is beside the point. The heart of the matter is not how much more the super-rich earn and possess compared to the ordinary wage earner, but the core of the problem is to reduce poverty. It was the improvement of the fate of the poor where modern capitalism achieved its greatest triumphs. One cannot eradicate mass poverty without capitalism.

The decline in extreme poverty has come about because more countries have turned to the capitalist economic order as has been the case in China and Eastern Europe since the 1990s. During this development, income worldwide has risen, and its distribution has widened.

Before the triumph of monetary profit-oriented entrepreneurial capitalism, most of the people of a country were poor, while it is a minority in industrialized countries today. Even these poor people have a higher level of prosperity than the rich social classes of the past.

Elimination of Poverty

While about 95% of the world's population of the one billion people who lived before the Industrial Revolution suffered from extreme poverty, this figure fell below 10% by 2015. During this same period, world population has risen to over seven billion.

In the period since 1980, the number of people living in poverty (according to the line established by the World Bank) has fallen from close to 90 percent to under 10 percent.

Decline of extreme poverty since 1820

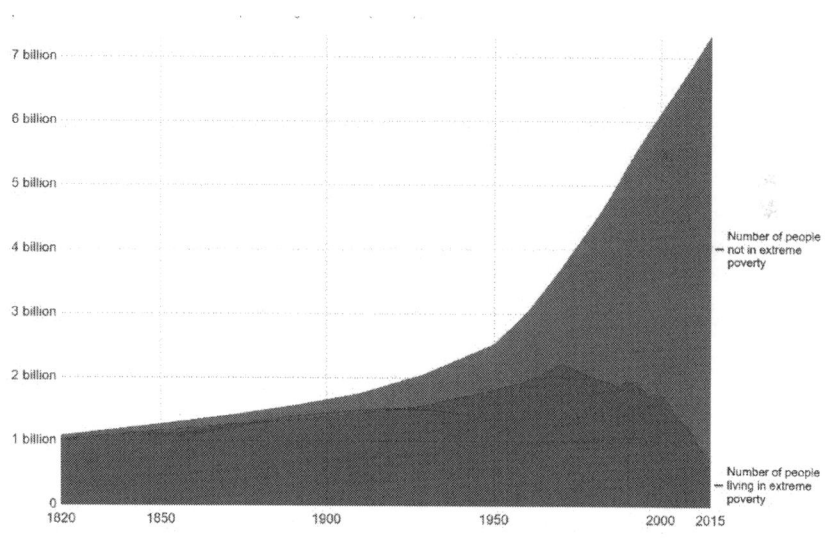

World population living in extreme poverty defined as living at a consumption (of income) level below 1.9 international dollars per day.
Source: Our World in Data. Global extreme poverty

The more capitalism has spread across the globe, however imperfect it still is, the more a middle-class has emerged, and the lower the number of people in extreme poverty has become. In China, poverty has been falling when the country changed course and moved to a capitalist system. A similar development takes place in India. Although in India, there never has been an outright communism, India practiced development socialism and is just beginning to reduce the influence, which the government exerts over the economy. The more India will abandon its old way, the faster misery will disappear as well as in the other countries that change their prevailing economic system to more capitalism.

***

China and India at a crossroads

Since the economic reforms and the move to a market economy, China gross domestic product per capita at purchasing power parity has grown from under 2,000 dollars to over 14,000 dollars per year.

India, whose gross domestic product per capita at purchasing power parity was similar to that of China in 1990, has increased its per capita income to over 6,000 dollars, less than half of that of China.

Both countries, China and India, face the challenge of going on with pro-market reforms against political obstacles and to avoid of getting stuck in the middle-income trap. Both China and India must go ahead with political reforms and curb the role of the state, of the bureaucracy, and of party politics. Yet it seems that China is taking the opposite direction.

The attempt of the ruling Communist Party of China to impose a comprehensive system of surveillance and control will abort the economic take-off and lead to economic stagnation with the income per capita staying low. In this respect, China would not be the first developing county that experienced a dramatic take-off yet remains stuck in the middle-income trap. The outcome of the race between India and China is still open.

Origins of Western Capitalism

The inception of modern capitalism took place towards the end of the 18th century. Nevertheless, the foundations for the industrial revolution existed before. The ground-breaking invention, which laid the cornerstone for the modern world, was, besides establishing the principles of double bookkeeping by the Franciscan monk Luca Bartolomeo de Pacioli in 1494, the invention of the printing press with movable letters by Johannes Gutenberg around 1450.

The double-entry bookkeeping system promoted the rational management of a business enterprise, and from then on, with the printing press in place, it was possible to make ideas accessible to interested parties at a fraction of the former costs. Until the spread of the modern printing press, reading and writing were a privilege of the authorities and reserved to the upper clergy and to high officials who could exercise a comprehensive control over the people. Few common people learned to read. As long as the costs of books and of other reading material were beyond the reach of most people, this skill was of little use. With the spread of the printing press, the affordable access to reading material made it worthwhile for the public to learn to read.

In 1517, the proclamation of Martin Luther's theses in Wittenberg started a strong incentive for learning to read. The Reformation proclaimed the personal study of the Bible as an obligation for the believers. Because there was no central authority, the new creed took hold in the individual geographical units, primarily at first in the independent city-states in the Northern parts of Europe. Books, pamphlets, and articles about God and the world spread across Europe, whereas the Chinese emperor and the Sultanate of the Islamic world would suppress what seemed to endanger their autocratic rule. Europe differed from other regions of the world through the unity of a common language for the educated in form of the Latin of the Church, yet politically Europe comprised many individual political units of a diverse composition in which free, independent cities played an important role as autonomous political institutions. The attempts to control written material and to forbid the modern printing press failed in Europe - unlike as it was the case in many other regions of the world, where censorship prevailed. The 'Great Divergence' began when Europe took off, while these regions consequently fell back relative to Europe in terms of economic prosperity, scientific progress, and individual liberty.

***

Economic, technical and scientific progress lives on ideas. Yet ideas do not spread by themselves. Equally important as the idea itself is that it spreads quickly and widely. The printing press made a wide distribution of ideas possible. Movable letters made printing cheaper. From the end of the 15th century onward, ideas traveled across the European continent at an accelerating speed. From then on, invention and discovery went hand in hand with the rapid distribution of the new findings in science, technology, the arts, and their application in the production process.

Printing press and literacy led to the enlightenment and scientific revolution of the 17th century. The economic rise of Europe began as modern capitalism took shape. Leading the way was liberty, competition, and innovation along with reason, protecting the individual and of his property.

Capitalism came not by way of orders from the authorities but emerged from practical wants and needs as a spontaneous order. Modern capitalism blossomed where the private initiative could unfold.

The new type of the profit-seeking enterprise grew out of the world of the common people. The entrepreneurial pioneers at the dawn of the industrial revolution were artisans, traders, and engineers. These new leaders - the capitalist entrepreneurs - built the first industrial machines and invented mass products. They founded companies and became factory-owners - from Thomas Newcomen (1664-1729), the inventor of the steam engine (1712), Friedrich Krupp (1787-1826) in steel, and Werner von Siemens (1816-1892) in electricity, to Gottlieb Daimler (1834-1900) in the automobile, and to Thomas Edison (1847-1936), the inventor of the usable light bulb (1880).

Fundamentals of modern capitalism

The intellectual foundation of modern capitalism, which took shape in the two to three centuries before the industrial revolution, comprised the triad of the market, literacy, and the freedom of speech. Scientific thinking as a logical and experimental approach could, therefore, gain ground. The Enlightenment in the 18th century made independent thought and the artistic and scientific creativity its basic pillars.

Besides the political-spiritual factors such as individuality, personal freedom, and more, economic-material factors laid the groundwork for the take-off of modern capitalism in Europe. Besides accounting and the emergence of companies and run by profit-oriented entrepreneurs, the discovery of America contributed through the access to new sources of food and the supply of silver and gold. The discovery of America also contributed to the intensification of global commerce.

The entrepreneur is the motor of modern capitalism. The entrepreneurial task is to enforce innovations. In contrast to management and engineering knowledge, entrepreneurship is not a teachable subject because it is the opposite of routine, rules, and conventions. The entrepreneurial activity in capitalism consists in violating the standards, in abandoning the familiar and in bringing new things and new processes toward a breakthrough. Neither socialism nor feudalism or the ancient slave societies has a place for this person.

The discovery of gold and silver in America contributed to developing the monetary underpinnings of capitalism. Introducing double bookkeeping in Italy in the 15th century inspired modern mathematical thinking and provided business with the accounting tool to direct large enterprises. A network of payment and credit institutions spread across Europe. These developments happened spontaneously, locally and without a central power. As such, they were not the result of legislation but these individual areas, such as the foreign trade, developed their own legal principles, their own rules and their own ethics of business. Modern capitalism did not arise through the state, but it emerged and developed alongside the state as a parallel society.

Foundational factors of modern capitalism

Political-spiritual factors
- individuality
- personal freedom
- rationality
- empiricism,
- experimentation
- tolerance
- legality
- skepticism
- legality

Economic-material factors
- new sources of food
- increased supply of silver and gold
- printer with mobile letters
- global commerce
- accounting
- profit-oriented entrepreneurship

Antony P. Mueller

Market Process and Competition

Economic competition is not the same kind as competition is in sports. In sports, the goal - and thus the criterion of performance - is pre-determined. The competition is about to jump higher or farther, to run faster or to score more goals than the opponents. The 'end-product', so to speak, is given. In the market economy, however, competition is different. In economic competition what matters is to find out what the customers want and then to produce it at a favorable price. Contrary to sports with its rule-books, the machinations of economic competition are tacit and change with the competition process. The entrepreneurial behavior comprises advancement and imitation. For some time, a firm can earn excess profits by offering a product that more than that of the other vendors meets the tastes and wants of the customers. The economic game is about innovations, which change the rules, either in small steps by incremental advancements or by leaps due to major technological breakthroughs.

Successful projects find imitators. Imitation reduces the pioneers' profits and provides lower prices to the customers. As innovations diffuse over time throughout the economies and raise the economic productivity in all countries that take part in world trade, prosperity spreads around the globe.

Capitalism rests on special ownership of the means of production. The more intense competition, the more private property will serve the community. Competition functions as a control mechanism. The more competition prevails, the less it is necessary for the government to interfere with the property.

The more dynamic competition, the less the need for legal consumer protection.

Competition serves the public. The more there is economic competition, the less there is space for economic power. With a restricted market entry, private ownership loses its economic function. This was the case before the industrial revolution. The rulers granted monopolies to secure their power and gain a stream of income for themselves from the sale of the monopoly right. When the state grants such monopolies, property loses its capitalist meaning and becomes a domain. This economic system is far away from free capitalism.

Private ownership allows self-initiative and motivates one to manage the constant adjustment to the changing circumstances. Private ownership ensures the incentive to control costs and strive for innovation. Property rights, in their essence, begin with one's own person. A minimum state in this sense is thus always a state of law since it has the right of the individual as its first principle.

The value of a good is not an objective category. Value is individual and subjective according to the situation in which the individual finds himself with his needs and wants. The relative value of a good is not fixed but changes with the external and internal conditions. The economic actor must revalue the goods according to the current and expected circumstances and the changing personal needs and tastes. A meal has a different value, depending on whether one begins to eat the meal, or one has just ended eating a meal. It is therefore impermissible to infer from the overall benefit to the price, or even to justify the socialization of the production of certain goods because these are indispensable for human survival.

Backgrounder: Utility, value, and price

The utility is subjective and varies from person to person. Units of goods with objectively the same characteristics have different utilities for different persons. Universally, however, the law of decreasing marginal utility holds, which says that the more units of the same goods one consumes, the less is the marginal utility of each additional unit.

This 'saturation law', according to which, in an act of consumption, the respective following unit creates a diminishing limit value until the marginal utility disappears at the saturation point, was first formulated in 1854 by Hermann Heinrich Gossen (1810-1858).

Since the same good can serve in different ways and for different purposes, the utility of the good varies. Water, for example, can be used to drink, or to take a bath, or to wash one's car.

As a rule, the valuation of a good is given by the usefulness of the last unity of this good in the ranking of the available amount.

Eugen von Boehm-Bawerk (1851-1914) shows this principle by the example of Robinson Crusoe who has five sacks of grains of objectively the same quantity and quality but values each individual sack differently according to the urgency of his needs and ranks them accordingly.

In line with his subjective valuation, Robinson places at the first rank the unit which serves him to produce bread as his basic meal. The contents of the second sack of grain is to make cakes. The grain in the third sack serves to feed the chickens while the purpose of the grain in the fourth sack is to produce beverages and the fifth sack of grain is for his parrot as a pet.

According to the marginal theory, the utility of the five sacks of grain depend on the value of the last sack on the ranking. The ranking is not as to the good but concerns the purpose of the use of the good. The ranking is an act of human valuation. The order of preference is not in the goods but in the mind of the acting person. It would be erroneous to assume that the grain in the first sack on the rank order because it serves the livelihood, had the greatest value. This consideration neglects that the contents of the bags are identical and therefore interchangeable. For example, if the grain of the sack of grain that should provide the basic food is lost, the grain of the last sack serves to substitute it and is used for making bread. This may continue until the last bag. Accordingly, the availability of the last unit of the order of the rank, which the economic actor assigns to the same commodity units, determines the value of the individual units.

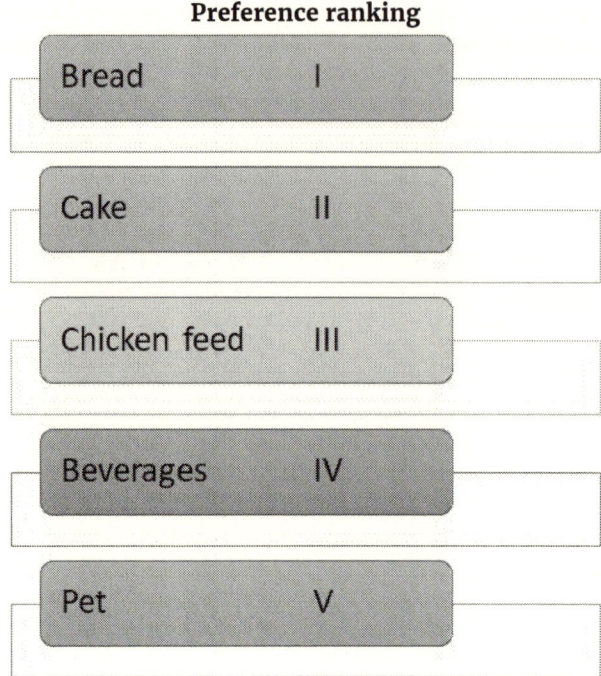

Preference ranking

- Bread — I
- Cake — II
- Chicken feed — III
- Beverages — IV
- Pet — V

The willingness to pay a certain price for a good depends on the marginal utility of the last unit, and not on the average or the overall value of the good. Although water, for example, is necessary for human survival, the price per unit is low, so long as enough units are available to satisfy the many uses of water. As long as there is enough water to wash one's car, the price of water to drink will likewise be cheap.

The value of a meal is different whether one is hungry or full. A specific medicine, which is necessary for the survival of one person, is useless for the person without the ailment.

The same context applies to production. The opportunity costs determine the value of a production factor as to its contribution to producing a good. Value, therefore, depends on the extent to which its marginal contribution is substitutable. This explains, for example, why the wage for a professional activity does not depend on how difficult it is to acquire this ability, but to what extent the activity is substitutable for the current production process to produce a good of high demand.

The value of a production factor, such as of labor or of capital, in its contribution to produce a good, depends on its opportunity costs, that is, on the extent to which its marginal contribution is substitutable. This explains, for example, that the remuneration of an activity does not depend on how difficult or painful it is to acquire a skill but to what extent the activity is substitutable for the current production process or not, and whether customers will pay for this product.

Determinants of value

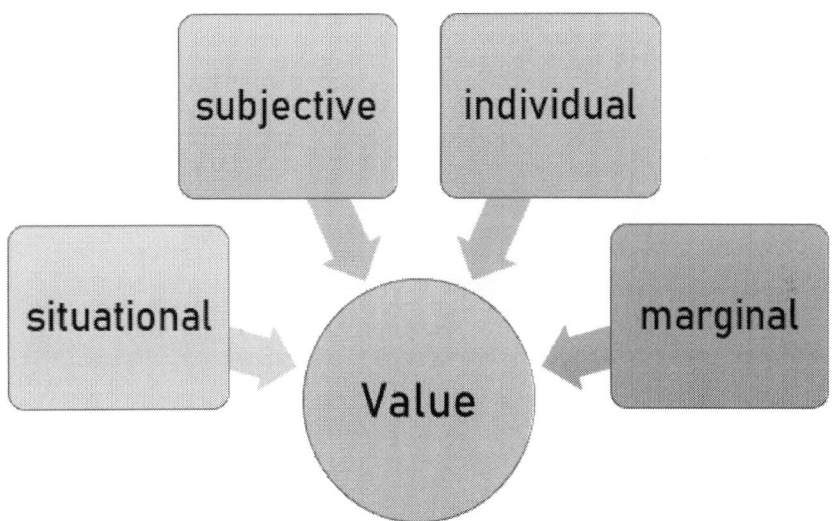

The value that the consumers contribute to the consumption good determines the value of the investment good. Not costs determine price, but the price that one can get for a consumption good determines the value of the investment good and consequently that of the factors of production.

The sale price of the consumer good provides the yardstick for the profitability of the investment and determines the remuneration of the factors of production in terms of wages and profits.

Chain of value determination

```
┌─────────────────────┐
│   Value of the      │
│   consumer good     │
└─────────────────────┘
           ▼
┌─────────────────────┐
│   Value of the      │
│   investment good   │
└─────────────────────┘
           ▼
┌─────────────────────┐
│ Value of the factors│
│   of production     │
└─────────────────────┘
```

Chain of determinants of remuneration

```
┌─────────────────────┐
│  Sale price of the  │
│  consumption good   │
└─────────────────────┘
           ▼
┌─────────────────────┐
│   Profitability of  │
│     investment      │
└─────────────────────┘
           ▼
┌─────────────────────┐
│ Remuneration of the │
│ factors of production│
└─────────────────────┘
```

Prices and their function

Prices represent income for the seller and are costs for the buyer. Prices inform about income and costs. They provide incentives for the seller to sell more if prices rise and to cut sales when prices fall.

Different from the buyer, for whom prices are costs, the incentives of the price call for buying less when prices rise and buy more when they fall.

This way, the prices on free markets move toward an equilibrium although they may never reach the condition of equilibrium in the sense of 'rest' and 'stability'.

The price-driven market process unfolds in response to a higher demand with an increasing quantity offered due to higher prices. Rising profits in the product segment, where a demand increase takes place, induce the entry of new suppliers along with expanding the production by the established firms. Suppliers thus expand the offer and increase the companies' capacity to deliver.

The market grows, and the prices fall. Lower prices lift the quantity demanded. The market enjoys a larger supply of goods at lower prices. A new market equilibrium takes hold.

To become effective, the price system must work properly, and this requires the absence of political interventions. When evaluating the market efficiency of concrete cases, one must keep in mind that already beginning with taxes, many political effects are at work that distort the system. It is wrong to assume perfect competition when capitalism is not free. The freer capitalism is, the more the markets will move to the ideal of perfect competition.

According to the individual assessment of benefits, the buyer determines his willingness to pay. In a market economy, all roads begin with the consumer. He is at the center of the system. His wishes and his preferences serve as input to shape the structure of the production apparatus. The demands of the consumers determine the value of the investment goods.

Entrepreneurs must act on behalf of the customer to earn a profit. The consumer as the end-user is the ultimate customer. The system works best when it can operate without distorting interferences. This is the meaning of the laissez-faire principle. A laissez-faire economy is an economy in which there is free space for the private initiative. The idea of 'laissez-faire' is not 'let it be' but rather 'let us do it'. As such, the saying refers to the role of entrepreneurs to satisfy the consumers' wishes without requiring state approval.

Market process

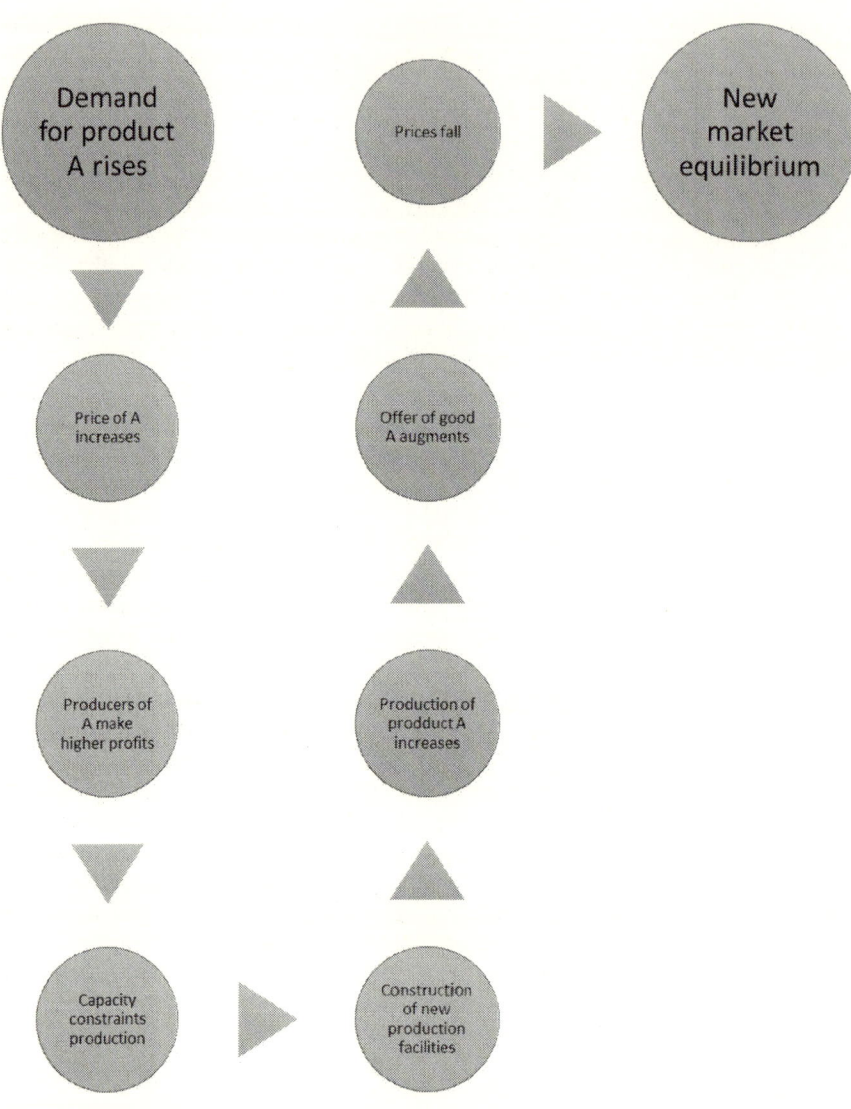

Once the legal system recognizes and guarantees the private ownership of the means of production, the market economy arises with the price system as its central facility.

Prices have two functions. They provide information on scarcity, and secondly, the price of a product signals the cost for the buyer and the income to the vendor. Prices function as signals and serve as economic incentives. The areas that are under state regulation in a socialist system, emerge spontaneously and automatically in a market economy.

If competition with unrestricted market access prevails, monopolies cannot last long. Monopolistic positions on the basis of technological progress disappear when further innovation makes the former obsolete. Stable monopolies require a charter by the state. Pure capitalism is not a monopoly capitalism. Monopoly capitalism is the consequence of crony capitalism. As in feudalism, such a system leads to economic stagnation and to a loss of productivity because the incentive to cost control and to innovation is lost.

In a market economy, even if a monopoly should exist, but the entry barriers are low, the monopolistic company cannot take advantage of its monopoly position, as it must face potential competition. Competition in contestable markets means that if a company abuses its monopoly, new firms would enter the market and the monopolistic position would be gone.

The control of competitive markets takes place through the price system. Competition means auto-control. Relatively high prices indicate that there is a scarcity of this good. Since prices represent income for the seller and costs for the buyer, there is an automatism on competitive markets, which leads to the alleviation of the scarcity. The producers will supply more goods when the price rises whereas the buyers of this commodity will demand less and use the product more economically when it becomes expensive. In order to function this way, the property must be private, and the costs must be borne by the individual owner.

In a free competition, there is a tendency to equilibrium on the market, which corresponds to the best use of the resources. This condition, however, is only temporary, since neither the wishes of the consumers nor the technology remains constant.

Higher relative prices show that there is inadequate production in relation to the demand for this product. In the first phase, this will lead to better utilization of existing production facilities. There is an increase in the quantity offered. In the second phase, there will be an increase in the supply when investments have enlarged the production capacity.

The signaling and incentive mechanisms of the price system on competitive markets provide the conditions that suppliers and demanders adapt their behavior according to price changes in the area where there is a discrepancy between demand and supply. The interplay of supply and demand thus ensures, by means of entrepreneurial action, that capital flows into such areas where demand is high relative to the supply, while entrepreneurs remove capital from areas where there is an abundance of capital and where overcapacity exists. This is the basic principle of the allocative efficiency of the market economy.

It is a boon and a tragedy that even with severe interventions, the price system works well. While the price system is robust enough to support many interventions, it is not immune and invulnerable. Each individual intervention weakens the market so that the quality of its performance decreases. With each intervention, the malfunctions accumulate. The capacity of markets to adapt slows down. It takes longer for the supply to respond to demand shifts. Gaps widen between supply and demand. It is as much paradoxical as it is tragic that these gaps, which result from excessive intervention, serve the interventionist to demand more interventions. The result is the interventionist spiral which says that each interference will lead to new additional interventions because the interference before has deteriorated the market performance, to begin with.

The efficient allocation of capital means that capital flows into those areas where it yields the highest returns. Because of this shift in the capital structure, the bottlenecks of supply disappear, and excess profits vanish. The faster and the more capital flows into the area where most of the scarcity prevails, quicker the bottlenecks vanish and the faster extraordinary capital gains dissolve.

It is the essence of the market economy that special profits arise and that because of that, individual companies and their owners accumulate wealth. At the same time, however, the market system functions in such a way that, when the allocation process can go on in an unhampered way, extra profits disappear. The more dynamic the economy is in the sense that there are open markets and that entrepreneurial action has great leeway, the less is there a persistent deficiency of supply. The more capitalist the economy, the faster extra profits dissipate.

The price system does not always work to perfection. The criticism of the 'market failure', however, misses the crucial point because in the real world it does not so much matter whether markets are perfect but how robust the price system works and whether even under unfavorable conditions it is still functioning to indicate scarcity.

Interventionist cost spiral

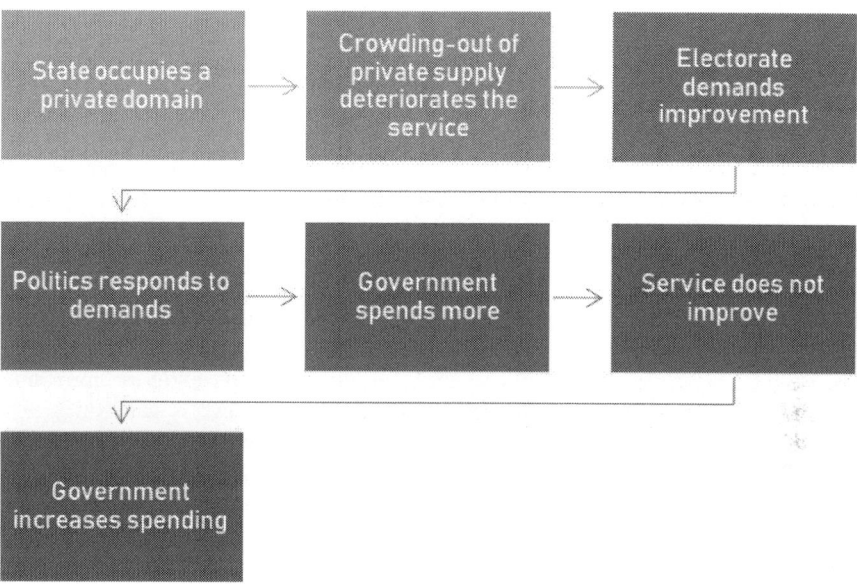

Some interventionists conclude that the market economy is indestructible and that one can intervene as much as one wants. This view is as erroneous as the theory of market failure that uses perfection as the criterion. Errors as these, form the intellectual basis of the interventionist spiral. A perceived, yet de facto non-existent, market failure leads to market intervention whereby this interference into the market produces the market failure the interventionist claims to cure when in fact it was the interference that brought the failure into existence. This way, the interventionist receives the confirmation of his claim and he will go on with further interventions although it was the market intervention itself that provoked the apparent 'market failure'.

Prices and Competition

The price of a good or service results from the interplay of supply and demand and the estimation of the commodity's utility by the individual market participants. Pricing in competitive markets means that the market price tends towards the minimum average costs where it equals marginal costs. The interplay of demand and supply is in constant change and relative prices move according to the relative degrees of scarcity. The market equilibrium balances the quantity demanded with the quantity offered. The law of supply and demand says that the higher the price, the higher the quantity offered and the lower the quantity demanded.

The interplay between supply and demand, on the one hand, and, on the other hand, the subjective utility and the opportunity costs, determine the price. The utility estimate of the individual market participant determines the individual value of the goods. The value of a good is not equal to its price.

While the price is an objective category, its value is subjective. The determinants of the value are subjective, individual, and situational. The value estimation changes marginally depending on the situation in which the individual operates. Scarcity means that goods are less available than people want. As determinants of prices (not as an accounting tool) costs are opportunity costs and, in this sense, as subjective as the utility.

Determinants of price

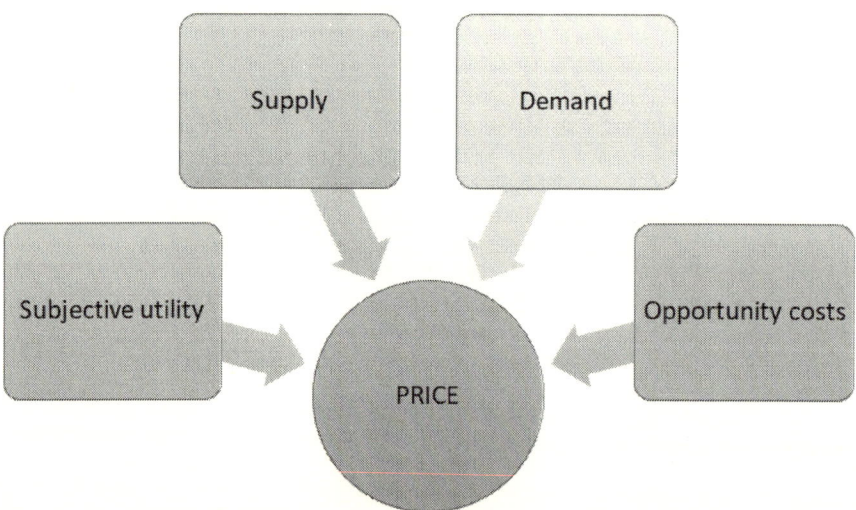

Scarcity is not an objective, but a subjective category. For a good to be scarce, it is not sufficient to be just rare. Scarcity describes the relation between the supply of a specific good and a person's subjective valuation of this good. Thus, the same kind of meal is scarce for a person who is hungry, yet no longer scarce after the person has eaten and is full. The relative prices of goods are numerical market phenomena. They come about through the interaction of the market participants. The equilibrium rate indicates at which price the highest possible number of transactions takes place in a market. The dynamism of capitalist competition unfolds from innovations that lead to pioneering profits. This market dominance due to a new product or a new process is only temporary.

If there is a free market entry, competitors will try to mimic the new products and processes, thereby differentiating and improving innovation.

The temporary monopoly profits diminish with the additional offer on the market. A new market equilibrium is emerging.

Product and process renewals spread across the market according to demand. At the pioneer company, profits go down to normal, while consumers' purchasing power and their real income increase to a higher level.

Competitive process

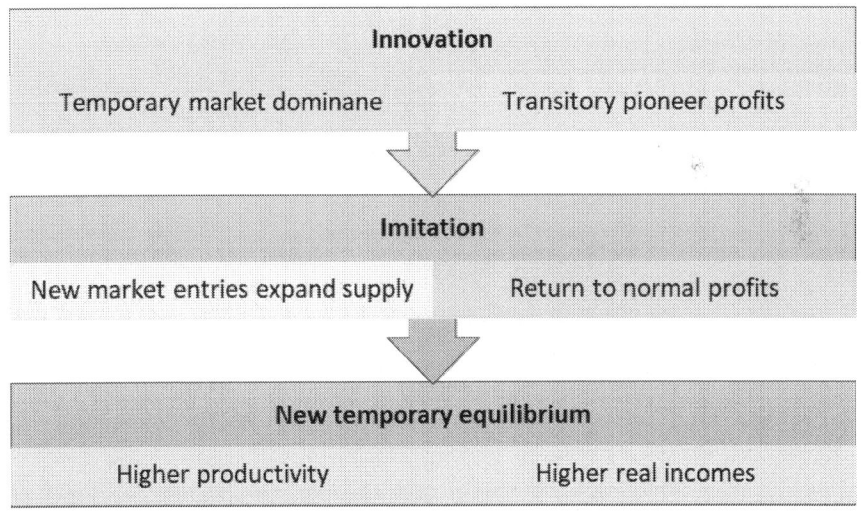

Mass production

The French king Louis XIV (1638-1715) had more than a thousand servants in his Palace of Versailles. Yet that would not change the fact that, despite this large group of subordinates, there was no hot water shower in the palace, and many other items of comfort were lacking, which nowadays are in every apartment of a social housing project. The sun king wore an impressive wig, and he was perfumed, yet this was necessary because there was no shampoo and the equipment of the palace with 'toilets' was well below any modern standards.

Before the industrial revolution, the rich were poorer than the poor today in the capitalist industrialized countries. Nowadays, the common tourist travels to Versailles by coach or by car. When he has finished his sightseeing, thousands of waiters and other servants in thousands of restaurants, cafes, bars, and hotels are waiting in Paris to entertain this tourist with food, drink, and bed.

Features of modern capitalism

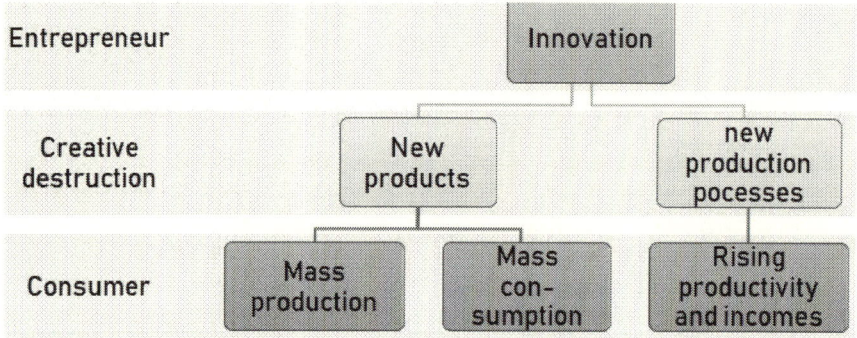

Modern capitalism serves the mass of the consumers. Those who work in the factories are the same people who consume the goods, which are manufactured there.

The equipment of US households with durable consumer goods such as telephone, electricity, automobile, radio, refrigerator, cooker, washing machine, tumble dryer, color-TV, air conditioning, dishwasher, microwave, video player, computer, mobile phones, and the Internet.

The process of spreading the consumer goods among the population is speeding up. While it took more than half a century for the phone and the car to reach over 80% of the households, it only took a decade for the video players and the mobile phones.

What is remarkable about this process is that many of the modern consumer goods not only make life easier and more enjoyable, such as a microwave oven or the access to hot water, but the modern goods also increase the value of leisure, such as the radio, television, video games, and the Internet.

***

Prosperity finds its expression not only in more consumption but also in the access to a better quality of goods and to a greater variety of products. Nowadays, a medium-sized supermarket runs an assortment that goes into the tens of thousands of different products.

The difference between the past and the present shows up in the general life expectancy. Two hundred years ago, average life expectancy was under forty years. In the meantime, life expectancy has doubled, and the average purchasing power has risen by a multiple. Compared to the past, not only the quantity of the goods has increased but likewise their quality and even more so the variety of goods.

Life expectancy has increased since 1800. Before the industrial revolution, life expectancy was around 30 years in all regions of the world. Since 1800, the global average life expectancy has more than doubled and is now around 70 years on average and over 80 years in some advanced countries.

Life expectancy has not only increased because of a falling child mortality. In 1841, a 5-year-old could expect to live 55 years. Today a 5-year-old can expect to live 82 years. At higher ages, mortality patterns have also changed, so that compared to the time before the industrial revolution, the life expectancy of a 50-year-old has increased from 20 years to 33 years. (Max Roser, Our World in Data. Life Expectancy. https://ourworldindata.org/life-expectancy/)

***

Economic growth is a false term if it denotes bigger and more. Growth in capitalism consists in using new, better, and cheaper goods. The basis of economic growth is higher productivity and technical progress in all its variants. In the course of this development, more people are enjoying goods, which were accessible only to the rich. No other economic system has brought as much prosperity to ordinary people than modern capitalism. This economic system creates new wealth through the ongoing process of 'creative destruction'. Technological progress is the motor of the entrepreneurial monetary economy, and production for the masses is its hallmark. The capitalist system promotes adaptable and efficient firms and eliminates the less productive enterprises. The basic conflict of modern capitalism does not consist in the struggle of capitalists against proletarians but in the conflict between pioneers and laggards, between those who produce change and adapt to change, and those who fall behind because they fail to change and to innovate. The conflict is between losers and winners, and workers and capitalists are found in both categories.

Corporate management is a constant endeavor for the highest possible productivity. Those companies will win the market competition that fulfill the wishes of the customer faster, better, and more cost-efficient than their competitors. In the long term, the rise of productivity will benefit everyone and reach the masses. The benefit comes at different times to different people. In the short term, there are losers in a relative way. Yet in the long run, capitalism makes everyone a winner.

Impatience is the enemy of economic growth. By redistribution, people want more goods now through political means even if they would get them through the natural process of economic growth in greater abundance later. People seldom notice that the market interventions, which they demand and the distributive benefits, which they receive, do not speed up to provide the goods but prolong the time of delivery because these measures slow down the dynamics of capitalism and because of these measures, productivity rises slower. The greatest enemy of the poor is redistribution because it keeps the poor in lethargic dependence.

Capitalism is a dynamic system. Uncertainty and risk are the prices of progress. Yet in this respect, the past was no different. On the contrary. Much more than today, people had to confront diseases, the weather, and the fluctuations of food production. A life of hunger, poverty, and misery marked most of the humankind before the industrial revolution. While there is never and nowhere a system of complete security in this world, free capitalism ends absolute poverty and makes the way free for individual success irrespective of one's origin. Need and care are the eternal companions of human existence. Even free capitalism does not lead to a carefree life. Yet capitalism liberates humankind from absolute misery and bondage.

In the pre-capitalist period, the inequality of wealth was greater than today. It is true that capitalism as an entrepreneurial monetary economy leads to accumulating wealth and income in some hands, but these extremes are now rather less than they were in the past, and above all, the relative wealth positions are not permanent in capitalism.

Since 1820, the world has become both richer and more equal. This development occurred because more countries have been moving to a capitalist economic order over the past 200 years. See Max Roser: What on Earth is going on? https://ourworldindata.org/income-inequality/

Before the industrial revolution, the upper class was small. Much of the population lived in extreme poverty and need. Since then, poverty has declined in those regions, which have adopted and developed the system of entrepreneurial monetary capitalism. Earlier economic systems made a few persons rich, but the rest remained poor. Capitalism makes a few persons extremely rich, but it makes also the rest wealthier than in any other system.

Capitalism makes not only some people rich, but also the rest much more prosperous than it has ever been in history.

***

The value of an investment project depends on the extent to which it contributes to satisfying the subjective individual utilities of the final consumers. The cost calculation is an indispensable tool to assess the profit chances of a project. The final judgment on the profits, however, is in the hands of the consumer. This also applies to investment goods, which have value as intermediate goods in so far as they contribute to the producing the consumer goods as the final goods. The individual additions to the value at each step along the stages of production receive their compensation when the final consumer pays for the goods.

The management of a company must fulfill the functions to estimate the future demand of the buyer and to produce the goods at the minimum cost. The attainment of these objectives requires experimentation to succeed. Business is trial and error. One can plan the trial but not its success. Competition serves to find out what consumers want and how to manufacture the goods in the most cost-effective way.

Modern capitalism serves the people through mass production and provides goods for mass consumption. In capitalism, there is no end to this process because the economy will grow with the pace of productivity. In order to understand this connection, one must keep in mind that in a competitive economy, economic profits result from higher productivity. In a market economy, economic growth is linked to profits, and profits result from productivity gains.

The function of the entrepreneur is to implement innovations.

The entrepreneur fulfills the task of creative destruction by overcoming the resistance against new products and new processes.

Different from the inventor or administrator, the entrepreneur is the one who has the specific ability to bring new products and new production methods to the market.

Innovation involves creative destruction as it breaks the prevailing market conditions and makes existing products and production processes obsolete.

Innovation benefits the consumers in the form of mass production and mass consumption, and due to higher productivity brings rising incomes and an increase of the purchasing power.

***

Capitalism means permanent revolution. In the market economy, there is no standstill and no equilibrium. New companies enter the scene; established companies disappear. Entrepreneurial activity creates new goods and modifies existing goods while obsolete products disappear from the market just as it happens with old production methods. Because of this dynamism, the structure of the market economy is changing and what was the case yesterday is no longer valid today. This means that new opportunities surface for new rivals to enter the market. In the market economy, the cards are re-distributed again and again. Crises are windows of opportunity when the asset prices fall. These crises offer chances for new companies with new projects. Instead of lamenting the crises, one should take them as a signal of the phases of economic transformation.

Capitalism is not perfect, but there is no other economic system where the advantages so outweigh the disadvantages. The capitalist economic system benefits above all the broad mass of the population. Capitalism delivers the goods, which at first were available only for the wealthy, to ever more people. Capitalism produces not only masses of goods, but also more so new and improved goods.

Freedom and Capitalism

Modern capitalism originated in Europe. Its cornerstones are commerce, cooperative competition, and decentralization along with private ownership of the means of production and the cultural ingredients such as individual dignity, love of truth, literacy, experimental (scientific) thinking, bookkeeping, and arithmetic. This modern capitalism experiences its legitimacy through the prosperity that it spreads. This prosperity is beneficial to the masses. Inequality exists, but under capitalism, inequality has an economic function; it serves as an incentive to achieve economic progress, i.e., to realize innovation and promote inventions.

The price system of the market economy ensures that supply and demand adapt to the conditions of scarcity. In this sense, there are no limits to growth. The scarcer a commodity, the more expensive it is on the market and the higher are the incentives to find substitutes and economize its use. Economic progress in capitalism results from constant efforts to produce goods of better quality at lower prices. The hallmark of entrepreneurial capitalism is the constant pressure to innovate.

The tendency to innovation, which is inherent in capitalism, provokes social change. These social commotions that come with capitalism call the anti-capitalists to the scene. In the resistance to accepting change as the essence of this economic system, modern history unfolds as a grand conflict. Since its emergence, modern capitalism must confront two separate opponents: Communism, born of utopian thought, and conservatism with its roots in the past. Communism and conservatism both continue to live on as great illusions. The socialist paradise does not come, and there is no way to go back in time.

In the market economy, every market participant pursues his own interest and promotes the common good because capital moves into those areas where scarcity is the highest. The consumer wants to increase his utility while the company's aim is to make profits. The universal language of the market is money in its expression as prices, costs, and profits. With the help of money prices, one can compare the goods with one another and relate the prices to one's income. The individual consumer can compare each good with every other good and weigh their price and value according to his personal preferences. This process happens also in production where the investment goods receive their valuation according to the extent to which they contribute to the profit of a company.

The monetary system, and thus the system of money-prices, does not function without error, but economic calculation without money is not possible when the process of production exceeds simple forms. In a household or in a small homestead, each associate can supervise all other members without the help of monetary calculation. Yet when the economic activities become more complex, one needs money and price calculation. Even that the purchasing value of money does not remain constant, does not outweigh the disadvantages of non-monetary management. Capital, for example, exists as a collection of production goods, but only its expression in monetary units makes it possible to speak of capital in terms of an entity and to relate it to other numbers, such as the yield, for example.

Summary

There is no perfect economic system. Scarcity does not disappear. The earthly human life is limited in time, and time is the ultimate scarce resource of human existence. The necessity to evaluate trade-offs will persist. Yet capitalism fulfills its function of providing prosperity and freedom. Capitalism removes absolute poverty from the life of the masses. We are not at the end of capitalism but still at its beginning. There is still a long way to free capitalism. In order to improve this system, fundamental reforms of the financial system, of politics, and of the legal system are necessary. More capitalism does not mean disorder. On the contrary. The freer the economy, the higher the productivity and thus the income. Rising income means less poverty. This is the great achievement of modern capitalism. Since the industrial revolution over two hundred years ago, the percentage of people living in poverty has declined worldwide. This development has come about because more countries have dropped their feudal and socialist regimes in favor of capitalism.

That the future belongs to capitalism must be understood in such a way that the future belongs to those countries, which put the least obstacles into place against the development of a free economy. It should be clear to everyone that if Europe or America will not do it, other countries and regions are already on the way to a free capitalism.

III.

WEALTH CREATION

BEYOND THE STATE AND POLITICS

> *"Innovation is the outstanding fact in the economic history of capitalist society or in what is purely economic in this history, and it is also largely responsible for most of what we would at first glance trace to other factors."*
>
> Joseph Schumpeter: Business Cycles: A Theoretical, Historical, and Statistical Analysis of the Capitalist Process 1939 (New York: McGraw-Hill), p. 86

- *The meaning of economic growth -*
- *Growth traps -*
- *The rise and fall of parasitic economies -*
- *Economics of wealth creation -*
- *Backgrounder: time preference -*
- *Backgrounder: Interest, consumption, and savings*
- *Value creation and capital structure -*
- *The state as an enemy of growth -*
- *Creative destruction -*
- *Obstacles to innovation -*
- *Free trade -*
- *Summary*

Productivity is the key to prosperity. Without productivity gains, there is no rise in incomes. Escaping from poverty requires economic growth. Yet what brings about economic growth? The term 'growth', when applied to the economy, is misleading. Although economic growth means a higher production and a higher per capita income of the population, it is that the economy must not only grow bigger, but it must become more productive. If one were to produce always more with the same methods of production as in the past without technical progress, the economy would reach the limits of growth. The key to understanding economic growth is productivity.

In capitalism, there are no limits to growth because innovation is the motor of economic change. Because of the technological progress, the economy becomes more productive. When productivity rises, it takes less input to produce the same amount of output or with the same amount of input one can produce a higher output.

The price system tackles the problem of scarcity. If certain resources become scarcer, their price will rise in a free market economy. The self-interest of consumers and producers leads them to use the scarce goods more carefully and to look for a replacement. The higher the relative price for an existing product, the more rewarding is it to change to its substitute.

The Meaning of Economic Growth

Economic growth in terms of a rise in per capita income is a child of the industrial revolution. The passage toward rising productivity came because of companies that systematically put a part of their profits back into expanding their businesses. This principle still holds today. In a country where the population is still too poor to save enough, it is up to the companies to finance investment from their own profits. England has shown this path during its leadership of the industrial revolution. The other countries, which have industrialized, have followed this model. The economic recoveries of Germany and Japan after World War II used this method. China's development policy uses re-investing profits as the main means of funding investment. Countries failed in economic growth where the state installed monopolies where the profitability of the companies remained suppressed or where – because of the danger of expropriation – the reinvestment of profit has been too risky and the outcomes too uncertain. In principle, capital accumulation has failed where investment was not in private hands but largely in the hands of state companies.

Types of savings

One must distinguish between private and public savings. Public savings refer to the balance of the government's receipts in relation to its spending. Having a budget deficit means that public saving is negative. As such, it will diminish the level of national savings. Private savings comprise the savings of families and businesses. Net savings of families takes place when consumption is lower than income. Reinvested profits by companies count as savings. Savings in the form of reinvested profits foster economic growth because it allows the funding new ventures with one's own financial means.

The gross domestic product (GDP) is the sum of the production of the individual companies of a country's private and public companies. Not 'the' national economy produces the GDP, but the national product is the output of the multitude of a country's private and public firms. In order to achieve a higher total product, the factories, offices, and the other production units that sell their products on the market must produce more. Economic growth happens at the level of the individual companies. The growth dynamics of an economy depends on the constellation of factors that determine the incentives for companies to produce more or whether the entrepreneurial creation of value confronts obstacles that inhibit and block wealth accumulation. In so far as the public expenditures depend on taxation, all economic growth rests on the shoulders of the productivity of a country's companies.

Economic growth serves as the prominent standard for measuring the performance of an economy. However, what gets published as the gross domestic product (GDP) does not represent production but reports overall spending. Calculating economic growth is based on the nominal gross domestic product deflated by a price index.

The figure for economic growth is subject to two distortions: the indicator does not measure production but reports expenditures, and, second, the number for 'real gross domestic product' depends on the techniques to calculate the price index.

Components of national savings

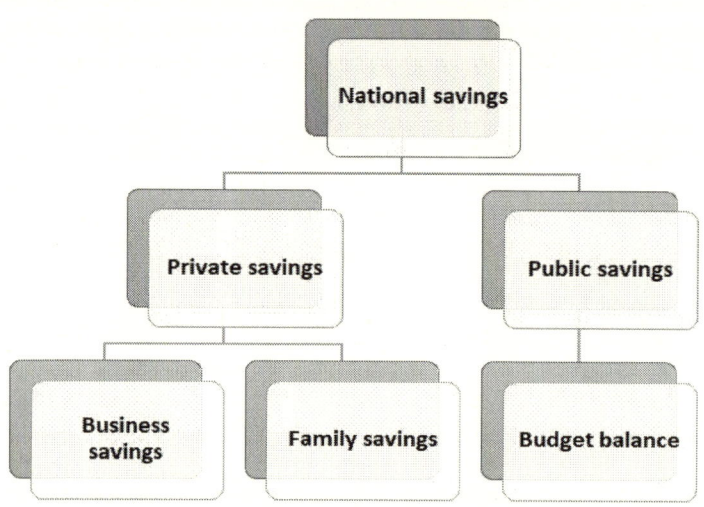

Economic growth figures can be determined fairly accurate for an economy, which is in a primitive state when a few identifiable and compoundable items are being produced, as it is the case with basic agricultural products. In the 1950s and 1960s, one used also tons of steel, for example, as a proxy for a timely estimate of a country's economic performance. Nowadays, the figure for the gross domestic production gets all the attention, although the basis for its calculation is more fragile than before.

Economic growth had its heyday with the spread of the social gospel that it is up to the state and its government to guarantee general welfare by managing the economy and to redistribute income. In this context, economic growth was conceptualized as an increase in standardized goods production, and the output served as the benchmark for the standard of living. It was for such aims that the modern system of national income accounting with the concept of economic growth at its heart was established, and this measurement device has never lost its link to mass production.

National income statistics and macroeconomic models use as a premise the identity between spending and production based on the tautology that sold production equals expenditures. What is being calculated here is this: income and – as its tautological counterpart – spending. However, the production itself could only be measured in uniform units of goods or services. When heterogeneous goods and complex services get produced, overall aggregation is not possible in a non-monetary form.

Calculating economic growth in terms of 'real GDP' requires deflating the nominal values of expenditures. To do that, the statistical offices create a basket of goods and compare the prices of the goods in this basket to those of the respective reference periods. But there is no objective representative basket of GDP other than as a statistical construct constructed with the help of many disputable assumptions. There is no common standard, which would allow the comparison of one period's production to the other when in fact current output consists in an ensemble of new and modified goods and services that differ from those of the past. Neither for an individual nor a family or a nation, the 'basket of purchases' stays constant. It changes from day to day, and from months to months, not to speak of years and decades. There is no way how a statistical office or any other agency could trace all these changes.

Measuring the economy as a whole as it is the aim the GDP-figure owes its popularity to the Cold War and that its origins have their roots in managing the war economy of the first half of the 20th century. Before World War I, economists worked in a tradition that was for peace, free trade, and for limited government. Thereafter, the perspective changed. With the experience of the industrialized warfare machinery and of the welfare state, economists found a new expanding field of job opportunities for them in government activism. Consequently, the dominant philosophy of the discipline changed from laissez-faire to interventionism. It was in this context that the statistical and aggregate approach to economic issues gained its momentum.

The managers of a war economy want to measure output and its growth because the economy is at the service of the war aims. Then, the central planning authority can know whether the goods and services that it needs get produced and at which proportions the factors of production it should allocate. In a war economy, the distribution of the production is in the hand of the government. Under such conditions, the planners rank the increase in output, and economic growth, as it is measured as an increase in output, serves as the indicator of economic performance. For a private economy, this procedure makes no sense because only individual goals count, different from the 'collective purpose' of winning a war.

The more we move away from basic goods, and that we have an advanced and dynamic, non-stationary economy, with many heterogeneous goods and services, attempts to measure 'the economy' have become more complicated, and these calculations have lost much of their economic meaning. The concept of total output and its measurement and thus of economic growth is a statistical construct that lacks informational value for an economy characterized by a wide variety of goods and services and in which producing new types of goods and services occurs while many other items become obsolete.

The economy is not like a pumpkin that grows to maturity and whose size can be measured at each stage and whose weight can be compared from one season to the next. Also, the economy is not a cake we all bake and then consume together. It is this pumpkin-like and cake-like understanding of economic activity that has provided the basis for most of the popular fallacies regarding production, distribution, and economic policy-making.

For governments, using the figure of the GDP as an indicator of economic performance has contributed to severe illusions of fiscal and monetary policy such as when spending for consumption is said to produce wealth or when government spending should boost economic growth as it happens – among others – with military expenditures.

Times of war and the preparation for it come along with high economic growth rates. Festive state acts produce peaks of production. Likewise, GDP got a boost after a pharaoh had died in ancient Egypt and the economy under the order to build a new pyramid. Yet this growth has no benefit for the people. On the contrary.

The problem with economic growth goes beyond statistics. Approaching the economic problem in terms of growth and stability is a severe obstacle to understanding the true nature of the economic activity as an exchange-oriented action directed at improving personal conditions. Economic growth as measured by the gross domestic product directs the policymakers to the lump sum of an imaginary output instead of allowing a market-driven adaptation to the diverse needs, wants, and wishes of the individuals.

In the context of a non-collectivist economic theory, economic growth, as it is measured by real GDP, has no place. Likewise, in a non-collectivist economic system, the focus would be not on economic growth, but on the conditions of market exchange as the way to economic amelioration. Given that the criteria for assessing economic improvement are individual and subject to change, no guideline is adequate other than that there are unhampered markets, protection of property rights, and the freedom of private initiative.

In a non-collectivist economic system, the focus would not be on 'sustained economic growth' as the oxymoronic expression says for the 'common good' in economic policy. The individualistic economic theory would focus on the prevalent conditions of market exchange as the way to economic amelioration. In this view, what brings about improvement, comes not from economic growth or from stability, but through the economic transformation under the guidance of entrepreneurial action within an open market system.

The grand-scale interventions that monetary and fiscal policy perform in the name of growth and stability disrupt and misguide the plans of the individual economic actor. They distort the decisions at the business level. Applying macroeconomic growth models has caused havoc when economic leaders adopt the interventionist creed and believe that it just takes the handling of a few economic policy variables – like easy money or government expenditures – to achieve the blissful state of economic plenty.

Instead of its fixation on economic growth and stability, a non-interventionist system would favor leeway for individual decision-making to pursue his own preferences. The interventionist system, in contrast, puts the individual under serfdom where 'output' or rather 'expenditure' become the criteria. Economic growth puts a criterion of performance upon the individual that is detrimental to change and adaptation and to the individual pursuit of benefit. Not unlike the slave masters of the past, the modern interventionist state uses its levers to push the individual by incentives and constraints towards an obscure output that is called 'economic growth'.

Growth Traps

The productivity of human labor rises when more capital becomes available and when this capital finds productive use. Total factor productivity signifies an increase of output without an increase in labor and capital or other factors of production. Labor productivity – which determines the wage level – increases with capital accumulation, which requires investments and thus savings. The poverty trap comprises the vicious circle that savings will be low when income is low. Low-income per capita implies low savings per capita, and low savings per capita imply low investment. Because the capital stock does not grow, income per capita remains low. How can one save enough if the income is meager? This is the poverty trap, which had kept humankind in deprivation until the industrial revolution. Saving requires an income above the subsistence level. Yet to have a high per capita income one must accumulate capital first. This requires saving, which, in turn, depends on the income available.

Poverty trap

The poverty trap consists in the vicious circle that low income allows only a low level of savings, and therefore of small investment. A low level of capital formation implies little production and income. If the investment is small, capital accumulation is also weak. A low level of capital goods means that income is also low. So long as there are no companies that earn and reinvest profits, there is no escape from the poverty trap.

The poverty trap transforms into a wealth cycle when companies reinvest their profits. Capital formation in companies is the path to a higher production. The increase in productivity leads to higher incomes. When incomes rise, more savings are available and more capital formation and productivity gains become possible. The economy experiences its 'take-off'.

Poverty cycle

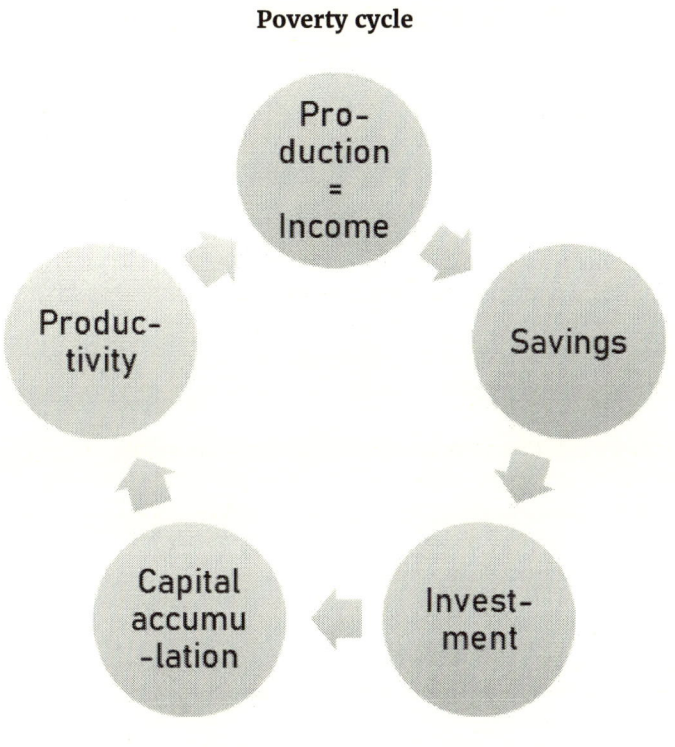

***

The violence trap aggravates the poverty trap. The world's history is a history of acts of violence because, throughout most of history, robbery was the preferred path to wealth. The state rose to historical prominence as a plundering machine. States represent the political means to gain a living different from the economical method. Every state is extractive in contrast to the economy, which is productive.

In the past, the great empires came into existence when one horde concentrated its efforts on martial purposes to prepare for the plundering of those groups that had settled to produce for consumption goods. Looting, however, works only until there is nothing left to loot. This way, all ancient empires were bound to fall.

As Franz Oppenheimer explains in his treatise on "The State" (German original "Der Staat" 1929), conquest and slavery have served as the means of exploitation throughout history. Plundering is a parasitic economy. When humans became sedentary, they dealt with nature no longer only in an extractive way, but productively as they began to plan crops and to cultivate domesticated animals and plants. Yet this did not put an end to poverty and violence. Robbery and oppression continued to gain a living when it came in the form of an organized state or as a state-like entity on a grand scale.

The problem of the parasitic economy is that parasites can survive only as a minority because their living depends on the surplus product of the hosts. Yet the incentives structure that prevails in a parasitic economy provokes the proliferation of consumption by the parasites and a diminished production by the exploited part of the population. Therefore, parasitic wealth is not permanent.

The robber state disintegrates society. Raiding annihilates the incentive to accumulate capital and thus leads to a decline in productivity. The output of goods and services dwindles whereas the exigencies of the exploiters keep on rising. The basis of such parasitic societies erodes. In the end, the parasites perish together with their hosts.

Backgrounder:
The rise and fall of parasitic economies

Parasitic robber economies are not sustainable. They strengthen the parasites at the expense of the host in the first phase but lead in the second phase to the death of the host and thus of the parasite as well.

The more a country finds its way to prosperity, a more attractive victim it becomes for the parasites.

While the parasite grows through exploitation, the host gets weaker. The incentives in favor of parasitism are increasing while those for productive activity are shrinking.

The result is a decline of the host and the weakening of the parasite.

An economy based on robbery and parasitism is not sustainable. The capital stock decays, knowledge gets lost. In a parasitic state, distribution conflicts are always present and, therefore, the costs of production are high. Parasitic economies are inefficient. The exploitative economy and society arises through violence, maintains itself through violence, and disintegrates through violence. At the end of the process, both the host and the parasite will perish.

Modern societies suppress the private exertion of violence and arm themselves against robbery and violence from abroad, but this does not exclude institutionalized robbery by the state itself against its own citizens. While the state holds the monopoly of the use of force in modern societies, subtle ways of extraction have replaced the open exploitation of the empires of the past.

***

The history of humanity is a history of parasitic robber economies. Before the industrial revolution, a warlike orientation of a country's economy was superior to a society that focused on the peaceful production of consumption goods. Modern capitalism has changed this balance. Since modern capitalism has taken hold, those countries that have a consumer-oriented economy are also militarily strong. However, exploitation and violence have not ended. Today, while the wealth in the industrialized countries is less in danger from private violence and from foreign invasion, wealth creation is at risk from the state itself.

The state, whose original function was to protect property, has become its fiercest violator. Although property rights still enjoy recognition, these rights are under attack by the state itself, most prominently by taxation and other forms of redistribution. In a perverse twist of history, to achieve domestic peace and security against external attacks has not closed the doors to domestic parasitism. The modern parasitism hides behind the mask of social justice and equality.

Backgrounder: Population Growth and Income

Until the industrial revolution, humankind found itself in the demographic trap. As more food became available per capita, there were more offspring. With the rise of the population, the increase in food per capita would disappear.

It took until the industrial revolution around 1800 that technical progress accelerated so that the rate of food production exceeded that of human reproduction.

Before the industrial revolution, gains in production did not compensate for the increase of the population that came with a better provision of goods.

The rise of income per capita in the first phase such made the way to the fall of income per capita in the following phase.

Despite the sharp increase in the population since the start of the industrial revolution, there has been no food shortage in the capitalist countries except for wars or other conflicts.

In the thousands of years before Christ, the world's population grew slowly. For the time around the birth of Christ, the estimates are between 150 and 300 million people in the world. Around 1850 the number of people on earth reached a billion for the first time.

In the meantime, the world's population has risen to seven billion.

Yet there is no reason to worry about a so-called 'overpopulation'. First, the growth rate of the population decreases after passing through the so-called 'demographic transition', and, second, there is enough space on earth. For a population density, such as exists in Paris, for example, the entire world population would occupy less space than is available in the State of Texas.

The population growth is about to stop because the reproduction rate is falling which is already the case.

From an annual growth rate of 2.1 % in the 1960s, the projections say that the annual growth rate of the world is to fall to a rate of 0.1 % in 2100.

In the early stages of development, the poverty, violence and population trap threaten economic progress. For the advanced economies, the hazards are the middle-income trap along with the imperialism and welfare trap.

***

Development Traps

Traps in the early stages of development
Poverty Trap
Insufficient savings inhibit capital accumulation, which in turn limits income and thereby savings
Violence Trap
In the short run, robbery is more effective than production, yet parasitic economies are not sustainable as they lead to the rise and fall of empires

Population Trap
While absolute production rises, per capita income stagnates as the rate of population growth exceeds the rate of the growth of production

Traps in the advanced stages of development
Middle Income Trap
Society opposes creative destruction and inhibits productivity advances. Politics strangles entrepreneurship through high taxes and bureaucracy
Imperialism Trap
In the short run, robbery is more effective than production, yet parasitic economies are not sustainable as they lead to the rise and fall of empires
Welfare Trap
Extensive welfare and social benefits undermine economic dynamic and lead to economic slowdown and rising government debt.

Economics of Wealth Creation

Before the industrial revolution had brought about rising output per capita, higher incomes showed up only for short periods. Economic growth was too weak to compensate for the increase of the population that came with better nourishment. The increase of the population reverted the advantage of higher incomes. After a temporary rise, per capita income fell again. Over the millenniums before the capitalist economic take-off, the world population had grown but the per capita income had not risen. On average, the population before 1800 was not much richer than in the hundreds of hundreds of years before.

Before the industrial revolution, only the families in power achieved a high consumption level. Living standards depended on one's social rank in the hierarchy of exploitation, i.e. whether one belonged to the conquerors or to those who were the conquered. Throughout history, conquerors achieved higher living standards at the expense of the subjugated peoples. Yet the peace that conquerors have tried to establish after their settlement has remained precarious and all parasitic robbery economies have failed.

In order to achieve wealth through capital accumulation, peaceful conditions are necessary. The means to gain one's living must shift from the political to the economical method. Property rights must gain universal respect. They require protection - both domestically and against violence from the outside. Secure property rights is an essential requisite of capital accumulation. Accumulating capital consists of investments that will yield its income in the future while the consumption loss takes place in the present. If there is too much uncertainty as to the future returns, investment will not take place because then it would be more rational to consume than to save for later.

Backgrounder: Time Preference

Time-preference denotes how much an individual prefers immediate consumption over future consumption. The time preference trade-off requires reducing the present consumption level to get more consumption in the future. The lower the time preference the more the individual prefers higher future consumption and will give up present consumption to realize this preference. Economic growth requires diminishing time-preference and have less consumption now as the way to consume more later.

Human action in time confronts the choice between earlier or later. Time-preference is not a psychological concept but follows from the theory of human action. Time-preference is a praxeological principle. Without preference for earlier over later consumption, action could not take place but would turn itself into eternal waiting.

Human valuation takes place in the presence although the time horizon of individual valuation may go beyond one's lifetime and even towards eternity. The orientation towards the future results from the principle of human action, and preference-ranking pertaining to the future is its necessary condition. Any human action involves sequence and thus implies a ranking process that extends into the future.

There is no such thing as the so-called 'paradox of savings'. What is important for an economy to grow is a low time preference. Time preference is the tendency of human action to estimate the value of current and near consumption higher than the future consumption.

Time preference is necessary to survive from day to day. Yet in as much as economic growth requires investment and therefore savings, a lower time preference is necessary to gain a higher future consumption level. It is of little help to have a hundred-fold meal in a month if there is no food on the table for the next few weeks. Time preference is therefore reasonable. On the other hand, capital accumulation results in a higher income only later, which makes a lower time preference necessary.

Less consumption now is the way to have a higher consumption later. The meaning of savings is not austerity but to have more. The time preference rises when gaining profits is risky, and when uncertainty rises. In the face of the risks of confiscation, savings and investment come to a standstill because time preference will rise. This has been the case most of the time throughout history. As a consequence, economic growth and thus the income per capita has been stagnating.

***

It was not until around 1800 that the industrial revolution broke the vicious cycle of poverty, violence, and demography. Based on the knowledge from the preceding centuries and its diffusion through books and magazines as well as because of the rise of education, humankind could free itself from the shackles of the traps that had inhibited wealth creation before.

As incomes in the industry rose and women could free themselves from family dependency on their own merit - first as factory girls and later as professionals - the birth rate fell while productivity progressed. In the course of this development, the wealth per capita of the population in Western societies has risen manifold over the past two hundred years.

After overcoming the population trap and taming violence, protecting property gained importance, a process which led to the modern legal systems. Western industrialized countries established a system of law, which institutionalized private property of the means of production.

The decoupling of economic progress from population growth took place when the pace of technological progress surpassed the rate of reproduction. The key for this to happen was when companies emerged as profit-seeking entities that invested large parts of their current profits back into new enterprises to earn more profits.

***

In the world of political ideas, the liberalism of the 19th century put forth the right of private ownership of the goods of production. The violence that had been the essence of the state found a new task is to protect property. In the past, the state derived a precarious legitimacy from its function of serving as a political means of getting the livelihood of a ruling class. The classical liberal state, in contrast, received its legitimacy as the guarantor of the property rights in the interests of the whole population. Protection of property by state power is the core of the economic and social doctrine of classical liberalism. Consequently, protecting individual property was the point at which socialism directed its assault.

Classical liberalism

Classical liberalism is based on individualism and 'right' is not an issue of groups but of individual persons.

An individual has a natural right to property, including the property of the means of production (capital). For classical liberalism, justice does not pertain to the equality of results but what matters is the equality of opportunity. Classical liberalism does not negate the role of the state. However, it wants to limit its scope.

***

The socialist ideology does not oppose property rights but wants to change them from a private right into a public domain. The socialists argue that with protecting the property rights of the means of production, the modern economy produces a class society the same way as it had been before in history. They lament exploitation under capitalism as if there were a strict division between those who suffer from the exploitation and those who exploit. Yet modern capitalism differs from the class societies of the past and from the caste societies. First, under capitalism, the social ranks do no longer come through birth; second, the workforce of the modern economy does not exist only in capitalists and proletarians but there are many intermediate forms; third, in the capitalist market economy, social positions change because innovation makes existing privileges obsolete.

Capital and Knowledge

Capitalism triumphed because it is that economic system, which leads to prosperity and because with wealth comes power. Capitalism spread by imitation because it was more successful as a source of supremacy than the other economic systems. A capitalist economy means market competition based on the right of private ownership of means of production. The essence of capitalism is the private right of capital accumulation and thus of the right to the income from the use of capital. Economic growth as a rising per capita income results from capital and knowledge as it began with the industrial revolution. The industrial revolution is the consequence of the triumph of capitalism over other forms of production.

The capitalist economies entered the wealth cycle, according to which a high income makes a high saving volume possible and thus provides the means to invest, which again leads to more wealth. This way, the world escaped the vicious circle of poverty and entered the circle of wealth creation. Growth in this sense comprises capital accumulation, which is possible because it comes along with technical progress. The resulting higher productivity enables rising wages and incomes, which, in turn, lead to more capital: physical, financial, and human capital. Capitalism puts an end to the poverty trap. Before the industrial revolution, there was the vicious circle in existence that low-income allowed only a low level of savings and therefore there had always been a scarcity of productive investment.

Productivity

Productivity relates output (production) to input. According to the type input-factor, one distinguishes between total factor productivity, labor productivity, capital productivity and national productivity.

Total factor productivity:
- Total output/Total input

Labor (hour) productivity
- Output per unit of labor
- Output per hour worked

Capital productivity
- Output per unit of capital

National productivity
- Output (gross domestic product) per capita
- National income per capita

Total factor productivity relates total output to total input. As such, input includes all factors of production such as labor, capital, and technology.

Labor productivity usually refers to non-farm output and labor. Labor productivity is an important determinant of wages.

Capital productivity measures output per unit of capital.

The indicator 'gross domestic product per capita' represents output in terms of the gross domestic product divided by the number of the residents in a country.

***

Capitalism is an economic system, in which capital accumulation comes along with expanding knowledge in the form of technical progress. Because of innovations, capitalist growth is not quantitative, but qualitative. Capitalist economic growth results from the supply of better, cheaper and more diverse products, which originate from a production process whose focus is cost-efficiency and innovation.

Technological progress is crucial since the mere accumulation of capital finds its limit in diminishing marginal returns of capital. Each additional unity of capital produces less marginal returns when technical knowledge and population remain constant. At the same time, the costs to preserve capital continue to rise. Without technical progress, the economy would come to a halt when the costs to uphold the capital are higher than the yield of capital. Then the capital stock must shrink.

No economy can maintain a production process where the depreciation rate exceeds the necessary amount of investment for its maintenance. For an economy to grow in terms of income per capita there must be technical progress. The richer a national economy and consequently the higher the capital stock already is, the more important is technical progress. The more mature an economy, the more important become human capital and technology.

For some period, economic growth can take place based on savings and capital accumulation. More investment leads to a higher capital stock and to a higher income. This process, however, works only until the economy confronts the fundamental dilemma that the rates of return on capital fall behind the marginal costs of maintaining the capital stock. Capitalism means a permanent change, and this applies to the capital structure. Without technical progress, the economy falls into stagnation.

If capital accumulation happens because of the incentives that come from expansive economic policies, the marginal costs of capital maintenance surpass the returns of the additional capital accumulation. Such policies must fail because the stimulus leads to a constellation where the income from capital is lower than the costs of capital preservation. Therefore, investment is not always beneficial. An expansive economic policy results in the opposite of the intention when the measures stimulate the accumulation of more capital than savings can support. The driving force of economic growth must not be government but private business on an unhampered market.

Human capital means having productive skills. A higher level of human capital leads to more returns of the existing stock of physical capital. An increase in human capital results in higher incomes with no increasing the share of physical capital because human capital allows a better use of the available capital goods.

Beyond the physical and human capital, income will rise when commerce intensifies because it allows a more intense division of labor. Domestically and internationally, free trade allows the economic actors to specialize in those activities where they enjoy a comparative advantage. Under free trade, all participants will enjoy a higher income because of this productivity effect. Increasing commercialization at the local, regional, national and global level means that the economic performance improves and that incomes rise.

Fundamentals of wealth creation

Economic growth occurs as roundabout production. Instead of producing a product directly, the production of an intermediate good takes place.

Capitalist wealth creation

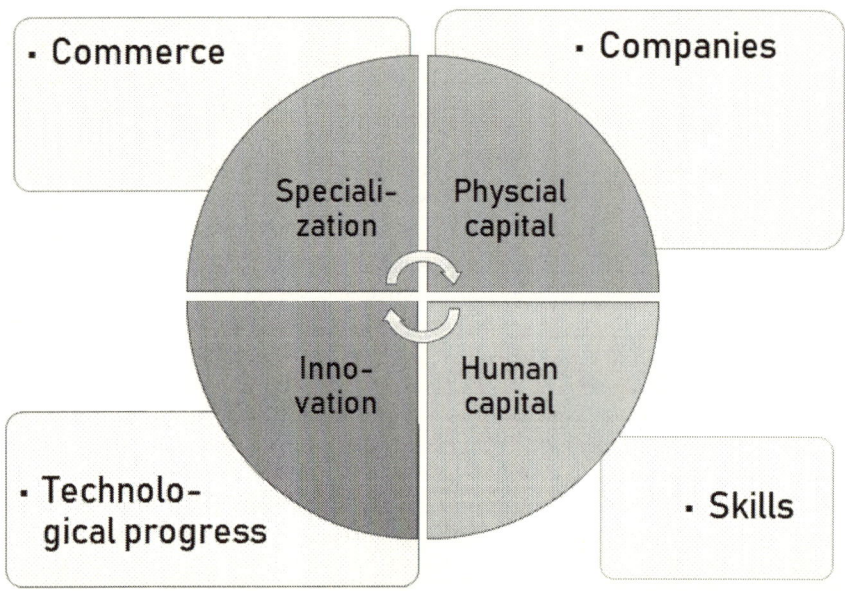

The intermediate production good, once finished, then serves to increase the productivity. The capital stock represents the totality of the production goods in its role as means to produce other goods.

Human capital includes the quality of human work, which comes from training and gaining skills.

Innovation is the application of new ideas to the production process. Innovation includes new products, new production methods, the opening of new markets and implementing new organizational forms. Ideas lead to new products, better and products, and to a greater variety and quality of goods.

***

Innovation is the entrepreneurial realization of business ideas. The function of the entrepreneur is to put ideas into practice to increase productivity and to earn higher profits. Business ideas express human creativity. They are an intellectual phenomenon. Economic progress happens when resolute entrepreneurs put these creative thoughts into practice. Economic growth depends on the ability of industry to generate innovation. Yet economic growth requires also a society, which tolerates and favors technological progress. Throughout history, technical progress has met with resistance. Technological knowledge is a recipe or a manual about how one can increase the productive effects of human labor in its interplay with capital and nature. Economic growth results from ideas put into profitable market operations. Only a few new ideas qualify as an innovation. Whether a business idea becomes an innovation depends on the market – whether the product finds buyers. In a market economy, the profitability determines the quality of an innovation.

One cannot realize innovations smoothly and without disruption. By its nature, innovation is disruptive and as such, it encounters resistance. The opposition to economic progress includes not only technical and financial obstacles but also the social barriers, the resistance that some parts of the population mobilize against technical progress.

Combined with technical progress, capital accumulation overcomes the limits of decreasing marginal return of capital. Yet realizing innovation demands investments, and therefore there must be savings to launch innovations. Innovation requires capital, and capital requires savings. Savings necessitate foregoing current consumption in favor of investment to gain a higher consumption level in the future.

The meaning of saving is not austerity but more future consumption. Saving is the opposite of austerity. Saving is a technique that refrains from using up all the wood for heating so that there is wood left for building a house or a bridge and have enough left to plant new trees. The purpose of saving is better living, not less consumption. The same holds for human capital. Instead of using all available labor time in the present, a part of it goes into training to have better abilities and skills. Besides savings, innovation requires experimentation. The innovators try out new ideas or production forms instead of using the same process of production or always producing the same products. Therefore, economic growth needs liberty.

Economic Freedom

Innovation is the basis of economic growth. Innovation requires freedom in all its forms. Therefore, liberty is the foundation of economic growth and thus of prosperity. Innovation needs the liberty of private initiative and the freedom of information. Mere ideas are not enough. Innovation requires communication. Sharing ideas needs means of making new ideas public. This is, on the one hand, a technical problem and touches on the question of the means of the available communication techniques. On the other hand, the spread of economic progress requires open markets and entrepreneurial freedom. Both thrive where there is a high general level of freedom of expression.

Political and commercial freedom go hand in hand. Innovation must become public to find a market. Whether an innovation is successful or not depends to a large degree on how fast it turns into profitable sales. Product promotion is important for new products. In this respect, the invention of book printing with movable letters was a crucial precursor to the industrial revolution, since it made the production of books and the distribution of ideas inexpensive and more effective than before. Only modern electronic communication, particularly the Internet, has a comparable effect.

Innovation is creative destruction, and as such, it encounters resistance. The more economic and political might are interconnected, the easier it is for the owners of the economic power to block innovations with political means. This was the case in many places in the past. America was the first great exception.

The economic triumph of the United States rests, among other things, on the fact that there have been fewer obstacles to the spread of ideas in the United States than in most other countries. As early as in the eighteenth century, because of freedom of religion, there was freedom of expression and freedom of publication, while in most other parts of the world political censorship prevailed. Early in the history of United States, its newspaper industry began to flourish. America was also a leader in literacy and in general education. After all, the US was the country, which, with its independence, also introduced freedom of trade among its States, thus laying the foundations for American entrepreneurship. The more a country or region prescribes itself to the free market economy, the more it promotes economic advancement. The protectionist policy of the United States in the 19th century was not aimed against free trade as such. The US trade policy served to divert trade from Europe to trade among the States of the Union where a new area of free trade was being created.

In the USA, freedom of religion, freedom of expression, and freedom of the press existed together with the freedom of entrepreneurial activity, which owned little or nothing to political power. If one did not like the East Coast or did not fit, Americans would move to the West and escape the established powers with every mile they went further away. After the end of the American War of Secession

(1861-1865), an extended period of economic growth began, which led to a long series of consumption-oriented innovations, especially at the turn of the century. While on the old continent, the breakthroughs of inventions happened mainly with investment goods, there were significant innovations going on in the consumer goods market in the US towards the end of the 19th century. In a short time, the reality of mass consumption should come into existence and change the economy, first in the United States and then, step by step, in the rest of the world.

Life today differs from that of our ancestors because innovations such as telephone, refrigerator, radio, movies, TV, automobiles, and restaurant chains have changed everyday life.

Economic growth has brought things into the hands of ordinary people, about which even the mightiest rulers of the past could only dream of and not even that because they did not understand that such things as any ordinary consumer nowadays can buy, could even exist. Today, the average wage earner in the developed industrialized countries is much better off than the richest and most powerful persons were before the industrial revolution. Even poor families possess most of the modern standard goods. The reason for this success is the freedom of expression and of the free entrepreneurial activity based on private initiative and the market economy. Nevertheless, both fundaments are always in danger, also in America.

Yet even the United States is not immune from a relapse into censorship. This was so during the War of Independence, the War of Secession, and during the First and Second World Wars. Today, a new form of censorship is taking shape, as freedom of expression is restricted under the tyranny of political correctness and the influence of special interests. In addition, there is a growing power in the hands of a jurisprudence that operates against business and innovation. It is not surprising that with suppressing the freedom of expression came the time of the decline of economic freedom. In the USA, towards the end of the second decade of the new millennium, entrepreneurial activity is in danger. In the international ranking of economic freedom, the US is moving downwards in the ranks while censorship ravages university campuses in the form of political correctness.

United States. Economic Freedom

The United States faces the risk of falling into the trap of the downward spiral where economic weakness leads to policies that reinforce the decline. The more the United States falls back in growth in the future, the more other countries will have the courage to step forth and to establish full freedom of expression and freedom of the press and of entrepreneurial activity.

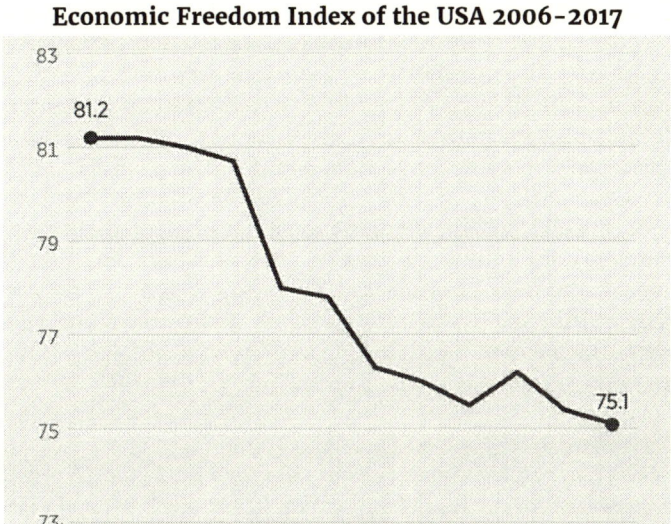

Source: Heritage Foundation. Index of Economic Freedom
https://www.heritage.org/index/

The United States suffers from the growth of government. Size and scope of the state are expanding, and the regulatory and tax burdens are rising. Among the broad population the feeling gains momentum that the game is rigged. The perception is growing that America suffers from cronyism, elite privilege, and corruption. America's competitiveness is declining. Domestic and foreign debt is on the rise.

The US economic freedom index of the Heritage Foundation has fallen from 81 points and number in 2006 to an overall score of 75.1 and a world rank of 17 in 2017.

Economic growth is the source of prosperity. The opposition to economic growth means to be against affluence and to favor misery. Growth requires as its basis a solid ownership structure of private property, entrepreneurial freedom, and a competitive market order. This is the basic idea of Laissez-faire. To be against Laissez-faire means to be against economic growth and implies to be in favor of keeping people poor instead of making the world more prosperous.

The institutions that will replace the traditional state after its abolishment must confine itself to protect property rights. The more reliable such a protective institution will accomplish its task the more business can concentrate on production. The present state does neither protect property nor life. On the contrary, the modern administrative state is the most severe violator of property rights – more than private criminals. State intervention begins with the imposition of taxation and ends with the draft. First, the state demands your property, then your life. This way, the state, which supposedly represents the organ of protection of property rights, sabotages economic activity. Instead of fostering entrepreneurship and commitment to work, the state regulates and taxes capital and work up to the hilt.

The modern administrative state imposes taxes on labor like it does on tobacco and on alcohol as if work were venom, which government must tax to restrict its commerce. Taxes and contributions make labor more expensive and reduce its use. The absurdity of the modern tax state shows up in the fact that it burdens the activities with taxes on which the existence of the fiscal state itself depends. The income tax is a child of the 20th century. It is the indispensable complement of the war-and-welfare state, as it began to unfold already before the world plunged into World War I. The personal income tax is the most anti-liberal taxation and the worst of all taxes.

The labor force suffers not only from the burden of taxes and contributions. The state also intervenes in the wage-setting - whether by means of minimum wages or by the many other labor market regulations. Before someone can work, i.e. perform the all-natural human activity, one must obtain a permit. In many countries of the world, the legal process to open a business is a bureaucratic hurdle that is lengthy, expensive and unpredictable. It is no wonder that those countries are poor where it is the most difficult to set up a company and that countries with a high per capita income have a low threshold to entrepreneurship. The consequence of this interference is subdued economic growth.

Political power is an enemy of economic growth. This has been the case throughout history. Nowadays likewise, the powerful groups in society try to exclude new competitors. They do this with the help of the state by means of difficult bureaucratic regulations, complicated tax laws, and high barriers to market entry. The larger and the older a company the easier is it for such a firm to cope with the regulations. Bureaucracy and taxes are a serious obstacle for new companies that want to enter a market. Regulations push up the costs and establish barriers to entry. Opaque and contradictory bureaucratic legislation means that fewer companies will surmount these barriers to challenge established companies. Those few new companies that enter markets often could only do that not because of the quality of their product but because of their legal savvy and political connections.

Laws against the dismissal of redundant labor force make it difficult to reduce the costs when a project should fail. Job protection means that the existing work-places become more secure at the cost of job creation that would come with new projects. To avoid risks, the creation of new jobs falls, particularly for positions that come with a new project when there is no flexible labor market and the company must bear the risk to remain stuck with an overload of workers who cannot be fired. The more innovative, the more daring a project the more it must face the risk of failure. As such, start-up companies as innovators must consider fiasco and prepare for it. The more regulation and tax burden business face the more companies will refrain from new ventures. The government wants to 'save jobs', but what it does is to reduce the number of jobs available, particularly jobs that would be more productive.

Technological progress means increased productivity and thus a higher wage level. Trade unions are unable to raise the general average wage when productivity stagnates. Trade union power can only redistribute income among the workers themselves. Therefore, a strike aims in the first instance against the other workers in the other industries, which do not or do not yet go on strike. Whatever the idealistic intentions may be, union power hinders economic growth, prevents creating new and better jobs, and stifles economic growth. Yet because prosperity depends on economic growth, the workers themselves bear the costs of strikes and excessive wage claims. Apparent protection comes with the loss of the chance of higher prosperity. Under socialism, the state manages the economy. The jobs, wages, and prices are stable the same way as they are for the inmates of a prison. The protection that the administrative state provides comes with the stagnation of income and mass poverty of the working population. Prosperity needs economic growth, and economic growth needs entrepreneurial freedom.

Economic freedom and social progress

There is a strong link between economic freedom and income, and between economic freedom and social progress.

The freer the economy of a country, the more pronounced social mobility and the more favorable are other measures of social progress such as health, environment, human development, participation, and reduction of poverty. The causal chain runs from economic freedom to economic growth and higher income, and thus to social progress.

Economic growth is not just about getting bigger, but about a better adaption of the production structure to the wants and needs of the consumers. All inventions serve to satisfy existing basic needs - food, clothing, housing, transport, communication, entertainment, etc. - in a cheaper and better way. Investing involves dispensing with current consumption in some cases to achieve a higher consumption level in the future.

Economic growth requires material and human capital and presupposes the reduction of temporary consumption. Saving provides the funding of investments and forms the basis of economic growth when capital accumulation comes along with innovation. However, no saving takes place in the economy at the aggregate when the savings of a person A serves for the consumption of another person B as it is the case when people buy government bonds. If someone invests in bonds, it looks as though this person is saving, but, in fact, while this person abstains from consumption he provides the funds to the state that spends it to finance the consumption of other groups of persons and provide funds for wasteful public projects. Money that comes from the sale of bonds serves to pay pensions and other consumptive expenditures by the state. When a government incurs a budget deficit, the state is de facto dis-saving and by the amount of the deficit, overall macroeconomic savings fall.

Time preference is a necessity for human survival. Time preference urges human action to eat, to sleep, and not to postpone consumption forever to tomorrow and beyond.

However, economic growth requires temporary abstention from consumption, which means that the time preference must be subject to voluntary control. In general, countries with a population that have a low time preference, where a culture of disciplined waiting prevails, have a higher tendency to save and invest. A lower time preference results in a higher rate of accumulation of capital and leads to a higher growth rate compared to populations with a higher time preference. The cultural foundation of economic growth exists in the degree to which some people control their time preference.

There is a similar dilemma regarding the time preference as is the poverty trap. The poorer the people are the more urgent is the satisfaction of the immediate desires. This urge involves high time preference. In contrast, pre-existing wealth facilitates the temporary renunciation of desires in the expectation that a higher level of prosperity will come later by this postponement of present wishes.

A low time preference promotes saving and thus investment and capital formation as the basis for economic growth and thus the increase in wealth. As time goes by, the time preference decreases as capital accumulation progresses.

Backgrounder:
Interest, Consumption, and Savings

The nominal market interest rate results from the interaction between the money supply and the current and expected price level.

The time preference determines the natural real interest rate as the discount rate between current and future goods and thus the relationship between consumption and saving.

A high time preference means that present goods are highly valued compared to future goods of the same type. Accordingly, the natural interest rate increases. The more uncertain the future, the more the time preferences increases and the higher is the natural interest rate. If one were to know for certain, for example, that the world would go under tomorrow, the time preference would become infinite and correspondingly would the natural interest rate. Conversely, eternal life would imply a zero-rate time preference and a zero-interest rate. The degree of time preference depends on expectations.

The natural interest rate is the relative distribution of consumption and saving. The higher the time preference and thus the natural interest rate, the more people prefer consumption over savings.

Insofar as the savings volume determines the level of investment, investments depend on the time preference. This explains why a falling market rate does not necessarily lead to an increase in investment.

The central bank determines the policy interest rate based on the control of the monetary base. Inflationary expectations of the market participants determine the market rate.

However, the actual volume of consumption and savings, and thus the investment, depends on the time preference.

In extreme cases, the interest rate may fall to zero or even below zero, and still not stimulate investment when the time preference is high and therefore a high natural interest rate prevails.

Determinants of the market interest rate

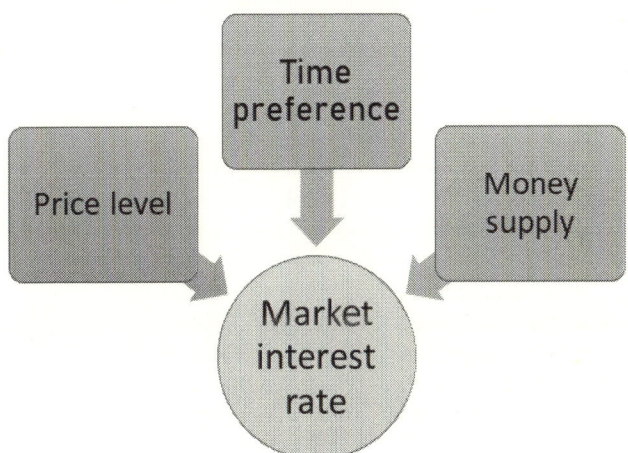

***

In order to carry out productive roundabout ways of production, there must be reserves available, which ensure that the workers and their families receive provision during the process of producing the investment goods. Roundabout production implies that investment does not yet yield a return, which will come only at the end of the process and not during the investment phase. While routine capital accumulation is less uncertain than an innovation, it brings less marginal returns. Innovation, in contrast, while it results in higher margins, suffers from uncertainty about success or failure. Therefore, it is crucial that there are companies that generate profits and that reinvest these profits. Excessive corporate taxes quash technological progress. Different from routine production, new projects are uncertain, but if they succeed, they bring high returns. Economic progress depends on making such innovative investments.

Value creation and capital structure

The production process extends over numerous stages, but the proceeds show up only at the end of the process when the goods arrive at the consumer and the latter pays for them. So long as the consumer does not pay for the final product, capitalists must pre-finance all the previous stages of production. The capitalist production process takes place as roundabout production. Instead of procuring one's livelihood directly with the mere force of pure labor, an intermediate material is produced as an investment good which facilitates the production of the desired consumer goods. Roundabout production increases the productivity of human labor.

To have the production process running, one must maintain the capital structure. Yet the salaried workers demand their payment before the products are ready for consumption. The function of the capitalists lies in providing the funds that are necessary to maintain the capital structure. The contribution of the capitalists to the production is to maintain and expand the capital structure and to advance the salaries and wages before the consumers buy the product.

The extent of roundabout production depends on the size of the means of subsistence. Therefore, one cannot take the highest degree of productivity as the guideline, but to which extent resources are available for the period during which the intermediate product is on its way to final consumption. During roundabout production, the labor force that is employed in the roundabout process does not immediately produce goods that serve for consumption. Those who are active in roundabout production must receive their subsistence out of a present fund of available consumption goods. It is only later, when the consumers pay for the goods, that the capitalists receive their compensation. Capitalists have been waiting for the completion of the roundabout production process and have assumed the risks whether production will come to a successful end, and they only get their reward at the end of the process when the consumer pays.

The State as an Enemy of Growth

In a free market economy, there is a natural tendency to expand production and to innovate. Stagnation afflicts the market economy through wrong economic policies. While the poverty trap hampers the way out of poverty, and the violence trap and the population trap block the road to wealth, the 'middle-income trap' hits the emerging economies when they oppose creative destruction. When a country has surpassed the traps of poverty, violence, and population, the path to prosperity is not open if the society does not yet embrace creative destruction. If at this stage of development, a country prefers social security to innovation, it will remain stuck in the middle-income trap. This is the case with many developing countries. The dominant class in these countries does not tolerate the changes that come with innovation and which challenge established positions of wealth. Consequently, economic progress slows down and comes to a standstill. The security that comes with social policy appears at first as a rise of prosperity – as more 'welfare' and more 'social justice' - when in fact it is the first step to economic stagnation. In the end, average incomes will fall as much as welfare policies diminish or block innovation and thereby lower the economy's productivity rate.

People opt for welfare and a 'social state' because they believe that it comes at no costs and provides only benefits. If people knew how the social benefits now imply less income later, the population, in general, would have a critical attitude towards the welfare state and politicians would have a harder time selling their fraud. Just as it is with security over liberty, a society that attributes a higher value to social security than to prosperity loses both. Promoting short-termism as it is inherent to a democracy run by political parties promotes the distribution of the cake and neglects that the goods must be produced before they can be distributed, and that the production should also grow over time. The illusion is widespread and propagated by the political machinery that production is independent of its distribution so that one could redistribute without weakening production.

Most of the 'distributive justice' is practiced at the expense of the 'commutative justice'. The justice of the distribution has its other side in the justice pertaining to the production of things. One cannot limit the idea of justice to distribution without contradictions. The rules of righteousness for the values of a society must include principles that reward personal achievement. The disregard of the commutative aspect of justice is itself unjust. It is also irrational since distribution is possible only when there is something to distribute, i.e. that production takes place after at all. Redistribution is unjust and economically irrational because it punishes those who carry on production and its advancement. When redistributing income and wealth becomes excessive, the active part of the population withdraws from production and parasitism takes over. This way, society will impoverish, and the poor are left with nothing. In the end, the poor themselves will pay the price because they will be the hardest hit when growth falters and unemployment rise.

It is problematic to strife towards more justice. Justice is often a false concern. The reality of life proves that coincidences in the form of happiness and misfortune undermine intentional righteousness. Justice and equality are not of this world. The costs to impose equality exceed its benefits because we are all children of luck – good and bad. It is important to stop the welfare state in time because its negative effect on economic growth is not visible. For some time, capital consumption compensates for weak economic growth. When this happens, it does not yet show in the national statistics. Statistically, consumption counts as a contribution to national production. An increase in consumption, even if it comes at the cost of capital formation and is due to the consumption of capital, gets counted as economic growth, although it is a statistical illusion.

An insidious form of capital consumption takes place through government debt. A deficit of the government budget means that the national savings volume falls, and that the economic investment potential has become smaller. In the economic statistics, the expenditures - whether they are from the state or from the private side - are equally a contribution to the social product. Yet while the spending benefits the current receivers of the government expenditures, the lower capital formation will later show up in a weaker economic growth. In as much as public debt is an enemy of economic growth, it is also an enemy of wealth creation. The benefits that a government distributes in the short run financed by higher public debt will reduce further economic growth and make poverty persistent in the long run.

A new phase of weak economic growth has arisen in the industrialized countries because of the expanding national debt, which began in the 1970s and has continued until our present days. The industrialized nations must now learn how difficult it is to get out of the whirlpool. This is most noticeable in the decline in the rate of productivity progress experienced by large industrialized countries since the 1970s, along with the strong expansion of the welfare state and the rise in public debt.

Government debt diminishes the economic growth dynamics. Weak economic growth, in turn, leads to higher government expenditures and thus a rising debt burden. When an economy experiences faltering growth, the demand for social benefits increases even more. This redistribution leads again to less growth. Numerous countries have fallen into the trap where social expenditures weaken the economy and where this weakness requires more spending, which in turn weakens the economy. A dangerous side effect of this fall into a downward moving spiral is that the anti-capitalistic attitude in the population increases, since for most citizens, the causal links are difficult to ascertain.

Cycle of welfare spending and economic stagnation

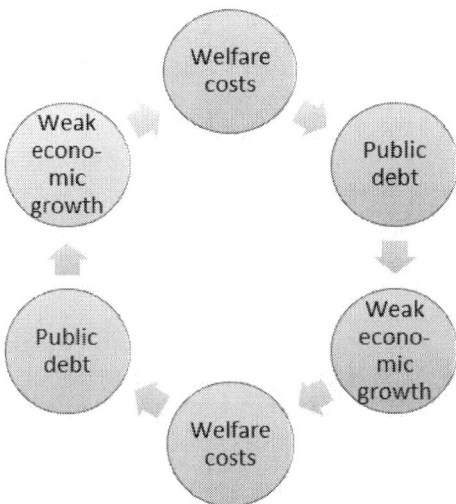

The welfare state and public debt are the main causes of the decline in the productivity rates. The productivity of a country determines the income level.

Over the past decades, the rates of the annual increase of productivity of the major industrialized countries have fallen from an average of five percent in the late to around two percent in the 1990s and keep on falling.

Without productivity gains, there is no increase in real per capita income.

The expansion of the welfare state leads to a rising public debt, which weakens the economic performance. A weakening economy entails more welfare spending and leads to a further rise of public debt, which, in turn, leads to more welfare spending.

Antony P. Mueller

Creative Destruction

The progress that comes with innovation makes other goods obsolete. Modernization means that some other forms of the production of goods become outdated. Less competitive forms of production must disappear from the market or the companies must change their production methods. With the disappearance of obsolete goods, the sources of income related to their production do also vanish. Any new production technology or new organizational form renders a part of the existing economic structure useless. Any new, better product makes the old goods less attractive.

Innovation is creative destruction. The effects of technological progress go beyond the economy and affect society and politics. If the social resistance is strong enough so that it can take a hold of the policy, and when social movements succeed in blocking innovation, the gate to economic progress shuts down. The more politics takes up the resistance from those whom innovation affects negatively, the more the future economic growth will falter. Such blockades have existed for thousands of years. The barriers fell at the time of the industrial revolution. There is no guarantee that the dark times will not come back. The same way that some countries never adopted capitalism, the modern industrialized countries are not free from the risk of abandoning the free market economy. The fact that the gates to the road of prosperity opened about two hundred years ago does not guarantee that innovations will go on forever. The enemies of economic growth never rest.

Obstacles to innovation

It is not only the bureaucracy, which hinders innovation, but also traditions and institutions. Tradition will result in social resistance and abort innovation because of superstition. The modern superstitions come in a scientific clad. There are also institutions that hamper innovation and its propagation along with underdeveloped financial markets and closed markets.

The best promotion of innovation is not through subsidies but to reduce the obstacles to innovation, such as bureaucratic regulations and high taxes.

***

The opponents to innovation find their allies not only in politics but also with some business leaders who are afraid of losing their pre-eminence when innovations threaten their realms. While the effect of protection is visible to those who receive its benefits, the indirect loss of prosperity remains undetected and therefore has no representation in the political play. When the spirit of innovation and economic progress declines, the economy grows less, falls into stagnation, and shrinks. Then, even more, the call for action by the state rises, albeit the policy itself has caused the problem. The voters want higher income and redistribution in their favor, and the government follows the call - just to make things worse.

Nowadays, governments are doing both: on the one hand, they suppress and slow down the structural change caused by the innovation; on the other hand, especially in the military sector, they promote 'research'. While it is obvious that the state that suppresses innovation hinders economic growth, it is less clear that this is also the case when the state promotes innovation and research for the state's particular aims.

While in the case of private research projects, business companies must bear the costs of research from the outset and will receive a remuneration only if the result of the project is successful on the market, public funds cover the costs of research. For state funding - both for university research and with the private company subsidies - the grants flow already during the development phase and not at the end. In other words, the state does not reward innovation but participates in the cost of a project that promises innovation. The problem of public funding begins with the standards of selection. Government agencies are in no way better in foreseeing the technological future than private business. To obtain public funds, the applications for the grants of subsidies need not correspond to the aim of earning a profit in the market-place but must please the evaluators. Too often, the whole project of 'research funding' ends with only the expenses covered and nothing gained. A more effective promotion of innovation would be low tax rates on profits, which would incite companies to innovate and develop new marketable products.

The competition itself is the discovery process. The market test does not consist in innovation as such or in the so-called 'research' but rather to the extent to which the innovation can maintain itself in the market, which means that it must be profitable.

The problem with innovations is not just to invent something new. The challenge is to market the new product so that it will find buyers and that the sales generate profit for the company. Inventions are not rare. There is an abundance of useless inventions and there is no lack of fascinating business ideas without a proper market. There is no reason for the state to promote more ideas. What is lacking in using inventions is capital, and capital is in short supply because too little is saved. Due to capital shortages, there are usually much more potential technological projects available that could be profitably realized.

Barriers to innovation

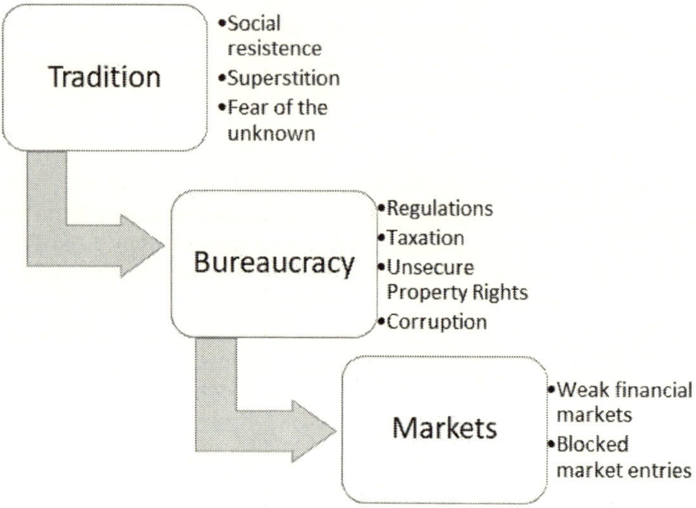

Tradition
- Social resistance
- Superstition
- Fear of the unknown

Bureaucracy
- Regulations
- Taxation
- Unsecure Property Rights
- Corruption

Markets
- Weak financial markets
- Blocked market entries

There is an overhang of productivity-enhancing possibilities that find no use when savings are too low. If the economy is not yet rich enough to afford the new technology, inventions remain unused. Just as a low-income person can only afford a bicycle but not a motorcycle although the motorcycle is much faster, an economy cannot have the most productive standard of capital in all its sectors. The limit of economic growth does not come from an absence of technological ideas but from a lack of capital to realize the ideas.

Public debt is an enemy of economic growth. Because budget deficits reduce overall savings, investment suffers and economic growth falters. If the government promotes innovation and accumulates debt, it will hamper economic growth in two ways: first, by lowering the efficiency of the economy, and, second, by crowding-out private research through the less productive public research funding.

The implementation of profitable innovations characterizes the entrepreneur as depicted by Joseph Alois Schumpeter (1883-1950) in his work on the economic development of 1911. The entrepreneur is not necessarily an inventor or a manager but someone who directs production and markets ideas with the aim of turning them into a profitable enterprise on the market. Entrepreneurs are rare. If their income moves to dizzying heights, this is because of their exceptional performance. Most of the entrepreneurial performance remains obscured to the observers. One sees the success that shines in the daylight, forgets the failed attempts, and disregards those entrepreneurs who have remained unsuccessful, and therefore have disappeared.

If the free market is functioning, competition eradicates the weaker businesses so that the system approaches an optimum without ever reaching it. In competitive markets, profits must be high enough to compensate for the high risk of failure. When a successful company emerges and gains prominence, it faces competition from imitation of the product and its improvement. Competitive innovation erodes the profit of the pioneer. Monopoly gains resulting from innovation are not permanent. Economic progress makes products obsolete. This is why profits must be high for the pioneer to maintain the incentive to innovate.

The basis for growth is industrial clusters, which do not owe their existence to an organization but appear as spontaneous orders, which do not obey hierarchical commands but thrive following their own laws of development. The rules of a spontaneous order are not explicit. A spontaneous order has neither a syllabus nor an organizational map. To know the rules of such a spontaneous order, one must participate in the game. One cannot learn the tricks of the trade outside of the circus. To be successful, one must be an insider and participate in the activity of the spontaneous order itself. One cannot transplant and simply imitate a spontaneous order. Innovation requires being a player. This is the way to become familiar with the details that are necessary for the success of the innovation. The problem with the state is not only that it is not a team player but that the state is as much a collaborator as an opponent with divergent interests and mutually exclusive projects.

In development policy, the lack of insight that simple imitation in the form of a state-run 'industrial policy' will fail has cost a high price to the poor countries that adopted such policies. With the industrial policy in the developed countries, it is not much different. The planning of new industries by the state is an unsolvable task and a sign of hubris because the technological future is unforeseeable. New technologies and industries themselves must discover the paths to success because there is no way that could be known before some venture proves that it works. The way of economic progress is experimental and cannot be planned. Innovations emerge, they are not implanted. Innovations thrive in the environment of a spontaneous order, not in organizations.

Return Matrix of Venture Capital Projects

	Consensus	No consensus
Failure	negative	negative
Success	neutral	positive

Failure means a negative result whether there was a consensus or not. The project earns no profit. Normal profits emerge when the project is successful but came into being based on consensus. Many other investors also spotted the opportunity and invested in the project as well. The result is neutral. No exceptional profits come about. Only a project that is successful and was launched without consensus reaps positive results and earns extraordinary profits.

The need to propose projects that meet consensus condemns the public financing of innovation projects to notorious underperformers. Promotion for research and development with the assistance of government usually takes place for ordinary projects, which, even when they are successful, will earn only meager profits.

Projects that earn a high return are naturally those that do not find a consensus at their beginning.

Economic Knowledge

One can imagine the competitive exploration process as a procedure where the pioneer companies explore the unknown terrain and develop the new markets while the rest imitates and improves the innovation. Pioneer profits serve as an incentive to take the risk of innovation.

The freer an economy is, the more the companies can embark upon an economic discovery process and create new products and new measures of production. In due course, the profit of the pioneer company melts away and the gains pass on to the consumers in the form of more goods and cheaper and improved products.

Dimensions of economic knowledge

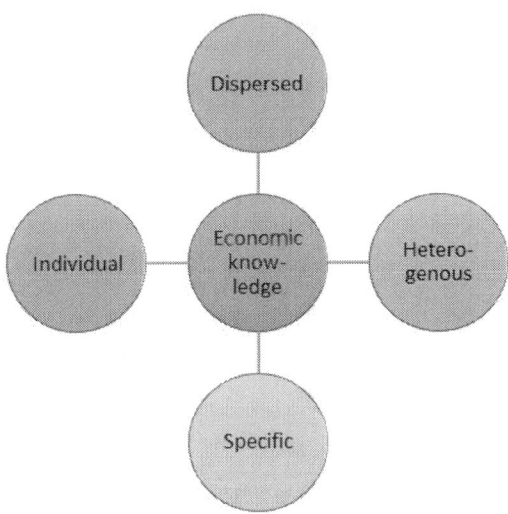

Innovation requires individual companies, which explore like scouts the path to the future. Nobody knows from the outset, which new products will find acceptance in the market, and how and where the technological breakthroughs will happen. Following the terminology of Friedrich Hayek, competition is a procedure of discovery.

Competition is a procedure to generate economic knowledge. The competitive process reveals knowledge that is specific to time and place. As such it exists in the mind of the individual. Economic knowledge is neither homogenous nor concentrated but dispersed and heterogeneous. It is the essence of the competitive process that the knowledge of the actors differs from individual to individual and changes with the situational setting.

The innovation, which first manifests itself in the success of the pioneer enterprise, reaches the consumers as a higher standard of living. Imitation follows and spreads the innovation in various new forms throughout the economy. Imitation is more difficult than it seems. One must be part of the competition process to imitate in a smart way. Innovation does not come out of nowhere but forms part of the market process. Therefore, the catch-up process of the developing countries is so cumbersome.

Developing countries suffer from the lack of deep markets. Even when there should be generous financing available to launch an individual investment projects, development does not spread across the economy because a product never stands alone in the market but forms part of a larger grouping of goods and industries that operate as clusters and whose ramifications reach across regions, nations, and continents. The barrier to development is not the lack of funds but the lack of a competitive market system where many firms try to gain profits and reinvest these profits to launch new and better goods.

Free Trade

International trade expands the size of the market. The individual firms have more potential customers and the companies can become more specialized and more productive. Higher productivity increases wages. The economies involved in international trade get richer, while the isolated, self-sufficient economies remain poor.

In order to participate in international trade, it is not necessary that a company is more productive in all its branches than its competitors abroad. Trade does not depend on the absolute level of productivity but on the comparative cost advantages. This means that also those companies and their employees benefit from free trade, whose competitiveness is lower than other companies. There is no reason to withdraw from international competition because one is less productive if the productive unit has a comparative cost advantage. Comparative advantage means to give up those areas of production where one is very much at a disadvantage and concentrate on those economic activities where one is less disadvantaged. Even in the case that companies in one country are less competitive than those abroad, foreign trade would be beneficial. External trade allows abandoning the activities of the lowest relative productivity in favor of those areas where the disadvantage is less. International competition has the same effect as to how competition works on the domestic markets. For the high-productivity country, international trade opens the possibility that its companies concentrate on the areas where they are not only more productive than the companies in other countries abut to focus on those areas of production where the companies are much more productive. In small markets, specialization is limited and thus production must include activities where productivity is low.

With the expansion of markets, the structure of the economy changes. The production in those areas where there are the greatest competitive disadvantages falls, while those where productivity is relatively strong, increases. If the trading partner has a higher level of productivity, the firms concentrate on the activities where they have the comparatively highest productivity. In the countries that participate in free trade, the general level of productivity increases because there is a shift of production to those companies that are relatively more productive. The less efficient enterprises focus on activities where the distance in productivity to the companies with the higher performance is lower. In terms of higher productivity, international trade benefits all participants. In each of the countries that begin to trade with one another, a re-allocation takes place according to the comparative advantages.

Wealth creation through free trade

The effect of global trade on wealth comes through specialization, which lifts productivity.

International trade means larger markets, and larger markets augment the scope of specialization. Rather than focusing on countries as the entities that specialize, it is individual companies that count. The larger the market becomes because of global trade the more individual companies can specialize and raise their productivity. Companies that produce goods that enjoy economies scale experience additional scale effects that comes with a larger market.

The competitive process compels the participating companies to move into areas where the opportunity costs are the lowest and to abandon the activities where they are high. International trade induces the firms to concentrate in those fields of production where their relative productivity is the highest. As each company produces those goods where its productivity is higher, the overall level of productivity increases. The wage level depends on productivity. By increasing the productivity, globalization increases the general level of world incomes. International competition boosts productivity and leads to more prosperity. Free trade makes the world rich - protectionism makes the world poor.

Higher productivity means that one achieves more output with the same amount of input of labor and capital. This way, the increase in productivity leads to rising profits. Higher profits encourage the expansion of production. The more intense competition and the more companies take part the faster productivity gains spread throughout the economy and the faster productivity benefits consumers in the form of lower prices, better quality and a greater variety of products.

With most economic phenomena, people recognize only what is at the surface and see what happens in the short term. When discussing free trade, people favor protectionism because they think this is the way to help 'our industry' and to save 'our jobs'. Protectionists focus on that aspect of free trade that leads to extraordinary profits for some companies while in some other production areas, jobs get lost and even entire industries fail. While some companies prosper, other firms must close their doors. Some industries disappear in one country and emerge in another as they change location according to relative productivity. Yet what the protectionists fail to see is that it is the structural change, which brings about overall productivity and the rising wages. Resistance to free trade is equal to the opposition against other forms of economic change as it comes, for example, from technological progress.

The more a country involves itself in the world trade, the more the companies of this country must concentrate their activities on the niches where they can achieve a relatively higher performance. The higher productivity emerges together with a rising purchasing power of the inhabitants of this country. World trade enlarges the markets and intensifies the competition; the power of national enterprises diminishes as their relative market size falls. Free trade is a strong antidote to a monopolization of the economy.

Extension of the market size

International trade is the geographical extension of the national market, which, in turn, is the extension of the local market and of family exchange. The larger the extension of the market, the more the individual and the companies can specialize and thereby increase their productivity. Specialization implies the division of labor and capital, which, in turn, require markets. The integration of a country into the global market provides the full potential of specialization for this country's individuals and firms.

Geographical market dimensions

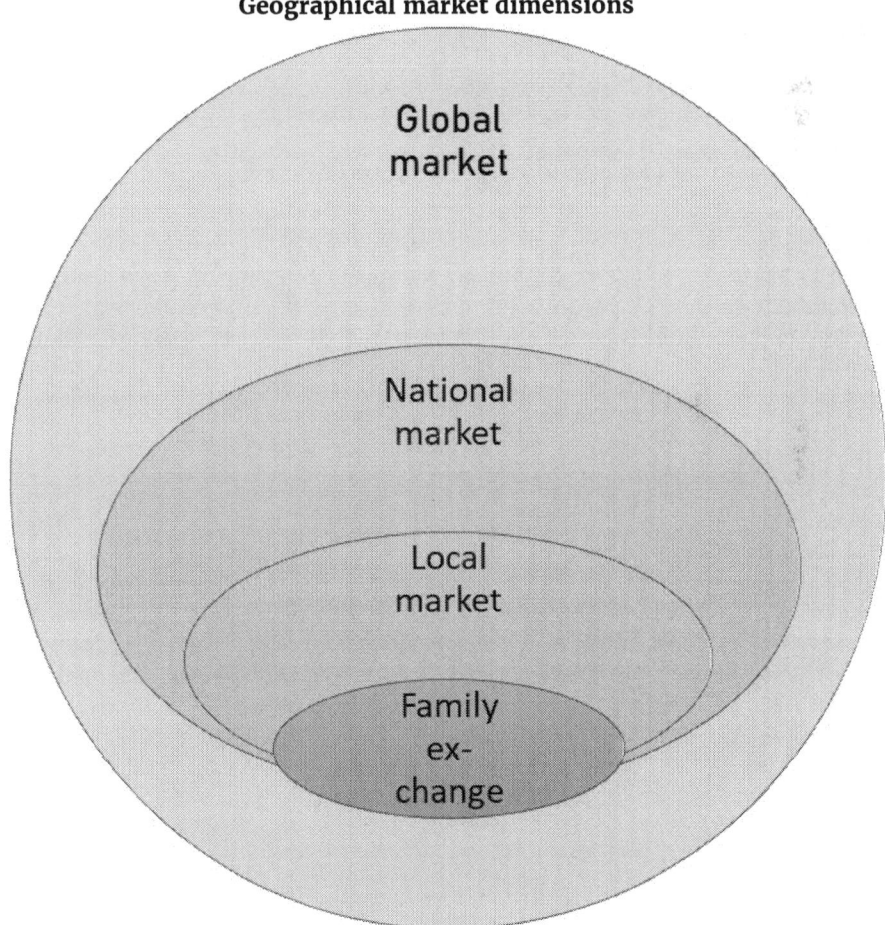

World trade extends the markets and lays the foundation for higher incomes as the expansion of the size of the economic area increases the potential for capital accumulation and innovation.

The larger the market, the more worthwhile becomes specialization and thus the acquisition of a specialized human capital.

The result of world trade is a higher level of productivity. Productivity gains come also to the less productive economies as the respective firms in these economies will gain the opportunity to specialize in those areas where they are relatively better and when they abandon those activities where they are relatively more unproductive than their competitors abroad.

Not countries specialize in a system of free world trade, but enterprises. Companies apply specific capital and specialized human capital. With international competition, the level of knowledge and the specialization of capital of the companies is rising. This increases productivity and income.

***

Like commerce on the local and national level, world trade is an interplay of competition and cooperation. This process of association begins with the individual in the family and continues in the local and regional spheres to extend to the national economy and to international relations and to the global economy. The protectionists take the nation-state as their criterion for the limits of free trade. They do not recognize that if their arguments in favor of protectionism were correct, they should also apply regional and local criteria. If protectionism were so good for the nation, why not also impose tariffs for a specific region within a country?

Effects of free trade

When a country opens to free trade, it expands the market. With the extension of the markets come higher productivity and more product diversity. More competition and increased productivity lead to lower prices and a better product quality.

Free trade has effects like technical progress. The less productive firms make room for the more competitive companies. There is a shift of the factors of production to the sectors of higher productivity at the expense of the less productive sectors. This process lays the foundation for higher incomes. Free world trade serves the consumer through a wider product variety, lower prices, and better quality of the goods and services.

Effects of free trade

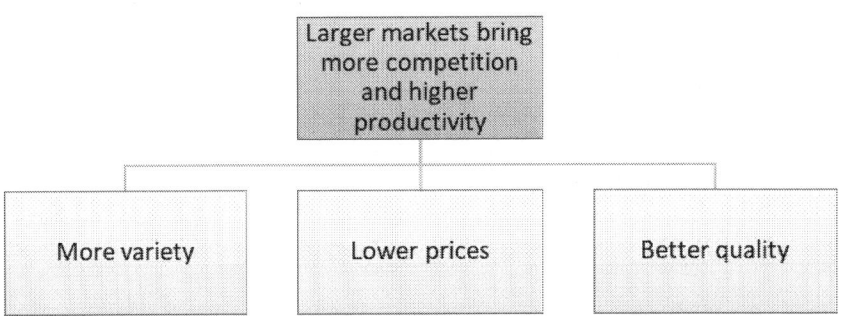

Summary

Economic growth is not a self-purpose but serves to achieve a higher degree of satisfaction of the consumers. In this sense, economic progress does not exist mainly in more but in better products and in more diverse goods. The purpose of economic growth is to free people from poverty and to ease the pain of work. No system other than capitalism makes this possible because, in capitalism, growth takes place through innovation and productivity gains.

Technical progress makes it possible to achieve a higher yield with the same input of labor and capital. Economic growth, therefore, means that one can produce the desired goods in a shorter time and thus gain leisure time.

The beneficial effect of economic growth is the reward of saving time. People can transform the saved time into leisure or use it to develop and apply new ideas, which further increase the productivity of human labor and capital. Modern capitalism is an entrepreneurial capitalism because economic success comes from transforming ideas into goods and processes that pass the market test.

One of the main errors of economic policy is to focus on economic growth and employment instead of productivity gains. Yet what matters is productivity, and the best way to promote productivity is having a capitalist order of free markets.

The sources of wealth creation are commerce and innovation. Human creativity and the benefits of exchange are the keys to wealth. Those societies do well, which put the least resistance to these natural expressions of human action.

IV.

SOCIALISM

Antony P. Mueller

> "Socialism is the fantastic younger brother of the despised despotism, which it wishes to inherit; its endeavors are thus, in the deepest sense, reactionary. For it desires an abundance of the power of the state, as only the despotism has had, and indeed it surpasses all the past by striving for the formal annihilation of the individual."
> Friedrich Nietzsche: "Human, All Too Human", Chapter 10.
> Item Eight "A Look at the State" (1878)

- *A deadly utopia*
- *Command economy*
- *Backgrounder: Friedrich Hayek on central planning and totalitarianism*
- *Economic calculation*
- *Planned chaos*
- *Marxist errors*
- *Backgrounder: Marx's' theory of the collapse of capitalism*
- *A dream becomes a nightmare*
- *Systemic Misery*
- *Summary*

A moral person cannot be a socialist other than because of ignorance. The fatal attraction to socialism results from the wishful thinking of people that there could be an economic system, which would be as productive as capitalism and come with equality. Socialism appears as the ideal that realizes heaven on earth. 'From each according to his ability, to each according to his needs.' - Who would not agree? Who would not want a society that guarantees prosperity for all but does not ask for an equivalent contributory effort?

Socialism promises equality and that everyone would receive what he needs -whether one adds little or nothing to produce the goods. According to the socialist ideology, this promise, however, is not an invitation to parasitism since, according to the socialist thesis, a 'new man' would emerge in the socialist community. Instead of the capitalist egoist, a new creature would rise under socialism, someone whose prime attitude is altruism and universal benevolence. According to the socialist utopia, only those people would ask for assistance who truly need help while all other individuals would contribute as much as possible to produce the goods and services for the community. The socialist dream says that under socialism, there would be both: abundance and equality.

There is no end to discussing such possibilities. Yet the real problem why socialism cannot work is not because of ethics, but that under a socialist regime rational economic calculation is not feasible. Even if the promised 'new man' would have appeared and a new human creature would have come into being - socialism would fail. The problem of socialism is not egoism versus altruism but that it is impossible to calculate in a rational way how to produce. Because there are no money prices, no markets, and no private property, socialist economies cannot properly function. Instead of abundance, there is misery and instead of equality, there is suppression in socialism.

Socialism, when put into practice, leads to a command economy. In as much as some command and others must follow, equality ends. Where there is no private property, the state must determine the use of the goods through orders and commandos. Freedom vanishes and productivity sinks. This fate becomes already visible before full socialism has arrived.

Each step closer to socialism brings less productivity, less income, and less wealth. The idea of 'society as a whole' is an absurd concept. When production is 'socialized', it is not the 'society' that decides what to produce, how, and for whom, but a band of commissars. When there are no markets and no prices to guide economic decisions, the commissars will have to threaten and apply physical force to get their plans implemented.

A Deadly Utopia

As soon as the Communists conquered the power in Russia in 1917, the new rulers established an oppressive apparatus grew into horrendous proportions. During the compulsory collectivization of agriculture, in the early 1920s and in further waves in the late 1920s and the early 1930s, the so-called 'Holodomor' cost the lives of millions of people who died due to executions, deportations, and famine. The human tragedy happened again in Communist China when Mao Zedong (1893-1976) prescribed the 'great leap forward' from 1958 to 1961.

State Murders by Socialist Regimes 1917-1979

REGIME	VICTIMS	PERIOD
Russian Soviet Communism	62 million	1917-1987
Chinese Communism	35 million	1949-1987
National Socialism	21 million	1933-1945
Cambodian Communism	2.0 million	1975-1979
North Korean Communism	1.7 million	1948-1987
Polish Communism	1.6 million	1945-1948
TOTAL	123.3 million	1917-1979

Figures are the average between the highest and the lowest estimate Source: R. J. Rummel, Death by Government, Transaction Publisher 1997
Website: https://www.hawaii.edu/powerkills/NOTE1.HTM

    A real abyss appears when one considers that National Socialism is socialism. As it says in its name, 'National Socialism' (Nazism) is the national version of socialism, while Soviet Communism is the international variant of socialism. Communist terror, however, came before the National Socialist era. In many respects, National Socialism was a reaction to international socialism. The Holodomor happened at the doorstep of Western Europe. The horrors of collectivization and the slaughtering of innocents by the Communist terror machine drove many people into the hands of Nazism and Fascism.
    It was the declared goal of the Soviet power to establish Communism on a worldwide scale through a world revolution. Germany was the number one on the list of countries to include in the Communist power range. The leading Communists (Leon Trotsky: 'What Next? Vital Questions for the German Proletariat'. January 1932) knew well that who owns Europe, owns the world, and that who owns Germany, owns Europe. At the beginning of the thirties, the leftist German Social Democratic Party, together with the Communist Party, gained more than half of the votes in the general election. That Germany would become Communist and thus surrender to the Soviet rule seemed a matter of time. While the Communist coups had failed at the end of World War I in 1919 in Bavaria, some

other German States, and in various parts of Eastern Europe, a Communist takeover seemed inescapable in the early 1930s when the Great Depression raged.

In March 1919, leading members of the Russian Communist Party founded the Communist International (Comintern). The aim of this organization was to establish Communism in Europe and then in the world. The plan was to fight 'with all available means, including the armed forces, for the overthrow of the international bourgeoisie and to establish an international Soviet republic'. For a political party to join the Communist International under the leadership of the Soviet Communists, twenty-one conditions were necessary to comply with, among them

- to lead truly Communist propaganda and agitation and to preserve the idea of a dictatorship of the proletariat;
- remove all reformists from the responsible posts;
- in addition to the legal, create an illegal organization for subversive work.

The term 'state murder' – 'democide' - refers to mass murders carried out by the force of state apart from wars. Elimination of its own citizens is the stamp of socialism. In a command economy, anyone who opposes the state becomes an enemy of the people. As it is impossible to obey the dictates of the command economy in its entirety, and as non-compliance counts as sabotage, one persecution wave follows the other.

***

States are fatal - not only for its foreign enemies but also for its own citizens. The rule holds that the more comprehensive the rule of the state and the more totalitarian its ideology, the more destructive is this state for its citizens. Since the socialist state is totalitarian, socialism is a regime that carries out mass murders.

If a socialist world government would come into existence, the known historical dimensions of killings would dwarf before the new potential of terror. Although under such a world socialist regime, there would be no more wars in the conventional sense, the democide - the killing of one's own citizens by such a world government - would ravage without restraint. 'World peace' under a socialist global government would eliminate international wars at the cost of an all-encompassing terror regime and an everlasting civil war. The way to prevent such a catastrophe demands to limit the role of state and politics wherever one can and oppose all plans of a world government. The libertarian agenda includes abolishing international institutions such as the United Nations, the International Monetary Fund, the World Bank, the World Climate Conference, and all the rest of the plethora of international institutions and organizations because they are the springboard of a world government.

In socialism, everything becomes a question of political power, not only the economy. Politics is the magnet that attracts those who seek dominance. The relentless pursuit of control over other people is a psychological trait common to all leaders in all political parties. Because of the overriding role of politics in a socialist system, everything in this society is subject to the vicissitudes of the power play.

A socialist system requires hierarchical command structures. Under the socialist rule, the 'new man' promised by the ideology comes into existence not as an angel but as an apparatchik and underling. The 'dictatorship of the proletariat' becomes a reality - not as an egalitarian rule but as a military regime. Deception and trickery rule everyday life in socialism. The system compels the individual to lie and to cheat systematically to survive.

Once the socialist regime is established, idealism vanishes, and the promised altruism makes way to crude selfishness. The dream becomes a nightmare. The revolutionaries turn into bureaucrats who block the attempts to transform the system since a change would put their position of power at risk. This lack of adaptability continues from the top down to the lower ranks and spreads throughout the economy and includes the cultural life. Together with the state, the economy falters and comes to a standstill. Culture becomes as blunt and drab as the socialist nightlife. After the decline follows stagnation. At the end of this process, a society emerges in which the military along with the Communist Party become the dominant institutions to rule over a corpse-like society and economy.

The rule of the socialist command economy begins by abolishing the price system and to do away with the private ownership of the means of production. War economy and military rule replace the market system. If socialism were to rule the world, it would lead to a global economic stagnation and to a worldwide decline. World socialism would mean global dictatorship based on a system of comprehensive military rule. This horror would happen without intention, due to the logic of a socialist system. Under the conditions of world communism, the population would become impoverished and suppressed and the opponents of the regime would suffer constant persecution and perish in camps or get killed right away.

Only in so far as there is space for a market-based commerce, a socialist system can somewhat still work. That Soviet communism could last from 1917 to 1991 is because that in Russia and in the countries dominated by the Soviets, the market economy was not fully eliminated and that these countries did not cut themselves off from the capitalist environment. Under a system of global Communism, however, it would no longer be possible to find orientation by imitating the price system of the capitalist countries. Then, the economy would be on the brink of total collapse and the regime could only sustain itself through the unremitting application of brutal force. The victory of world communism would surpass any known historical dimensions of terror and misery. Yet this was the plan that lay at the foundation of the Soviet Union and at the Communist plans of a world revolution.

From the inception of the Soviet rule onwards, the Soviet economy existed as a war economy. Until the beginning of World War II, the Red Army waged wars against Poland (1919-21 and 1939), the Baltic countries (1918-20), Finland (1939), and Japan (1939). The Red Army invaded Poland in 1939 and took its share of the country's Eastern part in an accord with Nazi Germany that grabbed the Western part of Poland. The Red Army waged the civil war (1917-1922) against the White Army and carried out the forced collectivization of agriculture with military force at the end of the 1920s into the 1930s. The Soviet economy developed as a war economy and remained one until the end of the Soviet Union on December 26, 1991.

Democides by the Soviet regime

PERIOD	VICTIMS (in millions)	YEAR OF INCEPTION
Civil War	3.3	1917
New Economic Policy	2.2	1923
Collectivization	11.4	1929
The Great Terror	4.4	1936
Pre-World War II	5.1	1939
World War II	13.1	1941
Post-World War II	15.6	1946
Post-Stalin Era	6.9	1954
Total	61.9	1917

Source: Rummel, R. J.: Lethal Politics: Soviet Genocide and Mass Murder Since 1917. New Brunswick, N.J.: Transaction Publishers, 1990, Table 1.1. https://www.hawaii.edu/powerkills/USSR.TAB1.1.GIF

The Soviet Union existed as 13 military districts. The Soviet army relied on conscription for its personnel. Together with a huge contingent of female soldiers, the Soviet Union could mobilize over ten million soldiers. The construction of large factories had already begun in the 1920s to produce attack-capable weaponry. By the 1930s, the Soviet Union had the most advanced paratrooper army ready to invade its neighboring countries and to go beyond. In 1941, the Soviet Union had thousands of tanks, more than all other armies combined and four times as many as Nazi Germany.

While the mass of the population in Soviet Russia lived in poverty and without freedom, Soviet Communism established itself as a powerful militarist regime. After the Soviet Union came into existence, the Soviet Communist Party became the leader of the Communist world. Using the military counted as a legitimate means to conquer the world and put it under Communist rule. The purpose of taking power in Russia was not to liberate the Russian people from the oppressive Tsarist rule but the Communist revolution was to serve as the first step on the road to world revolution and global dominance.

The history of the Soviet Union is a history of murder waves. Already on the way to establishing the Soviet power in the civil war, millions of people had to let their lives. Introducing socialist production forms in the new Soviet territory required further millions of victims, and the collectivization of agriculture from 1929 cost the life of over ten million people. The victims of the Soviet class warfare were not only 'capitalists', but prominent intellectuals, the priests of the Orthodox church, millions of common people, and all anti-Communists.

Even during World War II, the democide did not cease. Without counting the victims of war, 13 million people lost their lives - among them 10 million Soviet citizens - during the war. After the Second World War, the murders continued, and the Soviet regime engineered a further 15 million victims.

After the fall of the Soviet Union, the new accessible KGB documents revealed that from 1929 to 1953 some 28 million people fell victim to deportations and forced labor in the GULAG and that millions perished in the Holodomor of the 1930s. (For more details see Yuri Maltsev: Mass Murder and Public Slavery: The Soviet Experience. The Independent Review. Fall 2017). For the development of the Soviet Economy see: Peter Boettke: The Political Economy of Soviet Socialism.

Bibliography of Communist democides in the 20th century

- Applebaum, Anne. Gulag : A History. Doubleday, 2003.
- Becker, Jasper. Hungry Ghosts: Mao's Secret Famine. The Free Press, 1997.
- Conquest, Robert. The Harvest of Sorrow: Soviet Collectivization and the Terror-Famine. University of Alberta Press, 1986.
- Conquest, Robert. Kolyma: The Arctic Death Camps. Viking Press, 1978.
- Conquest, Robert. The Nation Killers: The Soviet Deportation of Nationalities. Macmillan, 1970. (I have not read Conquest's later Stalin: Breaker of Nations (Viking, 1991), but I believe that it incorporates additional material.)
- Heller, Mikhail and Nekrich, Aleksandr. Utopia in Power The History of the Soviet Union from 1917 to the Present. Summit Books, 1986.
- Rummell, R. J. Death by Government. Transaction Publishers, 1994.
- Solzhenitsyn, Aleksandr. The Gulag Archipelago (Volumes I-III). Harper & Row, 1973-1978.
- Werth, Nicolas; Panne, Jean-Louis; Paczkowski, Andrzej; Bartosek, Karel; Margolin, Jean-Louis; Courtois, Stephane. The Black Book of Communism: Crimes, Terror, Repression. Harvard University Press, 1999.

The Second World War merged into the Cold War so that the Soviet economy existed as a war economy also in the second half of the 20th century until the Soviet Union collapsed. The dominance of the military in a Communist state is not accidental as it is also evident in the two Communist states that still exist: North Korea and Cuba.

In its nationalist form, too, Socialism works as a war economy to the extent that the national economy serves for the war aims. National Socialism, like the Soviet Communism, is unsuitable to satisfy the variety of the consumers' wishes. As an economic system, socialism, be it nationalist or internationalist, functions as a war economy. As soon as the economic planners try to include consumers' preferences beyond the military requirements, production falters, and distribution becomes precarious. Be it Soviet Communism or National Socialism, socialism creates not prosperity but poverty and oppression.

Command Economy

In socialism, commandments rule and people must obey. Those who do not take part in the Communist Party must lead an existence at the margin. In as much as there is still supply of high-quality consumer goods, it is possible because socialist countries coexist with market economies and have some foreign trade. The Socialist planners could copy the price relations from the capitalist countries thus try to adapt their plans to these indications of scarcity. Without such price signals, the socialist economic leaders would lose orientation about the costs of the input factors of production. Beyond market prices, there are no gauges with which amount and kind of capital goods and by how much work one should produce a commodity - and be it only a pencil or a cooker. Socialism means economic blindness. The price tag disappears, and so both, the consumers and the planners, lose informational orientation about rational economic conduct.

Socialists suppose that to implant their rule all that is necessary is to socialize the private companies, replace the management, and install workers councils, and the new economic order would flourish. The socialists ignore that the socialization of the means of production is just a beginning. What matters is how to run a business.

The planners may know what type of technology a specific production would require, and they can count on the professionalism of the engineers to use their knowledge. The error of socialist economic planning, however, lies in believing that business management could also continue as before after socialist operators take over the capitalist management. While the socialist regime can train administrators and engineers, and put the party members in leadership positions, these new leaders cannot decide according to relative scarcities because there is no longer a private property-based entrepreneurial price system available.

Many supporters of socialism believe business management is nothing more than a kind of registration or simple bookkeeping. Vladimir Ilyich Lenin (1870-1924), the Soviet revolutionary leader, believed ("State and Revolution") that for the conduct of business operations the knowledge of reading and writing, as well as some expertise in the use of the four basic arithmetic operations and some training in accounting, would be enough to manage a company. The socialists then and now ignore the fundamental economic problem, which consists in determining what to produce, for whom, and how. The socialist planners assume that a plan can stipulate these three tasks and ignore how and where such a plan should find its standard of valuation. The basic error of the socialists is the presumption that one could manage a complex economy without capitalists and entrepreneurs.

Even if, for example, the plan should stipulate to produce a certain number of pencils for the literacy campaign, and that the order would go to the respective factories, the question arises how to design and by which combination of the factors of production the manufacturing should take place. When prices and markets disappear, one loses the orientation about which factors of production are more and which are less scarce along with the loss of knowledge of the costs of the goods used in the production process.

Scarcity makes goods valuable, and that something is valuable, expresses itself in its higher relative price in the market economy. Observing the prices, the market participants receive information about scarcity and align their economic decisions to the market signals. Yet when there is no market, information about the relation between the wants for goods and their supply vanishes. In a market economy, the economic participants need only partial knowledge to act rationally.

The price system informs about the scarcity relation and makes it possible to decide according to one's own best interests. There is no need for comprehensive information since markets enable to weigh the advantages and disadvantages of economic actions by way of the relative prices because the price system reduces complexity for the individual decision maker to the single number of the price.

In socialism, however, private ownership of the means of production no longer exists, and thus there is no price system for capital goods available. Institutionally, socialism consists in abolishing the market economy and replacing it with a planned economy. Yet beyond the loss of private property, the fundamental problem comes from the consequence that by doing away with private property of the means of production, one wipes-out information as well. Even if prices for consumer goods continue to exist, and if there is private ownership of consumer goods, the orientation about the relative scarcity of capital goods is lost as the socialist system removes the private ownership of the production goods and eliminates the role of the entrepreneur.

> **Friedrich Hayek on central planning and totalitarianism**
>
> "The reasons why the adoption of a system of central planning necessarily produces a totalitarian system are fairly simple. Whoever controls the means must decide which ends they are to serve. As under modern conditions control of economic activity means control of the material means for practically all our ends, it means control over nearly all our activities. The nature of the detailed scale of values which must guide the planning makes it impossible that it should be determined by anything like democratic means. The director of the planned system would have to impose his scale of values, his hierarchy of ends, which, if it is to be sufficient to determine the plan, must include a definite order of rank in which the status of each person is laid down. If the plan is to succeed or the planner to appear successful, the people must be made to believe that the objectives chosen are the right ones. Every criticism of the plan or the ideology underlying it must be treated as sabotage. There can be no freedom of thought, no freedom of the Press, where it is necessary that everything should be governed by

> a single system of thought. In theory, Socialism may wish to enhance freedom, but in practice, every kind of collectivism consistently carried thought must produce the characteristic features which Fascism, Nazism, and Communism have in common. Totalitarianism is nothing but consistent collectivism, the ruthless execution of the principle that 'the whole comes before the individual' and the direction of all members of society by a single will supposed to represent the 'whole'."
>
> (Friedrich A. Hayek, 1941, p. 583 in: "Planning, Science and Freedom", Nature 148 (15 November 1941), also available as "Planning, Science, and Freedom," Mises Daily (Auburn, AL: The Ludwig von Mises Institute, 27 September 2010)

Organization of the planned economy

The management plan in socialism shows a hierarchical structure of the command path from top to bottom (by way of commandos and force) and the information obligation from bottom to top (confirmation of the execution of the order). The consumer appears in the system only at the margin.

The socialist economy does not serve the consumers. The point of reference for proper management is to execute the commands – the same as in the military. To fulfill plans refers to the respective level in the hierarchy of the command order - not to the consumer.

Production faces the problems that there is an almost unlimited number of ways how to produce a good. One can manufacture a commodity with very different raw materials, technologies, and combinations of the production factors. The industrial feasibility and its technical optimum can only give a partial sign since many ways of construction are possible.

Before the aspects of technological feasibility could be considered, producing a good requires applying economic principles – the calculation of its potential profitability. Without cost calculation in relation to sales, a technical evaluation makes no sense. What is technically possible is not economically recommended, and what appears optimal from a technical point of view need not be so in terms of profits. With costs left out of consideration, socialist production is blind to the risk of producing goods that would cost more than they are worth. Who determines value? In a market economy, it is the client, and, in the last instance, the consumer.

In central planning economy, it is up to the planners to determine the value. This, however, they cannot accomplish because preferences and technologies change, and the complexity of the relationship among the goods exceeds the capacity of anyone's mind or that of a planning committee to grasp.

Without a price system, the constructors of a product cannot know whether the resources the plan foresees to use are in demand to produce other goods that may be more urgent. In the market economy, the price is the signal whether a certain commodity is scarce or abundant. If a good is expensive, it shows that many other economic agents also want to use this product or the resources that one needs to produce this commodity. The market price expresses the prevailing socio-economic conditions. Socialism means economic blindness. Information is lost along with the incentive to act according to the price signals. In capitalism, the motivations of gaining profits and to avoid costs work as an incentive to behave rationally. In a market economy, the prices fulfill the double function to inform and to incentivize the producer and the buyer.

Organizational structure of the centrally planned economy

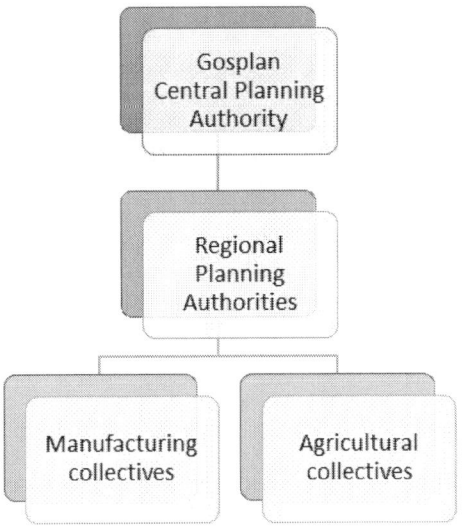

Capitalism is a system in which the higher profits come to those who are best at satisfying the wishes of the customers concerning type, quality, and price of the product. Even if one would want to satisfy the wants of the masses under socialism, this is not possible because the system has purged the information necessary to do. Socialism eliminates both: information and incentives. The economic actors must operate in the dark. They may have a sense of what the consumers might want and may want to produce it, but this diffuse knowledge differs from the way economic knowledge exists in a market economy, where the prices and the acts of purchases of a company's products show the customers' willingness to pay by the penny and the result appears as profit and loss.

At the beginning of socialization, the planners may still find points of orientation in the former capitalist price conditions. The socialist managers then come to grips with this residual knowledge in the early stages of socialist production. Yet the longer the socialist system is in place, the less reliable the former price relations to guide the production process. The conditions change, but the socialist steering apparatus has no mechanism to register these changes and to implement this knowledge. The longer the socialists rule, the more they shove the economy into misallocation. The longer socialism exists, the less the system can learn - opposite to a market economy, in which the economic actors become more knowledgeable the longer and the more intensive the market system operates. Capitalism is a learning system - socialism is a system of diminishing degrees of knowledge.

The socialism of the Soviet Union and its satellite states did not collapse right away because the remnants of the market economy were still around, international trade with capitalist countries was not completely cut off, and because a private shadow economy existed. If one considers that socialism will encompass the entire world, the planning problem would become overwhelming. Under a worldwide communist regime, the planning authority would create an uncoordinated economy. Such a system would deal lavishly with scarce resources but ignore abundant resources. The system would generate vast misallocations. Of some commodities, too many would be produced, while other more urgent goods would be in short supply. Not the actual demand would count but the vicissitudes of the production plans. As a result, goods would be of bad quality and very costly relative to the wage level.

A centrally planned economy suffers from a long command and information chain. It takes a long time for the commands to get down from the central planning body to the local production units, and it takes a long time for the information about the execution of the order to go back up to the central planning body.

Under a global socialism, the economies would fall into deep misery even more so than it is already the case under a single socialist economy. A global socialist system would descend into an economic abyss even if at the beginning it would seem as if the opposite were to happen when the wealth that had been accumulated by the capitalist economic order serves for the promised 'just' distribution.

Command and information chain of a centrally planned economy

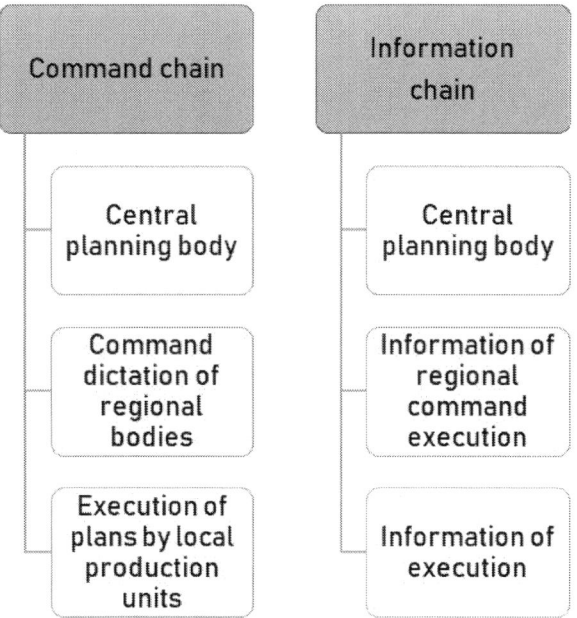

Antony P. Mueller

Economic Calculation

As early as in 1922, five years after the Communist takeover in Russia, Ludwig von Mises (1881-1973) wrote his profound analysis of the consequences of the lack of economic calculation in the socialist economy. Mises' approach was novel because he showed that the fundamental problem of a socialist economy is not a moral one but an economic issue. Without a price system and property rights, the economic entities lose the basis of calculation and thus of rational economic conduct.

In a market economy, the relative prices of the goods serve as a guide for the proper economic action. These price ratios reflect the combination of the production factors that best satisfy consumers' needs. Relative prices show what consumers want and guide the production process into this direction because this is where the profits emerge. The competition provides the incentives for cost-effectiveness so that consumers receive the goods at the lowest prices based on the best use of the factors of production.

In capitalism, the wishes of the clients determine the overall structure of the price relations. The preferences of the consumers determine also the values of the investment goods. This imputation of the value estimation goes from the consumers to the value of the production goods. It takes place according to the contribution of the investment goods to the value of the final consumption good that is produced by the capital good. The value of the final product determines the value of the intermediate goods. The anchor for the value structure of the entire wealth in a market economy is the final use of the goods by the consumer.

Under capitalism, it is not a planning authority that controls the production structure, but the consumers decide. These control the economy because only those entrepreneurs that obey the calls of the consumers can gain an extra profit. In a capitalist economy, the production follows the wishes of the consumers. Businesses must restructure the production according to the changes of consumer wants, needs and tastes. Therefore, business management is not an uncomplicated undertaking as Lenin had presumed.

Production direction and value creation

The expected prices of the consumer goods determine the prices of the investment goods.

The costs of capital goods do not determine the value of the consumer goods, but the value of the consumer goods determines the value of the production goods that is used producing the consumer goods.

The direction of valuation of the value of capital goods runs from the value of consumer goods to capital goods while the direction of the production process in time runs from the early stages of production to the present.

The capitalist mode of production uses market prices, which result from the interplay of individual subjective estimates of subjective utility to assess the value of capital goods in this process.

Market prices objectively indicate how wants are distributed in society in terms of the economic actors' willingness to pay.

Directions of production and valuation

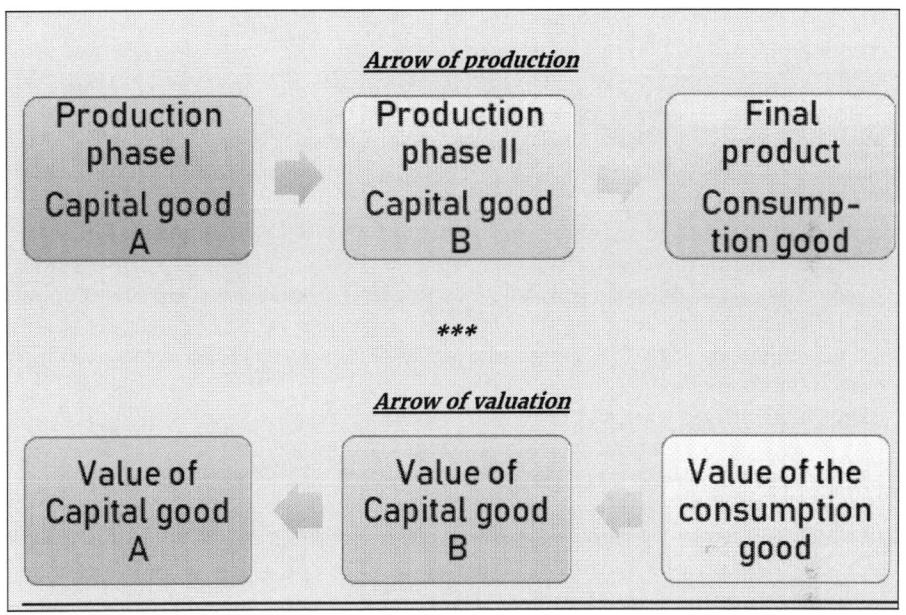

***

Ludwig von Mises shows in his analysis of the economy under socialism that a private property-based pricing system must be available to evaluate the goods used in production. The price is objective in the sense as it bundles the various subjective valuations present in the society. The values of the consumption goods depend on the wishes of the consumers as they reveal their wants by their willingness to pay. The link between the value of a consumer good and a capital good becomes clear when the production process moves closer to the end of the production chain. The further away from consumption that the capital good stands in the time order of the production structure, the less does the subjective valuation of the consumer goods determine the value of the production good. Without a price system, no individual and no expert planning team, no matter how excellent, could survey and appraise the almost endless variety of combinations in the production process.

In order to gain an orientation in this maze, one needs price ratios, which reflect the exchange conditions on the market. It is the function of entrepreneurs to appraise these price ratios and to make business decisions. The more extensive the market, and the more intensive the competition, the more and the better the information input in the system.

There are also socialized enterprises in a market economy system. However, these state enterprises, including municipal enterprises, can behave economically when they follow the guidance of the private price system of the capitalist environment. This is possible if the market economy is still the dominant system. The same applies to the socialist economies when they use international prices from the capitalist countries. In the system of global socialism, however, these points of reference are no longer present. The planners are then unaware of the conditions of scarcity.

As Mises explains in his essay on economic calculation under socialism, any economic endeavor "becomes a feat whose success can neither be estimated in advance nor can it be evaluated later in retrospect ... Socialism is the abolition of the rationality of the economy". Only the monetary calculation of business based on prices offers a guide through the "overwhelming abundance of economic possibilities". Without the calculation of prices by means of money, "all production with far-reaching processes would be a tapping in the dark." (Ludwig von Mises: Economic Calculation in the Socialist Commonwealth)

The value of an investment project does not follow from its cost but from the extent to which the investment contributes to satisfying the subjective utility of the consumer. Due to this connection between value and price, the entrepreneur will gain the information whether it is worthwhile to bear the costs of a project or to refrain from its realization. The cost calculation is an indispensable tool for estimating the profit chances of a project, yet the final judgment about the profits is in the hands of the consumers according to their willingness to pay a price. This also applies to investment goods, which have value only in as much as they contribute to producing consumables. The entrepreneurial contribution to each production stage along the production chain will get its final financial compensation only when the consumers have paid the goods.

From an economic point of view, the entrepreneur must fulfill two functions: first, estimate the future wants of the buyer and, second, produce these goods at the minimum cost. These tasks require experimentation. Trial and error lie at the heart of the market-based competition process. If there is no competition, the companies lose both the orientation what consumers want and about how to manufacture the goods in a cost-efficient way. Even if the socialist planners wanted the best for the consumers, they could not determine the optimal production structure because they do not have the information of the market prices about the degree of the prevalent degrees of scarcity.

Socialism as an economic system had already failed in the early phase of the Soviet Union. The Soviet economy survived as a war economy. The main purpose of the economic activity was to serve the needs of the military. The wishes of the consumers found only marginal consideration. It would be wrong, however, to conclude that the Soviet economy could not be a consumer economy because the Soviet Union was compelled to give priority to the military. The war economy was the only way that the Soviet planned economy could at least somewhat function.

Why socialism cannot work

Socialism suffers from four fundamental defects. Each one of them alone makes socialism already inoperative. Together they multiply the effect.

First, socialism eradicates private property and markets and thus eliminates rational calculation.

Second, socialism allows soft budgets, so there is no mechanism in place to discards inefficient production methods.

Third, abolishing private property and replacing it by the state promotes distorted incentives.

Fourth, the socialist system with its absence of private property and of free markets inhibits economic coordination of the system of division of labor and capital.

Socialism means economic blindness. Information gets lost along with the incentive to act according to the price signals. In capitalism, the motivations of gaining profits and to avoid costs work as an incentive to behave rationally. In a market economy, the prices fulfill the double function to inform and to incentivize the seller and the buyer.

It is no wonder that even a degenerate capitalism produces more prosperity than the best socialism. Therefore, the task ahead cannot be to remove capitalism in favor of socialism but to make capitalism better which means to make it more capitalist.

Fundamental defects of socialism

Abolition of private property and markets eliminates rational calculation.	Soft budgets untermine the mechanism to eliminate inefficient production methods
The absence of private property and of free markets inhibits economic coordination	Abolishing private property and replacing it by the state promotes distorted incentives

Defects of Socialism

Planned Chaos

Socialists accuse the market economy of the anarchy of production, yet it is, in fact, the socialist economic system, which suffers from chaos. Scarcity requires economic behavior. Prices indicate the relative availability of a good. Profit and loss, which arise from the difference between sales and costs, inform the business owner about the profitability of the company. If profit and loss disappear under socialism, the indicator of how well production serves the consumers also vanishes. Without such signals, production takes place by happenstance and production may cost more than the goods are worth for the final user. The socialist economy absorbs more material and human resources than the production generates in utility. The lamented 'exploitation' of human labor, which socialist blame to exist in capitalism, is the systematic reality under socialism. This negative-sum economy of socialism cost a colossal toll in human lives and labor in the Soviet efforts to industrialize Russia. In the second decade of the new millennium, this exploration of the masses continuous in Cuba, North Korea, and Venezuela.

Planners can provide schemes to produce consumers goods based on surveys of the conditions among the population. For example, planners could try to determine how many pairs of shoes the population needs. Yet the planners cannot achieve these goals because they have no reliable and detailed knowledge about what consumers want but also do not have the guidelines as to the costs that producing the shoes would absorb in relation to satisfy urgent consumer wants, such as clothing, housing, and food. In a market economy, the solution to this problem lies not in the hands of one central planning authority, but all market participants cooperate in the assessment process and delegate the production of the goods to different entrepreneurial units according to the specific capabilities of these individual companies that the market competition reveals. Each individual consumer expresses his subjective valuation in the act of purchase. The prices and the sold quantities are signals and incentives. In a capitalist market economy, the owners of the means of production are involved at each stage of the production process to solve the valuation problem. In the end, the valuation of the consumers determines the value of the capital that is employed in the production process.

In socialism, however, workers and engineers work without entrepreneurship in the absence of the capitalists and of the capitalist managers. The socialists want to make the entrepreneurs superfluous and put the production apparatus into the hands of the workers and their leaders. The socialists believe that they can achieve a better economic performance through the socialization of the enterprises. The anti-capitalists come to this false idea because they do neither understand the function of the entrepreneur nor that of the capitalist.

Unlike the administrator, the entrepreneur represents the creative force of the business. The task of the entrepreneur - who may or may not be the owner or co-owner of a company – is to realize business ideas. The entrepreneur is the one looking for the best way to satisfy customers' wishes, how best to produce with the production equipment, and how best to organize the plant. An entrepreneur is someone who enforces these ideas. Different from the entrepreneur, the function of the capitalist is to maintain the capital structure. Capitalists finance the production process. They receive their compensation only with the sale of the final good while the workers receive their salaries already during the time of the production process. When the capitalists and the entrepreneurs disappear, and the socialists seize power, the capital structure disintegrates because there is no one left with a personal interest in financing and managing the edifice of capital with the final consumer in mind.

Marxist Errors

Karl Marx (1818-1883) ignored the role played by the capitalist and entrepreneur in the market economy. Marx saw the capitalist as someone who, like it was the case with Marx' collaborator Friedrich Engels (1820-1895), owns a fortune and receives dividends and interest payments without an accomplishment of one's own. Biographers of the communist labor movement leader claim that Marx never saw a factory from within. Friedrich Engels, the financial sponsor of the Marxist project to conquer the world, was the heir of a fortune that his father had accumulated, and that the son would spend not only as a supporter of Karl Marx and the socialist movement but also as a playboy. Friedrich Engels was neither a capitalist nor an entrepreneur, but an inheritor and a parasite like Marx. Engels kept Karl Marx financially above water, particularly in the period after the socialist author had squandered the inheritance of his noble wife.

Marx and his successors ignore that the capitalists pre-finance and preserve the capital structure of the economy. Capital formation requires before everything else, abstention from using one's full potential of consumption. The capitalists are those who do this by financing the production processes until the commodity reaches the consumer as the finished product ready for use.

In order to understand the role of the capitalists in the market economy, one must consider that each product runs through a lengthy production process until it reaches the consumers. This production process extends from the planning process onward through the different processing stages until the goods get to the warehouses and the exhibition and sales rooms and includes the marketing to sell the goods. The receipts come only with the sale of the final good.

By the time when the capitalist receives income from the consumer, time passes, and the entire process is subject to risk and uncertainty. The capitalists receive their reward because of waiting and of bearing risks and uncertainties while the wage earners receive their remuneration regularly long before the product reaches the final consumer.

Under market competition, only the successful entrepreneurs and capitalists, those who master the challenges of satisfying the customers, will remain in business. The failed entrepreneurs disappear from the market together with their projects and their associated firms. The socialists see those who have accumulated a fortune. They lament the inequality and ignore the fact that the capitalist process is an elimination process that roots out the losers of the game.

The market process creates inequality because the failed projects vanish. The inequality in capitalism is the result of the elimination process, which is the reason why capitalism is so productive. The market competition forces the unsuccessful entrepreneurs to disappear and to make room for those who are better in satisfying the customer's wishes. In the reality of the market economy, the Marxist construct of a 'capitalist class' does not exist because each member must struggle for his membership every day and both the entry and the exit doors are wide open.

Backgrounder:
Marx' Theory of the Collapse of Capitalism

According to the Marxist doctrine, the characteristic feature of capitalism is that the use of money serves to produce goods to earn more money.

Marx put this idea in his 'formula' of M-G-M', which means that money (M) serves to produce goods(G) to earn more money (M').

In the Marxian model, the capitalist profits result from the exploitation of the workers because capitalists gain the surplus value, which the workers create. The surplus value depends on the so-called 'organic composition of the capital', which includes the 'constant capital' of machines and property and the 'variable capital', which represents the labor force in the production process.

Following Marx, the capitalist competition compels the companies to increase the constant capital. This reduces the relative share of the variable capital and the profitability of the capitalist firm falls since the extraction of the surplus value as the rate of exploitation depends on the relative size of labor in relation to constant capital.

'Das Kapital' Volume I was published in 1867. Volume II and III were published after the death of Karl Marx (1883) in 1885 and 1894 respectively.

The focal point of the Marxist model is the thesis that entrepreneurial profit results from the exploitation of the labor force and that in as much as the concentration of capital reduces the extraction of surplus value, profits will shrink, and capitalism will collapse.

For Marx, the solution is socialism as a system under which the workers retain that part of the work which capitalist extract as surplus value from the working proletariat.

The central problem of the Marxist model is the assumption that the value of a product is equal to the labor effort needed for its production. Marx took this error from the classical economists who already had noted its paradoxical implications and the clash of the labor theory of value with reality.

Only five years after Marx published the first volume of "Capital", the neoclassical revolution happened, which corrected the fundamental error of classical economics.

Neoclassical economic theory resolved the paradox of value. The neoclassical approach clarifies that the value of goods and services depends on the subjective valuation of the individual buyers and is determined not in terms of averages and totals but on the margin.

***

According to the Marxist doctrine, capitalism suffers from crises that become more severe and destructive over time, and finally, bring the complete collapse of capitalism. The capitalist competition leads to an army of unemployed persons and to the impoverishment of the working class and to a growing concentration of capital. According to this theory, the mass of the proletarians will grow, while the number of the capitalists will shrink.

The Marxist theory concludes that to the extent that the volume of the active labor force falls in the production process, the profits will decrease and thereby capitalism brings about its own downfall.

Yet during the 150 years that have elapsed since 'Das Kapital' (1867) appeared in print, the opposite development has occurred:

Instead of mass impoverishment, a new middle class has emerged, and extreme poverty has decreased worldwide the more countries have turned to capitalism. Today, there are more companies than ever in the world, where profits expand production, to introduce technical progress, and to raise productivity and with it the wages.

Marxist process of the collapse of capitalism

Surplus extraction

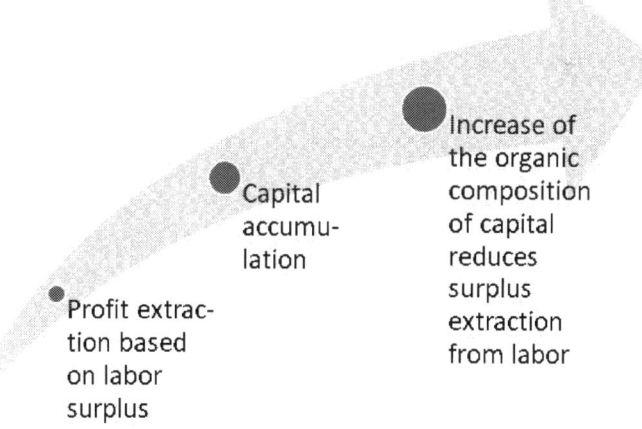

Profit contraction

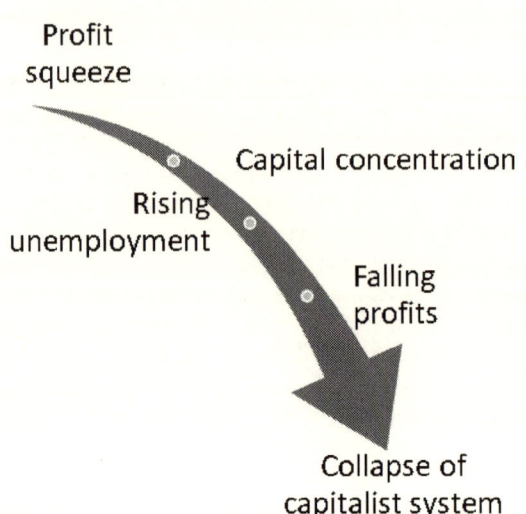

A Dream Becomes a Nightmare

Socialism demands the socialization of the means of production. Central management will replace the market. The original idea of Karl Marx was that socialism would lead to the death of the state. The opposite has happened.

Under no other form of economic production has the state become larger, stronger, more powerful, and more suppressive than under socialism. The internal contradictions of this economic system were soon recognized. This insight, however, did not bring the utopians to discard their dream into the dustbin of history, but rather the socialists ignored the criticism of their utopia. For the dream that the socialist way of production could work, idealist revolutionaries and the dictators who followed them sacrificed millions of people. While some of those who were in favor of socialism at the beginning of the movement may be dispensed of their error because of their inexperience, yet the socialists of today can no longer claim ignorance after the dimension of the brutal repression that came with the socialist system have become known.

Karl Marx, who opposed the socialist utopians, avoided answering the question how socialism would function. In his writings, he concentrated on the criticism of capitalism and he lost only a few words on how socialism may look like and how it could operate. Yet how far from reality the ideas about the future communist reality of Marx and Engels were, shows up in the following quotation. According to this Marx-Engels citation, it would be possible under communism "to do this today, to do that tomorrow, and to hunt in the morning, to fish in the afternoons, to breed cattle in the evening, to criticize after eating, without ever becoming a hunter, a fisherman, a shepherd, or a critic." (Marx-Engels-Werke, Vol. 3, Berlin 1969, p. 33). Apart from these promises, Marx did not much to elaborate the practical aspects of socialism. Instead, he would put forth the assertion of the historical inevitability of socialism. Marx took the postulate of historical necessity from his philosophical master G. W. F. Hegel (1770-1831) yet transported the Hegel's concept of the world spirit into economic history. What for Hegel was the path to freedom, became for Marx the road to bondage. The intellectual development towards liberty in the philosophy of Hegel turned into the deterministic historical materialism in the philosophy of Karl Marx.

According to the Marxist idea of the ultimate determination of the historical development, the march to the socialist rule can be slowed down or accelerated, but ultimately cannot be stopped. In the end, socialism will be victorious - the sooner the better. For the daily political struggle, this position meant that all opponents of socialism were reactionaries who prevent the socialist paradise from becoming the new heavenly reality now already. The postulate of the historical necessity of socialism implies that the socialist front as the leaders of the proletariat have the right and the obligation to eliminate those persons who resist the socialist movement because they postpone the coming of the socialist paradise. In the perspective of historical materialism, the predestined coming of the socialist paradise justifies and requires the physical removal of the opponents of socialism.

The supposedly scientific nature of historical materialism underpins the claim of determinism. This belief was effective when, in the middle of the nineteenth century, science had gained a religious status. The members of this new hybrid class of intellectuals who belong neither to the bourgeoisie nor to the nobility or to the working class had abandoned the traditional religious beliefs to assume a secular religion with as much fervor as they distanced themselves from the faith that they once held in childhood. he revolutionaries regarded religion as an obstacle to the unlimited progress that would come with socialism. Socialism and atheism were to be inseparable. With the claim of being scientific, the fantastic pronouncement of the utopia of a land of plenty for all finds its anchor in the belief of a heaven on earth.

As a child of his time, Marx was a naïve believer in science as determinism. Marxists assert that criticism of their theory is unscientific when, in fact, Marxism itself is unscientific as it sells a belief system as a proven theory. Since the times of Marx, the promoters of the socialist movement accuse anyone who turns against it as being an advocate of inequality, and as someone who does not want justice for the world but favors exploitation and inequality to continue.

The fusion of determinism and science with the promises of justice and happiness for all leads to a striking combination, which has been appealing to intellectuals. Up to the present day mainly academics believe in Marxism. Workers, after all, are a part of the economic reality of the production process and know that the socialist promises are rubbish. Nowhere has socialism established itself as the result of a workers' movement. The workers have never been the perpetrators of socialism but always its victim. The leaders of the revolution have been party politicians and military men. It was up to the intellectuals and artists to conceal the brutality of the socialist regimes through articles and books and by films, songs, and paintings, and to give socialism a scientific-intellectual, aesthetic and moral appearance. In the socialist propaganda, the new system appears to be both fair and productive.

While Marxism has disappeared from the workers' movement, Marxist theory flourishes today in culture, the academic world, and in the mass media. This 'cultural Marxism' goes back to Antonio Gramsci (1891-1937) and the Frankfurt School. The theorists of Marxism recognized that the proletariat would not play the expected historical role as a 'revolutionary subject'. Therefore, for the revolution to happen, the movement must depend on the cultural leaders to destroy the existing Christian culture and morality and then drive the disoriented masses to Communism as their new creed.

The final goal of this movement is to establish a world government in which the Marxist intellectuals have the say. The Russian Revolution was neither Russian nor proletarian. It had not come from a labor movement, but from a group of professional revolutionaries. A closer look at the personal composition of the Bolshevist party and the at first governments of the Soviet state and its repressive apparatus reveals the true character of the Soviet revolution as a project that did not aim at freeing the Russian people from the Tsarist joke but planned to launch a world revolution.

The supporters of socialism recognized that their preferred system could not function without a dictatorship. In order to succeed, the dictatorship must come in disguise, in the form of a mind control. For that purpose, the cultural Marxists postulate and exaggerate the role of social, sexual and racial differences. They play a game of confusion by promulgating that socialism can be democratic and that true communism has not yet existed but was to come - all the while calling themselves 'liberals' to usurp a label that connotes freedom.

When the murderous reality of communism in the Soviet system became known, the term 'communism' fell out of favor and was replaced by the less burdened concept of 'socialism'. When the concept of 'socialism' became less radiant, the expression 'left' came to the fore. When 'left' got a bad name, 'liberal' became the brand name, as it happened in the United States. In the US, the socialists have usurped the concept of 'liberal', so that 'a liberal' is now the opposite of its true meaning as being in favor of liberty. By these conceptual confusions, the socialists try to conceal the fact that socialism has been and always will be an inhuman system.

Systemic Misery

Besides eliminating the rest of their opponents, redistribution marks the socialist seizure of power. Expulsion and liquidation go hand in hand.

Without economic, redistribution becomes pure capital consumption, and the shrinking capital stock makes the people poor. Income depends on production. And more income requires economic growth. One cannot distribute more than gets produced. If there is less production, there is less for consumption and less for investment. The income level depends on the capital stock and on the rate of innovation. If both decline, the wage rate must fall. Instead of a realm of plenty, socialism creates misery.

Paradoxically, the longing to realize the socialist dream comes in part from the great success of capitalism as an engine of prosperity. The modern entrepreneurial economy proves the enormous economic achievements that humanity can generate. The socialists believe that this great success would become even greater when one combines the productive capacity of capitalism with an equalitarian redistribution under the control of the state. This illusion was already evident in the Communist Manifesto of 1848, in which Karl Marx and his sponsor Friedrich Engels formulated their enthusiastic praise of the capitalist achievements of the so-called bourgeoisie.

In the same pamphlet, there is also a programmatic list of goals to transform capitalism into the socialist ideal.

Among the ten points, some party planks show how far socialism has already engulfed the economic systems of today:

- Strongly progressive taxes
- Centralization of credit in the hands of the state by a national bank with state capital and an exclusive monopoly
- Centralization of the transport system in the hands of the state
- Installation of national factories and production instruments, cultivation and improvement of the countryside according to a Community Plan
- Unification of the farmlands of agriculture and industry with the aim of gradually eliminating the contrast between town and country
- Public and paid education of all children, elimination of factory work of children in its present form, union of education with material production.

According to this Communist Decalogue, the items left to achieve full socialism are

- Requirement 1 - Expropriation of the landed property and use of the basic rent for state expenditure
- Requirement 4 - Confiscation of the property of all emigrants and rebels
- Requirement 8 - Equal obligation to work for all, establishment of an industrial army including in agriculture

If one compares these demands of the Communist Manifesto with the theses of the Party Program of the Nazis, whose official name was NSDAP, which means 'National Socialist German Workers Party', the similarity of the two catalogs show up regarding the individual demands and the spirit from which they are derived. In the NSDAP program of 1920, personally drawn up by Adolf Hitler, there are demands such as:
- Socialization of monopoly companies
- Municipalization of large department stores
- Expropriation of land for charitable purposes
- Prevention of real estate speculation
- Expansion of the entire education system
- Comprehensive system of scholarship stipends

along with goals as to health, fitness and a clean environment.

This selection of planks from both catalogs shows how similar the two lines of thought are. The two lists also show how far the claims of both ideologies have become a modern reality. It comes as no surprise that both the communist and the national-socialist governments have acted as repressive regimes that brought neither prosperity nor equality nor peace.

Socialism – whatever its kind - cannot exist without violence. If prices as an information and incentive system no longer exist, a command system must replace it. The socialist project leads to a command economy. The image of the 'new man' propagated by the socialists who contributes to production without self-interest or of the Aryan superman of the Nazis, turn out to be the opposite. In practice, socialism works by fear. When the Soviet Union was no longer able to exert terror, the regime collapsed. If the Hitler regime had not ended through war, it would have collapsed from its inner contradictions.

Under capitalism, in contrast, the economic actors adjust their behavior following their own interests in the face of scarcity because prices represent costs for the buyer and income and profits for the seller. The same applies to the entrepreneurial profit. In the capitalist economy, profits serve as an incentive and as an indicator of the extent to which the firm does the right thing according to the consumer's wishes. Losses signal inefficient production and coerce the company change its ways or leave the marketplace and thus make room for the more productive firms, which produce goods in a better way. Even if one assumes that under socialism only good and educated persons would populate the country, socialism would fail nevertheless because the structure of the system does not provide the conditions to act rationally in the economy.

Antony P. Mueller

Summary

The socialist utopia still attracts many people - despite the catastrophic outcomes that happened in all places where socialist systems took hold. Wherever there was socialism, there was also mass murder, oppression, and massacres. Social utopias are attractive. They satisfy the human wish for a paradise. Socialism shares with the other social utopias that the more one wants to realize the paradise on earth with the use of force the more one will create a hell. Not only did socialism fail to deliver the cherished expectations - the tragedy is that the reality of socialism has surpassed the worst expectations. It is the discrepancy between claim and reality that frightens and how much this system of horror was desired by many people and still is an ideal for some in our days.

The rulers need coercion so that everyone will follow the central plans. Under a socialist system, one cannot avoid becoming a law-transgressor because one could not survive without breaking the laws. In practice, socialism installs a power center, the Communist Party, which cooperates with the central economic planning apparatus, the secret police, and the military to suppress any dissent and to make sure that the voice of the people keeps silent and that the companies fulfill the plans.

Without market prices, following plans is always precarious because nobody knows how to fulfill the plan. Liquidation and deportation thus become a vital part a socialist rule. If everyone must break the laws and commands because it is impossible to follow them, there is also a secret list about each citizen, which compiles a person's inevitable trespassing and 'crimes'. Thereby, under socialism, everybody is a suspect and a criminal, first on paper, and, if need be, in front of the tribunal. In order to declare someone as guilty, the courts do not have to resort to prove the dissidence of the accused as the real cause of his prosecution, but it suffices to condemn the defendant because of an economic delinquency. Therefore, everyone in socialism is always at risk of persecution and incarceration. No one can feel safe since no one can remain innocent under such a regime.

When profit and loss no longer play a role, economic actors lose the orientation about what and how to produce. Even if socialism could have created this 'new man', and the ideal socialist man had emerged, he could not act economically, even if he wanted it to do, for lack of a price system to guide the allocation of resources. In socialism, there is an automatic tendency towards misallocation, waste, and inefficiency. 'Social prices' disregard scarcity. If the price of bread is made cheap, and at the same time there is no meat in the shops, consumers feed the cheap bread to pigs and chickens in their homes.

V.

INTERVENTIONISM

Antony P. Mueller

> "A government founded on the principle of benevolence to the people as a father to his children... is the greatest conceivable despotism .... The Sovereign will make the people happy according to his concepts and become despotism; the people will not let the universal human claim of their own happiness be taken and become a rebel."
> Immanuel Kant: On the common saying: That may be correct in theory, but is not suitable for practice (1793)

- *Fascist roots of interventionism -*
- *Origins of modern state capitalism –*
- *Rational irrationality -*
- *Legacy of interventionism -*
- *Backgrounder: Effects of price interventionism -*
- *Interventionism and the market process -*
- *Employment –*
- *Power and economic law –*
- *Welfare: more costs than benefits –*
- *Healthcare costs –*
- *Cost explosion in education -*
- *Social policy –*
- *Backgrounder: origins of social policy -*
- *Missing standards –*
- *The chimera of social justice –*
- *Backgrounder: concepts of justice -*
- *Perpetual financial crisis –*
- *Backgrounder: the economics of the public debt -*
- *Backgrounder: where does the money comes from? -*
- *Capital, savings, and entrepreneurship -*
- *Summary*

The belief in interventionism has become so deep it resembles a religion. State activity is the new salvation without God. With the help from the state, the interventionist seeks to relief society from all ailments. The state has become the ultimate *'Deus ex machina'*. Yet the evils that the interventionist wants to cure through government intervention were often caused by the state itself. This way, interventionism does not solve problems but creates new troubles.

Interventionism is the so-called Third Way, an economic system between capitalism and socialism. This economic regime comes along with political populism and results in state capitalism and the growth of government. People like to praise this mixed system as a welfare state, but they fail to recognize that this kind of governance does not lead to the hoped-for Eldorado but is the path to stagnation.

Interventionism means a state-controlled economy and produces a perverse form of capitalism. Government intervention weakens the economic performance. The intervention in the market economy by the state leads first to disorientation among the economic agents, then to allocative distortions, and ends in a prolonged process when the economic activity slows down until it stagnates at a low level.

When the system has become fragile, it seems as if a failure of capitalism had occurred. The interventionists then conclude that new and even more comprehensive state intervention would be necessary to save the economy. Therefore, interventionism knows no end. It will always go on because intervention itself brings about the evils, which the government claims to remove.

The welfare state produces most of the social ailments, which the government claims to heal. The more generous the social assistance, the larger the number of social welfare recipients, the higher the burden of the social tax contributions, and the more the shadow economy will flourish. More complicated the tax code, more tax evasion takes place. The more access to public healthcare and medication, the sicker people become. The higher the percentage of a populational cohort that attends high schools and colleges, the lower the educational level.

Rational Irrationality

Interventionism suffers from the conceit of knowledge. In his Nobel Prize speech of 1974, Friedrich Hayek diagnoses that the state planners overestimate their cognitive ability. They ignore that the more diverse the economy and society become, the more the economic coordination depends on a spontaneous order. The more complex the economy, the more important and indispensable are the markets.

The knowledge relevant to economic decision-making does not exist in a systematized form and is not available as a concentrated, organized set, but is tacit, fleeting, specific, and dispersed. Economic market knowledge relates to the specificity of place, time and people.

Characteristics of market knowledge

Market knowledge is	is not
specific	organized
heterogenous'	homogeneous
dispersed	concentrated
tacit	public
fleeting	stable
uncertain	certain

The division of labor in the market economy goes together with the division of knowledge in price-driven competitive markets.

The state intervention in economic life takes place without sufficient knowledge of the relevant circumstances. The motive of government intervention is not to resolve concrete problems, but to address political concerns. Without the explicit interest of specific groups, governmental action will not come into play.

Politics is not about solving problems; it is about to respond to special interests that brings forth specific concerns. The articulation of issues by the various groups is one-sided and influenced by the respective interests. Reliable statistics and detailed knowledge of facts about public issues are not available. Official statistics take a long time from the original collection data and their statistical treatment to their publication. Until the statistics reach the decision-makers, the actual situation has already changed. All statistics are history. Until the economic data reveal a clear picture and before the most relevant facts are gathered, the situation has changed again, and the social concerns have become different. Even if one could solve the information problem, the next barrier is how to reach a proper diagnosis and decide. The political process exists in a struggle to bundle, equalize or displace the diverse interests. The political decision-making is never about the issue itself. Politics is about interests and the representatives of certain interests are the issue.

By way of biased public discussion of socio-economic problems, even absurd political decisions receive popular support. The public debate is about values, which reflect interests. The representatives of special interest present their issue as a priority and as an absolute value. They do not consider that resources are limited in the face of the variety and of the plentitude of other needs and wishes. At the level of an individual, a family or a company, scarcity compels the decision-maker to weigh among the desires and to bring them into a ranking order so that the limited funds find an optimal use. Yet when public agencies decide, limited resources find no concern. Instead, specific interests dominate the discourse as these push their aims as unique absolute values. This happens because, in politics, not the same group which represents the specific interest bears the costs of a project but the collective of the taxpayers.

Even if a proper consensus about the diagnosis of the problem were available, it does not follow that politicians would use the appropriate means to solve the problem. Means are not neutral. Their use raises different costs, and the question is always to ask who will bear the costs associated with the project. Individual interests distort not only the political diagnoses and the objectives but also the use of the means.

In the political struggle, the loss in the fight for an issue of a relevant power group requires compensation. Concessions to one group raise demands from some other group. The wider the state distributes benefits the more other groups will emerge to claim their share. Consequently, there is no end to spending until the government runs out of money. When the game is over, everyone has been deceived and everyone feels betrayed. Therefore, the lobby never rests, and one negotiation session is only the prelude to the next. The more redistribution takes place, the more the people regard the system as unjust.

Interventionism suffers also from the problem that a considerable time elapses between information and diagnosis, and between the decision on the use of the means and the effect. Most times, the time span exceeds the regular legislative period. The government will not take sensible measures if the means bring costs now and only benefits later as it would be the case when the government reduces expenditures. In contrast, those measures receive priority that will offer present benefits and attract electoral votes now even when later the costs will exceed the benefits.

The monetarist economist Milton Friedman supported his doubts of a rational monetary policy by arguing that discretionary policies suffer from the lags of observation, decision, and effect. Yet not only monetary policy, but all types of public policies suffer from lags.

The decisions of governments take a long time to be made and a long time to take effect with the result that the pollical issue to be addressed has already fundamentally changed when the means begin to take effect. The problem runs even deeper than Friedman envisioned when one applies an individualist approach. All economic phenomena exist in human action. Thus, to gain complete picture the analysis must take human action into account. The lag problem is much wider and deeper when one considers that the political issues begins with individual expectation and the policy measures feeds back on the expectations before they can become effective.

Lags of interventionist policy measures

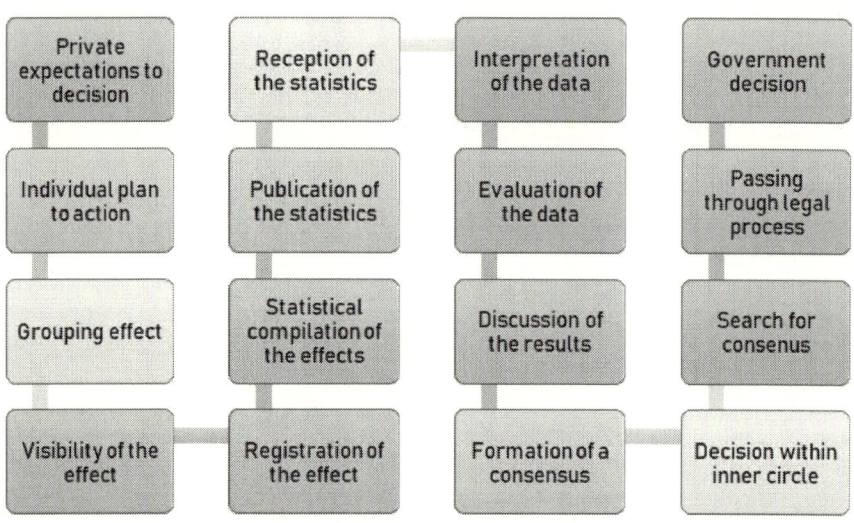

The popular view holds the present government responsible for what happens now - even if the current prosperity results from past actions or if the present gaiety of public spending will cause future misery. Under the system of party democracy, sensible decisions get through the political decision process only if they bring short-term benefits. Other measures must wait in the pipeline – often forever. Interventionism is populism. Interventionism hinders rational economic conduct. Therefore, interventionism, like socialism, does not represent a rational economic order.

It takes a long time for the government to become aware of an issue and come to a decision and likewise it takes a long time until the effects of the governmental decisions become visible. Public policies are always out of sync with the de facto situations.

Antony P. Mueller

Legacy of Interventionism

Over the past decades, the rate of economic growth has decreased. The more the USA and other countries maintained and try to expand the welfare state, the more the economic momentum subsided. The victim of the welfare state is capitalism and as much as capitalism was curtailed, the population has suffered. The rate of economic output is going down, and the debt levels are going up. The state, the government, and the political system restrict the free development of the economy. The weaker the economy gets, the more there is a reason, according to the prevailing perverse considerations, to take new interventionist measures.

A planned economy cannot cope with multiple aims the same way as the market economy can. This is also the case with interventionism, albeit here there are no fixed goals. Socialism is planned chaos. Interventionism is a chaotic planning.

The interventionist spiral takes hold of the economic policy as hyper-activism. If the economy does not recover with one interest rate cut, then the interest rate must fall further. When one government-spending program fizzles, a new one must follow. The more interventionism increases, the more capitalism gets the blame, even though the capitalist order is the victim of the interventionism. With all this political activism, one forgets that the cure for a weak economic performance is not more intervention but less government activity. Not more interventionism is the solution but more capitalism.

In the United States, the annual growth rate of the economy fell from around five percent in the 1950s and 1960s, to an annual rate of around two percent since 2000.

The publicized official growth rates would be smaller if the statistical bureaus of the governments would use the older methods of calculating the real GDP rate.

In as much as the official rate of inflation becomes lower, real gross domestic product and productivity will become statistically higher.

In Germany, the rate of economic growth of the gross domestic product fell from 8.2% in the 1950s to 1.6% in the 1990s and to 0.9% in the period 2000 to 2010. In Japan, the annual economic growth averaged 10 % from 1955 to 1970, around 5 % in the 1970s and 1980s, and has been in a slump ever since.

***

Interventionism hampers the dynamics of the markets and falsifies the price system. The administrative state perverts the market economy and reduces the effectiveness of the market as a coordination mechanism. The economic system gets weaker. Interventionism discourages innovation and leads to a waste of resources due to the cost of regulation and the misallocation brought about by the state intervention. The modern welfare-warfare state absorbs about half of the overall national production.

The central bank controls the money supply and the interest rate. All economic transactions are under bureaucratic authority. To speak of a 'savage capitalism' is evidence of grave ignorance and of ideological blindness. Capitalism in its present form is not a free capitalism. There is no predatory capitalism but a predatory state. While markets fail occasionally, governments fail systematically.

While socialism brings misery, distress, suppression of freedom, and a broken economy, this obvious failure of socialism does not quench the craving of the anti-capitalists to condemn the market economy. The critics denounce capitalism because it does not bring a paradise and because markets are not 'perfect' according to their imagination. The desire for the impossible is the reason for the popularity of the 'Third Way'. It promises a system beyond capitalism and socialism with the claim the best of the two worlds would merge. Yet there is no such thing as a perfect economic system where scarcity would disappear and social justice for all would find a home. The pretensions of the progressive movement that is behind the 'third way' is that there is an elite who has a special insight into what is right to improve the world. In their view, it is the government through which this progress will come about. In practice, however, the 'third way' makes capitalism less efficient. Progressivism is one more variant of the many socialist delusions.

The interventionists unite with special interest groups, who cloak their specific concerns as a common good. Under interventionism, the market competition perverts into a competition about subsidies and bailouts. The winners are no longer those who best contribute to the growth of the economy and serve the consumers, but those receive the largest share who have the best political contacts. In the end, no one is better off. In the long run, everyone is paying the price when the economy falters, including those who got a big share from the government when the economy was still flourishing.

In contrast to socialism, the interventions of the third way do not take place according to a central plan but happen ad hoc following populist-political criteria. Interventionism comprises a special order, which relates to the use of private property. A rental control, for example, leaves the private property formally intact but restricts the scope of pricing. The 'third way' leads to the fiscal state, to the gradual erosion of private property, and to the creeping confiscation of private income and wealth.

While there is little controversy about the harmfulness and economic inefficiencies of direct price interventions, the government bureaucrats ignore the effects of indirect interventions. Most economists know how price interventions, as it is the case in agriculture, for example, lead to misallocation. Yet there are few who likewise condemn the interventionism that comes with welfare policy, labor market regulation, environmental policy, pension and health policy, education, taxation, financial market regulation, and monetary policy. Nevertheless, a look at these areas of intervention reveals that these are the same areas where the misallocation of recourses is the greatest and the dissatisfaction of the population is most widespread. The interventionist policies are to solve problems when in fact more new problems emerge as the result of interventionism than old problems get solved.

The great illusion of our time is the expectation that special state interventions can settle our problems. But there are no perfect solutions available, to begin with. Public problems have no solutions, only trade-offs. Here is the poodle's core: the state is notoriously unable to evaluate the available options and weigh benefits against costs. The government either makes no trade-off at all or, when it does, comes to the wrong results because of one-sidedness and public pressure. The members of the bureaucracy know very well that government activity lacks wisdom and if there is a reasonable decision, it comes more from accident than by design.

The state bureaucracy must replace evaluation and judgment by statistical indicators, reference numbers and the whole flood of quantitative controls and political criteria. Cases are not rare when grotesque misallocations occur. The assessment of medical doctors takes place in line with the number of their operations, and more patients get surgeries than necessary. The evaluation of science comes not from scientific content, but by the number and place of publications. Teachers receive their assessment according to the failure rate of their students and grade inflation sets in.

The problem with state interventionism is that it fails not only to solve the problems and that it creates new ones, but that state intervention systematically excludes private solutions. Interventionism makes society less open to opportunities for success. It reduces the innovative power and paralyzes the private initiative both directly through regulation and indirectly through the tax burden. Interventionism closes the space for innovations.

Any alleged solution entails specific costs. These costs are not just the immediate costs that are obvious but also the plethora of undetected consequential costs that are difficult to discover and impossible to quantify and to forecast. Since there are no definitive solutions, problems remain, and this is the reason there seems to be a constant need for renewed interventionist efforts. Each government intervention aims at a specific problem and promises its 'solution'. Yet with the growing number of interventions, a network of problematic constellations arises, so that with each new state intervention the problems do not decrease, but they multiply. Interventionism, in contrast to markets, cannot cope with complexity. In a modern economy, interventionism must fail.

Types of government intervention

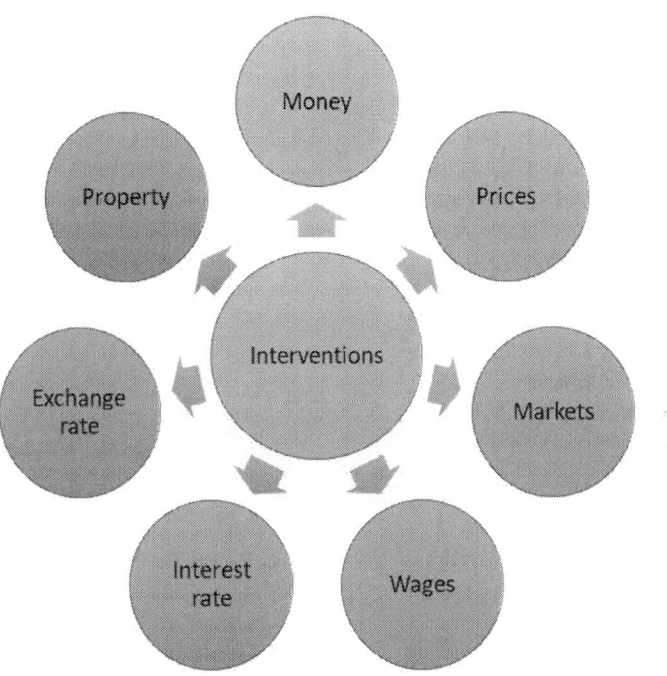

Policy interventions produce confusion, disgust, and indolence among the population, yet people demand more, and politicians are keen to promise delivery. Popular talk denounces the politicians, but hardly anyone names evil by its name: interventionism. There is no one who could have all the knowledge about the intricacies of the tax code or of the social legislation. If the government adopts a new measure, no official, secretary, or minister can state what would be its effects. The scientific reports of alleged governmental advisors are worthless. First, because experts also do not have complete information, and second because if they should expose deviating opinions they would diminish their chances of being hired for the next project. The larger an institution, be it a private company or a state, the higher the transaction costs and the less the transparency. Companies know there are not only advantages of size but also costs of size and limit the expansion of their production units. If a company grows beyond its optimal size, profits fall. Yet with no system of profit and loss in the public sector, there is no warning signal of misallocation with interventionist policies.

Effects of Price Interventionism

Interventions change the market outcome and produce distortions. When government installs a price ceiling, prices are kept low. Instead of doing away with the shortage, this policy leads to a contraction of supply and an increase in demand. Because producers do not receive the market price, there will also be less investment to produce this good. Therefore, price ceilings produce not only a temporary shortage but perpetuate the market disequilibrium.

In the case of a price floor, when the government sets prices above the equilibrium price, supply rises while demand falls. This discrepancy will become more severe over time because a price above the equilibrium incentivizes the producers to invest more and thus future supply will increase.

Effect of price ceiling

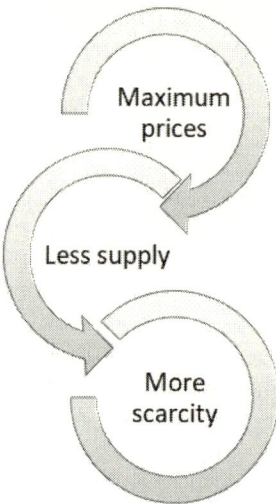

In contrast to price ceilings, which lead to persistent scarcity, price floors generate a persistent oversupply.

The European Union has applied price floors in many areas of agricultural production with the result of a massive overproduction. The responsible agencies had to buy the excess production and store it or dump it on the world market at subsidized prices.

Effect of price floor

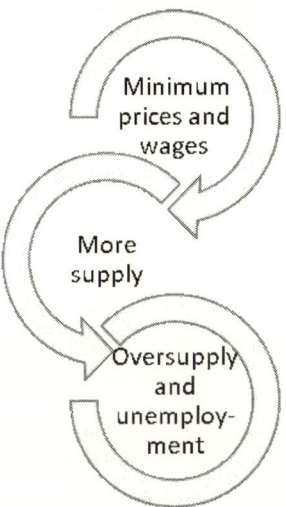

In addition to the market interventions, the state's activities include monetary affairs and interventions in property rights.

Market interventions refer to price and quantity controls as well as to competition policy. The Constitution protects private property only to a limited extent. Money is under direct state control. Issuing of circulating money in the form of notes is the responsibility of the central bank which also has powers to control the distribution of money by the private commercial banks.

Interventionism and the Market Process

Among the three basic ways of coping with the uncertainty of the future -- gambling, speculation, and engineering -- speculation is the way of human action when dealing with economic and financial matters. Speculation is the basic mode of entrepreneurial judgment. Even more so, speculation is how human action deals with the future.

Speculation as the entrepreneurial judgment would be unnecessary if the future were not uncertain. Then it would be possible to calculate the future structure of the market and economics could become a reliable forecasting profession. Yet "the entrepreneurial idea that carries on and brings profit is precisely that idea which did not occur to the majority. It is not correct foresight as such that yields profits, but foresight better than that of the rest. The prize goes only to those dissenters who do not let them be misled by the errors accepted by the multitude. What makes profits emerge is the provision for future needs for which others have neglected to make adequate provision." (Ludwig von Mises in Human Action, p. 867)

In this view, it is futile to base economic decisions on formulas. Human action must use relative prices as the guideposts for making plans, but information and the numbers which appear as prices do not speak for themselves and instead one must assess, compare and relate them to one's personal value system. The same original bit of information has various shades of meaning for different persons and often it is of a very different quality as to its practical relevance. Prices cannot substitute judgment. They are tools to make judgments.

The market process exists in action and reaction of extreme complexity even at the level of simple goods. The market process coordinates the diverse subjective valuations of the immense variety of individual plans all of which are not observable beyond the prices. The structure of relative prices does not reflect agreement on valuations, but the observable exchange ratios in the market are the product of a discrepancy in attributing values. Prices, although they convey information, do not imply that these are correct or efficient. Prices coordinate, they neither measure nor evaluate.

What is available to the observer as 'present prices' are in fact past prices as they reflect the conditions of the past. Past prices do not determine future prices - but to anticipate future prices determine the current prices. Expected prices are also those prices, which are relevant to price complementary goods and to remunerate the factors of production. What counts for the entrepreneurial judgment are neither past nor present prices, but the expected prices.

Without entrepreneurial judgment that deals with expected prices instead of current prices, as bureaucrats must, there is no way to cope with the vicissitudes of a dynamic economy. Present prices suffice to allocate the resources in a stagnant economy; they do not coordinate economic activities in a growing economy.

Equilibrium in terms of fulfillment of expectations is temporary. Market prices are volatile because they reflect the uncertainty of our expectations, which is even more pronounced when evaluating the value of assets. Governments that presume that due to their position of authority they could do away with this instability, base their cause on the belief that bureaucracies are better equipped to deal with the uncertainties of the future than the individual entrepreneurs and the individual consumers. By doing so, they disregard the essence of markets.

Market interventions mislead the adaptation process of individual actors. They add further elements of uncertainty to the formation of expectations and frustrate the expected courses of action. The popularity of interventionism -- defined as the efforts of political authorities to reallocate resources other than in a free market -- can be explained in terms of political interests. Epistemologically, however, interventionism stands on very weak grounds once the assumption of determinism gets discarded.

Not less so than the direct interventions in individual product markets, macroeconomic intervention and the stabilization of the price level disrupt the coordination process. Macroeconomic aggregates are ill-defined concepts and of dubious statistical validity. The conceptual units that are used in macroeconomic policy are statistical constructs and their presumed causal connection lacks reliability. Statistical averages neither act nor can they cause a phenomenon.

The stabilizers and interventionists ignore that error is essential to human action. They postulate failures of the market yet for themselves they claim to be free of the errors. The stabilizers ignore their own fallibility and negate that in a world where the future is unknown, the occurrence of errors -- or disequilibria when defined in terms of the fulfillment of expectations -- is a necessary part of the human action in a complex and dynamic environment with numerous interactions. Unhampered markets receive their privileged status in this context, not from the chimera of being perfect but because they allow continuous adaptation, i.e. the constant correction of misallocations as they are identified by subjective valuations. All models of the so-called market failure suffer from the deficiency that they take the perceived errors for permanent and ignore that what matters is not that errors occur, which is unavoidable, but that the market as a process works to correct the errors.

In a market economy, there is no such thing as certainty about the future prices. The status of wealth, which is attributed to a certain arrangement of capital goods by the market process, is always at stake. It is this insight into the changing nature of wealth that differentiates the Austrian approach from the preachers of stabilization. Likewise, the idea of social justice has no place in a capitalist economy. The problems with just or unjust distribution pertain to pre-capitalist societies with quasi-stationary economies where the ownership of resources -- predominantly land and serfs -- implies the automatic access to a yield. Under capitalist conditions, however, there is a need for an on-going re-pricing of capital goods with the consequence of a permanent process of redistribution.

We live in a world of unexpected change. "The maintenance of wealth is always problematical; and in the long run it may be said to be impossible." (Ludwig Lachmann)

The market process is the great leveler. By coordinating demand and supply, the market process also redistributes wealth.

In socialism, the ultimate rationale for state control is the deceitful promise of social justice. A similar kind of pretense continues to form the basis of the apparent legitimacy for government interventions when it comes to the stability of the economy or to social security and equal redistribution. In the light of these concepts, a market economy always must appear as deficient. By applying the ideas of stability and social justice as policy guides, each failed interventionist policy measure will only provide one more reason for additional measures. In the light of the theory of the market process, the dramatic failure of socialism comes as no surprise. Likewise, the fixation of modern governments with stability, social security, and redistribution must fail; and the more these goals are being pursued the more likely these policies will end in a collapse.

Employment

The declaration of a 'right to work' has no rational foundation because it disregards who will provide the capital that enables employment. The problem is not 'work' but having a workplace. To look for a job is, in fact, the search for a place to work, and the search for a workplace is the search for capital. If there were no need for capital, then the unemployed could work right away as self-employed. Unemployment means that there is a lack of capital in this economy.

The stock of capital determines the potential of employment and the level of productivity. Unemployment occurs when the productivity of the worker is too low compared to the wage rate. The wage rate must fall, or productivity must increase to do away with unemployment. Therefore, as the classical economics pointed out, only voluntary unemployment happens in a market economy. Unemployment means that wage claims are too high compared to labor productivity. The productivity of labor, in turn, is too low when the economy does not have sufficient capital and lacks technological progress. Rising wages and more jobs require capital formation. It is only with the corresponding capital stock that the labor force becomes productive. Unemployment disappears when the wage rates adjust to productivity. To do away with unemployment, either wage rates must fall, or productivity must rise.

If workers raise wage rates through trade union power that exceed productivity, unemployment occurs because companies must reduce their workforce. Power, including trade union power, cannot break the fundamental economic laws. As with other markets, in the labor market, too, price interventions lead to quantitative reactions. If the price of labor is too high, the result is the dismissals of workers and a decline in the number of jobs offered by the companies.

It is a common error to believe the use of machines in production would lead to unemployment when in fact capital accumulation makes it possible that workers move from less productive jobs into those with higher productivity where they can earn higher salaries. The increase in wages results from more capital and from technical progress in these advanced sectors of the economy. Not trade unions and government intervention lift wages, but capital accumulation and technological progress.

In the 1930s, the link between wage level and employment, which classical economics had well elaborated, came under fire by the doctrine of the English economist John Maynard Keynes (1883-1946). According to Lord Keynes, employment depends on aggregate demand. For Keynes, the cause of unemployment is not the shortage of capital but the insufficient overall demand. The Keynesian recipe of bringing down unemployment is to increase spending by the state financed by an increase of the government debt. This school claims that the expenditure program would pay for itself because spending creates income, and incomes serve to stimulate the demand. The plain fact that public debt has been rising since the 1970s indicates the failure of Keynesian doctrine. The legacy of Keynes is not full employment and economic growth but inflation and stagnation.

Types of unemployment

Like with the 'wage mismatch', it is questionable to categorize 'skills mismatch' as involuntary unemployment. After all, the workmen are obliged to gain marketable skills.

Skills mismatch, like frictional unemployment, is not necessarily 'involuntary' because it happens as the effect of the structural changes that come with a dynamic economy. As such, they are a normal ingredient of a market economy. Skills mismatch is comparable to falling sales and profits of a company that has an obsolete product line and will go out of business when it does not adapt to the new market conditions. Keynes' theory of involuntary unemployment postulates that persistently high unemployment is neither lack of capital nor of a wage mismatch but results from a lack of aggregate demand. If this theory were correct, one could do away with unemployment as fast as the government would spend more.

***

The Keynesian theory of aggregate demand ignores scarcity and costs. While it is true that the income, which some person spends, is income received by someone else, it is also true that wages – while income for the worker – are costs for the employer. In the Keynesian perspective, wages can never be too high because they represent income and thus spending. Yet if labor costs are higher than the contribution of labor to production, it does not matter whether there is more demand or less demand because losses result when labor costs exceed the contribution of labor to production. Business cannot survive without profit, whatever the demand.

The relationship between aggregate demand and employment runs in the opposite direction as postulated in the Keynesian model. Wage rates that are too high in terms of productivity lead to unemployment, and unemployment leads to a fall in demand. As the classical economic theory states, not lack of demand causes unemployment, but wage rates that exceed productivity lead to layoffs. The true cause of the lack of demand is falling employment, which reduces the wage sum and diminishes aggregate demand. Not the economic weakness leads to unemployment, but the unemployment - caused by high wages - causes the economic weakness. The Keynesians mistake the effect for the cause.

Keynesian and classical model of unemployment

The Keynesian theory postulates without further ado a 'lack of demand', which causes unemployment and leads to a downward spiral where lack of demand increases unemployment, and the unemployment reduces demand.

The Keynesian solution is government intervention: the injection of extra demand through 'deficit spending'.

The Keynesian crisis circle

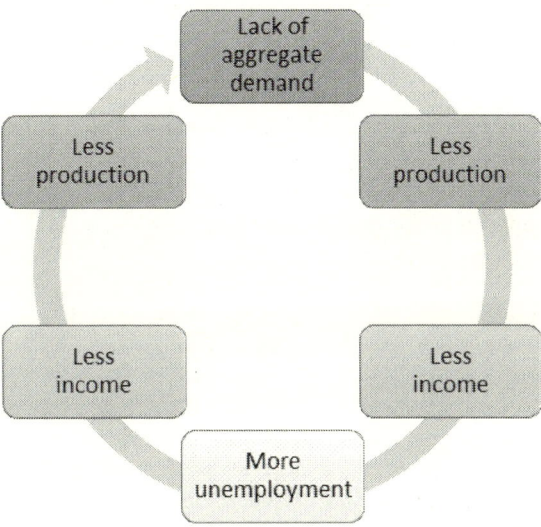

The Keynesian model suggests a permanent disequilibrium of the economy. There is no automatic mechanism that would link aggregate demand to aggregate supply. Therefore, thus says the Keynesian theory, stabilization policy is a permanent task of government.

The classical model, in contrast, has a theory about the causes of unemployment and how a free labor market eliminates unemployment. According to the classical sequence, unemployment results when the wage rates exceed productivity and compels business to reduce employment. Rising unemployment, however, brings down the wage rate and thus leads a new equilibrium with no involuntary unemployment.

Classical self-regulating unemployment model

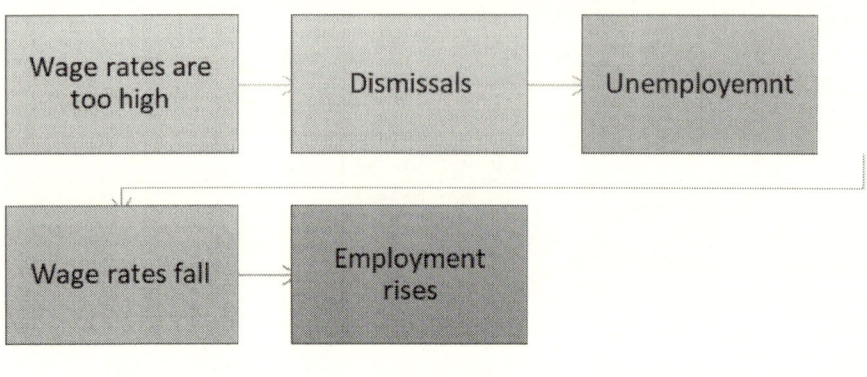

***

Not different from earlier times, contemporary doomsayers fear mass unemployment due to the automation of production by robots. They put forth the same arguments as was the case at the time of the industrial revolution. Then, the weavers and other craftsmen feared the loss of their workplace because of the steam engine as the result of more sophisticated production devices. However, it is a historical fact that the technological advances that accompanied the industrial revolution have created a multiplicity of jobs. While the new machines saved labor in agriculture, jobs expanded by the multiples in the new industries.

While over two-thirds of the workforce still worked in agriculture at the beginning of the 19th century, they now account for about two percent in the industrialized countries.

In as much as the new technologies eliminate jobs, including sophisticated positions, productivity counts to bring down the costs of living. A policy of keeping the jobs safe would be the wrong approach because it would hold the economy down on a low productivity level and thus keep people poor.

In a free economy, technological unemployment loses its threat. This warning ignores that the automation of the economy drives up productivity. High wage rates require a high technological standard. Productivity determines the wage level. Wages are higher in the industrialized countries because their productivity is higher than that of poor countries. Because of the high level of productivity, simple activities, too, receive a better remuneration. The high remuneration for ordinary jobs drives the people from the poor countries to migrate to the rich places. The Mexican agricultural worker in California multiplies his earnings in the United States doing the same work as at home because the general productivity in the US is higher than in Mexico. Excess labor is the scourge of the poor countries because they lack capital and therefore suffer from low productivity.

While the dearth of capital is the fundamental cause of persistent unemployment in the developing countries, in the developed market economies with their high stock of capital, there is no reason of enduring unemployment beyond the effects of wrong economic policy measures.

Since 1975, the rates of productivity gains have been sinking in the industrialized countries, and since about 2007, productivity growth in the advanced industrialized countries has been almost stagnating. This means that wage increases and working time reductions will be limited for the years to come. In such a situation, a politically motivated expansive spending policy would be poison for the national economy. The answer to this challenge is less state, less bureaucracy, and less government debt.

Antony P. Mueller

Power and Economic Law

In the same way that government cannot eliminate the natural laws, state intervention cannot do away with the market laws. Under interventionism, the laws of economics maintain their validity, albeit in a distorted way. This rule applies to trade union power. A single union can raise the wage rate for its members but when all trade unions go on strike and achieve higher wage rates in tandem, no worker will be better off. On the contrary, if the wage rate increases at the expense profits, the pace of accumulation of capital falls. When the capital stock gets smaller, wage rates must fall, and less hiring will take place. The chain of causation goes from higher wage rate to less capital, and from less capital to lower productivity to unemployment and to lower wage rates.

Trade union power may push wage rates higher, yet when they exceed productivity, profits fall, and less capital accumulation will take place. Rising labor costs cause the demand for labor to fall and lay-offs to rise. Higher unemployment implies that aggregate labor income falls, and mass unemployment follows. Instead of improving the fate of the workers, the excessive demand for higher wages has achieved the opposite.

One can contrast the neoclassical answer and the Keynesian policy recipe in one sentence: Neoclassical economics says that wage rates should fall, while Keynesian economics says that aggregate demand should rise.

***

When government introduces price controls, the outcome of the law of supply and demand changes from price to quantity. If the legislative body abolishes the private property rights to eliminate supposed deficiencies, more scarcity results since the production incentives are lost. Despite this, authoritarian thinking prevails in the public sphere and the belief prevails that the laws of the state could overcome the laws of economics. Many people still think all it would take to make things better were the promulgating of more laws. Yet while a government can arbitrarily oblige the people to drive on the right side as opposed to the left, the state cannot oblige the water to flow upwards and violate gravity or to induce economic agents to act against the law of supply and demand.

The concept of the law, including that of natural laws and the market laws, comes originally from the sphere of legislation. Until the eighteenth century, the idea prevailed that man was subject to religion and authority, and ultimately to God. The same way as nature has its own laws, the economy and the society have their own principles.

In the Scottish Enlightenment of the 18th century and with Immanuel Kant (1724-1804), the new science of the economy and society showed that the economy and society have laws of their own. It was Adam Smith (1723-1790), who

– with Adam Ferguson (1723-1816) and David Hume (1711-1776) – formulated such laws for the society. In his "Theory of Moral Sentiments" (1759) and for the economy in his work about "The Wealth of the Nations" (1776), Adam Smith elaborates the basic statement of economic liberalism that this nation comes to prosperity which respects the market laws, and that keeps the state activity and the tax burden small. In Smith' view, the way to the prosperity of a nation is not the activity of the state, but individual freedom. In his "Lectures" (1755), Adam Smith states that little else is needed to lead a state to the highest wealth from the lowest barbarism as peace, light taxes, and a tolerable legal system: everything else comes by the natural course of things. "Little else is requisite to carry a state to the highest degree of opulence from the lowest barbarism, but peace, easy taxes, and a tolerable administration of justice..."

In his "Wealth of Nations" (Book One, Chapter 2), Adam Smith points out that the supply of food and drink does not depend on the benevolence of the butcher, the brewer or the baker that we get our meal but because they pursue their own interest. "We address ourselves, not to their humanity but to their self-love, and never talk to them of our own necessities but of their advantage." The state intervention is not only unnecessary but also harmful, explains Adam Smith, because the statesman, who was to instruct private people about how they were to invest their capital, would not only be burdened with a very unnecessary task, but also would seize an authority, which is nowhere so dangerous as in the hands of a man who has enough folly and arrogance to feel capable of exercising that authority. (Book IV, Chapter 2).

In politics, however, it is common to ignore the laws of the economy. On the political battlefield, the guiding principle is that one could shape the economy and society at will – and be it by applying brute force. This conviction comes along with the positivist legal thinking, according to which law is what the legislator decides to be legal. This belief in the omnipotence of legislation and of the state dominates the expansion of the welfare state and promotes interventionism.

With the claim to arbitrary legislation, the legal positivists ignore the original idea of the law and violate the principle of the validity of law beyond the will of man. The modern lawgivers act as if they were gods and could declare at will anything they want as 'the law of the state'. Yet the basic idea of law is that it is not a creation but a discovery. In the traditional, pre-positivist legal theory, to be deemed legitimate, laws had to conform to the physical world and to the essence of the human nature. The principle says that man cannot and must not shape his environment to one's own predilections but that one must respect the laws of nature and of society. For economic and social policy, this means that the person who opposes the economic laws must pay the corresponding price. In this sense, the rule holds that when one chooses a system against the human nature, such as socialism, society will earn poverty and suppression. Equally, although at a different level, if the trade unions succeed to push up the wage rate above the equilibrium level which productivity sets, retribution in terms of unemployment sets in. When the state inflates the money supply to counteract unemployment, inflation is the result. A man is free in his choice, but not in the consequences of his choice.

Welfare: More Costs Than Benefits

For many people, the welfare state is a great achievement. Yet few people recognize that the more comprehensively the welfare state extends its realm, the more the beneficiaries themselves must bear the costs. The citizens pay for what they receive and, in addition to it, they pay also for the apparatus that has emerged around the distributive state in the form of administrative expenses and the rent-seeking by special interest groups. There is a welfare industry in existence that ranges from the medical-pharmaceutical complex to the employment opportunities of social workers.

The wealthy persons of the society will care for the poor if redistribution remains small and if the circle of the needy is well defined. This is the case with voluntary charity. Yet when the state expands into the welfare state, the beneficiaries of the social transfers must de facto assume the costs themselves for what they seem to get free from the state. The more the general population falls into the grip of the welfare state, the more diffuse the definition of need becomes and the larger the number of the contributors will grow. In the end, all pay more than they get.

At a deeper level, the evils that many citizens attribute to 'capitalism' are the result of the fact that these very same citizens demand from the political parties what they lament. As the French libertarian pamphleteer Frédéric Bastiat (1801-1850) observed, the state is that fiction where each one tries to live at the expense of all other people. The social state means that the services it provides become more expensive than they would be under private supply. For example, under a system of general health insurance, medical services cost more than they would cost in the free market if there were no state insurance schemes. Because an insurance exists, demand for its services rises, including for many superfluous purposes. Instead of utility-driven, the system becomes cost-driven. Prices continue to rise even when the benefits of the services sink. As the costs rise, the quality of the supply falls.

The term 'moral hazard' comes from the insurance industry. The concept designates the phenomenon that insurance produces incentives to provoke the damage that the insurance covers. The prices of the insured product and services will rise. The profiteers from insurance are those groups that provide the good, which the insurance covers. With the car insurance, it is auto repair shops and with health, it is the health providers, the medical doctors, and the pharmaceutical industry. For the healthcare system, moral hazard signifies that the great beneficiary of a comprehensive health insurance system is the medical establishment - such as hospitals, medical doctors, and the health industry, while the clients are the losers as they must bear the extra costs. An obligatory insurance is financially a magic boon to the suppliers of the goods and services for which there is an insurance. Likewise, the largest beneficiaries of the subsidies that students receive from the state to study are the employees of colleges, with their administrators at the top.

Since its inception, dissatisfaction with the welfare state has increased at the same tempo as the costs of the welfare state have risen. Since its beginning, social security was sold to the public as an offer that apparently would come costless. Since then, this illusion is also upheld as to the whole range of programs of the comprehensive welfare state. Consequently, the demand for all kinds of social policies systematically exceeds the supply, even if almost everyone is dissatisfied with the performance of the system.

Backgrounder: Healthcare Costs

The more comprehensive the insurance coverage is, the more the additional costs caused by the moral risk (moral hazard) will rise. The health care system has become so expensive because of the high number of insured persons who have easy access to healthcare.

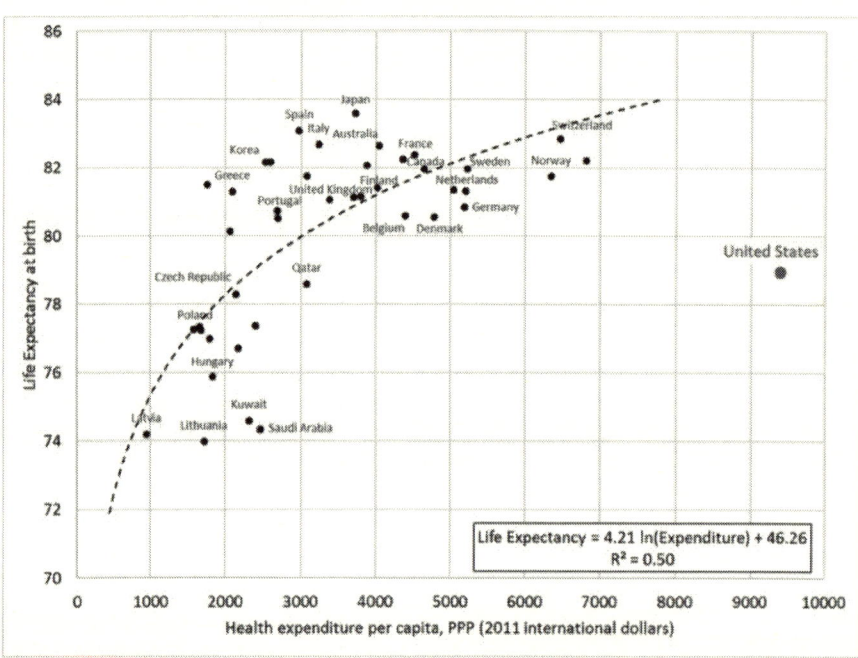

Source: World Bank
https://www.moneyandbanking.com/commentary/2017/3/12/improving-us-healthcare-and-coverage

The existence of a state-run health insurance system drives up the costs for the private insurers and the private consumers as well. A rarely noticed effect of a widespread healthcare system is that it pushes up the costs for the private payer. The higher the number of the insured, the more increases the incentive of the uninsured to get an insurance, which makes the system even more inefficient.

The data of the United States support this thesis. Although the United States has the highest per capita spending on health, life expectancy is lower than in that of comparable countries. At present, the limit of the best general life expectancy is about 80 years. Expenditure on health spending of over 2,000 dollars a year does not increase this limit.

> Health care spending does not provide a significant increase in life expectancy if the expenditure is more than about two hundred US dollars per month. The curve indicates that the medical spending reaches is maximum positive effect at about two thousand dollars per year. Even this sum may be too high because spending on health up to $ 2,000 happens thanks to the benefits that come with the growth of the economy, so that part of the increase in life expectancy is not due to health spending, but rather to the growth-related increase of the overall quality of life (Max Roser https://ourworldindata.org/life-expectancy/)

Due to the demographic development and the further expansion of the medical-pharmaceutical complex, studies predict that health care contribution rates would rise to between 25% and 30% of the personal income in the coming decades when no system change will take place without much benefit in terms of longevity.

***

Today, the healthcare system has become an institution where a massive redistribution takes place from the young people and the active workforce to the old and inactive part of the population. While the benefits of the care for the elderly are questionable and an ethical issue, the burden that falls on the active part of the population is obvious. Expenditure on healthcare is a deadly trend. Incurable patients absorb increasingly resources as expenditure flow into the diagnosis because no therapy works and because of the costs for the individual patient concentrate in the last few years or often just months of one's life with dubious benefits and immense costs.

It is difficult to answer the question for which activity more public spending is a waste: for health or for education. In any case, both areas suffer from the rise in costs, which exceed that of the rise of the cost of living in general. Both systems suffer from a fundamental deficiency of control because there is no direct linkage between the costs and the individual demand. Without personal cost bearing, the insured consult the doctor, even if it were unnecessary and may even be harmful, and the young attend the subsidized educational institutions, even if one learns useless stuff or not even that but nothing at all.

Taking the contribution of medicine to the extension of life as the criterion, a modest sum of expenditure on health would suffice. The same would hold for education. If these systems were private, costs would sink. However, since the benefits are independent of the direct contribution payment of the user, there is no upper limit of the expenditure, and costs continue to rise. This applies both to a state health system as to a system that makes insurance compulsory and that covers almost the entire population.

Like the healthcare system, the educational system suffers from the separation between those who benefit and those who carry the costs. In the education system, too, demand has no fixed saturation point. If the costs for the providers do not play a role, the demand increases. Consumers and suppliers share the common interest to expand production and consumption.

A new thinking is necessary for healthcare and education. For the healthcare system, medical and technical progress means that spending goes into efforts for a goal that it cannot achieve: eternal life. It is as if one wanted to continue using an automobile forever despite the wear and tear that comes with aging. It is obvious that the repair costs would increase while the marginal benefits of the repairs would fall. The older the car, the shorter the time span between the repairs and the less the benefit. When maintenance becomes the exclusive objective, technical progress brings rising costs with little benefit. Such systems set a cost expansion into motion that leads to their bankruptcy. One can wish it were different, but it is not.

It has become common to ignore that human nature aims at reproducing life and not only at life extension and its maintenance. If everyone were to bear the costs personally, demand would stop when marginal utility no longer exceeds marginal costs. This would also be the case for health services, since some questionable treatments, which would be technically possible, would no longer be in demand. With insurance, however, there is no resistance from the patient concerning the interest of the suppliers of health services to apply as many services as possible at prices - and therefore of costs - that are as high as possible.

An insurance scheme, when organized as a collective system as it is the case with health insurance, brings with it that the users will ignore the principle of marginal utility and marginal costs. The gates are thus open to a cost avalanche. If no change of the system will occur, the healthcare Moloch will absorb increasingly of the income of the population, until at the theoretical limit health costs would use up a person's entire income. The patient would then have access to the most comprehensive range of healthcare according to the most advanced standards, but this privilege would come with a financial ruin because no buying power would be left for any other expenses beyond the medical expenditures. The healthcare system in its present form moves towards this absurdity.

In education, the situation is similar, albeit with a different emphasis. Both education and health are so-called superior goods, where the demand rises to income more than proportional. This would be no problem if the beneficiary of the product were to bear the costs. It is different, however, with health and education. The recipients of the service are not the same who pay. An excessive demand is a result. Over-consumption occurs with both, health and education. The costs are exploding because neither from the buyer nor on the side of the supplier is a wedge in place. Demand is individual, but the costs are borne by the collective of the insured. The logic of the system drives to its expansion and to rising costs.

While individual consumption ceases when the marginal utility no longer covers the marginal costs in the case that the recipient pays the price, consideration of benefits and costs play almost no role in the demand and supply of education and health. Here, the beneficiaries continue to consume even if the additional costs exceed the marginal benefit. Goods like education and health have no natural saturation points. Since finding the optimum is not an option, the demand moves to the maximum. Even if each patient had his personal physician, there would be further demand. This is also the case with education. Demand shifts from the optimum to the maximum and questions such as why not give each student his own special teacher appear no longer absurd. When healthcare and education are apparently free, supply will never satisfy demand. Over the past several decades, it has become almost an obligation for the young to go to college – even for those who neither want it nor who are qualified for a university that deserves its name. The absence of the price system has eliminated cost control.

The interaction of demand and supply works no longer as an equilibrating process but as an accelerator toward an avalanche of expenditures. If everyone were a self-payer, the providers would have to focus on the financial capacities of the individual. Medical progress would take different paths from those which are happening now. In the same way, the role of universities and schools as diploma factories would have long since disappeared, and different forms of education would have emerged if there were a free market in this area. Yet because the state acts as a provider that apparently delivers the goods for free, alternative suppliers cannot effectively compete. Because of the quasi-monopolistic position of the public educational agencies, the offers from private suppliers are crowded-out. The supply of alternatives shrinks although these would be better and cheaper than the official provision. The same applies to modern medical practices, where the potential for cost saving remains under-used since no significant incentives for efficiency exist.

A free capitalism would end with the collectivism that prevails in the education and health system. Disposable income would rise, and people could spend it according to one's personal preferences - different from the present system where one must pay for the use about which the contributor has little if any say. As with healthcare, the costs of education exceed the marginal benefits.

Consequently, the services become more comprehensive and more expensive. In the educational system, the larger the proportion of people in each cohort who go to college and the higher the formal level of education of this group, the more the relative costs per pupil and student increase while their qualifications sink.

Backgrounder: Cost Explosion in Education

The rise of the costs of the American educational system began when 'education insurance' became the norm according to which students gained easy access to government-subsidized loans. This system came about because the education policy did no longer focus on the best education as an objective but on its expansion. The new aim was to have as many students as possible in college. The higher, albeit loan-financed, ability to pay for the students led universities and colleges to raise prices and expand those areas, which had little to do with the educational goal. As a result, many campuses of U.S-universities became more like sports and amusement parks than places of higher learning. As the academic program is no longer the focus of attention, but the quantity of students, the proportion of part-time instructors and substitute teachers has expanded at the expense of qualified professors. The number and salaries of those who work in the university administration rose and the incomes of the directors and coaches of the various sports teams with whom the colleges promote their 'branding' rose to astronomical levels.

For the United States, the increase in the cost of a university education compared to the general consumer price index and to other consumer goods and services. Along with hospital costs, college education shows the highest increases. Studies that show that graduates earn higher salaries than those without studies are correct, but they ignore that this unequal distribution of income would also have come about when these more talented and dedicated persons had not attended a university.

Studies show that getting a college degree serves as a signaling for employers. Having absolved a college serves as a sign of certain levels of discipline, intelligence, and obedience – traits, which employers esteem and are much more important than what one has learned at the college. Students themselves care less about what they learn than how to pass a course and to get the desired diploma. Tests confirm that students forget most of the contents of what they have studied at the schools. With some exceptions, many academic disciplines teach useless subjects.

Selected consumer goods and wages compared to general price level 1997-2017

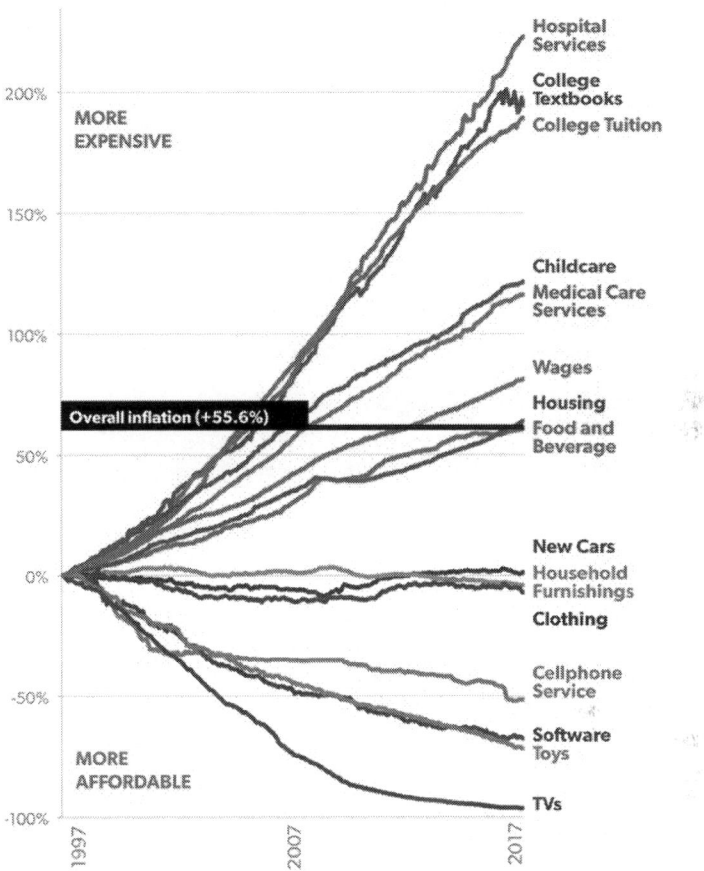

Source: Bureau of Labor Statistics. American Enterprise Institute AEI

This thesis finds support from analyses that show that the role of the 'prestige' and 'selectivity' of the educational institutions has almost no significance for salaries. It is not where one studies, but what subject one has chosen that is the crucial factor for career development in terms of salaries.

There are no significant differences between the low-barrier colleges and the selective universities. The main difference in income comes not from where but from what one studied. Students who studied technical and mathematical disciplines earn a higher income than those who study disciplines of the humanities, irrespective of the status of the university where they have studied.

There is comprehensive evidence to show that what to study is more important than where to study. Even more so: anything that one would want to study now, is the Internet - free of charge. For education, there has never been a need for public funding, and nowadays this is even more so the case.

Selectivity of institution and income by study area

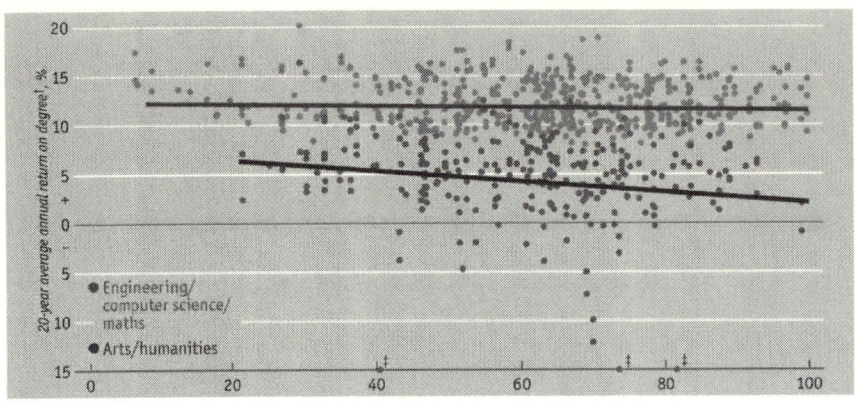

Source: PayScale, National Center for Education Statistics. The Economist: https://www.economist.com/gallery/2015-03-06/20150307-universities

***

The problem with the modern educational system is that it has fallen almost completely under the authority of the state. Therefore, the system has become more bureaucratic as it has become less educational. Disguised as a public good of immense 'social value', education has evolved into a multi-billion dollars industry whose main benefactor are not the students but the group of organized providers of educational services. Not unlike the medical establishment, a credulous public accepts the apparent benefits of education without a trace of doubt.

Higher academic degrees serve the individual to get more personal remuneration but for the cohort, education means that one does out-compete those with lower degrees while more education for the whole group does not make the economy more productive. Tests and other types of examination do not serve as ways to find out the qualification of the candidates for doing useful work but how they match up with their colleagues in terms of such yardsticks as general intelligence, perseverance, and conformity.

The modern state-run and state-certified system of education would collapse when employers discard academic degrees as a screening device. Education would become useful when it focuses on specific skills that people can learn at specialized institutions that cooperate with firms which business finances. In a free capitalism, there is no room for state-run and union-controlled schools. People would not spend the best years of their lives as college kids but learn early on how the world works.

Social Policy

Since its inception, social policy has been a tool to gain mass loyalty and win electoral votes. This concept was already at the heart of Bismarck's social policy when he implanted a 'white revolution' from above to fight the 'red revolution' from below in his struggle against the social democracy and the other socialist movements in the late 19th century. Today, as in the past, social policy is neither left nor right in the political spectrum, but it is a populist-nationalist project.

Under the current democracy, political parties try to outdo each other with new designs for 'social security' and 'welfare' and 'justice for all'. In politics, however, 'better' means more spending and higher costs. Therefore, these proposals come down to nothing more than to increase the costs for the general population. In the modern democracies, almost the complete population is under the cover of the social state - be it because of membership in the statutory health and pension insurance schemes or in the obligatory unemployment insurance and occupational accident insurance or because of the U.S. programs Medicaid and Medicare. In addition, there are family subsidies and child allowances, and social assistance programs.

Despite the broadening and deepening of the social programs, social issues have not diminished. Not only in the European countries, but also as to the United States, one could observe that new social policy plans have augmented the hardships and widened the number of people in need instead of reducing the social ailments and to diminish the dependency on the programs. Never in America have the poor been 'losing ground' so much as under the social welfare expansion that came with the launch of the 'Great Society' in the 1960s.

Originally, the design of social policy was for a society in which there was the family help and that of the community before the state aid and where 'to live on welfare' was a disgrace. This has changed. The traditional family associations have broken down, and the state support has become a 'human right'. While in the past, the recipient of social welfare suffered from a stigma, now, who does not take advantage of the system is the dupe.

The modern economy and society are no longer an industrial society in the traditional sense. The idea of social insurance was to protect the industrial workers. This model assumed that the employee would remain in the same field of activity and even stay in the same company until the statutory age of retirement. Additionally, the design of the social security systems presumed that the period during which a pensioner would receive the old-age pension was only a few years. As to illness and unemployment, too, the design of the system assumed these periods without own earnings from work as temporary emergencies. For this purpose, it was necessary to include the individual in a collective of solidarity and to protect the industrial worker against the financial consequences of illness, disability, unemployment, and old age.

In the modern technological society, there are less fixed and lifelong employment relationships. Horizontal and vertical mobility has become indispensable. Although workplace and society have changed, most governments still cling to the traditional concept of social policy. Yet the modern economy and society are moving away from the model of the old industrial society as it still existed in the 1950s and 1960s. The social policymakers, however, stick to the old model and wonder that the reforms do not work. The solution to the problem does not consist in reforms to maintain and expand the system but to make the system leaner and to abolish it.

The consequence of the sprawling social policy is that governments stumble from one deficit to the next, that politicians with the appropriate slogans win the election and then lose support after the voters wake up to the insight that these politicians, when they are in the government, cannot deliver what they promised in the election campaign. Then comes the next tentative, and the cycle starts again with the next election. Over time, the parties and their representatives will become more like each other and indistinguishable as to their policies when in power. Each party in power contributes in its own way to bring down the economy.

The policy is stuck in a permanent conflict of an ongoing ambivalence between too much government activities and less populism. In the first case, the economy produces less while in the second case politics does not get its share and the success at the elections wanes. The modern state is politics with an affiliated economy. Yet in a system dominated by populism, politicians come to power by squeezing the productive economy and distributing the benefits according to their political calculus. It is obvious that the productive sector of the economy does not favor this approach. The insight has been lost that the best social policy is a good economic policy and that the best economic policy is as little policy as possible or better even none.

Government spending

All industrialized countries have experienced an increase in the relative share of government expenditure as a share of the gross domestic product since the end of the 19th century.

In Italy and Germany, the rate rose from around ten percent to around 50 percent, and for the United States from less than five percent to around 45 percent, and in Japan to over 40 percent. Even in Switzerland, the share of the state rose to about 35 percent. From a level of less than a tenth of gross domestic product around 1880, government spending has increased to almost half to the GDP in the 1970s in many industrialized countries.

Government spending in percent of gross domestic product since 1880

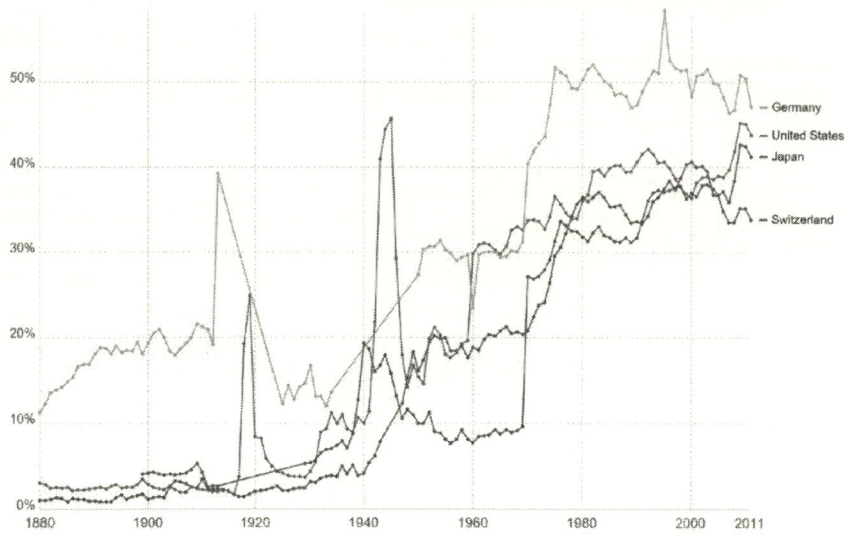

Source: Out World in Data: https://ourworldindata.org/public-spending

The compilation shows that the major sources of the expansion of social government spending over the past decades have been healthcare and old age. Given that the process of aging will continue and speed up, social government spending will take a growing share in decades to come if the present system remains unchanged.

Backgrounder: Origins of Social Policy

Implementing social security systems and providing so-called welfare and social justice as governmental goals have become the outstanding features of the state since the late 19th century.

Germany is a case worth studying. This country was a pioneer in creating a comprehensive system of social policy, and it is now one of the prime examples where a maze of regulations and the fiscal burden that has come with this kind policy is paralyzing the economy. A historical analysis of the German welfare state also reveals the close link between the welfare and the warfare state.

When Otto von Bismarck (1815-1898) as Chancellor of Germany from 1871 to 1890 conceived a system of social security for the industrial workers in the late 19th century he had a clear aim in mind. Along with strengthening the geostrategic position of the Reich, he set out to bring the industrial workers under the control of the state. Integrating the masses into the body of the unified German state was the objective, and a comprehensive social insurance system provided the means to achieve this aim.

The social policy began as national policy, and the social security system has remained an instrument to lure the citizens away from private and communitarian systems into the arms of the government. In the eyes of Bismarck, it was the state that had created national unity and this agent was also necessary to maintain the social unity by a system of mutual obligation between the state and its citizens.

Originally, Bismarck's set up social security to be specific as to its target, limited in depth, and light in terms of the financial burden for the productive sector of the economy. When the first steps were taken towards establishing a social security system in 1883 with the inception of a health insurance system and with its expansion to cover old age, working place accidents and unemployment, the maximum contribution to social security was six percent of the gross wage. Social security was limited to the new class of the industrial workers. Regular old age pensions received only persons over 70 years of age, and the payout would amount to the subsistence level.

Adolph Wagner (1835-1917) is one of the intellectual fathers of social policy. He is the author of the 'law of increasing state activity'. Wagner foresaw that the expansion of the state functions into the 'social era' would change the character of the state and lead to an ongoing financial expansion of governmental activity. He predicted that the new 'social epoch' would be the age of interventionism when the governments would 'correct' the capitalist process of production and distribution.

While the practice and institutional forms of social policy vary from country to country, the idea that the government must protect and promote social justice and progress has become the paramount modern ideology. Following in the footsteps of Bismarck, the construction of social policy systems has emerged as the distinctive feature of the modern state.

Periods of war, depression and prosperity alike were the major propellants to expand the system when social policy became the favorite means to offer the carrot along with the stick of governmental control. Social policy ushered the way into the age of the unfettered growth of taxation, government expenditures, and bureaucracy -making the modern welfare state totalitarian as a guardian of the individual from the cradle to the grave.

In accordance with its historical roots, social policy has maintained its nationalistic aims, its paternalistic schemes, and its authoritarian practice. As such, the social policy represents the modern complement to the traditional role of the state as an agency of warfare. Social security has served as a formidable instrument in the hands of governments to obtain popular loyalty and the allegiance of special interest groups. Under democratically elected governments and dictatorships alike, the temptation has been the same: expanding the coverage of social security and of welfare has been the foremost instrument in search of government power and presumed state legitimacy.

In Germany, it was first during World War I and its aftermath, and later under the Third Reich in the 1930s when the welfare state experienced its greatest expansions. Under the national-socialist regime, the appeal to 'social justice' and to expand the social security systems flourished, together with the buildup of the warfare state. In the first couple of years of the Nazi dictatorship, social policy was one of the major legal projects of codification to create an all-encompassing 'social state'. The systematization of social policy was so profound that almost all major bodies of law that rule Germany's current social security system go back to their original formulation in the national-socialist era. While minor adaptations happened to fit the current needs, the original spirit of the social policy laws lives on with its roots in the class distinctions and the paternalistic-authoritarian schemes of the past.

Under the Third Reich, social policy measures extended to protect and promote ideologically defined standards of reproduction, health, and the environment. The carrot of social policy served as the main means to facilitate the application of the stick of repression. It also happened in this period that the labor market came under the control of the totalitarian state making the dismissal and hiring of personnel dependent on governmental permission (issued by the local Labor Office).

Grown for over a period of more than a hundred years, the various branches of the obligatory social security system have put the entire population under intensive bureaucratic care. Social policy has become a labyrinth formed by laws and regulations, individual judicial decisions and cases of special considerations that make it impossible to determine who are the net payers or who are the net beneficiaries.

The coverage of old age, sickness, and unemployment insurance, along with social aid, and disability insurance and with all the numerous special branches of social policy have become an Eldorado for those seeking a free ride. Often described as 'generous', the German social welfare system provides a plethora of incentives for becoming unemployed, seeking early retirement and fulfilling the requirements to become eligible for social aid and disability payments.

By promoting 'social progress', the modern welfare state has dissolved all limits to the governmental constraint. Together with the traditional goals of protection and social justice, the extension to social progress has opened the way to all kinds of absurdities, abuses, and interventions.

With social policy becoming ever more comprehensive, it has turned into a severe and suffocating burden for the economy. The boon—however great or small it may have been in its early stages for a specific group—has turned into a plague. Now, the dismantling of the welfare state emerges as the major policy challenge of the 21st century.

Missing Standards

It is a common misunderstanding to allow the state to take over the areas where the market economy apparently cannot work well. Expecting that through regulation the performance would improve, is the grand illusion of our time. Interventionist economic theory invented the concept of 'public' goods and 'merit' goods as different categories besides private goods. This classification claims there are goods whose usefulness is unrecognized by the individual consumer and therefore requires extra incentives that increase their consumption.

These 'merit goods' do not share the characteristics of a public good such as non-excludability and non-rivalry of consumption but are like private goods. The presumed systematic under-consumption of these goods requires state intervention. As if it were a matter of fact, the state takes over health care and education, jurisprudence, and security on the assumption that there is no other alternative. Even if it were the case that these goods are 'public' and 'merit', the problem arises by which standards production and distribution should take place when markets instead of the market, the state operates in these areas.

The regulatory state eliminates competition where it is in place, as it is the case, for example, in the financial sector, yet at the same time introduces an artificial competition where it does not fit, as it is the case with medicine and education. This way, the economic competition gets a bad name and the market economy is discredited because the market mechanism apparently does not work in these areas when in fact the market mechanism was never meant to work here. State intervention does not cure the proclaimed market failure but makes matters worse.

When the state assumes the allocation in areas such as medical care, the individual provider of medical services no longer places the patient in the center but the bureaucratic regulations of the provider of health insurance because this is the place from where the doctors and the other suppliers of healthcare services receive their financial remuneration. The performance criterion shifts from the therapeutic success to the number of points that the respective insurance company stipulates. The patient is the loser. He rarely notices this scheme, and if one does, he does not care much, because one must pay the contribution anyway and therefore one is interested in regaining the largest part out from the obligatory payments. As everybody does so, costs explode, and the contributions rise.

State activity requires justification and faces the problem of how one can justify state intervention. One tries to solve this task by objectifying the value of a good albeit value is subjective. In the private sector, each one assesses individually the benefits of a good or service according to one's own discretion. There is no such guideline for the public sector. Before the state took over such areas as education and health, they were under the care of private charitable and religious organizations. Churches, for example, were such institutions, which consciously cultivated altruism and charity.

Before the state became to dominate these systems, there were also numerous private associations, which provided social services for specific groups. The members themselves of these private associations controlled the operations of the institution. Expanding education, healthcare, and social aid to the dimensions of the modern territorial state, the contributors have lost the knowledge about the specific trade-off between costs and benefits. People lose their status as members of the association and to become mere numbers relevant only as paying contributors. They can no longer exert effective control over the system, which has taken on a dynamic of its own. The more the state spends for healthcare, public assistance, and education, the more these areas become bureaucratic madhouses.

The usurpation by the state means that private spontaneous aid and private initiative suffer from the crowding-out by the state. When this has happened, and the bad outcomes show up, public opinion now says that the state must intervene even more because there is no alternative as there is no private supply. Yet it was the usurpation by the state that destroyed private social services since the start of the welfare state at the end of the 19th century.

Publicly funded research policy no longer aims primarily at gaining knowledge, but it is about output as defined by the norms that the state has imposed. Public medicine is no longer about healing but is concerned mainly with medical measures. Public schooling is not about education, but the concern has shifted to the score and the position in domestic and international rankings of the educational institution be it a school or a university. The result of these interventions is to abandon the original objectives in favor of - often meaningless - bureaucratic indicators.

This process occurs slowly and even the members of the apparatus themselves hardly notice it. Professors then spend a major part of their time developing research assignments and producing expert opinions for the research projects of their colleagues instead of doing own research and care for good teaching. Physicians no longer focus their diagnoses and therapy measures to heal their patients, but rather modify their activities according to the rules of financial compensation that the health care institutions stipulate. Education disappears from the school plans while the new standards come from the measurement systems of achievement as a means to climb up to the ladder of the rankings.

That the state could do better because the market economy does not do well, is a common error. In fact, free competition can also coordinate supply and demand where the market economy in the narrow sense, i.e. the price system, does not work perfectly. Competition can provide the so-called public and merit goods among the providers – different from the state, which acts as a monopoly. It is not true that there is no education without a state or no roads would be built without government spending. Public opinion laments the broad failure of the supply of goods and services under the state but takes it as a given while even small problems with private providers meet immediately the stain of a market failure with the consequent request that the government must jump in with state intervention. Throughout history, different religious groups and other non-state organizations have competed with one another to provide goods and services that have public characteristics and the features of merit goods. Over the past century, the state has wiped-out these services and established itself as a monopoly.

The state has become an obstacle to social progress. Under government tutelage, social policy has lost its original meaning and purpose. Social policy is a prominent example of the general law according to which bureaucratic organizations continue to operate the same way as before even if their original function has been lost over time.

Antony P. Mueller

The Chimera of Social Justice

The 'march through the institutions' on the part of the cultural Marxists not only intends to undermine the political parties but also, in addition to the school system and the media, the judiciary. The judiciary is the area where the infiltration of the cultural Marxists has advanced and has grasped many who are not an active part of the movement. The judiciary has become a force that no longer promotes freedom but stifles and strangles individual freedom and the private initiative. No longer is liberty the guiding principle of jurisprudence, but 'social justice', 'social protection', and 'social inclusion'.

The concept of 'social justice' has become the substitute for communism and socialism. Because these terms suffer from negative connotations and even the word 'left' incites no longer much attraction, today's communists hide behind the concept of 'social justice'. Social justice is an invocation. It is the keyword to practice the terror of 'political correctness' and thus to suppress the freedom of expression as a preparation to eliminate all other liberties as well. Social justice is neither definable nor can it be realized. This opens the door to interventionism because social injustice lurks everywhere. In one way or another, ultimately everything is 'socially unjust'.

As soon as interventionism seemingly eliminates one aspect of the manifold appearance of injustice, new injustices show up, which equally demand urgent elimination. If it is no longer about women's rights, then the lesbians need care; and when it is no longer about the poor, another disadvantaged group needs assistance. If it is no longer the poor of the own nation, it must be those of the world that require compassion and help in the name of social justice. The zeal of those who have put social justice on their flag never rests, for their principal goal is not prosperity for all but to gain power, to realize their idea of communism, which is the deeper motive of this movement.

The way toward the rule of the cultural Marxists is the moral corruption of the people. To accomplish this, the mass media and public education must not enlighten but confuse and mislead. The media and the educational establishment work to put one part of the society against the other part. The list of the identification specifications gets larger while the groups' catalog of victimization and history of oppression becomes more detailed. To become a recognized victim of suppression is the way to gain social status and to gain the right to special assistance and to get social inclusion.

The demand for social justice creates an endless stream of expenditures deemed essential - for health, education, old age, and for all those people who are 'needy', 'persecuted' and 'oppressed', be it real or imaginary. The flood of never-ending spending in these areas corrupts the state finances and produces fiscal crises. This helps the Neo-Marxists to accuse 'capitalism' of all evils when, in fact, it is the regulatory state that provokes the systemic failures and when in fact it is the excess of public debt that causes the financial fragility.

Politics, the media, and the judiciary never pause at waging the new endless wars: the war on drugs or against high blood pressure or the campaigns that assert the struggle against obesity. The list of the enemies grows every day when one item gets dropped, new enemies such as fat, butter, eggs, and salt are on the list along with racism and xenophobia. The next stage, which is already in full preparation, is the war against one's own opinion. While the public tolerates an increasingly disgusting exposition of behavior, particularly under the cult of art, the list of prohibited words and opinions grows daily. Public opinion must not go beyond a few well-defined positions. Yet while the public debate impoverishes, the diversity of radical opinion flourishes in the hidden. From there, the counterrevolution will come – as a rebellion at the risk of a civil war.

***

The cultural Marxists drive society morally into an identity crisis by the means of the false standards of a hypocritical ethics. The aim is no longer the 'dictatorship of the proletariat', because this project has failed, but the 'dictatorship of political correctness' whose supreme authority lies in the hands of the cultural Marxists. As a new class of priests, the guardians of the 'politically correct' rule the institutions whose power they sneakily try to extend over all parts of the society. The moral destruction of the individual is a necessary step to accomplish the final victory.

It is the hallmark of all ruling groups to know how to hide their true power behind the pretense of a legitimate function, which gets the name 'justice'. Yet history demonstrates that no deceptive power lasts forever. If the rule is not yet total, and this is rarely possible, counter forces are at work to topple the ruling group, typically through a movement whose battle cry is 'freedom'. In this respect, we are at the final stage of a struggle, at the end of which either a new totalitarianism or more freedom will emerge. In the universities, the triumph of cultural Marxism is the most advanced. From the young people, the counter movement must start, or it will never come.

Backgrounder: Concepts of Justice

People are different from each other beginning with age, sex, and physical appearance. The difference among people is the foundation of society. If we all were equal, societal interchange and the economic transaction would make no sense. In this perspective, individual differences form the basis of society. We come together not despite, but because we differ from each other.

The principle of reciprocity lies at the heart of social relations. A society that systematically violates fair dealings cannot survive and will not prosper. This also holds for the procedural justice which requires fair play and restorative justice, which demands the compensation of wrongs. While these principles are essential for the maintenance and progress of society, distributive or social justice is ambivalent. In a strictly philosophical sense, it remains problematic to justify social justice as a right. While the principles of reciprocal justice refer to the relationship of person to person, with the procedural justice to the dispute resolution among dissenting individuals, social justice has no individual as its basis but refers of the right of a group against society. This deviance makes 'social justice' a tricky and a false construct.

'Social justice' is a notion that one can fill at will with all kinds of claims. In the light of social justice, injustice is universal. Once that social justice is taken seriously, there is no end to the claim that society is obliged to manage the many ailments that anyone can bring forth in the name of the idea of social justice.

Because there is no such thing as social justice and never will be, the social justice movement works against society. Social justice is a hierarchical concept as it does not refer to the relations among equals but to the relationship of submission. Yet who is the suppressor? The society as a whole?

Procedural justice refers to fair play, restorative justice aims at the correction of wrongdoing while 'social justice' is hierarchical. It is based on political power in order to implement forced redistribution of income and wealth.

Concepts of justice

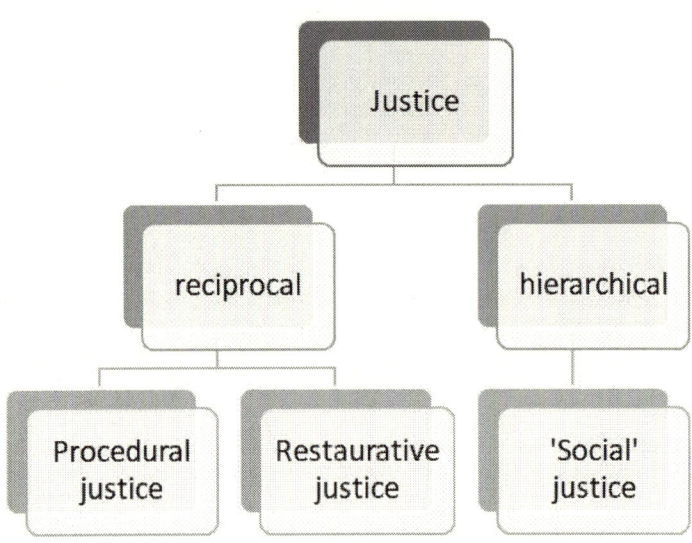

Perpetual Financial Crisis

The result of interventionism is a weaker economic performance. The other factor is government debt, which also contributes to lower the economic output. Not only in Greece and the other southern Eurozone countries, but also in the United States, Germany, and in Japan, government debt is moving steadily toward the collapse. Governments will not diminish indebtedness voluntarily without the urgent need that comes in the form of financial crisis. As soon as the gap between spending and revenue closes again because the economic situation is improving, new spending plans come into action. While the long-term trend towards more spending continues, revenues erode. Governments pursue a policy of debt financing so long as they legally and practically can. The question is not resolved by stipulating that there are limits to government spending. The fact is that governments spend as long and as much as they can. They do this to the extent that they can finance the budget deficits. Consequently, the discrepancy between spending and receipts increases while the government's funding needs are rising. This will go on until the debt collapse has become unavoidable.

U.S. Government debt is on the rise since the 1970s. It experienced two accelerations. The first happened after the start of the new millennium and the second one after the financial crisis of 2008. In December 2017, U.S. government reached a new high of 20,6 trillion US-dollars.

The chart shows the evolution of government debt ratio from its height at the end of World War II. In the 1950s and 1960s, the decrease of government debt came along with strong economic growth, which lasted until the 1970s. A new boost of public debt occurred from the mid-seventies to the mid-nineties, while the second big expansion of government debt took place after the turn of the millennium and has continued until today.

At the end of 2017, government debt reached 106% of the U.S. gross domestic product. After its fall from a high of 122% in 1946 to a low of 32% in 1974, the ratio rose again since the early 1980s and attained a new boost up to the current height after the financial crisis of 2008.

Official projections say that the U.S. federal debt per person will reach 70,000 dollars by 2019. After the rise in the 1980s, the debt level plateaued somewhat in the 1990s to take off again at the beginning of the new millennium and experiencing a dramatic increase since the financial crisis of 2008 from 30,000 to 60,000 dollars per capita in 2017.

***

Eventually, the relentless logic of government debt takes hold that one can no longer sustain the debt burden as economic growths will weaken because of the public debt. In addition to old debt and new borrowing, the level of the interest rate, the inflation rate, and the growth rate of national output determine the debt ratio (debt as a percentage of the gross domestic product). The debt ratio augments with new debt and when interest rates rise. The rate of government debt declines, the faster the economy grows. With growth is too low, the price inflation comes into play as a way out. Inflation and hyperinflation reduce the real burden of the debt. The government can avert official state bankruptcy through hyperinflation, yet this means the expropriation of the savers and the ruin of the national economy.

In many industrialized countries, the financial crisis goes hand in hand with a demographic predicament. The system of statutory pension insurance makes having children costly (in terms of opportunity costs) and thus is self-destructive. The collective pension insurance compels a young couple that wants to raise children to bear not only the cost of child-rearing but also to forgo a salary. With a part of the income lost, subsequent pension claims diminish in contrast to the couple that has no children and continues to receive two incomes and consequently gains two pension claims. The system of statutory pension insurance proves that the welfare state is suicidal. The welfare state eats its own children and grandchildren.

The specific problem of government debt results from the fact that government credit is unhinged from the productive capacity of the national economy. The status of government debt differs from private debt. The analysis of creditworthiness for a company limits the loan to the profitability of the company's projects. The debt capacity depends on the company's capability of generating profits that are high enough to pay interest and principal. Likewise, a consumer credit depends on the extent to which the applicant has income and how the lender assesses the borrower's future income situation. With the state, it is different. The state lives from the taxes at the expense of the population. What distinguishes the state as a debtor from the other debtors is the power of the state to exert its monopoly to tax by physical force. Not only that, the state also has the right to determine which money is valid to serve as the legal tender in its territory. The state has the authority over to produce money even if the central bank is autonomous. By lifting the amount of money from its anchor in gold and silver, the modern state is de facto more absolute than the state was under absolutism – most prominently in monetary affairs.

A sovereign debt crisis is a credit crisis and at the same time a currency crisis. How the money system depends on credit shows up in the fact that the modern money emerges as a credit at is the source as the commercial banks borrow currency at a nation's central bank. The commercial banks are indebted to the central bank where they obtain cash and general liquidity. On this basis, then, the commercial banks create additional money by granting loans to their customers, including the state.

The modern state-money is a currency without an intrinsic value and without an anchor to a specific economic good, such as gold, for example. The modern monetary system has no anchorage outside the state power to implement its will by force. If the tax revenue does not rise, the state privilege of money creation will produce money at the government's discretion. Instead of a tax on income and consumption, the government raises an inflation tax by increasing the amount of money.

Backgrounder: The Economics of the Public Debt

The size of a country's total public debt results from past budget deficits. A budget deficit comes into existence when a government spends more than it collects as revenue. If taxes and other sources of government receipts fall short of public spending, the government needs to borrow. With each new budget deficit, the size of debt increases and along with the principal the obligation to pay interest also rises.

As an indicator of the debt burden serves the so-called 'debt coefficient', which relates the government's overall debt to the country's gross domestic product (GDP).

In the light of this number, a rise of total debt need not necessarily denote an increase of the relative debt burden. If the total debt rises together with national income, relative debt as measured by the debt coefficient remains constant. By the same token, the relative debt burden would increase even without new debt if national production should shrink.

Coefficients of public debt

Country	Public debt in percent of gross national product as of December 2017
Japan	253.0
Greece	178.6
Italy	131.8
United States	105.4
France	97.0
United Kingdom	85.3
Euro Area	86.7
Brazil	74.04
Germany	64.4

Source: National data. Tradingeconomics.com

The distinction between the so-called 'primary deficit' and that part of the budget deficit, which pertains to interest payments, is important because the amount of interest payments varies not only with the size of outstanding debt but also with the interest rate.

When assessing the debt burden, the rate of price inflation makes up an important factor. Price inflation devalues outstanding debt. This happens slowly when inflation rates are low and rapidly when inflation rates are high. In the case of hyperinflation, even a gargantuan public debt would evaporate. However, a deliberate fabrication of hyperinflation to get rid of the debt burden is not a rational strategy because such a policy would come along with the collapse of the economy.

Determinants of the debt coefficient

The debt coefficient as overall debt in percentage of gross domestic product will rise (+) and fall (-) with the following variables

	Debt coefficient (public debt per gross domestic product) Rises: + Falls: -
More government spending	+
Less government spending	-
More government revenue	-
Less government revenue	+
Higher interest rate	+
Lower interest rate	-
Price inflation	-
Price deflation	+
Higher economic growth	-
Lower economic growth	+

In order to capture the impact of the price level on the debt burden, one must distinguish between the nominal rate and the real rate of interest. The current nominal interest rate comprises the real interest rate plus the expected inflation rate. While the real interest rate is relatively stable, the expected inflation rate and therefore nominal interest rates are volatile because if the uncertainty concerning the future inflation rate.

Public debt in terms of the debt coefficient – total debt in percent of gross domestic production – will rise or fall according to the movement of the following determinants.

It may appear easy to construct a package for bringing down the debt burden without cutting expenditures. Such a simplistic plan would include measures to
- raise taxes
- decrease the interest rate
- increase price inflation
- stimulate economic growth
- reduce the size of accumulated debt (by forgiveness or default).

The problem with such a policy is that while each measure would work in isolation, the factors are interdependent. Therefore, such a package would contain contradictory measures.

Taxes: A government cannot simply raise taxes. All it can do is to impose the tax rate. Higher tax rates do not imply higher tax revenue. A rate that is too high will lead to a lower tax revenue.

Interest rates: Central banks control the nominal interest rate for short maturities by setting the policy rate such as the federal funds rate in the case of the United States. The monetary authorities have much less power over the interest rate for longer maturities. An additional limitation of interest rate policy comes from the fact that when nominal interest rates hit zero-bound, price deflation would mean rising real interest rates.

Inflation: The monetary authorities can push the monetary base but the size of money in circulation results from the interaction of borrowers and lenders in the financial markets.

Economic growth: The long-term rate of economic growth depends on factors beyond manipulation by fiscal and monetary policies. Economic growth results from a confluence of hard and soft factors that include the quality of macroeconomic management, governance, and culture. Education, infrastructure and the legal framework exert their influence on economic growth over decades.

Debt reduction: One way to reduce the amount of past debt accumulation is debt forgiveness or default. Such a measure reduces the amount of the outstanding debt right away and lowers the coefficient. A well-negotiated debt reduction may contribute to lower interest rates and speed up an economic recovery. Economic expansion would mean an increase of government revenue particularly when it comes along with lower interest payments. Yet granting debt forgiveness and managing an orderly debt restructuring depends on the willingness of the lenders. Whether lenders agree on rescheduling to reduce the debt burden depends not only on financial factors but very much on the geostrategic position of the indebted country when foreign lending is involved as it is mostly the case with public debt.

Default: Another way of reducing the amount of current debt is by default. Yet deliberate nonpayment provides no way out of the debt trap. Such a policy would give up access to the capital market and crush economic growth right away. Any kind of default exacerbates a return to prosperity. The detrimental impact of default on economic growth may be long-lasting. As easy as it is to lose confidence as hard is it to regain trust.

***

An effective debt reduction strategy, which would bring down the debt coefficient, must address both variables of the debt quotient. Such a policy must seek to bring down total debt combined with lifting the rate of economic growth. It makes no sense to bring down debt when at the same time the economy would shrink, and the gross domestic product would fall. Likewise, the relative debt burden would not go away even with a larger gross domestic product, when the boost of economic growth rates has come mainly from more public spending. To bring down the debt coefficient, one needs to reduce absolute debt and have a growing economy.

The way to bring down total debt is to cut spending in combination with higher rates of economic growth which would require a boost in private investment. Only a very superficial analysis would point to lower interest rates as the way to get more investment. Confidence, secure property rights, and a positive profit outlook are the keys. If the central bank forces down interest rates to stimulate more investment, it will provoke investment errors. Because of the resulting economic distortions due to these malinvestments, such a kind of economic growth would not be sustainable.

In order to achieve debt reduction, spending cuts must be accompanied by an improvement of the investment climate for private enterprise. This happened after the end of World War II in the Western world when less military spending went hand in hand with a return to the principles of free markets. Different from Roosevelt's anti-capitalist rhetoric that had prolonged the Great Depression and the government's political sway over the war economy that has suppressed free enterprise, the decades after World War II saw the return to capitalist economic principles and economic growth accelerated despite massive budget cuts.

The failure of a country such a Greece to bring down the debt quotient results from the fact that the various Greek governments before and after the debt crisis have failed to coalesce the policy of spending cuts with adequate measures to increase private business confidence and to liberate the economy. Greece is the exemplary case how the march towards the debt crisis begins as a joy ride and ends in a horror trip. The higher the debt burden, the harder it is to restrain its future growth. Passing through the limit from the manageable to the unmanageable size of public debt goes with little notice. It is only after the barrier is broken that the trouble begins. Then it is often too late for a turnaround. The ride over the cliff into state bankruptcy happens as if programmed once the critical threshold is crossed.

Theory and evidence show that to overcome a debt crisis, the policy must combine the debt reduction program with incentives for private enterprise to fill up quickly and efficiently the space that the retreat of government opens. With the right incentives in place, private business will generate employment and income not despite but because the government cuts spending. The task ahead not only for the US but for all countries which are in a debt trap is to bring down debt in combined with a forceful surge towards free enterprise.

***

A loan is worth as much as the borrower can serve it by paying interest and principal. If the state can no longer finance its debt through tax revenues, it must make new debts to pay the old debts, and the confidence in the value of the money dissipates. Eventually, there will be a loss of trust in the currency, and the monetary system moves towards its collapse. Modern money as a legal tender has no value in use, only an exchange value. The acceptance of money rests on the confidence that money maintains its purchasing power and serves for the proximate spending acts. When this confidence falters, money loses its value. A reform must be fundamental: the money system itself.

A free capitalism requires abolishing the monetary monopoly of the state and the central bank. The way to do this is to legalize a competitive private monetary system. Free capitalism requires separating state and money not much different as in earlier times classical liberalism demanded the separation of state and church. Attempts to deal with government debt by proclaiming spending cuts are doomed to fail. One can curb the Moloch state only if one blocks its access to money creation. This requires that the system of public money must return into private hands.

Backgrounder: Where does money come from?

The basis of the circulating money is the creation of the money base by the central bank.

The monetary base reflects the stock of foreign exchange reserves while the largest part comprises credit of the central bank to the commercial banks.

The central bank money of the commercial banks (banknotes) comes into circulation through credit, i.e. by the borrowing of commercial banks from the central bank. On this basis, the commercial banking system creates book money (also known as depositary money) by granting credits to businesses, the consumers and to the government.

Central bank balance sheet

Assets	Liabilities
☐ Foreign currency reserves	☐ Circulation of cash (notes)
☐ Loans to commercial banks	☐ Deposits of commercial banks
☐ Bonds and other titles	☐ Deposits of government agencies
☐ Loans to government agencies	

The demand for credit by companies and consumers and by the state authorities at the commercial banks leads to additional money, which economic agents use for a bank transfer in the form of bank deposits and which can be converted into cash in the form of notes.

Commercial bank balance sheet

Assets	Liabilities
☐ Cash	☐ Capital
☐ Investments	☐ Reserves
☐ Loans	☐ Deposits
☐ Participations	☐ Borrowings

Money and assets

Money is the asset with the highest degree of liquidity. Money gives the holder the immediate general ability to pay. Shares, debt securities, and insurance policies have lower liquidity as they do not provide an immediate payment ability.

With these assets, one must sell the titles to raise money. How much money a bond or share can generate at a specific moment is subject to fluctuations.

There are two main money producers: the central bank and the commercial banks. Both institutions create money out of thin air through the act of lending.

The statistical calculation of the asset distribution among the population, which provokes so often heated discussion, can be nothing more than a blurry snapshot because beyond cash all other assets fluctuate in price.

Stock prices are constantly changing during trading hours and are experiencing considerable changes at certain times.

For real estate, there is no market price at all comparable to that of equities. In the case of real estate, prices fluctuate, too, yet, as each object is a single piece and as such, only partially substitutable, no reliable market price exists before the sale of the object.

Household goods and works of art may be valuable for the owner, but who knows their market value?

Cash, bank deposits, bonds, and life insurance are debt securities. The holder is a creditor. These titles, including the cash, come into the circulation as credit lines. Cash arises with the central bank which lends to the commercial banks.

Main monetary aggregates

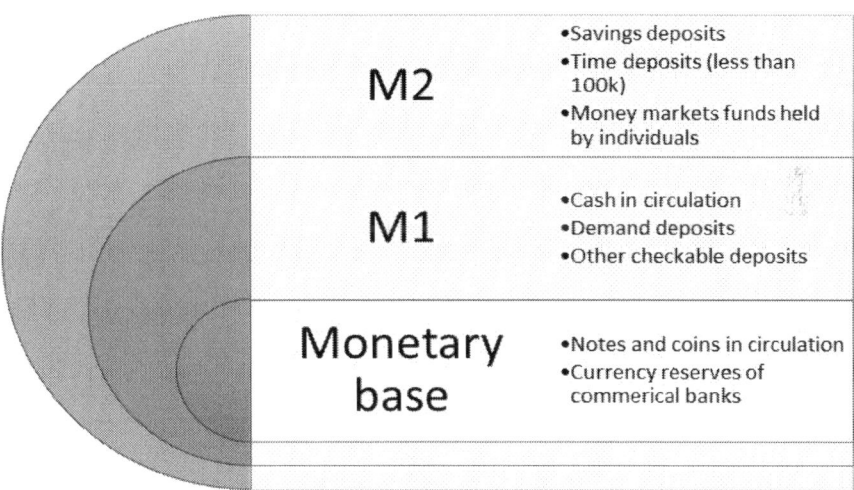

A small amount of cash covers the book money, which exists in the form of bank deposits. Commercial banks have more liabilities to their deposit owners than they have cash in their vaults.

Each act of lending by a commercial bank creates a chain of deposit creation as one man's spending becomes another man's income. Therefore, the amount of deposit money exceeds the amount of cash.

Capital, Savings, and Entrepreneurship

Monetary saving is not necessarily investment, and investment is not automatically capital formation, which renders yields and could bring forth appreciation by some compound interest formula. Real capital does not exist as a homogenous lump in the sense that there is a capital stock that enters the production function to produce the national income. Real capital exists in the form of diverse capital goods, and as such, they do not represent a source of a permanent revenue. Capital goods render an income stream only insofar as they are rearranged and renewed according to the changing market conditions. Capital without entrepreneurial activity is an empty concept.

The term 'capital' as it is frequently used and applied when calculating the financial state of households, companies, or investment funds is an accounting concept. Only in terms of monetary units can capital be treated as a sum. In contrast to monetary capital, real capital, as an ensemble of diverse capital goods, cannot be added up. As the means of production, capital is a mental concept that exists in the mind of the entrepreneur who puts the capital goods in their interaction to use. The means of production wear down by rendering the yield, and they become obsolete when the production process must be altered because of the technology or demand and competition change. Real capital left to itself does not bear fruits. On the contrary, left to itself, real capital as it exists in the form of capital goods deteriorates; capital in this sense does not grow but dies. Without entrepreneurial activity, capital is just a heap of heterogeneous capital goods. Without the entrepreneur, capital is dead. It takes the entrepreneurial activity to bring capital to life and keep capital alive.

The present consumption comes from the current production. Most of the goods that one needs to satisfy the future wants cannot be pre-produced now and saved for consumption later. It will be the state of the economy at the point of time in the future when the consumption needs arise that determines the degree of meeting the new specific demands. Because future demand will differ from today's, the capital structure currently in existence will become inadequate, and it is only by constant adaptation and new capital formation that the production process will provide the flow of consumption goods in the future periods. Higher productivity now does not guarantee that its level can be maintained, or that the areas where high productivity is presently the case will be the same that will be needed in the future. In order to preserve productivity, one needs on-going entrepreneurial management. Capital maintenance and its accumulation need perpetual savings and investment and continuous re-arrangements of the capital structure under entrepreneurial guidance.

The accumulation of financial assets may be an investment from a personal perspective, but it does not necessarily mean that real capital comes into existence. Most of the stock trade is only a rotation of ownership. Even less so does the lending to government make up the acquisition of capital goods. Governments spend most of the money on salaries and other items that are mainly consumption. In terms of saving via government bonds, there is little difference between a pension scheme of pay-as-you-go and a capital-based system, because in both cases the savings of one group is consumption by another one, and no real capital formation takes place.

Under a socialist economic system, savings and investment typically come along with capital destruction. But in the capitalist countries, too, savings, investment, and economic growth can deceive as an indicator of the future performance of an economy. If it were merely aggregate investment that mattered, economic development and swift wealth creation would be easy. Poor economies could become rich in a short time by borrowing abroad; and rich economies, where sufficient savings potential is available, could deliberately choose their desired future wealth levels. Yet economic growth requires more than saving and investment, and even together with technological progress, these conditions are not enough. Only insofar as the savings get into the hands of companies that adapt to market conditions will investment contribute to future prosperity. The entrepreneurial quality of the management and the overall socioeconomic conditions determine whether the savings are put to proper use or squandered.

Popular thinking about economic growth is still strongly influenced by the productivity theory of capital, which presumes that capital generates the yield like a tree begets its fruits. In the models of high aggregate macroeconomics, saving and investment along with technological progress are the main sources of growth. In this view, more savings imply more investment, and more investment means a higher capital stock, which in turn augments future yields. To assume a proper fertility of capital is sometimes even transferred to the accumulated monetary capital as it exists as an investment portfolio, which is said to grow automatically with its returns.

Only as an accounting tool - as 'monetary capital' - can capital be measured and said to grow or to diminish. But capital in the sense of capital goods cannot be expected to grow or to be stored over time. On the contrary. Capital goods deteriorate during production and finally disappear from the process of production. It is not accumulated monetary capital that brings forth output and renders profits and interest, but only capital in real terms as a heterogeneous ensemble of capital goods, and as such, it renders yield only insofar as it is constantly remodeled by entrepreneurs who buy labor, find and employ new techniques, and adapt the structure of production to changing conditions.

An individual member of a generational cohort may improve his future wealth position in relation to the average by saving more, but it will be the state of the economy in the future that determines the general level of well-being.

Individual savings will not contribute to the aim of maintaining an adequate capital structure by buying government bonds. Giving money to the government is more harmful than good because it means that the money does not go into the hand of entrepreneurs. The savings, which the government receives from the private investor helps the government to expand its activity. Therefore, buying government bonds will deteriorate the environment where the entrepreneurial spirit can thrive.

Expecting future returns from the stock market as a wealth-generation machine is as foolish an idea as the belief that the government pays for social security checks. The expectation that it is primarily financial investment now that guarantees the yields for the time to come is as illusory as to believe that more social security contributions now would guarantee higher pensions later. By concentrating on financial schemes, the focus is diverted from the real issue. Higher stock market valuations appear as real wealth creation, and it gets ignored that it is not the price of an asset that makes up wealth but the profits that come from the process of production.

There is no escape from permanent efforts to rearrange the production process. The future levels of wealth are linked to the overall conditions of the economy as it evolves over time. The need for constant renewal of real capital requires an on-going flow of funds in terms of free capital to maintain the production process. Financial assets will appreciate insofar as net savings continue to be generated in the future and as they get into the hands of able entrepreneurs. Saving and investment will be wasteful when companies are run by managers who lack foresight and prudence or when institutional settings emerge that hamper, transform, and destroy these entrepreneurial qualities.

Summary

Interventionism is the scourge of our time. Interventionism cannot hold its promises. On the contrary, governmental interference in the market processes creates new problems and generates new difficulties, while at the same time it suppresses and destroys opportunities and chances of improvement. The regulatory state leads not to prosperity but to stagnation and economic decline. For the welfare state, citizens end up paying more than they get, as the actual costs rise because of the seemingly free supply and because the social apparatus brings with it a growing bureaucracy.

The expectation that the so-called 'Third Way' would lead to a social and economic paradise has not come true. Both socialism and interventionism represent failed forms of economic governance. Weakening economic activity is the consequence of interventionism; the other cause is government debt, which contributes to lower economic output. The ultimate destiny of interventionism is the financial collapse of the state. On the one hand, expenditure for one specific item leads to new spending for another item and thus public expenditure continues to rise; on the other hand, the public debt burden lowers economic performance and the tax revenue. This way, two sides squeeze the modern interventionist welfare state: falling revenue and rising expenditures.

VI.

ECONOMIC STABILIZATION

Antony P. Mueller

> *"All that a good government can do to improve the well-being of the masses is the establishment and preservation of the institutional frameworks that do not hinder the accumulating of new capital and its use to improve the technical production methods."*
>
> Ludwig von Mises: 'Planning for Freedom' (1952)

- *The myth of crisis capitalism* –
- *Backgrounder: Stagflation* -
- *Backgrounder: Say's Law* -
- *Monetary policy* -
- *How small crises become big crises* –
- *A menu of models* –
- *Backgrounder: Survey of business cycle models* –
- *No crisis without a boom* -
- *What happened in the Great Depression?* -
- *Lessons yet to learn* -
- *Backgrounder: Misery Index* -
- *Backgrounder: the economics of inflation and deflation* –
- *The sorrows of central banking* –
- *Inflation-targeting* –
- *Bailouts and stimuli* –
- *The pitfalls of policy-making* -
- *The value of money* -
- *End the Fed* –
- *The crisis of 2008* -
- *Summary*

The declared goal of macroeconomic policy is to stabilize the economy. This claim implies the assumption that the market economy is inherently unstable. Yet what if it is not the market economy but politics which produces instability? What if the policy managers fabricate the opposite of their claim? What if they do not flatten the business cycle but make it more extreme? What if monetary policy does not cure inflation but instigates the fall of the purchasing power of money?

The great economic eruptions happen when the government and the central bank do not allow the small economic fluctuations to play out. The authorities hinder the return to a balance when false incentives and distorted market signals persist. When capital becomes scarcer, the interest rate should rise to signal this change. If, however, the central bank attempts to pump more money into the systems and to lower the interest rate, this policy will cover up the capital shortage. Cheap credit insinuates a profusion of funds that do not exist.

Economic policy claims to stabilize the economy and keep it on its growth path. For that purpose, economic policy is said to pursue the aims to fight inflation and deflation, to prevent recessions and depressions and to promote economic growth. Yet, often, these policies themselves produce what the policymakers claim to prevent and to cure.

Antony P. Mueller

The Myth of Crisis Capitalism

The business cycle comprises the ups and downs of economic activity. One must distinguish between fluctuations - the slight oscillations of the economic process - and the strong waves of the boom and the bust. The term 'cycle' - if it should evoke the image that the economy swings regularly between expansion and recession - is inappropriate because there are no regularities in the movements of economic activity. Each stage, be it recession, stagnation, or depression, can last for a long time. There are countries that do not escape their economic standstill, and there are those economies, which enjoy a good economic performance for decades, and experience only brief and slight dips or no recession at all for a long time.

The Marxists put the myth into the world that extreme crises were inherent to the market economy when in fact, the strong economic fluctuations have come from war and political unrest, or by natural events and acts of God, and are not due to the inner workings of capitalism. War, revolution, civil war, ethnic, and religious conflicts have been the main causes of economic collapse, long-lasting stagnation, and failed recoveries. Throughout history, it has been politics that has ruined the economic well-being of the people.

For the 20th century, one can say, all the evils of that century followed from the basic error of expecting to improve the human condition through politics. If we want to avoid similar catastrophes in the 21st century, we must stop politics and dismantle the state.

The Great Depression, which dates from 1929 to 1939 for the United States, but that began in Great Britain already in the early 1920s, was the consequence of the First World War and the world-political conflicts after the duplicitous Treaty of Versailles. It took until after the end of the Second World War until the Western nations could find their way back to cooperation again.

In Eastern Europe, the stagnation continued after the end of World War II because the Soviet Union imposed its socialist system on the countries that the Soviet leader Stalin gained with the consent of the British Prime Minister Churchill and the US-American President Roosevelt at the Yalta Conference in February 1945.

Western Europe received the American Marshall Plan from 1948 until 1952 and helped to launch the European recovery. The 'economic miracle' of the recovery of the Federal Republic of Germany in the post-war period is only partly the result of the Marshall Plan. Just as important was the program of economic liberalization that Ludwig Erhard (1897-1977) started with his monetary reform in June 1948. Yet towards the end of the 1960s, Germany, too, resorted to an activist economic policy.

Nowadays, there is little tolerance to the natural fluctuations in the economic process. Even the small natural swings of the economic activity lead to exaggerated reactions of economic policy. The fear is that even a small increase in unemployment would cost the government its reelection. Yet by not allowing the small fluctuations, economic policy earns the big fallout.

This way, the economic stimulus measures of the 1960s laid the foundation for the inflation in the 1970s and the excessive reaction to the stock market decline at the start of the new millennium led to the crisis of 2008.

In Japan, the central bank stimulated the excessive boom of the 1980s. When the crisis came 1990, neither expansive fiscal nor monetary policy helped to get the Japanese economy out of its slump - despite the size and duration of the measures. The massive fiscal and monetary stimuli to fight the downturn of 2008 has not produced a swift recovery but laid the groundwork for an even worse crisis.

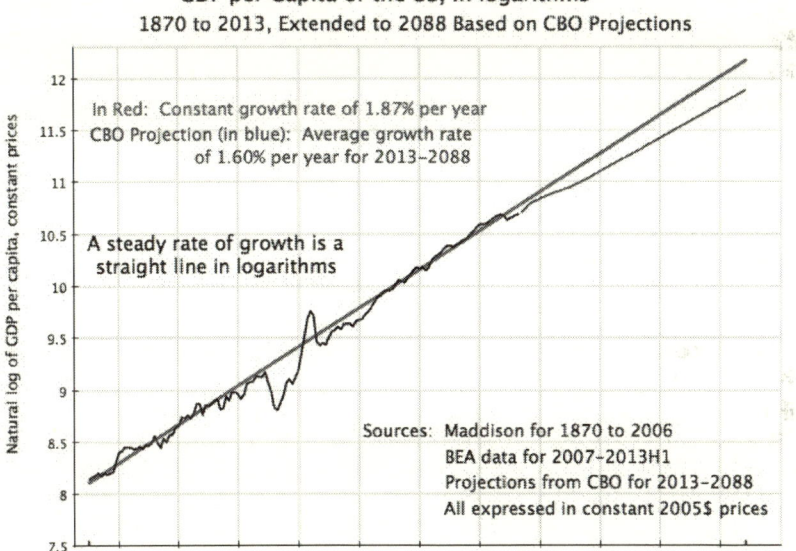

U.S. economic growth since 1870

GDP per Capita of the US, in logarithms
1870 to 2013, Extended to 2088 Based on CBO Projections

The long-term trend in the US economy of an increase in per capita income of 1.87% per year since 1789 and the projection from 2013 to 2088 of a growth rate of 1.6% per year. The major economic fluctuations in the 18th and 19th centuries resulted from war and domestic conflicts such as the Napoleonic Wars, the American civil war, and the wars of independence.

The 'Great Depression' is the most pronounced deviation from the trend. The crisis was longer and deeper because of the false monetary policy of the Federal Reserve System and the many economic policy errors of Franklin Delano

Roosevelt (President of the USA from March 4, 1933, to his death on April 12, 1945).

The boom of the post-war period came after Roosevelt's demise when a pro-market orientation of the American economic policy took hold. Yet things changed later again towards interventionism in the 1960s and in the 1970s. The 1980s and the 1990s saw respite, but since the start of the new millennium, monetary policy has become expansionist without being able to stimulate economic growth. Debt accumulation and interventionism demand their toll and have pushed the U.S. economy from the 'Great Moderation' into the 'Great Recession' that has become the 'Long Stagnation'.

***

In the United States, the welfare state, whose foundations came into existence during Roosevelt's New Deal of the 1930s, experienced a revival in the 1960s and continues its expansion since then. After the 1962 Cuban crisis and President John F. Kennedy' assassination in 1963, the hot phase of the Vietnam War began under the presidency of Lyndon B. Johnson (U.S. President from 1963 to 1969). With the Vietnam war, the welfare state grew at high rates in this period.

The American central bank, together with the other major central banks, helped to support this expansion of government expenditure with a loose monetary policy under the spell of the cheap money cult. When, during the war in the Middle East in October 1973 (the 'Yom-Kippur War' - from 6 to 25 of October 1973), the group of oil exporting countries (OPEC) launched a boycott of the supply of crude oil, the simultaneous occurrence of recession and inflation brought about the stagflation of the 1970s. Attempts to stimulate the economy through public expenditure programs combined with easy money failed. The economies did not recover despite massive government spending combined with strong monetary stimuli. What increased, was unemployment, the inflation rate, and government debt. The economic policy followed a Keynesian orientation. This economic doctrine as laid down by the English economist John Maynard Keynes (1883-1946) states that one must overcome an economic crisis by more government spending and more easy money.

Stagflation

The term 'stagflation' signifies the combined appearance of stagnation and inflation. In the 1970s, all major industrialized countries suffered from low growth, high rates of price inflation, persistent underemployment, and widening budget deficits. In the United States, both, the price inflation rate and the unemployment rate, reached double digits in the 1970s and early 1980s.

Deflationary and inflationary gap in Keynesian perspective

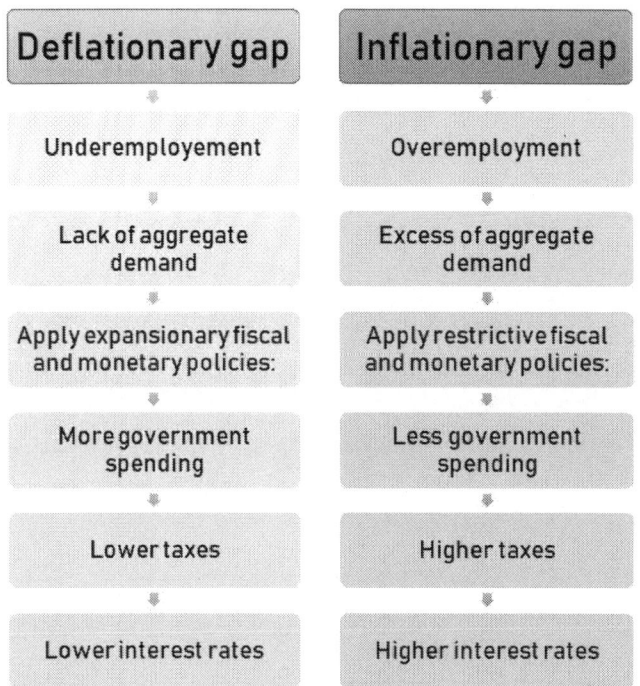

The dominant macroeconomic policy theory in the mid-1960s until the end of the 1970s was 'Keynesianism', according to which an economy is in the state of a 'deflationary' or an 'inflationary' gap.

A deflationary gap comes along with a falling price level and rising unemployment. As the Keynesian theory diagnoses these phenomena as the result of a lack of demand, the government must apply expansive monetary and fiscal policies. In contrast, thus says the Keynesian doctrine, an inflationary gap results from an excess of demand which leads to inflation and over-employment. Here, the right policy is a fiscal and monetary contraction.

Confronted with stagflation, the Keynesian policy knew no answer. While doing away with unemployment would require expansive policies, fighting inflation would need contracting measures. Additionally, the Keynesian policy paralyzed in the face of stagflation because high unemployment and stagnant growth meant widening budget deficits and a mounting public debt.

The principle of Keynesianism states that the government expenditures should not come with a balanced government budget, but that the extra spending should happen through borrowing. With the credit-financed expenses, the state assumes budget deficits.

The doctrine says the government should spend in place of the consumers and of the companies to overcome the investment weakness and the consumer restraint in the private sector. The problem with this theory is that it cannot explain why, after all, there was a falloff in investment activity in the first place.

Features of stagflation

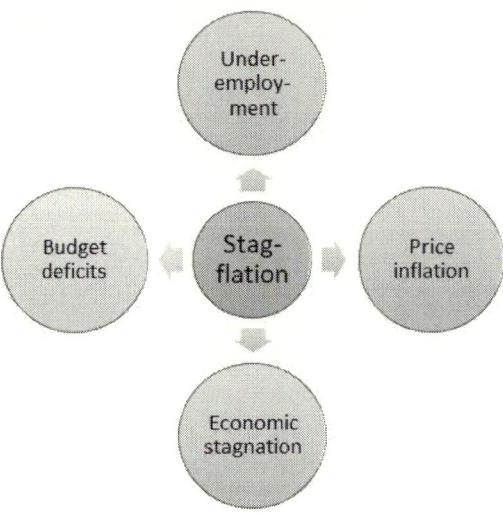

Defects of the Keynesian Theory

The Keynesian theory suffers from a series of fundamental problems. The model makes no clear distinction between the short and the long run as to the determinants of investments (long run) and the demand for money (short run). An insufficient distinction refers also to nominal and real variables. If the Keynesian model wants to explain unemployment, the model requires real variables. Then, however, additional government spending cannot expand the economy at will. More spending is not equal to real economic growth.

The Keynesian model cannot explain the breakdown of 'animal spirits' as the cause of the fall of investment and as the trigger to the business cycle. Extreme levels of aggregation conceal more than they reveal and a mechanistic interpretation of cause and effect between the variables makes the Keynesian model unrealistic.

***

The economic model of the Keynesians postulates that aggregate demand determines economic activity. Therefore, the policy recommendation says that if there is insufficient private demand, the public sector must jump in. With this theory, Keynesianism stands in contrast to classical economic theory according to which the growth of an economy depends on the production. For the classical economists, production generates the means demand goods, as stated by 'Say's law'. According to the classical theory, economic crises show that technical innovations or changes in consumer preferences or the political and social environment require restructuring the economy's supply side.

Structural deficiencies of the Keynesian economic model

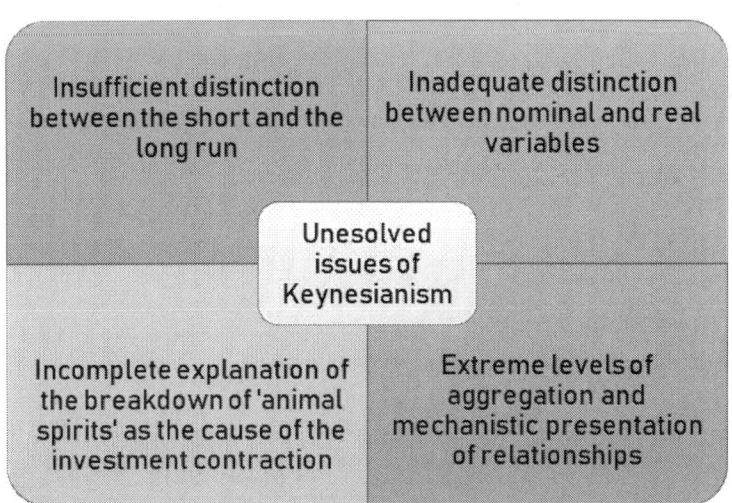

Backgrounder: Say's Law

Keynes and his followers distort 'Say's Law'. They claim it says 'supply creates its own demand' when in fact the theorem denotes the law of the market, which contends that supply equals demand and that to exercise demand one must have something to offer. Because for the economy a whole, credit and financial assets cancels out, and thus the demand that there is, must have an equal supply. Say's Law is not that supply creates its own demand but that for the economy in total, supply serves to exercise demand, and that both variables must match.

In a market economy, there cannot be an 'over-production' and an 'under-consumption' as the Marxists and their Keynesian followers claim. If a company produces an item that it cannot sell at the expected price, it must lower the price. When the price falls below the marginal cost of production, the company suffers losses and consequently must abandon producing this good. This happens all the time with individual companies and specific goods. If it were not so, business would be an easy game.

The Marxist term of 'under-consumption' signifies that workers would produce more than they earn. Yet this claim does not hold for a competitive market economy. As long as the remuneration of a worker is below its marginal revenue product, a company will increase its overall profits by hiring more workers. A firm will stop using more workers at the point where the marginal revenue product of labor equals the wage rate.

As long as the wage rate is below of what labor contributes to the sales revenue of the product, a company will hire additional workers and stop when the two rates are equal. When the wage rate exceeds the revenue product of the workers, the firm must lay-off labor until the two rates will be equal again.

A frequently used argument says that when companies dismiss workers, the overall volume of demand will shrink and thus the slump will deepen. The answer to this claim is that if wage rates do not fall to the level of productivity, business would make losses and inhibit capital accumulation. Yet capital accumulation along with technological progress must take place to lift productivity up to the wage level and to do away with unemployment. There is no other way but dismissal when the wage rate is too high because if the workers stayed in their jobs, they would provoke losses and thus inhibit the capital accumulation. Profits are a necessary condition of capital accumulation and a wage rate in tune with labor productivity is a necessary condition to make profits. Capital accumulation raises productivity and thereby more labor will be employed, and then the wage rate can rise.

***

In the perspective of classical economics, it is not the task state but that of the entrepreneurs to redirect the production structure and to adapt the production process to the altered conditions. According to the Keynesian doctrine, in contrast, the economy recovers due to government spending, which stimulates the economic actors to ask for more goods and services. When this happens, so the

Keynesian theory says, the economic engine will start again, and the cart moves out of the ditch. One must 'crank up' the economic motor. In order to stimulate the economy, the government must apply 'pump priming'.

At the heart of the Keynesian message lies the psychological thesis that in a crisis the entrepreneurs and the consumers fear spending their money. To compensate for this, the state would have to overcome this paralysis by credit-financed extra expenditures. As demand increases, economic activity would revive because entrepreneurs and consumers would regain confidence and spend more money again.

Three years before Keynes' monograph appeared, Germany's Nationalist Socialist government started a policy of government deficit spending in early 1933. This experiment influenced Keynes' thinking as it proves the English economist's preface to the German edition of his "General Theory of Employment, of Interest, and Money". The General Theory appeared in the English original in 1936 and received a German translation in the same year. In his preface to the German edition, Keynes elaborates that his theory would work better under an authoritarian regime than in a free democracy and that the Nazi economic policy was the first test case for his 'new economics'.

The Keynesian economic model works better under the conditions of a dictatorship than in a democracy because a state-sponsored demand policy requires additional compulsory measures to prevent that the money creation that comes with the government's spending policy would cause the price-wage spiral. The reason the Nazi variant of Keynesianism worked and because the mass unemployment in Germany disappeared without inflation in a few years was that this policy combined strict price and wage controls. After the fire of the Reichstag building on the night of February 27, 1933, the new government put the union leaders, together with leading Social Democrats and Communists, into 'protective custody'. The entrepreneurs, as far as they were loyal to the new regime, became operations managers and had to obey the government directives although private property in its formal legal sense remained intact.

The Third Reich completed the system of state capitalism, which had come into being during World War I and had continued in the 1920s. More radical than the Italian fascism, Nazism subjected the economy and society to totalitarianism. In contrast to the Soviet Socialism, National Socialism was a socialism that maintained private property in its positivist legal sense. Yet National Socialism put the economy also under a plan whose main aim was the military armament. Not only in this respect are National Socialist (NAZI) Germany and the Union of the Socialist Soviet Republics (USSR) twins. Both systems were socialist not only by name.

The circumstances are very different if one wants to practice demand policy under the conditions of a liberal democracy. If government finances its expenditures through deficits, the amount of money that circulates in the economy will increase. If the stock of money in circulation grows faster than production, prices will rise. Higher prices call for higher wage demands by the workers and their representatives. A price-wage spiral emerges. The irritations, which emanate from inflation, along with the ensuing labor struggles about wages and strikes, brings about the opposite of the desired economic recovery. Instead of an economic rebound, recession looms. As the money supply expands in line with the size of deficit spending, the simultaneous occurrence of economic stagnation and price inflation sets into motion.

Price-wage-price-spiral (PWP-Spiral)

An increase in government spending brings with it a monetary expansion, which leads to a higher price level. Price inflation will lead to demands for higher wages, which put further pressure on rising prices. Such a process can go on as long as the central bank aliments the process with monetary expansion. The longer the inflationary expansion last, the harsher will be the effects of the contraction.

The cleavage between deficit spending, price inflation and stagnation became a major topic in the 1970s. The 'stagflation' brought monetarism as an alternative policy concept to the forefront. In the late 1970s and the early 1980s, the industrialized countries tried to put an end to Keynesian policies and replace it with the monetarist 'counter-revolution'. The teachings of the monetarists say the economic cycle depends on the variations of the amount of money that circulates in the economy, and that the best way of practicing economic policy is keeping the money supply steady by having money grow at a pre-fixed annual rate.

The main representative of monetarism, Milton Friedman (1912-2006), showed that the US-American central bank prolonged and deepened the economic crisis of the Great Depression of the 1930s. According to his analysis, the US central bank allowed the money supply to shrink and thus price deflation to happen. As a result, real interest rates rose and there was a fall in consumption and investment.

Price-wage-price spiral

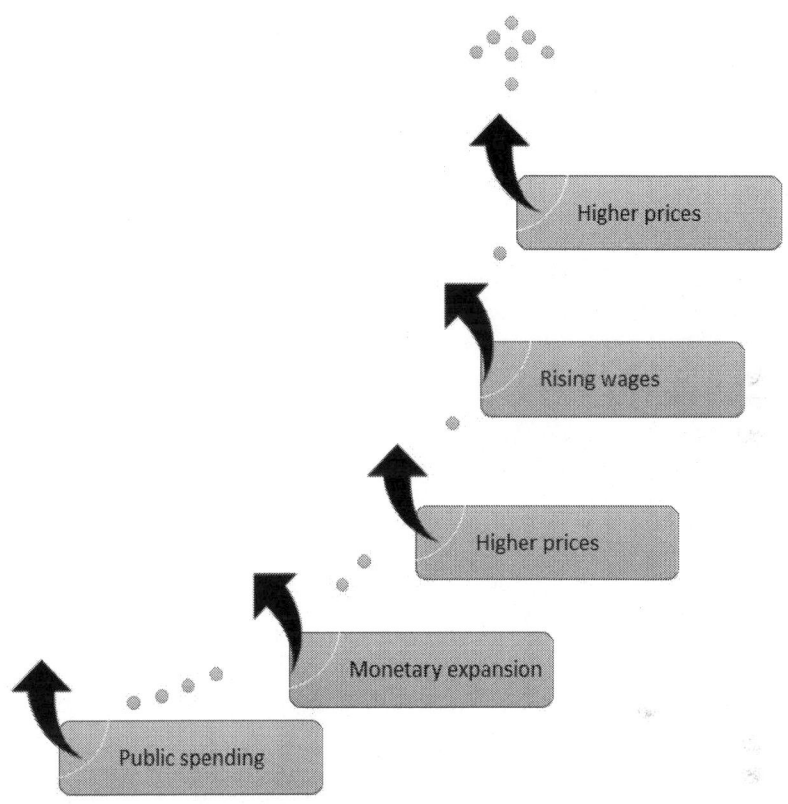

Keynesian, monetarist, and neo-classical models of economic contractions

For the Keynesians, the starting point of an economic crisis, which manifests itself in less production, is a fall in overall demand and the cure exists in stimulating aggregate demand. The policy recipe of the Keynesians is anticyclical government spending.

For the monetarists, the starting point of an economic downturn is a monetary contraction, which leads to less spending and to a fall of economic activity. In order to prevent less production, the monetary authorities should take care that the money supply does not contract. The policy recommendation of the monetarists is a stable growth rate of the monetary supply.

Classical economics explains a downturn as the result when the wages rates exceed the marginal productivity of labor. To forestall losses, companies must dismiss labor, and the economy enters a temporary contraction. After the wage rates have adapted to the marginal productivity of labor, new hiring sets in and the economy moves out of the dint.

The neo-classical sequence precedes both the Keynesian and the monetarist sequence. What these two opposing views take as the cause - the fall of aggregate demand and the monetary contraction - is, in fact, the outcome of a wage mismatch brought about by the trade unions that cooperate with the government.

Keynesian, monetarist, and neoclassical sequences

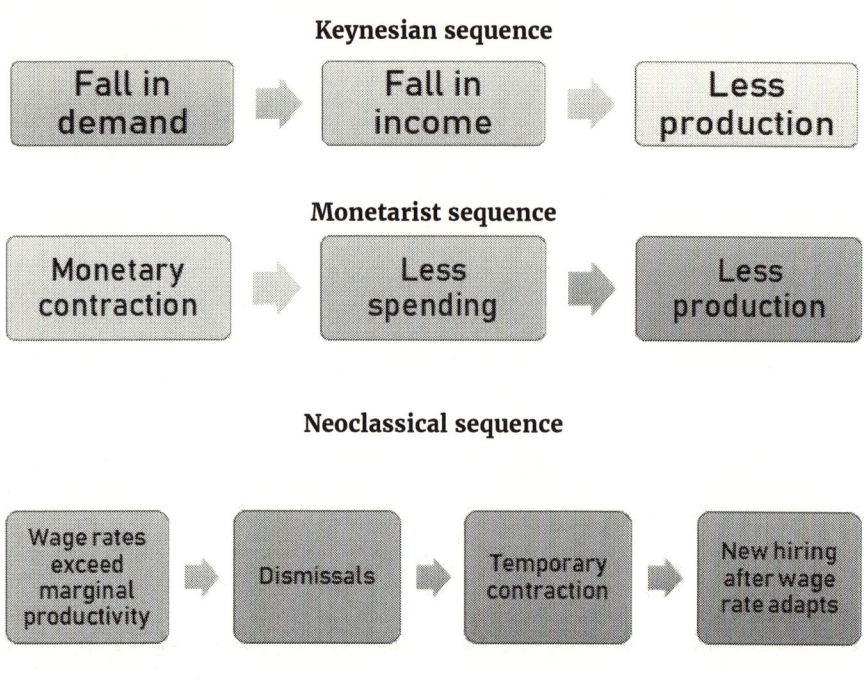

***

Friedman explained that not the market economy is to blame for the Great Depression but the American central bank's monetary policy. In the view of the monetarists, the lack of aggregate demand that the Keynesians deplore as the cause of the Great Depression was the fault of the monetary policy of the American Federal Reserve System (FED) and not a failure of the market economy. What the Keynesian diagnose as insufficient aggregate demand was a monetary contraction.

Yet Friedman ignored in his analysis that the Federal Reserve had committed two errors. It pursued a false policy not only because it was too restrictive in the crisis, but also because it was too expansive in the 1920s. By heating the boom in the decade preceding the Great Depression with low-interest rates, the FED prepared the path to the crash. American monetary policy instigated both: the boom and the subsequent bust.

From the 1960s onwards, monetarism gained influence in academia and replaced the Keynesian explanation of the crisis. The stagflation of the seventies gave Keynesianism its deathblow because their macroeconomic demand model was incapable of explaining how recession and inflation could occur at the same time. By the late 1970s, monetarism became a mainstay of monetary policy.

When the US inflation approached the fifteen percent mark towards the end of the 1970s, the time had come for a monetary policy turnaround. The President of the United States, Jimmy Carter (President from 1977 to 1981), appointed Paul Volcker as the chairman of the American central bank. Volcker took office in August 1979 and implemented a monetarist policy. During 1980, the US central bank, under the new directorship, conceived the monetarist experiment, which comprised shifting from the focus on the interest rate to the control of the money supply.

Defects of monetarism

The monetarist model establishes a relation between the money supply and the price level. According to the monetarist doctrine, rising prices come about when the money supply expands too much.

To reduce the rate of inflation, the rate of the increase of the amount of money in the economy must diminish. As a practical policy model, four questions arise:

First, which criteria fit the definition of the money supply to calibrate the monetary policy's interim policy aim? Second, which is the relation of the monetary aggregates (M0, M1, M2, M3, etc.) to the monetary base? Third, which is the appropriate monetary aggregate that the central bank can control? Is the management of the monetary base sufficient to control the other monetary aggregates? Fourth, how works the transmission mechanism in detail? What are the links from the money supply to the national income and to the price level? How does the monetary aggregate, which serves as the central bank's steering tool, affect the other monetary aggregates, the interest rate, investment, and consumption? Finally, how does money and the price level impact on the real gross domestic product and on employment?

***

When the central bank under Paul Volcker's chairmanship designed the new monetary policy, the experts knew of the causes of the Great Depression due to monetary contraction. The policymakers at the FED knew of the risk of pushing the economy into a depression if the money supply should shrink too much.

Therefore, the monetary policy aim was to avoid an abrupt contraction and not to provoke a recession or a new depression.

Structural defects of monetarism

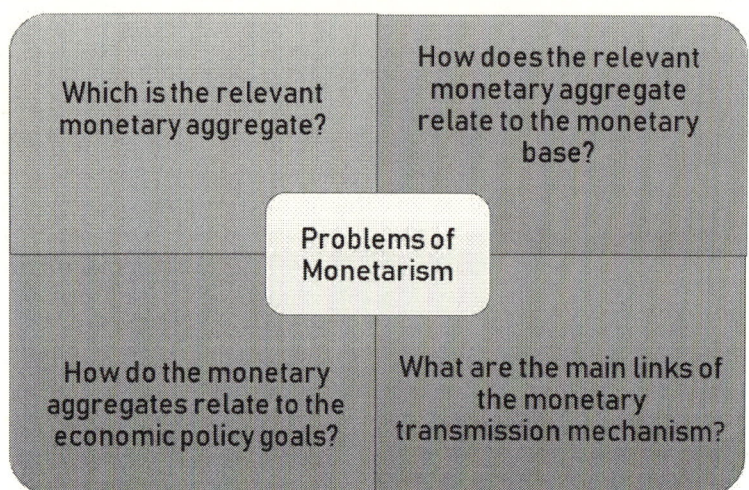

To plan a monetarist policy operation and to determine the monetary target, the monetarist policy projection must include the expected velocity of circulation in its calibration. As of 1980, the statistical data showed a continuous increase in velocity. For the several decades before 1980, econometric analyses established an almost perfect trajectory of the velocity of money. This way, so it seemed, the future rate of the velocity of transactions was to project with high confidence and one could put the number into the equation to expand the money supply. On these considerations, the US central bank decided upon a monetary target which corrected the rise of the money supply by the expected increase in circulation. Because the rate of velocity was rising, the amount of reducing the quantity of money had to fall more than otherwise to compensate for the increase in velocity. It came as a big surprise when the statisticians of the US central banks discovered after some time that as soon as the new monetary policy began, an abrupt change of the trend of the velocity of circulation had occurred. Instead of continuing to rise, the velocity of money had fallen. The planned moderately restrictive monetary policy turned into a strong contracting policy.

As a further irony of the story where one more error offsets another error, came into play that Ronald Reagan (President from 1981 to 1989), as the newly elected president, wanted to augment the defense budget. As the increase in spending requires to calculate in real terms, the estimated inflation rate played an important role to determine the size of nominal budget increases. In 1981, when preparing the first Reagan budget, none of the budget experts assumed a rapid decline of price inflation., which was around ten percent. Together with the other budget items, the projected defense spending rose by the desired real increment plus the compensation for the expected inflation rate. Public expenditure in real terms rose much stronger than intended when the rate of inflation fell more than expected. The following recession was deep but short. As a legacy remains the inception of a new cycle of higher national debt together with the myth that celebrates Paul Volcker as the daring inflation fighter. Inflationary expectations vanished from the system without a long-lasting recession not because of a superior policy design but by accident. The good performance of the U.S. economy in the years to come came as the result of the double error of a fiscal policy that was too expansive and a monetary policy that was too restrictive.

Monetary Policy

The 'Monetary History of the United States, 1867-1960', written by Milton Friedman with Anna Schwartz and published in 1963, identifies the monetary contraction as the cause of the Great Depression. The depression was deep and long because the US central bank did not counter the squeeze of liquidity with an appropriate increase in the money supply thereafter.

Friedman developed the concept of a quantitatively oriented monetary policy. According to this concept, monetary policy must not focus on the interest rate, but on the money supply. According to the monetarist doctrine, an increase in the price level, i.e. price inflation, results from expanding the money supply that exceeds the real growth of the economy. Therefore, a policy of combating inflation requires diminishing the rate of expansion of the money supply and in the more severe cases of inflation to reduce the absolute amount of money that circulates in the economy.

An indispensable premise for the practice of monetarist policy requires that the velocity of money would be constant or trend stable or that one could preview the price increases by some other prognostic technique. Yet if the velocity of money changes its course over time, these changes are not foreseeable, and the monetarist monetary policy will fail.

Velocity of circulation

The velocity of money refers to the frequency of transactions in an economy. One unit of money can serve for several transactions. The velocity of money can thus strengthen the effect of a change of the amount of money either to an expansion or to a contraction. Inflationary expectations lead to a rise in the velocity of money while deflationary and dis-inflationary expectations lead to lower velocity of transactions.

A monetarist monetary policy must fail if the velocity of the circulation of money is not stable. The effect of changes in the money supply is unpredictable because one cannot foresee how the velocity of money changes. The trends often last a long time and change abruptly. A reliable calculation of the future trend is not possible even if for the past many data points are available which seem to suggest a stable trend.

The velocity of money collapsed during the Great Depression. The long period of the increase of the velocity came from the 1950s until 1980 before the trend turned and the further decline of the rate of velocity that happened since the outbreak of the international financial crisis in 2007. The contraction of the velocity of circulation of money explains why the massive increase of the monetary base by the American central bank as a response to the financial crises has not increased the price inflation.

Source: Federal Reserve System. FRED: https://fred.stlouisfed.org/graph/?g=9wK

The downturn in the 1980s occurred after the American central bank had introduced its new monetary policy. It turned out that the measures taken were far more restrictive than intended. The U.S. interest rate rose, and the American economy plunged into a recession that dragged many of the indebted developing countries into insolvency. The deceptive relationship between the money supply and nominal gross domestic product before 1981 induced the American central bank to launch a much more restrictive monetary policy than it had planned.

Antony P. Mueller

How Small Crises Become Big Crises

Many people still hang on to the naïve belief that the economy needs an active policy to function, and that monetary and fiscal stimuli are necessary to achieve economic growth, 'full employment' and a 'stable' price level. Governments and central banks still stick to the concept of macroeconomic demand management. Economic policymakers and the electorate ignore that the economic policy itself is often the reason for economic weakness and unemployment and that monetary policy itself is the main cause of price inflation. Under the conditions of the current system of governance with its party democracy, those politicians gain most support who preach activism and promise to realize the impossible.

Although the macroeconomic demand theory is dead, it continues to live on as vulgar Keynesianism at the policy level. Since the economic downturn in the early 1990s, Japan has been trying to resolve its economic crisis with the quackery of a policy aimed at stimulating aggregate demand. Right from the start the recession, the Japanese government began with a series of expenditure programs to boost the economy. The Japanese central bank has pushed interest rates into negative territory, but the economy has not much recovered. In the meantime, the Japanese government debt has grown in dimensions that otherwise only occur in times of war. This policy has been a gigantic waste.

The immense sums that the government spent over the past quarter of a century did not help to lift the Japanese economy out from its stagnation. What remains of this policy is a vast debt overhang, which has paralyzed private economic activity. Savings are in decline, fears of coming tax increases are on the rise and the innovative zest has faltered. Among the top industrialized countries, Japan has become the country whose economy has experienced the sharpest decline in productivity increases since the 1990s.

Stagnation has become a permanent feature of the Japanese economy. Instead of fostering a swift recovery, the Japanese economic policy has made the structural distortions of the economy more rigid. Macroeconomic policy since the 1990s has wasted much of the wealth that Japan had accumulated in the decades after World War II.

The Case of Japan

By the end of 2016, Japanese government debt had reached 250% of the gross domestic product. Since the mid-1990s, the debt ratio has risen by 150 percentage points since the start of the low-interest rate policy of the Japanese central bank - which put its key rate close to zero and, in some periods, even into the minus territory.

The result of these massive stimulus packages that led to quasi-zero interest rates and a debt ratio of 250 percent was not only that Japan did not get out of the slump but also that its productivity rate, which had been in line with the other important industrialized countries until the 1990s, began to slump as well.

Japan. Interbank interest rate and public debt coefficient

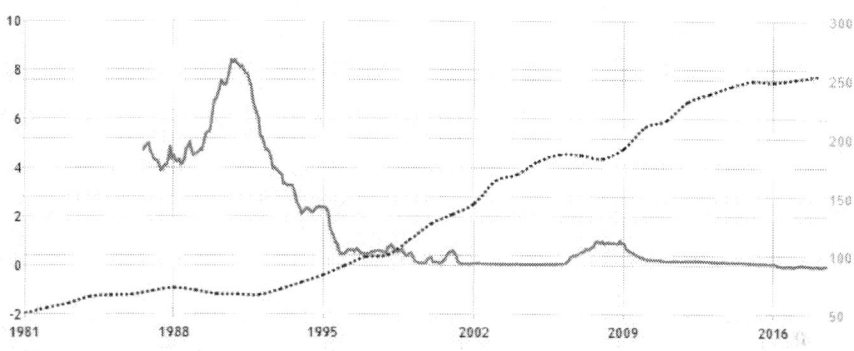

Source: tradingeconomics.com

Interbank interest rate (left hand side) and public debt in percent of gross domestic product (right hand side)

The graph shows the application of both fiscal and monetary stimulus policy in grand style. The public debt coefficient rose from around 50 % to 250 %, while the interbank interest was brought down into the zero and negative territory since the mid-1990s.

Nevertheless, economic growth has remained weak and productivity has stagnated.

The data (Penn World Table. Our World in Data. https://ourworldindata.org/economic-growtho) *show that Japan has been falling behind since the middle of the 1990s and enjoys less productivity per working hour than Italy and the United Kingdom and that Japan suffers from a big productivity gap with the United States, France, and Germany.*

***

Neither the American nor the European economic policymakers have drawn the right lessons from the Japanese disaster as the reaction to the 2008 crisis documents. In the USA and Europe, central banks have cut interest rates and governments have expanded government spending. Yet these measures have not led to a solid economic upturn.

Although Keynesianism is no longer a leading paradigm in academic economics, governments continue to follow its recipes with blind enthusiasm. Politicians favor Keynes' economic policy concept because it suits them well to justify spending and thus any sign of a recession legitimizes higher government debt. Yet while governments are exploiting economic downturns to increase government spending, they have a hard time to tackle the nation's debt burden.

No government wants to ruin its chances for re-election because of an increase of the interest rate, higher tax rates, and cuts in government spending, in particular for 'social' purposes. Governments follow the rule that the pain should come later while the pleasure is for now.

While the original theory of government deficit spending would call for anticyclical fiscal policy, budgetary policies follow an opportunistic line. The original theory of Keynes calls for a debt reduction when the economy is doing well. Yet for governments, Keynes has become an alibi which serves to justify extending the state's activities and to accumulate more debt in good and in bad times. Different from what Keynes envisioned, the national debt rises during a recession but does not fall when the economy is expanding.

Public debt cycle

Keynes' trust in the rationality of the state was so deep that he believed governments, which would boost public debt as deficit spending in the bust, would reduce the debt level in times of the boom. This way, John Maynard Keynes presumed the long-term debt level would remain constant.

Idealized public debt cycle

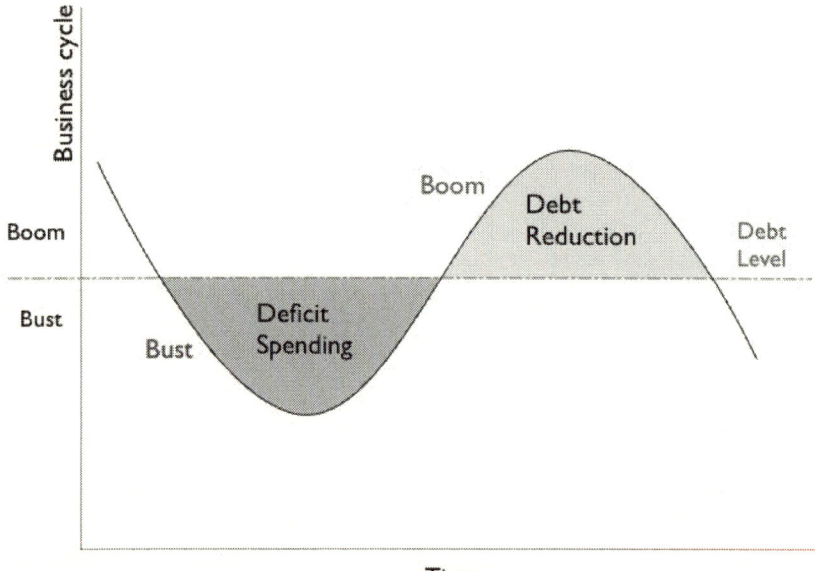

Things worked out differently. While governments took the Keynesian rationale to boost government spending in periods of the bust, they did not reduce public debt when the economy was doing well. This way, there has been a steady rise in public debt. Along with the demands as they come from healthcare and old age in particular – there is the ratchet effect of rising public debt that comes from boosting government spending in an economic crisis while not reducing debt when the economy booms.

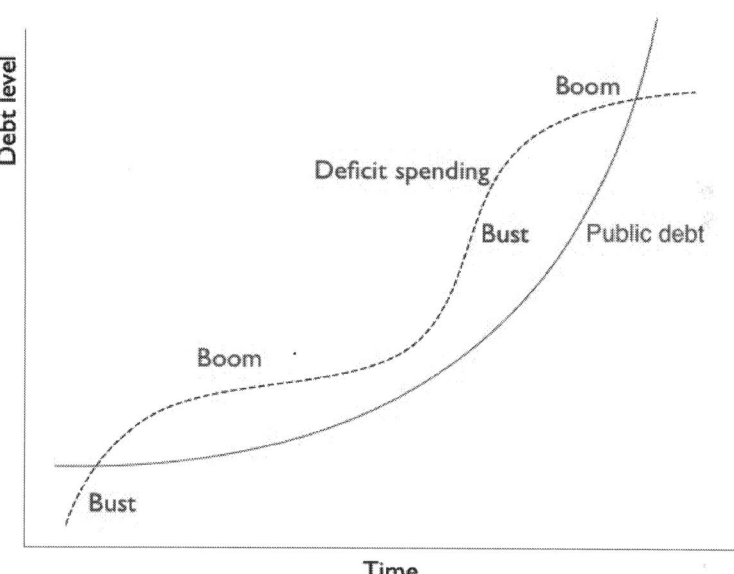

Ratchet effect of public deficits and debt

The leading industrialized countries are practicing a failed economic policy. As a result, the economies experience slow growth, and the productivity and the wage rates have stagnated, while public debt is on the rise. Almost all the economic progress that has occurred over the past decades was the result not of these countries' own economic policy but came from the economic liberation in Eastern Europe and Asia. The economic reforms toward a market economy of many countries that had adopted socialist regimes have led to creating many large new trade areas. One of the big beneficiaries of this development was Germany whose economic performance improved as the country developed close trade relations with the countries of Eastern Europe and Asia where reforms in favor of capitalism had taken place.

Antony P. Mueller

A Menu of Models

Other than as a crude psychology, the doctrine of Keynes cannot explain why the entrepreneurs should collectively cut down investment and cause a recession. Why should businessmen suddenly lose their 'animal spirits'? While it happens frequently that individually the leadership of a company will misjudge the future needs, the thesis that suddenly most members of the business community should lose their drive has no foundation. The crucial point left out by Keynes is to investigate the specific economic reasons investments drop. Instead of postulating obscure psychology, economics must investigate the difference between the fall of investment expenditure because of a shrinking demand when specific goods or certain product lines become obsolete on the one hand and the contraction as a macroeconomic phenomenon on the other hand. In a microeconomic perspective, a good that is no longer in demand on the market makes way for the demand for another commodity as its substitute. There is no fall in aggregate demand. What does the Keynesian theory mean when it postulates the fall of aggregate demand not as a consequence but as a cause for the economic downturn?

For the classical economics, a contraction of demand for the economy in the aggregate is not possible. This 'law of the markets', which goes back to Jean-Baptiste Say (1767-1832), pronounce that producing the goods is the basis for the demand for goods in exchange. Total supply is equal to total demand. The price mechanism corrects discrepancies in individual markets. The demand theorists, in contrast, use psychology to explain the business cycle. According to the Keynesian view, the moods of businesspersons fluctuate like that of maniacs between anxiety and euphoria. Such a thesis implies that economic actors are not only fools but also lunatics that suffer from chronic manic-depressive afflictions. This comes in handy for Keynes' solution, which is to take economic decisions, particularly those on investment, out of the hands of the private sector and turn the decision-making over to the government.

Keynes regards the state as an asylum of reason, in contrast to the irrational investors who act driven by fear and greed, and the consumers who spend according to what they get. To this day, this message from Lord Keynes delights all believers in the state as a supreme entity beyond the world of the mortals. Brought to its core, the Keynesian psychology postulates that businessmen are psychotic, consumers act like robots, and only government officials act wise, rational, and with foresight. Yet what appears as irrational to the Keynesians is, in fact, a rational reaction to the follies of the government.

Rising government spending and a higher public debt reduce investor confidence and increase uncertainty. The decisions in the private sector may seem irrational yet it is the capricious unpredictability of government decisions that drive the economic decision-makers nuts. Economic policies are a major source of uncertainty as they produce inflation, recessions, and depressions, and most of all, represent a constant source of uncertainty. If entrepreneurs observe that the government and the central bank will apply expansionary demand policy when signs of an economic downturn appear, business will postpone new investments because they can expect lower interest rates, new subsidies, and new tax reductions. To prevent a recession, economic policymakers turn slight economic downturns into deep recessions.

Producing the crisis that government said to cure happened also with the Great Depression. This tragedy was not due to a failure of the free market economy but of government. The Great Depression came about because World War I had wrecked the liberal monetary system of the gold standard and disrupted the system of an unregulated free world trade system. What came out of World War I (1914-1918) was interventionism, protectionism, communism, and Nazism. Toward the end of this bloody conflict, the international Communist movement had found a national power base with the Russian Revolution (1917) and in the Soviet Union (officially founded in 1922), which thereafter threatened the world for the next 70 years.

The First World War has brought with it not only material costs but also a moral and ideological destitution because of a profound spiritual crisis. In the war and afterward, a generation grew up, which had lost their religious faith together with the confidence in the value of individual freedom and the advantages of the market economy. Fascism and National Socialism along with world Communism and protectionism are all children of the same parent, namely World War I. What unites these various ideologies is their anti-capitalism. Theories of classical liberalism with individual freedom and private initiative at its base had to make room for collectivism and state interventionism. No wonder that 'animal spirits' faded in the face of the follies of politics, state, and governments.

Anti-capitalism

While Soviet Communism took a clear anti-capitalist stance, National Socialism was likewise anti-capitalist albeit in a more disguised form. The difference between Soviet Communism and National Socialism is that the Soviet version had international aspirations and wanted to implant a world communism, National Socialism represents the national version of socialism.

Permanent foes of capitalism are protectionism and interventionism. Interventionism justifies its activity as a way to improve capitalism while protectionism claims to protect the citizens against foreign competition. All four anti-capitalist forces are children of World War I.

After the neoclassical economic theory had amended the errors of classical economics in the 1870s, especially in value theory, a modern economic theory had emerged at the turn of the century. This new monetary theory identified the banking system as the origin of economic fluctuations. If there is an oversupply of money that pushes the monetary interest rate below its natural level, the economy experiences an artificial boom that will end in a bust.

The natural interest rate reflects the time preference in society, which determines savings and investment. Saving means to forego current consumption to get a higher level of consumption in the future. For the economy to grow, savings must become investment and turn into capital. If, however, the central bank, together with the commercial banks under its authority, expand the money supply and lowers the monetary interest rate, the economic agents take the increased money supply for actual savings when in fact the original time preference has not changed or has even deteriorated.

For the individual company, it looks as if there were more savings available than there are. A low-interest rate deceives about the state of scarcity in the economy and insinuates that it would be possible to realize longer-term and more costly investment projects. Yet when authentic savings have remained at the same level as before, the new projects, which the cheap money had induced, confront a lack of available resources and must be abandoned even before they get completed. The demand of the consumers remains at the former level and may speed up with the pace of the fall of the interest rate. Consequently, demand for investment is rising in tandem with the demand for consumer goods, while both demands clash in the face of insufficient real funds.

The spending for investment and consumption are in conflict as they wrestle for the scarce production resources. The increase in money combined with low-interest rates pushes economic activity beyond the normal utilization of the capacity and creates a false boom. At the onset, prices may not yet rise, and the price-wage spiral may not yet have begun if the wage-level persists. Yet the more the economic activity grows into a boom and moves to the limits of production, the more bottlenecks arise in the labor and capital markets and prices rise, first for capital goods, and then for the consumer goods.

The crisis, which follows the boom, reveals that the investments during the expansion phase were bad investments that do not yield the expected returns. The outlook for their profitability came from the erroneous calculation, which took the monetary variables for real and confounded more money with an increase of authentic savings. A correction requires liquidating the failed projects and the return to normalcy as fast as possible. If this happens, the crisis is solvable and may be short. Yet when government intervenes in favor of 'keeping the boom going', the adaptation does not take place. Failing to cure the wrong investment now lead to even more malinvestments and the costs will be higher when the next crisis comes.

During the process of abandoning the bad investment projects, unemployment rises, demand falls and liquidity contracts. Business must struggle with overcapacities. The profit outlook deteriorates, and some companies must go bankrupt. Financial problems emerge, and creditors lose their assets. Consequently, the offer of credit shrinks. The expansion becomes a contraction and price inflation turns into deflation. It seems as if there were a 'lack of aggregate demand' when in fact correcting the wrong investment projects takes place. While Keynes interpreted the fall of the propensity to invest and to consume as a psychological deficiency, this condition, in fact, is the rational consequence of the economic situation that came because of the policies of the government and the central bank.

In the perspective of the Austrian theory of the business cycle of the neoclassical economic theory, not the recession needs correction, but the recession corrects the false boom. The problem is not the recession, which is the healing process; the problem is the wrong boom because of the expansive monetary and fiscal policies, which the nation's central bank and the government have fabricated.

Backgrounder: Survey of Business Cycle Models

Business cycle models fall into three categories: models, which see the cycle inherent to a capitalist economy, models, which claim external factors cause the business cycle, and those models, which say government policies are the main cause of the business cycle.

The Marxist, Keynesian and Post-Keynesian theories fall into the categories of endogenous models, while for the New Keynesians, for Schumpeter, and for the Real Business Cycle models, the causes for the business cycle lie outside of the market economy and affect the economy in the form of external shocks.

The third group of policy-induced models blames economic policy as the cause of economic crises. Into this group fall the monetarist, the neoclassical, and the Austrian models of the business cycle.

Typology of business cycle models

Endogenous	Exogoneous	Policy-induced
Marxist	New Keynesian	Neo-classical
Keynesian	Schumpeterian	Monetarist
Post-Keynesian	Real Business Cycle	Austrian

A. Endogenous Models

The Marxist, Keynesian, and Post-Keynesian models postulate that the causes for the business cycle are inherent to the capitalist economy. Consequently, the remedy must be the abolishment of the capitalist system (Marxian theory) or the management of capitalism through macroeconomic policies (Keynesian theory) or by comprehensive regulation (Post-Keynesian theory).

The Marxist crisis model

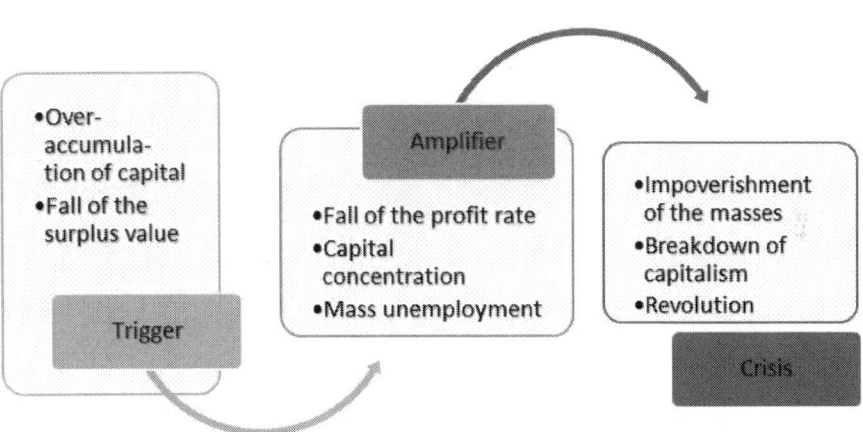

The Marxist theory of economic crises holds that capitalism brings about its own downfall because capitalist competition leads to the over-accumulation of capital and thus to the fall of the relative share of labor. According to the theory of Marx, the so-called 'exploitation rate' is equal to extracting 'surplus value' from the labor force. The profit rate shrinks with the relative share of labor in the production process.

According to the Marxian model, the decline of the surplus value leads to a fall in the profit rate. The concentration of capital increases and mass unemployment follows. Mass impoverishment prepares the collapse of capitalism. The socialist revolution puts an end to capitalism.

Contrary to the Marxian prognosis neither mass impoverishment nor the breakdown of capitalism have occurred. On the contrary. The freer the capitalism, the more technical progress has happened, and productivity increases. With higher labor productivity came rising income. The greatest beneficiaries of capitalism have been the members of the so-called working class, and they know it – different from their self-proclaimed leaders who either by intentions or intellectual deficiency propagate impoverishment and alienation to preach their gospel of revolution.

Keynesianism

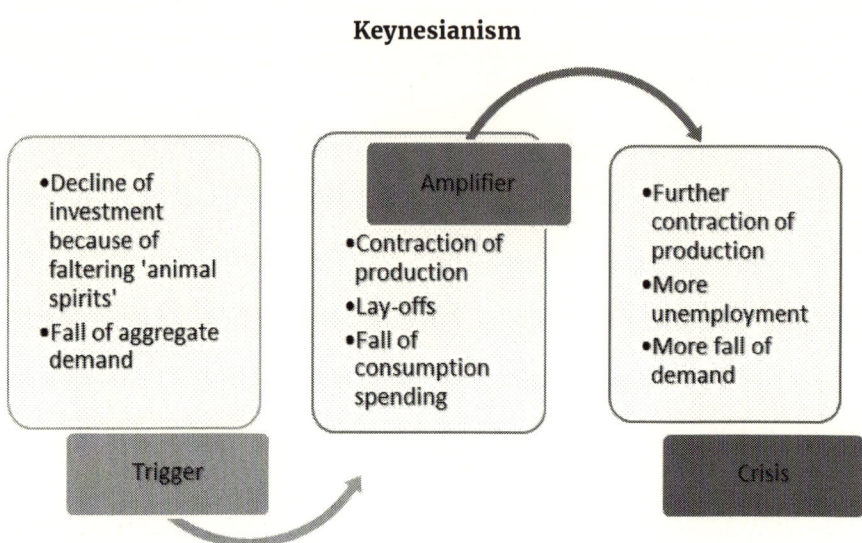

The Keynesian economic theory suffers from the omission that it does not explain the origin of the fall of aggregate demand. This theory makes use of the psychological hypothesis of a breakdown of the entrepreneurial drive ('animal spirit'). The Keynesian model depicts a vicious cycle where declining investment leads to layoffs and the rising unemployment provokes a further decline in production. In the Keynesian model, there is no return to full employment other than through state intervention in the form of more government spending.

Post-Keynesianism

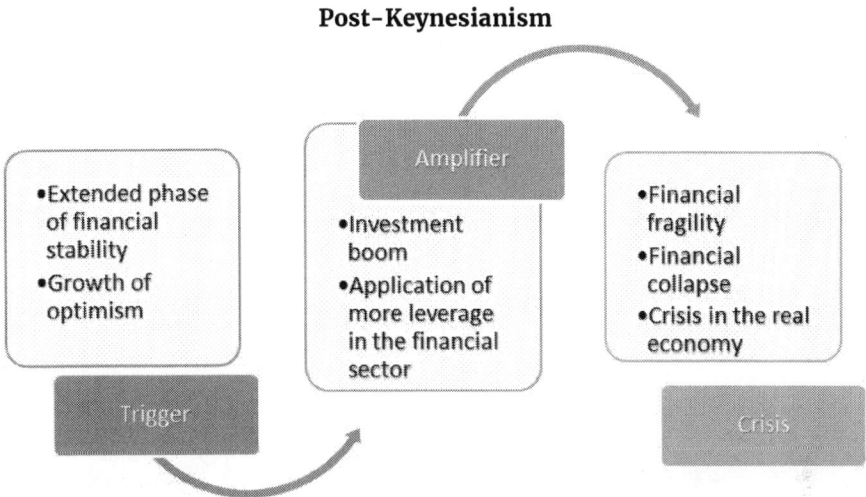

The post-Keynesian model of the economic crisis is 'endogenous' in the sense that this theory assumes that the downturn emerges from the financial system itself. Prolonged periods of stability lead to over-optimism. Rational exuberance makes it easier to get financing for investment. Stability turns into a boom. Problematic investment projects get financing. Applying financial leverage increases. Based on a narrowing capital base, more credit comes into existence. The financial system becomes fragile, and small shocks can trigger a contraction of the financial markets that will spread across the financial sector into the real economy.

The Post-Keynesian theory of the business cycle represents a poor tentative to solve the gap of Keynes' theory as to the causes of the fall of aggregate demand.

B. Exogenous Models

For the models in this group, the business cycle results from exogenous shocks. The economic actors react to these shocks, making that the economic activity speeds up or decelerates. It makes no sense to intervene in this adaptation process. Macroeconomic policy should concentrate on making the economic apparatus more flexible and take care of stabilizing the expectation, such as by a monetary policy of inflation-targeting.

New Keynesians

Trigger
- External shock hits the economy
- Costs rise

Amplifier
- Prices increase
- Production shrinks
- Lay-offs

Crisis
- Combination of recession (stagnation) and price inflation lead to stagflation

The model of New Keynesianism has been the preferred monetary policy model by the central banks since the 1980s.

The starting point of the economic cycle according to this model are positive and negative external shocks. A negative shock – such as the oil price hike of 1973 – leads to rising costs and prices and to a fall of production. The combination of stagnation and inflation push the economy into 'stagflation'.

The monetary policy rule of the New Keynesians recommends that instead of practicing fiscal policy, economic policy should focus on strengthening the supply side of the economy and increase its flexibility, particularly of the labor market. It is the purpose of monetary policy to maintain price stability and to align its measures with a pre-determined and published inflation target to stabilize expectations.

Schumpeter's business cycle model

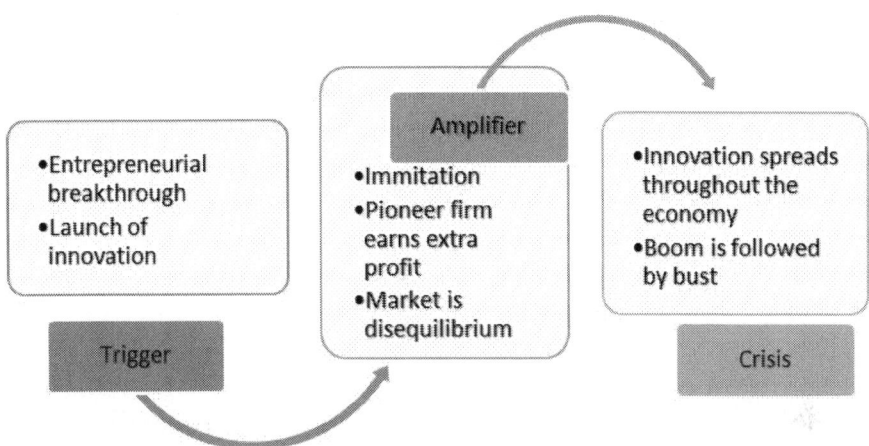

Joseph Alois Schumpeter (1883-1950) worked hard to attain his goal of developing a concise business cycle model. For this purpose, he studied to come up with a consistent framework. Yet he failed. The findings in his two-volume "Business Cycles. A Theoretical, Historical, and Statistical Analysis of the Capitalist Process", first published in 1939, show that the material is too heterogeneous to allow for a consistent model. From Schumpeter's efforts, only sketches of a theory have survived – most of it summarized in his late masterpiece 'Capitalism, Socialism, and Democracy' (first published in 1942).

According to Schumpeter, 'creative destruction' is the mark of modern capitalism and its motor is the innovative entrepreneur. Innovations disrupt existing equilibria and the innovative entrepreneur earns extra profits as long as he can hold on to a monopoly. Revolutionary innovations lead to new industries and the economy enters a long expansion.

When the innovative impetus peters out, the economy slows down, and capitalism experiences a crisis until a new cycle of innovation begins.

Real Business Cycle Theory

```
┌─────────────────────┐      ┌─────────────────────┐      ┌─────────────────────┐
│ • External random   │      │     Amplifier       │      │ • Propogation -     │
│   shocks            │      │ • Rational choice   │      │   spread of the     │
│ • Process of        │      │   as to             │      │   adaptation process│
│   adaptation by     │      │   consumption,      │      │   throughout the    │
│   economic agents   │      │   savings,          │      │   economy           │
│      Trigger        │      │   investment,       │      │                     │
│                     │      │   prices, work and  │      │       Crisis        │
└─────────────────────┘      │   leisure           │      └─────────────────────┘
                             └─────────────────────┘
```

The real business cycle theory considers economic fluctuations as the result of a rational adaptation process to external shocks. The changes in macroeconomic variables, including demand and labor supply, are because of the choices of rational economic operators.

Statistical-econometric studies show that the model captures a large part of the economic fluctuations, mainly the small-scale fluctuations. The model does not explain how the major cyclical upswing and the severe economic crises occur. The Austrian theory of the economic cycle answers these questions.

C. Policy-induced business cycle models

The policy-induced business cycle models claim the capitalist economic system works well if left to itself.

Government intervention produces dis-coordination and misallocation and moves the economy away from equilibrium.

The policy recommendation of these approaches includes abstention from interventionism, to install a rule-based monetary policy, and practice Laissez-faire.

Neoclassical crisis model

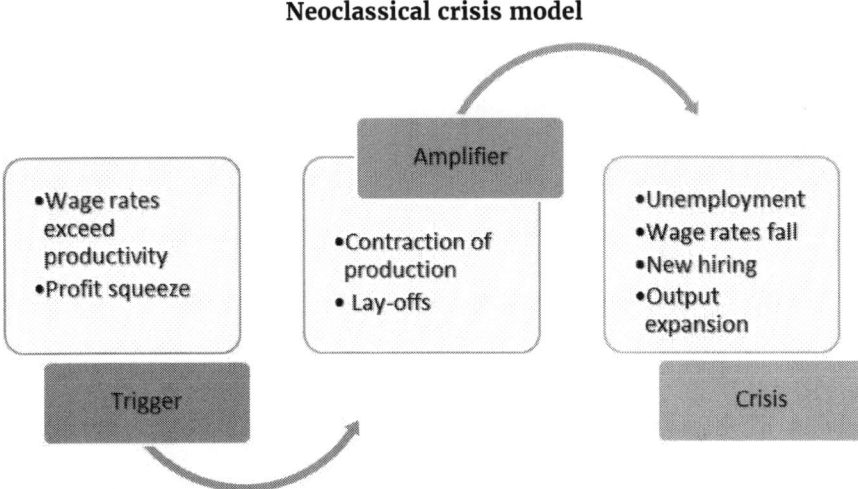

In contrast to the Keynesian model, the trigger of the crisis in the neoclassical model is well founded by economic theory.

By means of trade union power or by other types of pressure (also by the state), wage claims, which exceed the productivity level occur. Firms dismiss workers to compensate for the reduction in profits and to ward off future losses.

Increased unemployment leads to a reduction in consumption expenditures and provokes further restrictions on production, which lead to further redundancies and more unemployment and production restrictions.

In as much as wage rates adapt to the marginal productivity of labor, the economy stabilizes, and an upturn begins.

The causes of distortive wage rates include minimum wage policy, trade union power, labor laws, and other kinds of regulations such as licensing.

Monetarism

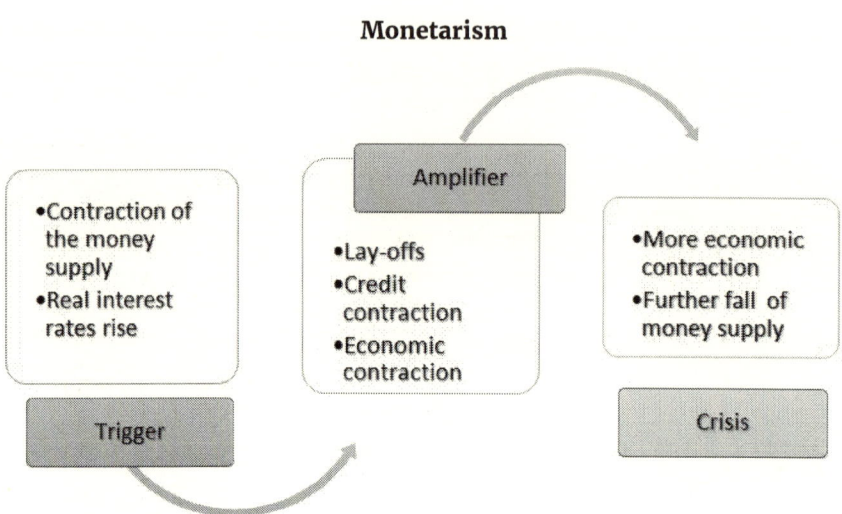

Monetarists regard money as the crucial variable of the economic cycle. The monetarist model postulates that a fall in the money supply is the trigger for an economic crisis while an expanding money supply beyond production causes price inflation. The monetarists conclude that monetary policy must take care of a stable monetary growth. They propose a constant annual increase of the money supply a little more than the rate of productivity increases. Monetarism was the leading paradigm of the central banks in the late 1970s before the New Keynesianism model replaced it.

The monetarist model postulates that an increase of the money supply beyond production causes price inflation.

Austrian Business Cycle Theory

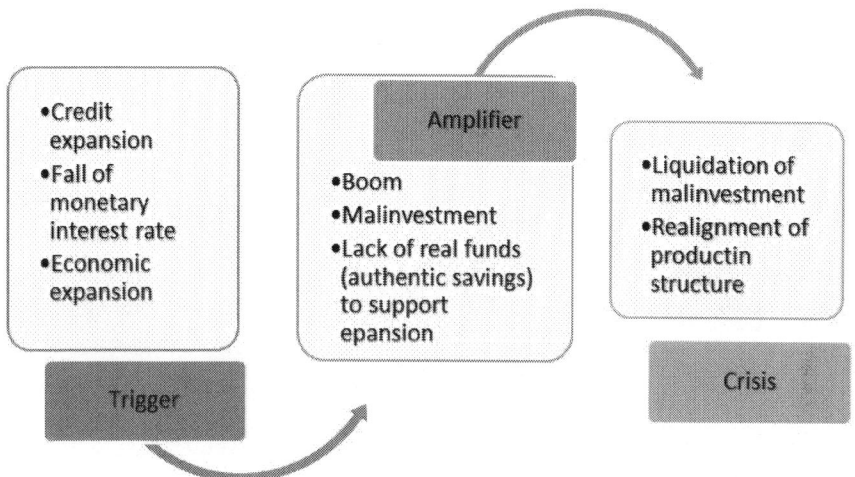

For the Austrians, the crisis comes through the boom which results from excessive credit expansion.

When the monetary interest rate falls below the natural interest rate due to a credit expansion, economic activity receives an artificial boost, and the economy overheats.

The credit expansion produces a false boom when authentic savings have not risen under the prerequisites of funding the prolongation of the investment projects. Because the new investments lack profitability, investors must abandon their projects. The economy falls into recession, and unemployment rises.

For the Austrians, the crisis is a process of healing since it leads to liquidate the unsustainable investment projects. The losses, real and potential, that come with the crisis, incentivize the efforts to adjust the existing capital arrangements and to move forward to establishing a new production structure.

The supporters of the Austrian school demand to abolish the central bank through either a return to the gold standard or by introducing private banking. There is also the model that calls for freezing the quantity of central bank money in combined with repealing the legal tender laws and thus leave the monetary system to the market forces.

Capital-based business cycle

```
                    Amplifier
•Expansion of                           •Lack of funds to
 macroeconomic      •Capital             maintain
 liquidity           investments rise    extended capital
•Demand increases    despite insufficient structure leads to
                     authentic savings   reduction of
                                         output

   Trigger                                Crisis
```

The model of the 'capital-based credit cycle' represents an advanced model of the Austrian School by integrating a few of the analytical approaches from other economic theories into the Austrian model.

The capital-based credit cycle model rests on the equation of exchange whereby the amount of money multiplied by the velocity of circulation is identical to the product of price level and the output. Each of these two parts of the quantity equation is, in turn, identical to the nominal social product.

The large swings in economic activity (not mere fluctuations, as modeled by the theory of the real cycle) come from the macroeconomic liquidity, which comprises the product of the money base, the money multiplier, and the velocity of circulation.

The rising investment volume collides with an insufficient level of savings, which means that the investments lack economic viability.

No Crisis Without a Boom

The Austrian school of economics claims both the Keynesian and the monetarist models of the Great Depression do not explain the global crises of the 1930s. According to the Austrian approach, the forced boom of the 1920s led to the Great Depression. In his book 'America's Great Depression' (1963), Murray Rothbard (1926-1995) shows how the interventionist economic policy first sped up and extended the boom and then deepened and prolonged the depression.

In contrast to the Keynesian doctrine, the Austrian school has a complete theory of the business cycle. It does not look only at the recession but sees the economic crisis as the result of the faulty economic policy of the boom. In the Austrian perspective, the full economic cycle begins not with the downturn, but with the boom.

The first phase of the cycle is the inflationary expansion triggered by expansive economic policy, with inflation lagging. A time gap opens between the economic expansion and the price inflation, which creates an illusionary Goldilocks economy where everything seems perfect for an economy that is neither too cool nor too hot. Only later, the problem becomes visible when the expansion speeds up and when it leads to a rising price level.

The second phase of the economic cycle consists in an inflationary contraction. While price inflation is on the rise, economic activity is stalling and the economy tips over into recession.

The third phase is a deflationary contraction when the debt overhang from the wrong investments becomes noticeable. The supply and the demand for loans decline; financial institutions collapse. The normal course of the economy would now be that a deflationary expansion follows the deflationary contraction in the fourth phase. Prices are falling, demand is picking up again, and the economy is recovering.

Austrians criticize that an active economic policy would prevent and delay this natural adaptation process. Economic policy lies at the origin of the crisis, and policy errors deepen and extend the crisis. When the central bank tries to fight the downturn with cheap money, it uses the same means that have caused the slump. The false economic policy stands at the start of the crisis when it produces the fake economic boom, and false economic policy is the culprit of the prolongation of the crisis when macroeconomic management tries to extend the expansion by additional monetary injections and a policy of low-interest rates.

Phases of an idealized business cycle

An expansive monetary and fiscal policy leads to speeding up the economic activity. If the stimulated demand exceeds real output, inflation will occur. The government's demand policy provokes bad investments, which provokes an inflationary boom that turns into a deflationary contraction.

If there are no interventions, a deflationary expansion follows the deflationary contraction, and the economy moves back to its growth trend. Yet when an expansive monetary and fiscal policy intervenes again, a new and stronger artificial boom follows. These cycles may go on for several rounds. With each one stimulus exacerbating the productions structure while at the surface, in terms of output and employment, it may seem that the economy is doing fine.

It is rare that governments will allow the economy to deflate. On the contrary: by policies of cheap money and higher government expenditures, the authorities attempt to stop the contraction. Such policies prolong and deepen the crisis.

In the end, the cycle will break down anyhow and leave the economy in a state that is much weaker than it would be if government intervention had never happened.

The depth of the crisis depends on the extent and duration of the false boom that preceded the bust. If the boom goes on, it is almost impossible to identify the false projects. The dimensions of the wrong investments become discernible when liquidity contracts and the funding becomes scarce. The boom ends in a credit crisis, which restrains the banks from granting new loans because they face credit losses. Investors reduce their credit demand because they fear their own solvency. In this phase, deflationary tendencies set in as overall demand falls.

When governments and central banks try to combat deflation, they worsen the misallocation. What matters is to liquidate bad investments and not to push them further ahead with cheap money. By prolonging the boom, the economic structure suffers more distortions. As long as there is a gap between the funding needs to maintain the capital structure and the available savings volume, an expansive policy in the name of economic stability achieves the opposite effect. Instead of ending the recession, the measures prolong and deepen the downturn.

More pivotal than aggregate demand is whether information and incentives work at the micro level on the markets. This is all the easier, the more flexible and adaptable business and labor is. The more that there is a free market economy, where competition prevails, and prices result from the unhampered interplay between supply and demand on competitive markets, the fewer downturns will happen and the quicker an economy will move out from a slump if one happens. The macro problems diagnosed by Keynes have microeconomic causes. To correct the macro problems - such as mass unemployment and inflation - the causes of the problems must disappear at the level of the markets.

Strong economic fluctuations are a symptom of a lack of a well-functioning coordination in the economy. An economic policy, which does not recognize this, deepens the disorder. Instead of stabilizing the economy and to promote economic growth, the maladjustment intensifies because of the extra demand. The economy enters the vicious cycle when failed economic stimulus measures lead to more wrong economic policies.

Bad policy re-enforcement

The worse the economy gets, the more the tendency rises that the government will pursue bad policies. Wrong economic policy measures in response to a poor economic situation worsen the economy. The spiral that failed policies beget more failed policy is in full swing.

Bad policy cycles

- Bad economic policies lead to stagnation and to recession
- Crisis incites more ruinous economic policy measures
- Economic crisis deepens – Worse economic policy measures follow

Once this spiral from bad to worse comes into existence, it is difficult to bring it to a halt. The economy gets out of balance and the policy, instead of restoring the equilibrium, reinforces the imbalances. The worse the economy, the more controversial becomes the public discussion and the phonier get the proposals.

A cascade of bad economic policies leads the path to a secular decline as it has happened to many a once prosperous country. No nation is immune to this risk.

What Happened in the Great Depression?

Policy-makers claim that laissez-faire capitalism is the culprit of a depression and that an active economic policy is necessary for the economy to recover. This claim, however, does neither hold for the present nor does it explain what happened in the Great Depression. What pushed the U.S. economy into a depression was an active economic policy in the boom years and what kept the American economy so long in the slump was the active interventionist policy after the bust.

Under the presidency of President Herbert Hoover from 1929 to 1933, policy interventionism flourished. Measures designed to prevent a fall in wages hindered the natural course of a rapid economic recovery. Instead of ending the recession, Hoover's interventionism deepened the downturn. President Franklin Delano Roosevelt, who ruled from 1933 until his death in 1945, continued thereafter not only the interventionist policy of Hoover but worsened the policies. Roosevelt practiced ruthless interventionism, which included wage and price controls. He did not hesitate to preach crude anti-capitalism to gain popularity among the masses by cheap and perfidious rhetoric. In the presidential election campaign in 1932, Franklin Delano Roosevelt presented himself as the new Messiah who would save America. Yet he did not know what to do when he took over the presidency in 1933. In practice, his plan comprised pointless hyperactivity. Just doing something was more important to him than doing the right thing. One can only wonder about his policies when one considers with which audacity the government under Roosevelt violated elementary laws of the market.

Roosevelt's New Deal

In order to support the prices of agricultural products, for example, Roosevelt forced the pig farmers to slaughter millions of piglets. To prop-up prices for cotton, the farmers had to plow under land. Despite high unemployment, the government prevented lower wage rates. Under Roosevelt's leadership, America came under the spell of a wave of anti-capitalism, and a wild rhetoric damned entrepreneurs and bankers by blaming them for the depression. Roosevelt established a network of informants who monitored prices and wages and spied on the American population. The Great Depression happened not because of the free market economy and it lasted so long because of state interventions. Not a savage capitalism caused the great crisis, but the duration and depth of the depression resulted from government interventions that first aimed at keeping the boom going beyond its natural cycle in the 1920s and then hampered the recovery with more interventionism after the downturn in the 1930s.

It is not surprising that private investment remained weak under this interventionist onslaught and that the American economy did not emerge from the depression. Until the end of the Roosevelt government in 1945, the American private sector remained in paralysis because of the fear that still more encroachments on the property rights were in the making.

New Deal Policies

Year		Description
1933	EBA	Emergency Banking Act March 9
"	CCC	Civilian Conservation Corps
"	TVA	Tennessee Valley Authority
"	AAA	Agricultural Adjustment Administration
"	FERA	Federal Emergency Relief Administration
"	NRA	National Recovery Administration
"	FDIC	Federal Deposit Insurance
	PWA	Public Works Administration
"	CWA	Civil Works Administration
"	FAA	Federal Aviation Administration
"	HOLC	Home Owners Loan Corporation
1934	FCC	Farm Credit Administration
	GRA	Gold Reserve Act - confiscation of private gold possessions
"	FHA	Federal Housing Administration
"	NLRB	National Labor Relations Board (Wagner Act)
"	SEC	Securities Exchange Commission
1935	NYA	National Youth Administration
"	SSA	Social Security Administration
"	FSA	Farm Security Administration
"	DRS	Drought Relief Service
"	RA	Resettlement Administration
1938	USHA	United States Housing Authority
1939	FWA	Federal Works Agency

International aspects of the Great Depression

The 'Great Depression' was not a failure of capitalism, but the result of the First World War, the Treaty of Versailles, and the departure from international free trade.

While the tariffs restricted the free movement of goods, the international financial transfers turned into an illusory carousel. The US banks extended loans to the Europeans, particularly to Germany, to pay for the war and reparation debts, which allowed them to pay their war debts against the United States.

A fatal blow came with the Smoot Hawley Tariff Act, which increased tariffs on about 20,000 items. The carousel which got its spin from the lending spree in the 1920s turned into a contracting spiral in the 1930s.

When the protectionist measures of the 'Smoot-Hawley Tariff Act' gained legal force in on June 17, 1930, the march on the road to the catastrophe speeded up when the world trade collapsed in the following years.

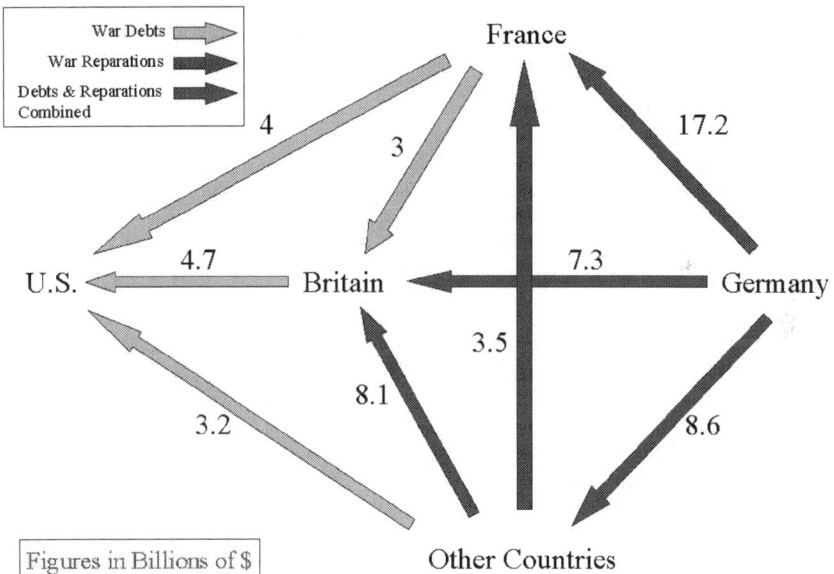

Source: http://spider.georgetowncollege.edu/htallant/courses/shared/dawes.gif

***

The American President Franklin Delano Roosevelt has not led the country out of the depression, but his economic policy has caused that the Great Depression would last so long and run so deep. Unemployment fell only when the

U.S.-government drafted millions of young men into the military service. The economic expansion in the war years came not from the economy as a productive place but in the form of a war economy.

In a full assault on capitalism, Roosevelt broke the spirit of the investors and brought down the drive of the entrepreneurs to increase production capacities, accumulate capital and maintain a well-functioning capital structure.

The capital base of the American economy eroded because capitalists refrained from providing the financial resources during the production process out of fear that the product will not receive its final payment at the end of the production line, when consumers pay, while the workers earn their wages during the time of production.

The International Financial System Under the Dawes Plan and Young Plan 1924-30

Source: http://ndynes.weebly.com/the-dawes-plan-1924--the-young-plan-1929.html

Insufficient savings illuminates the role of the capitalists to preserve the capital structure in contrast with the economic theory, which declares that economic crises result from a lack of demand. Not insufficient demand provokes the economic crisis, but excessive lending is the original cause why investors launch projects, which find no buyers as the consumers do not have the funds to pay. The problem of the crisis is not that there is a lack of effective demand, but that there are too few buyers because they can no longer afford certain goods.

A false boom begins when the excessive supply of liquidity pushes the interest rate below the natural rate. This constellation triggers a clash between the companies that will expand the capital stock and the consumers who do not save more but want to maintain their consumption level. When the goods reach the end of the production process and become final products ready for consumption, demand is deficient because consumers have already spent their funds for consumption and are unable to buy the additional amount. Then, the economy suffers from forced savings because voluntary abstention from consumption did not take place with a sufficient amount during the boom.

The low-interest rate set a false signal about the actual availability of investments. The capital structure expanded without corresponding savings. As a consequence, capital accumulation becomes a malinvestment. During the boom, no warning signal appeared because of the ample supply of credit and the low-interest rate. In the bust, the available funds are not large enough to maintain the extended production structure.

***
Kindleberger Spiral

As the "Kindleberger Spiral" chart shows, the protectionist measured pushed the world economy into contraction. The monthly decline in world trade from 2998 million to 992 million gold dollars based on the total world imports from January 1929 to March 1933. When the stock market crashed in October 1929, the American money lending ended, and the carousel stopped. The American financial crisis became a global economic contraction.

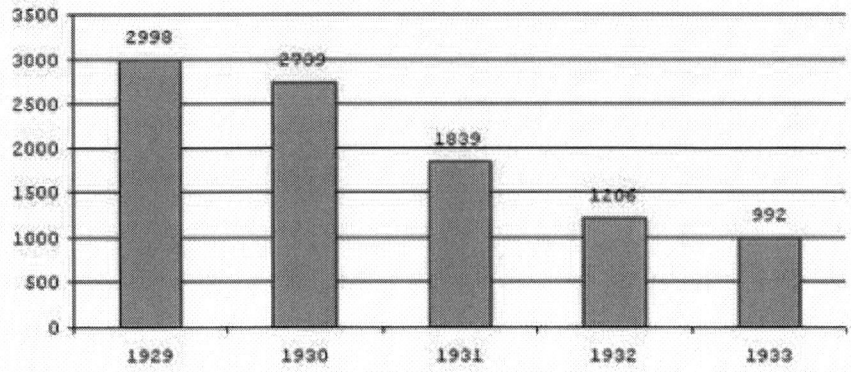

Contraction of world trade, 1929-1933

Contraction of world trade, 1929-1933
(Kindleberger Spiral)

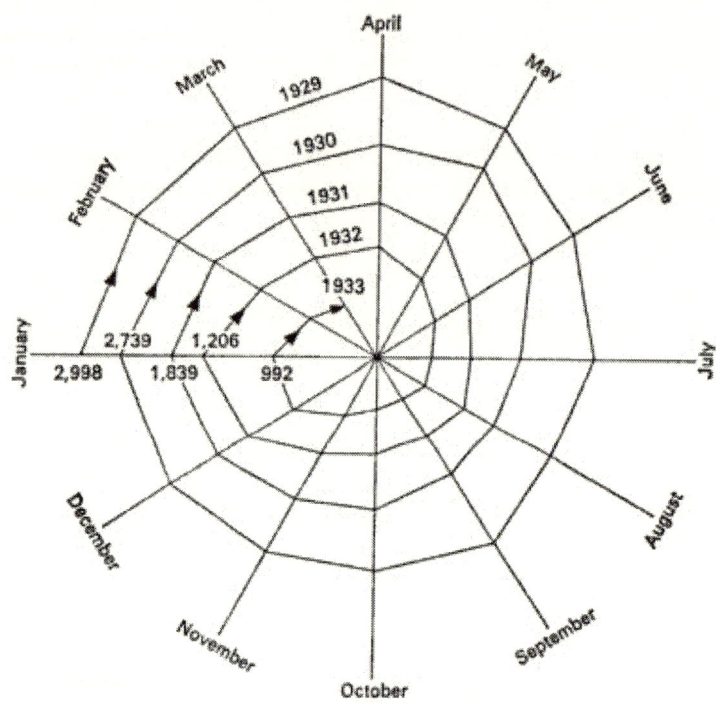

(in millions of dollars)

Source: Charles P. Kindleberger: "The World in Depression" (Anniversary Edition 2013)

According to Murray Rothbard (1926-1995), who elaborated the Austrian economic theory of the business cycle in his book on America's Great Depression (1963), the U.S. government applied a full catalog of false economic policy measures in the 1930s. These interventionist measures explain the depth and the length of the economic catastrophe of the Great Depression. Instead of remedying the mistakes that had developed during the boom of the twenties, the Hoover government, and then Roosevelt, took a whole series of actions that had the opposite effect of correcting the wrong investment and of liberating the forces to readjust the economy.

Roosevelt's economic policy implanted measures that delayed liquidating the malinvestments. High wage rates, promoted by the support that the Roosevelt administration gave to the trade unions, led to the high unemployment. The American Presidents Hoover and Roosevelt thus exacerbated the errors of the American central bank.

The American economy did not recover with Roosevelt's New Deal but that it took until 1939 when war preparations began that gross domestic product came back to the level of 1929. After the sharp deflation until 1932, the price level rose again until 1937 after which a second deflationary phase took place in 1938 and 1939.

Unemployment persisted throughout the decade. In 1940 the unemployment rate was still 15% - three times the rate of 1929 (St. Louis Federal Reserve Bank https://www.stlouisfed.org/the-great-depression/curriculum/lesson-plans)

Different from the United States, the recovery in Germany was swift.

The German economy - economic growth and inflation, 1926-1939
Annual change rates of the gross national income in prices of 1936 (columns) and Gross national product deflator (line)

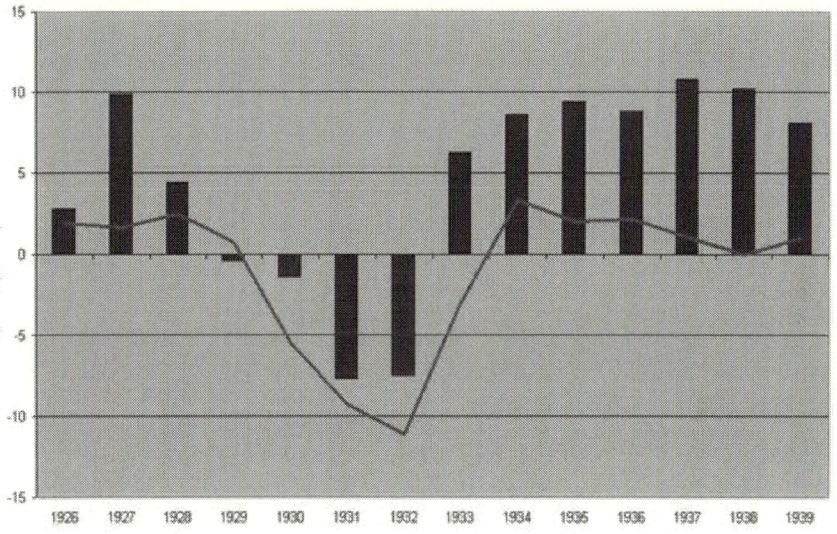

Source: Statistisches Bundesamt für Wirtschaft und Statistik 3/2009: https://www.destatis.de/DE/Publikationen/WirtschaftStatistik/Monatsausgaben/WistaMaerz09.pdf?__blob=publicationFile

The reason for that performance was that the Nazi government, which came to power in January 1933, applied dictatorial Keynesianism, which meant that it combined government spending with price and wage controls. The Nazi government could achieve this economic policy feat because it put trade union leaders and the leaders of the socialist and communist parties into preventive custody and – while keeping property rights as legal formality intact- degraded businessmen to agents of the government's central planning authority.

A tragic element comes into play when one considers that the German economy would have also recovered without the policy measures that the Nazis applied after they took over the government. Different from what had happened in the United States, the German governments in the years from 1929 until the end of 1932 had adopted a policy of austerity and forced liquidation. When Hitler took power in January 1933, he could use the plans that laid in the desks of the former governments and start his public works program such as the nation-wide construction of autobahns. The indications are very ample that a strong recovery in Germany would have come about also without the Keynesian-style public spending program.

Economic indicators of the Great Depression

The following data set shows that the economy did not recover with Roosevelt's New Deal but that it took until 1939 when war preparations began that gross domestic product came back to the level of 1929. Unemployment persisted throughout the decade. In 1940 the unemployment rate was still 15% - three times the rate of 1929.

After the sharp deflation until 1932, the price level rose again until 1937 after which a second deflationary phase took place in 1938 and 1939.

Dimension of the Great Depression
Change (in percent) of economic indicators 1929 to 1932

	USA	UK	France	Germany
Industrial production	- 46	- 23	- 24	-41
Wholesale prices	- 32	- 33	- 34	-29
Foreign trade	- 70	- 60	- 54	- 61
Unemployment	+ 607	+ 129	+ 214	+ 232

Source: Jerome Blum, Rondo Cameron, Thomas G. Barnes, The European World: A History (2nd edition, 1970) p. 885

Backgrounder: United States. Great Depression – Data 1929-1940
Real Gross Domestic Product, 1929-1940

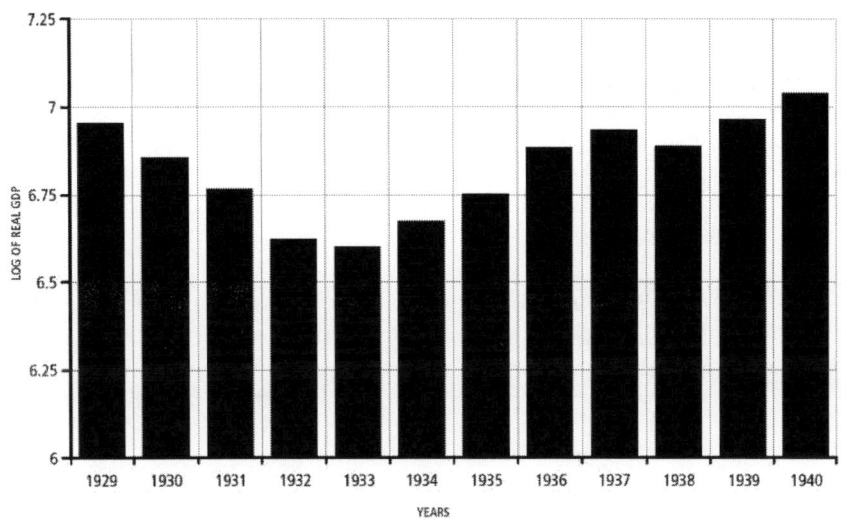

Civilian Unemployment Rate, 1929-1940

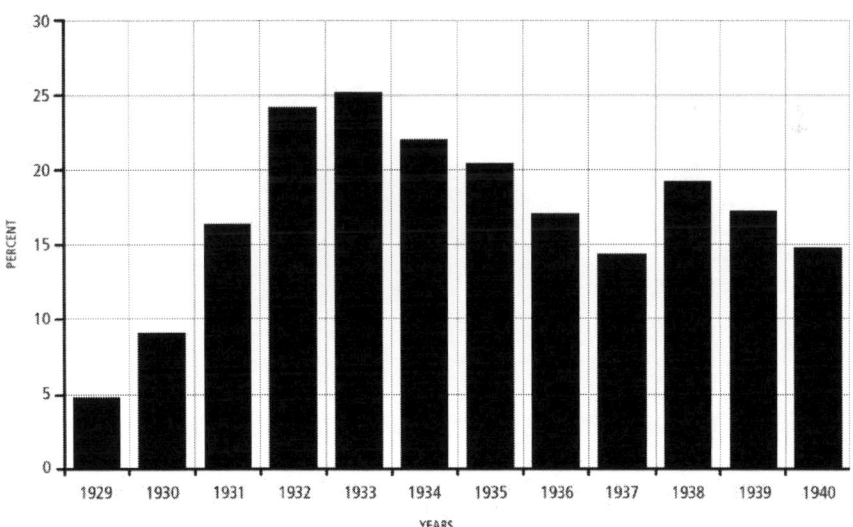

Consumer Price Index, 1929-1940

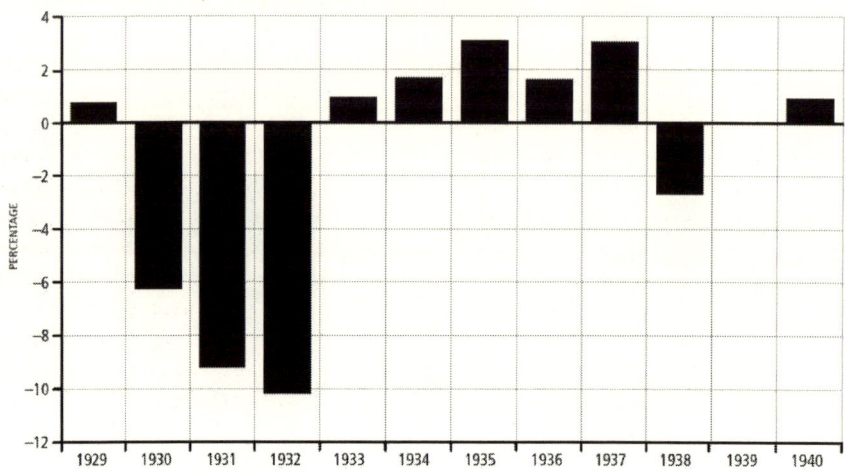

https://www.stlouisfed.org/the-great-depression/curriculum/lesson-plans

**

Lessons to Learn

Governments – irrespective of their brand - like to intervene because they like to do things, which other people pay for. Governments like to combat even a small recession because it gives them reasons to launch new spending programs. The financial markets welcome any boosts of liquidity. Economic policy is interventionism. 'Stabilization' policy is the major arena of political hyperactivism. Yet these policies of stimuli undermine the economy's performance. If the state interferes with the price system by means of maximum and minimum prices, subsidies, and other assistance programs or prohibitions - and last but not least by taxation, the interest rate, money supply, and government expenditure policies – government activities distort the original market signals. There will be mistakes in the allocation of resources and competition will lose its effectiveness. Governments claim to cure the ailment that they themselves are culpable of having brought about.

Rothbard on the Great Depression

In the perspective of Austrian Economics, the recession is the phase to cure the excesses of the boom. Therefore, any attempt to postpone the cure deepens the ailment. The best government can do to promote a swift recovery is to cut taxes and to curtail public spending.

As Murray Rothbard showed, the governments of both Hoover and Roosevelt prolonged the Depression because they delayed getting rid of bad investment projects. Instead of speeding up the liquidation, they tried to reflate the economy, instead of letting deflation run its course, they tried to reflate the economy. They kept wage rates high instead of letting wages and prices fall.

Rothbard's 'Do's and 'Don'ts' in a depression

Do:	Don't:
accelerate liquidation	delay liquidation
let deflation run its course	reflate the economy
augment savings	stimulate consumption
reduce government spending	increase government spending
cut taxes	raise taxes
let wage rates fall	stabilize wage rates

Source: Murray Rothbard: America's Great Depression (1963)

***

The main cause of the crises in the financial and monetary markets is a national monetary and fiscal policy when they inject liquidity in excess into the economy. There is no bust without a boom, and the boom results from excessive credit expansion. The attempt to combat the contraction exacerbates the maladjustment. A new credit expansion suppresses the price signals and aggravates the imbalances. The crises deepen, and the stagnation becomes longer. The stabilization measures and the guarantees of a bailout that central banks, governments, and the international monetary organizations pronounce, undermine the risk perception of the financial market operators. Attempts to control the financial markets according to inflation targets and to reduce the private liability of the market actors promote excessive risk-taking. It comes as no surprise that markets expose abrupt, strong price fluctuations.

Regulations produce hidden costs while the so-called 'market failures' seem obvious. Thus, in a superficial populist assessment, each intervention appears as justified, whereas, in fact, regulations bring more harm than good. Each state administrative regulation suffers from the problem of the interventionist dynamics, whereupon the affected action causes side effects, which then calls for renewed control as it is also the case with economic policy.

Backgrounder: Misery Index

The so-called 'misery index' was set up in the 1960s for the two prominent economic policy objectives of a stable price-level and low unemployment. At first, this index comprised the sum of the two variables inflation rate plus unemployment rate.

Steve Hanke has expanded the original 'misery index', which Robert Barro had extended by the interest rate, with the annual rate of growth of per capita income as a percentage to deduct from the sum of the other variables.

Hanke's comprehensive 'misery index' comprises the components inflation rate plus the unemployment rate (percentage of job seekers in the labor force) plus the interest rate (long-term nominal interest rate of government bonds) minus growth (real growth of per capita income).

Components of the misery index

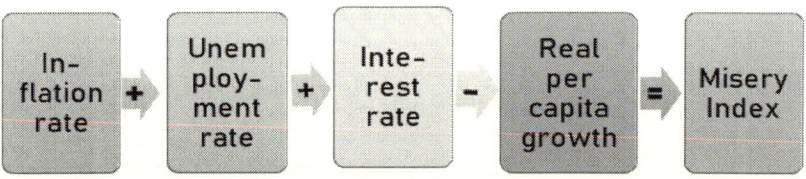

The misery index correlates with a country's overall crime rate and with the extent of corruption. The higher the misery index, the more there is criminality, and the more pronounced is the corruption. The causality goes from the latter to the first: the more corrupt a country, the higher the misery.

While more interventionism brings more corruption, there is a distinctly negative correlation between a high misery index and a high degree of freedom of the economy (according to the Heritage Economic Freedom Index). The worse the ranking of a country as to its misery index, the worse is the position of this country at the World Bank ranking of 'Doing Business', the annual survey of the extent to which governments (mainly through taxation and regulation) promote or hinder the free economic activity.

As a rule, one can say a country suffers less from macroeconomic misery the freer its economy. So why do people not choose freedom even if they could? Why do people choose their own misery? Why do democratic governments not promote the prosperity of the population but bring misery upon the people? This question leads to the theory of public choice, according to which politicians are not interested in the welfare of the people but pursue their own personal interests. For politicians, politics (sold as the public good) is not the aim but serves as a means to gain personal benefits. The politician's own well-being depends on the power which he executes. The men and women in government will gain more power by producing misery, including war, than by creating peace and prosperity. Historians do not give the title 'the Great' to the peacemakers but prefer the mass murderers. Who can blame the people for calling for the devil when they are desperate? If a politician wants to become an eminent leader of the state, he must create unrest and help create misery. This provides the opportunity that the politician can present himself as the savior of the country from the misery he himself together with his clique has produced from the beginning. So long as there is politics, as we know it, there will be no economic policy, which will serve the people. The decisive step on the way to keeping the misery index low is diminishing the role of politics and the power of the government. By abolishing politics, the state would shrink. This would make the way free for the prosperity of all and the end of misery.

***

Inflation and deflation differ from market-induced price changes if they result from monetary factors. With market-induced price changes, prices rise according to the interaction of supply and demand for this good. Prices will drop if the supply rises, and prices will rise, when demand increases, and vice versa. This is the universal law of the market. A functioning market system requires that rising and falling prices inform about the relative scarcity of a good. It is different with inflation and deflation. Here the price level rises and falls because there is more money or less money circulating in the economy. Inflation and deflation are not indicators of the relative scarcity of goods but concern the relationship between money supply and goods. Correctly defined, 'inflation' is a rising stock of money. When the money supply grows faster than the supply of goods, prices will rise.

Demand for a good comes through money. If the amount of money in an economy does not change, production corresponds to the national income. Only the relative price structure changes. Without inflation and deflation, the economic identity between the origin (production) and the use (consumption and investment) of the national product remains valid. Yet if the credit growth exceeds savings, there is additional money in the economy.

When economic actors use the excess money to demand goods and services, they will offset the relationship between the supply of the goods and their demand. Although production has not increased in line with the money in circulation, more funds are available to feed demand. There is more spending than real production. As a result, not only individual prices rise, but the price level. The relative price structure changes because the structure of production suffers from price inflation and from bad investments. Because of a monetary expansion, not only the general price level rises but also the price structure changes. Thus, a monetary inflation lays the groundwork for the next crisis.

With a proper evaluation of creditworthiness, the loan-capacity that a commercial bank grants to a company corresponds to the company's capacity of production in terms of the profit it can earn. With a consumer credit, creditworthiness depends on the debtor's ability to generate income. These factors determine the respective credit limit. This rule, however, does not apply to the loan to governments, which – at least for debt in the country's national currency - is unlimited because the state is the owner of the monetary monopoly. If the government is indebted in its own currency, it cannot go bankrupt because it can service its public debt by money creation without an end. Instead of default, which would bankrupt the state, governments opt for inflation, which bankrupts the whole country.

When there is no foreign borrowing, a government budget deficit absorbs at least a part of the savings surplus in the private sector. If the domestic savings volume is insufficient, or if the government's credit surpasses the private savings surplus, inflation will occur. The resulting loss of purchasing power of the private sector provokes forced savings later. Inflation comes into play when the demand for credit-financed demand surpasses production. Such an extra demand cannot come from the private sector because the creditors impose restrictions on the indebtedness of companies and consumers. Persistent excess credit is the privilege of governments.

The price level can also rise if the production shrinks and if the money supply remains unchanged. Here, the monetary surplus is not the result of the increased money supply, but of the relative decline in production. Hyperinflation results from two main causes – credit expansion combined with a falling production.

There are two kinds of deflation. The benign deflation results from productivity gains. It makes the products overall cheaper. If the money supply remains the same, the price level will drop. As a result, the purchasing power grows, and real wages rise. Such beneficial deflation occurs in small steps so that the economic entities can adjust their expectations and the market interest rate corresponds to the natural rate.

> **The German Hyperinflation**
>
> The German hyperinflation has its roots in the First World War when Germany left the gold standard in 1914 to finance the war expenditures through banknotes.
>
> In 1919, there was the first inflationary burst with a subsequent temporary stabilization of the level from 1920 to 1921.
>
> From 1921 on, the inflation rate of wholesale prices moved ahead. There was a collapse of confidence in the monetary value after the Allies presented the reparation claims to the German Reich on May 5, 1921, in the 'London Ultimatum'.
>
> In 1922/23, hyperinflation took off, after the confidence in the government's ability to service the debts accumulated during the war waned in the face of the reparations requirements of the Treaty of Versailles.
>
> The graph above shows that until 1919, the increase in the monetary base preceded the wholesale prices. Thereafter, when the inflation expectations became more manifest, the increase in the price level precedes the money supply.

A malignant deflation comes from a collapse of the financial markets. When an abrupt monetary contraction happens, there is no time to adjust the terms of the standing credit relationships. Credit-related defaults will emerge along with imbalances between the amount of old debt and the current market values of the assets. A sudden shrinkage of liquidity, combined with deflation, leads to an unexpected rise in the real interest rate, which makes existing investment projects unprofitable and speeds up the close of new investments.

The over-expansion of liquidity in the financial markets precedes the collapse of the financial markets. Expansive monetary policy, which floats the financial markets with liquidity, is the real reason for the financial markets to collapse. Deflation in the sense of a monetary contraction results from the preceding expansion of the money supply. After the central banks first make the mistake of inflating the money, they aggravate the contraction in the phase of the crisis, when they try to prevent the swift adjustment of the markets to the new circumstances by renewed credit injection.

Backgrounder: The Economics of Inflation and Deflation

Inflation and deflation are monetary phenomena that result from the growth of money in relation to the growth of production. When monetary demand falls short of the increase of the production of goods, the price level will fall. The price level will rise when monetary demand exceeds the supply of goods.

Deflation is not malicious. Deflation is benign when it results from an excess of goods production while the money supply has remained constant. This benign deflation differs from the malignant deflation, which occurs when a monetary contraction happens while production stagnates.

Of the two kinds of inflation, monetary price inflation occurs when an excess of liquidity meets a stagnant production. Goods-related inflation happens when there is a fall of the goods production while the money supply remains constant. This inflation happens during or in the aftermath of war and other catastrophes.

Waves of inflation and deflation remained in a narrow range before the US-central bank began its operations. The great price rises came after the inception of the US Federal Reserve System that assumed its function in January 1914.

The waves of inflation show up because of the wars: the independence war of 1775/76, the War of 1812, and the civil war 1861-65, the First (1914-18) and the Second World War (1939-1945) with the US entry in 1942.

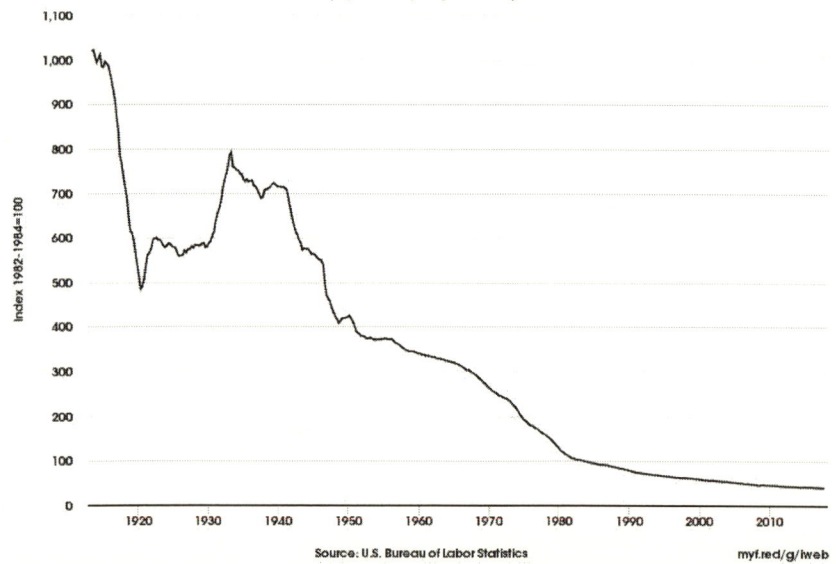

Purchasing Power of the U.S.-dollar, 1913-2017
(1982-1984 = 100)

Source: U.S. Bureau of Labor Statistics

The diagram depicts the phases of deflation after the War of 1812 until the Civil War and the 50 years of deflation after the War of Secession up to the First World War.

In 1913, the American central bank came into existence and began its work in 1914. After a period of relative stability after the end of the Second World War, a long phase of inflation started in 1970 that continues with short interruptions to this day.

As a consequence of the price inflation over the past hundred years, the U.S. dollar has lost 97 percent of its purchasing power.

The Sorrows of Central Banking

On September 30, 1979, at the depth of global stagflation, the former US central bank chairman Arthur Burns gave a speech at the meeting of the International Monetary Fund in Belgrade (at that time the capital of Yugoslavia) entitled "The Anguish of Central Banking". In his talk, Burns offered little hope for an escape from secular inflation. Current worldwide philosophical and political trends, Burns diagnosed, will continue to undermine wealth creation and curb incentives. These modern trends produce permanent budget deficits and have introduced a strong inflationary bias into the economy.

Reviewing central bank action in the 1960s and 1970s, Burns stated in his speech that '(v)iewed in the abstract, the Federal Reserve System had the power to abort the inflation at its incipient stage 15 years ago or at any later point, and it has the power to end it today. At any time within that period, it could have restricted money supply and created sufficient strains in the financial and industrial markets to terminate inflation with little delay. It did not do so because the Federal Reserve was itself caught up in the philosophic and political currents that were transforming American life and culture'.

It is the same in other parts of the world where almost all the modern central banks are functioning in a similar political environment and thus behave in the same fashion leading to the 'anguish of central banking'.

Central banks are not only hostages of their political environment, but they are also technically and intellectually not up to their job. Central bankers make errors and encounter surprises at practically every stage of the process of making monetary policy; misinterpretations of statistics abound, and there is also no reliable scientific guide for central banking: 'Monetary theory is a controversial area. It does not provide central bankers with decision rules that are at once firm and dependable'.

Burns ended his speech by saying: 'My conclusion that it is illusory to expect central banks to put an end to the inflation that now afflicts the industrial democracies does not mean that central banks are incapable of stabilizing actions; it simply means that their practical capacity for curbing an inflation that is continually driven by political forces is very limited'. Central bankers still meet surprises 'at practically every stage' of the process of making monetary policy, and modern interventionist academic monetary theory has contributed very little 'to provide central bankers with decision rules that are at once firm and dependable'.

What has changed since then? Are central banks up to their job by now? Have they learned how to interpret statistics correctly? Have they gained true independence? A superficial answer may say yes: Paul Volcker came in, put on the brakes, wiped out inflationary expectations, and opened the door to decades of stability. And then came Alan Greenspan to carry on and brought modern central banking to its epitome.

In a more realistic assessment, however, the answer must be that not much has changed. Inflation seems to be more benign nowadays, but it is a harsh twist of words to say that there is price stability when, since 1980, the official price index has more than doubled.

While the 1950s saw a phase of relative stability, the United States entered a long inflationary phase. In the late 1960s and experienced an inflationary surge in the late 1970s. Since 1980, the U.S. consumer price index has more than doubled from 100 to around 250 index points in 2017.

***

Seen in a long-term historical perspective, we still live in an inflationary age, and the turning point for the United States can be nailed down as the year 1914 when the US central bank began its operations. It took only a few years for the Federal Reserve System to create an inflationary boom ushering the way to the Great Depression later. The 'stability' of the 1930s and 1940s came about with the Great Depression and the price controls during the war. After that episode, prices began their steady rise, first slowly, then, since the late 1960s, more sped up. In a long-term perspective, the slowing of the price increases in the 1980s and 1990s is nothing more than a slight flattening of the curve.

Since abandoning the gold standard, we entrust two of the central prices in the economy—the interest rate and the exchange rate—to governmental bureaucrats for them to manipulate. Presumably, they know what they are doing, and they are doing it for the best of the country. Facts speak against this presumption.

After a short period of curbing the money supply in 1979 and 1980—more by accident in its impact than by deliberate design—the US central bank has turned again into a debt creation machine that inundates households, companies, government and the globe with dollars. Foreign central banks and governments are eager to join in, each of them pursuing to gain a temporary advantage by targeting the United States as the willing absorber of exports. What is going on now is global debt creation at an unprecedented pace, and the major players in this game are central banks under the obvious or implicit tutelage of their governments.

***

Registered inflation rates have been more subdued since the 1980s, but inflation is not 'dead', and the inflationary age has not yet ended, and it will not end as long as central banks and governments hold the lever to create money more or less at will. No less so when Burns practiced central banking, the interventionist policies of today's central banks lack a reliable basis in monetary theory, diagnostic errors abound, and the inherent inflationary bias of central banks is still alive. While until 2018 inflation was still benign, it may turn malicious again.

It seems an idle game to expect better central bankers or improved analytical tools or—for heaven's sake—more reliable econometric models. The right way to look for the escape is moving toward different institutional settings like that envisioned by Friedrich Hayek under the heading of a 'denationalization of money', by which it is suggested to dissolve the monopolistic structure that characterizes modern central banking.

Ludwig von Mises in "Human Action" put the problem this way: "Credit expansion is the government's foremost tool in their struggle against the market economy. In their hands it is the magic wand designed to conjure away the scarcity of capital goods, to lower the rate of interest or to abolish it altogether, to finance lavish government spending, to expropriate the capitalists, to contrive everlasting booms, and to make everybody prosperous"—with the consequence that such an artificial boom will lead to the bust.

***

Global money creation by central banks, 2008-2017

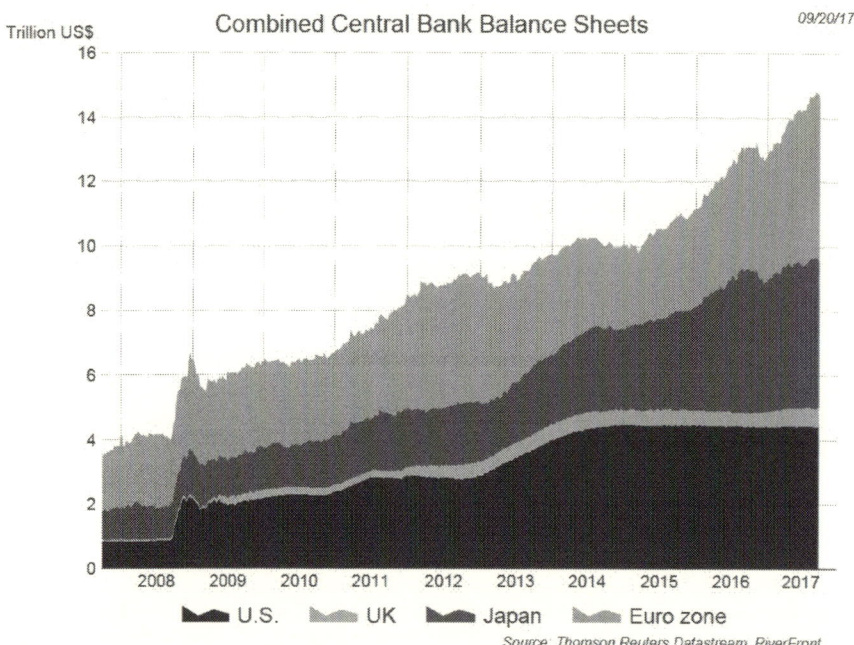

Source: Source: https://www.etftrends.com/end-qe-means-higher-rates-resilient-stock-markets-and-higher-volatility/

In the face of the international financial crisis of 2008, central banks have initiated an unprecedented program of feeding the world economy with liquidity. From less than four trillion US-dollars of central bank money of the four major central banks, this monetary aggregate has risen to over twelve trillion US-dollars.

Modern central banks will, at best, do little other than to 'undernourish' the trend towards inflation—when they are good at their job and helped by some luck. Faced with the choice between putting a serious strain on the financial markets and industry to end inflation or letting the boom go on beyond control, they will opt for the latter. In the current institutional setting, it is the natural tendency of central banks to produce unsustainable booms first and prolong the inevitable slump in the aftermath.

Inflation-targeting

A central bank that pursues an inflation-targeting monetary policy model would raise the policy interest rate (which in the case of the United States is the federal-funds rate) when the current price-inflation rate moves beyond the target. The central bank will reduce the policy interest rate when the inflation rate falls below the predetermined range. Operationally, the inflation rate is the target variable of this approach while the policy interest rate serves as the instrument variable. Different from monetarism, the monetary aggregates play only a secondary or no role at all in the inflation-targeting model.

Inflation targeting is not new. Its basic idea comes from the American economist Irving Fisher (1867–1947). The Fed implemented a rudimentary form of inflation targeting after it became operative in 1914 and practiced a policy of 'stabilizing the price level' in the 1920s, in the decade before the Great Depression.

The 1920s marked a period of rapid accumulation of debt that until 1929 came along with a rise in financial wealth due to a stock-market and a housing boom. The collapse of the stock market, which began on Thursday, October 24, 1929, ushered the American economy into the Great Depression, which lasted over a decade.

During the 1920s, the US monetary authorities were not much concerned with credit expansion because the focus was the 'price level' — a statistical construct that Irving Fisher had promoted. Noticing that the price level was 'stable', the Federal Reserve felt no need to change its course or to become preoccupied with what was going on. The Roaring Twenties were, in fact, exuberant times — albeit not for agriculture. Manufacturing and the related sectors celebrated the new era and most of all this decade was one more heyday for Wall Street after the financial bonanza that World War I had delivered as the great enrichment of the United States.

The focus on price inflation had induced the monetary authorities to ignore credit growth and monetary growth as well as to disregard the productivity gains of the US economy in this period. The Fed felt vindicated for letting the monetary aggregates expand because the price level remained stable. The monetary authorities paid no consideration to the notion that with productivity advances, the price level should fall as it had been when the United States was still on a full gold standard, and thus the quantity of money was constant. In the 1920s, with an almost exclusive focus on the price level, the American central bank did not hold the quantity of money constant, which would have meant deflation, but allowed expanding the money supply because there seemed to be no reason to worry if the price level stayed stable.

When the decline of the price level results from productivity gains, the fall of prices represents a benign deflation, and the central bank should not fight it. When it does, its monetary policy is de facto inflationary albeit prices do not rise. Inflation, correctly defined, means monetary expansion, and this took place in the 1920s.

The boom of the 1920s

From 1919 to 1929, the U.S. economy experienced a period of tremendous productivity gains, both for labor and capital.

While in the decade before, labor productivity rose 1.14 percent per year and in the 1930s the rate was 1.95 percent, it amounted to 5.44 in the 1920s. These high rates of labor productivity gains came with amazing rates for capital productivity, which rose by an annual rate of 4.21 from 1919 to 1929

United States. Labor and capital productivity, 1899-1937
(Average Annual Rates (%) of Labor and Capital Productivity Growth, 1899-1937)

Period	Labor Productivity	Capital Productivity
1899-1909	1.30	- 1.62
1909-1919	1.14	- 1.95
1919-1929	5.44	4.21
1929-1937	1.95	2.38

Source: Devine, Warren D., Jr. "From Shafts to Wires: Historical Perspectives on Electrification." The Journal of Economic History 43 (1983): 347-372, Table 3
https://eh.net/encyclopedia/the-u-s-economy-in-the-1920s/

During the Great American Boom that took off after the recession of 1921, the consumer price index remained stable, rising until 1926 and then falling until the outbreak of the Great Depression, which from the 1930s onwards experienced a malignant deflation. By not letting a benign deflation happen in the 1920s, the U.S.-American central bank provoked a malicious deflation in the 1930s.

In the years before the onset of the Great Depression, there was a massive increase of bank lending from 1923 to 1929, which did not concern the members of the policy-making committee of the Federal Reserve System because they deemed that everything was O.K. as long as the price level remained 'stable'.

According to data of the Federal Reserve System, U.S. bank lending rose from seven billion in 1923 to almost ten billion US dollars in 1929 from where it collapsed during the Great Depression to around five billion US dollars from 1933 to 1936.

What had happened in the 1920s was a wrong response of the monetary policy-makers to the widening divergence between the agricultural and industrial sector of the U.S.-economy. While agriculture fell into depression already after World War I, US industry experienced a monetary-induced boom. On average, the price level appeared steady, although its stability resulted from a leveling out due to a deflationary depression of the agriculture sector and an inflationary boom of the industrial sector. Particularly in phases when the unemployment rate was above the acceptable level, low rates of the consumer price index have served as a justification to bring down interest rates to low levels. In many parts of the world where monetary policy uses an inflation-targeting framework, it has become a rule to ignore the growth of the monetary aggregates and bringing down the interest rate. Inflation targeting has led monetary authorities to ignore not only money and credit growth but also asset prices along with other variables such as the exchange rate.

The latest episode of a mega boom occurred in the 1990s when, as in the 1920s, there was a stock-market bubble combined with a massive increase of indebtedness of consumers for housing and consumption goods. Central bankers did not pay much attention to the money supply and remained sanguine throughout the period that led up to the crisis of 2008. The mantra of monetary policy was that if the price level remained stable and with only moderate price inflation, interest rates could fall as low as they can drop, and the money supply could grow without restraint and get as large as the demand for money seemed to warrant.

There were a series of shocks in the 1990s and in the decade before and after. Yet up to the outbreak of the crisis of 2008, one could overcome the calamities, so it seemed, by bailing out the creditors and expanding the money supply. Inflation targeting entailed a pervasive policy of bailouts and thus laid the basis of a financial culture of moral hazard.

In 2007, financial markets froze, the flow of money in the interbank market came to a sudden standstill. It was as if a cardiac infarct had hit the heart of the financial markets. Albeit shocked, monetary policy-makers showed full confidence that a proper amount of liquidity injection would make the markets move again soon; thus, they believed in their naïve conviction, the economy would recover to full bloom again. Yet doom set in when it became clear that the old recipe didn't work anymore. Despite massive injections of liquidity, markets recovered somewhat, and in 2008 a wave of defaults of financial institutions occurred. In August 2011, the United States came close to bankruptcy when Congress was reluctant to raise the statutory debt limit. Shortly thereafter, the global financial crisis deteriorated into the European sovereign-debt crisis. Greece came close to bankruptcy and contagion hit Spain, Portugal, and Italy.

By early 2012, monetary policy had reached its limits. With interest rates close to zero in the major economies of the world, it was only through gargantuan amounts of liquidity injections that the financial system got propped up. By practicing a 'zero interest rate policy' (ZIRP), by buying assets of dubious quality from financial institutions through its Troubled Assets Relief Program (TARP), and by trying to pump more liquidity into the market through its policy of 'quantitative easing' (QE), an expansion of unprecedented proportions of the Federal Reserve's balance sheet has occurred. The real or imagined assumption that the financial system is on the verge of complete collapse has brought about massive government bailouts and stimulus programs that have resulted in rising fiscal deficits and unsustainable public debt burdens. Deflation has become the ultimate scare of governments and the dreadful nightmare of central bankers.

Bailouts and Stimuli

Under Alan Greenspan's rule at the Fed, the function of the central bank as a bailout institution experienced a golden age. He was the chairman of the Board of Governors of the Federal Reserve System from August 11, 1987, to January 31, 2006. Greenspan served almost two decades at the helm of the US central bank. He has left his mark like few before him.

As head of the Federal Reserve System, Alan Greenspan earned the highest esteem from the central bank's main clientele: the financial community. The adoration that the chairman received from the financial market operators and from the various governments by which he was re-appointed five times has come from the expectation he would stand ready as their bailout man.

It would be a vain endeavor to research modern mainstream economic textbooks to pin down the economic theory which guided Alan Greenspan's monetary policy. The chairman of the Board of Governors of the Federal Reserve System has let it be known that most of these models are irrelevant. The monetary school he represents is the traditional model of modern central banking. It is 'bailout economics'. It is an economic doctrine, which says whenever and for whatever reason the financial markets or the government should get into financial trouble, the central bank will bail them out by providing abundant liquidity.

As soon as the asset markets—and later the banks and the public in general—had learned about the bailout doctrine there was no stopping. Under such a cover, financial investing no longer needed prudent calculation, even more so as the chairman's visionary portraits of an imaginary world of abundance promised an oasis of prosperity on American soil. With the bailout guarantee verbally and practically in place and the vision of a new economic dawn firmly put forth, the shackles of fear that had restrained excessive debt accumulation in the past have been shed.

After the stock market crash of 1987 and Greenspan's bailout of the financial system, financial market operators have operated under a quasi-official charter, which says the central bank will protect its major actors from the risk of bankruptcy. Consequently, the reasoning emerged that when one succeeds in this game, one will reap high profits and gain market share, yet if one should lose, the authorities will save you, anyway. Under the protective shield provided by the central bank, the US financial system has become tilted toward relentless expansion. In a process that began as early as 1987, Greenspan's monetary policy has transformed the American economy toward the predominance of the financial sector and secured a bonanza for the financial market operators.

After just two months in office as Fed chairman, Greenspan set the norm when facing the stock market crash of October 19th, 1987, when he declared: 'The Federal Reserve, consistent with its responsibilities as the nation's central banker, affirmed today its readiness to serve as a source of liquidity to support the economic and financial system.'

Greenspan's prime monetary policy rule has remained the same since then. It is a rule which he formulated when referring to the response to the stock market debacle in 1987: 'It wasn't a question of whether you would open up the taps or not open up the taps. It was merely how you would do it, not if.' (quoted in David B. Sicilia and Jeffrey L. Cruikshank: The Greenspan Effect. Words that Move the World's Markets. New York et al.: McGraw-Hill, 2000, p. 11)

As Greenspan explained in his testimony before the U.S. Senate Committee on Banking, Housing, and Urban Affairs, on February 2, 1988, it is the 'crucial role' of the central bank to respond to 'episodes of acute financial distress'.

The chairman has lived up to that promise. Greenspan fulfilled his mission in the wake of the 1987 stock market debacle. He made sure that the government could finance two wars in the Middle East. Alan Greenspan performed his bailout job by saving the creditors of the Long-Term Capital Management (LTCM) hedge fund in 1998, he did it in the face of an expected Y2K liquidity squeeze at the turn of the millennium, and the chairman did it by fabricating the housing bubble that led up to the financial crisis of 2008.

What Greenspan has accomplished is in line with the original intentions of the Act that established the Federal Reserve System in 1913. This legislation passed under the pretense that protecting the major players of the financial industry from default means saving the system. By making the financial system more 'elastic', governments received the prospect that from now on golden fetters no longer would curb their encroachment.

By acting as the 'lender of the last resort' to guarantee 'financial system stability', central banks implant a safety net for their debt-ridden governments and for the big players in the financial industry. With the adage of 'too big to fail', a financial institution gets a free ticket to accumulate private wealth with almost no risk. Providing unlimited money supply establishes an incentive for the governments to expand without end and for the financial intermediaries to opt for asset expansion at the cost of prudence. As bailout institutions with the promise of unlimited liquidity, it the central banks themselves that lay the groundwork for 'financial distress' to emerge—not just as 'episodes', but that makes the modern financial system fragile.

There were recessions and changes of money values before the ascendance of modern central banking, but these were short and mild and most of the time they resulted from external factors such as bad harvests and wars. With modern central banking, hyperinflations and great depressions emerged. With all anchors severed that would curb debt expansion, modern central banks create the permanent boom, but while aiming at this illusory goal, they prepare the conditions that erupt as big slumps and hyperinflations.

Modern central banks function as the prime instigators of unsustainable booms. While imposing as the navigators, they act as the prime instigators of the instability they are to fight. Greenspan has played this game in all its virtuosity.

With a masterful hand, the chairman wielded the levers of monetary stimuli. He has given the financial markets what they want: a lender of the last resort that one can bank on. When one debt-driven boom had turned into a bust, he made sure that another one would begin.

The key to the power of a central bank is maintaining the illusion that fiduciary money is wealth. It is a con game, and in this respect, there can be few doubts that Alan Greenspan has been a master at this game. Under his rule, the arcane machinery of the central bank has turned into a fountain of cheap money, which has inundated the globe. This policy of repeated bailouts and providing unlimited funding for government expansion in the face of a decreasing savings rate and a shrinking productive sector is the way toward an economic Armageddon. By functioning as bailout agents, central banks use the power to create money as a power to destroy.

If one thought, however, that Alan Greenspan was peculiar in the respect, soon learned that his successor, Ben Bernanke, would open the floodgates of money even more. While under Greenspan, central bank money increased from 220 billion to 825 billion U.S.-dollars. Under the chairmanship of Ben Bernanke (chairman from 2006 to 2014), the U.S. monetary base rose from this level to over four trillion.

The Pitfalls of Macroeconomic Policy-Making

Macroeconomic policy pursues four major policy aims: a stable price level, steady economic growth, high employment and the maintenance of the country's international payment ability.

In its modern version, macroeconomic policy focuses on the price level in terms of 'inflation targeting'. By this policy, the monetary authorities announce an inflation goal such as an increase in the consumer price index of more than zero and less than two percent as it is explicitly the case with the European Central Bank (ECB). Different from the ECB, the U.S. law obliges the American central bank to include a low unemployment and low-interest rates as its goals. As spelled out by the U.S. Congress that the monetary policy should pursue 'maximum employment', 'stable prices', and 'moderate long-term interest rates', these goals are contradictory and beyond the reach of a central bank. Furthermore, Congress stipulated five areas for the central bank with mutually exclusive objectives such as conducting the nation's monetary policy, helping maintain the stability of the financial system, supervising and regulating financial institutions, fostering payment and settlement system safety and efficiency, and promoting consumer protection and community development. (see: Board of Governors of the Federal Reserve System. Purposes and Functions).

As to macroeconomic policy in the narrow sense, the policymakers have three tools at their disposal: Fiscal policy, monetary policy, and exchange rate, and trade policy (tariffs). There is a discrepancy between the complexity of the goals and the scope of the instruments. Such a construct is to fail by necessity.

Main objectives of macroeconomic policy

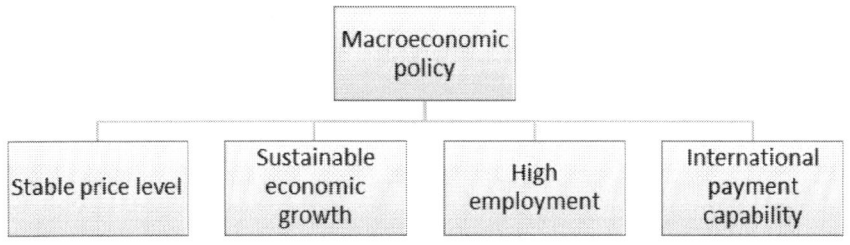

Because only a small part of government spending is discretionary, fiscal policy is useless as an effective policy instrument. On an operational level, fiscal policy plays a role only as an emergency instrument as it was the case when

President George Bush launched a stimulus package of 105 billion US-dollars in February 2008, and his successor Barack Obama followed suit with an additional package of 787 billion US-dollars in February 2009.

The problem with fiscal policy is that debt-financed expenditures increase public debt and therefore the effect will backfire. Tax policy is too cumbersome as an effective policy instrument. This leaves macroeconomic policy with only monetary policy. While monetarism favored the quantity of money, the emphasis has shifted back to interest rate policy after the problems of practical monetarism became apparent.

John Taylor (1946*), while working at the U.S. Treasury in the early 1990s, has captured this shift in a formula which became popular as the so-called 'Taylor Rule'. This rule assumes that the monetary policy follows an explicit inflation target and that the long-run real growth rate of the economy follows a natural path that is determined by factors outside of the control of the monetary policy – such as capital accumulation, education, and innovation. Taylor also postulates a natural real rate of interest. The formula stipulates quantitatively by how much the policy interest rate must change when the actual inflation rate deviates from the target rate and the actual economic performance deviates from the economy's potential. The modified Taylor Rule substitutes the natural unemployment rate for the indicator of the capacity utilization.

Main instruments of macroeconomic policy

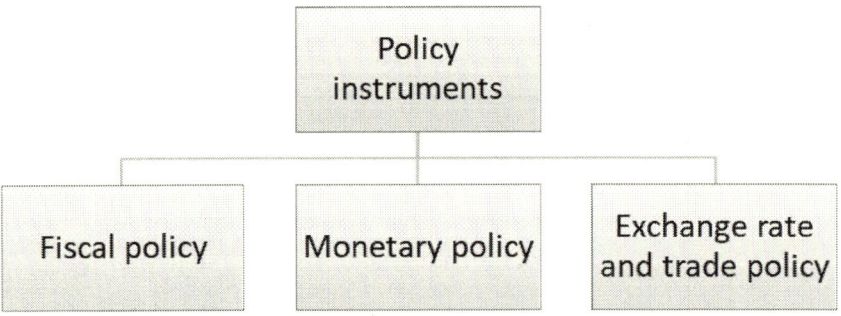

Things get complicated when international economic aspects come into play. The interest rate is not neutral as to the exchange rate and the exchange rate affects the price of imports and exports and feeds back on the price level and on the import and export sectors of the economy.

Even this cursory glance at the intricacies of economic policy should reveal that managing the economy is a mission impossible. Any ambition of improving economic policy to make it more effective will fail. The path to go is not the technical improvement but to abandon policy altogether and let the markets do the job. Not the vile attempt to improve economic policy is the way but less intervention. Instead of more activism, economic policy should find ways to promote such institutions that foster the autoregulation of the markets. The freer the markets, the less market intervention, the better is the economic performance and the less there is the need for economic policy.

The Value of Money

There is a sharp distinction to make between the changes of the price level and of the changes in relative prices. The price level changes because of the changes of the relation between the amount of money and the volume of goods in an economy. Relative prices change because of changes in demand and supply in the market. One must distinguish between relative prices and the price level. The price level results from the relation between the amount of money and the supply of goods. In contrast, relative prices reflect demand and supply for specific goods.

If the money supply is constant, the increase of the supply of goods would bring about a benevolent deflation. Yet often the monetary authorities expand the money supply more than the economy can produce goods and the result is the general price inflation. Relative prices are indispensable to guide the behavior of consumers and investors. Price inflation is a constant risk factor for entrepreneurial decision-making because price inflation affects both the level and the structure of prices. Because the price level affects relative prices, misallocations happen in the economy.

In order that prices fulfill their function as instruments of information and incentive, they must be flexible and responsive to changes in demand and supply. The concept of 'price stability' is a misplaced concept for this type of price changes. When the central bank speaks of 'price stability', the term does not refer to relative prices, but to the price level. The aim of the central bank is to keep the price index stable following the problematic concepts put forth by Irving Fisher and its current operation as inflation targeting.

The published 'consumer price index' and the other price indices represent a statistical hodgepodge. One can concoct such statistics in many ways, and one can do this without violating common statistical rules. 'Hedonic calculation', which attempts to take account of changes in quality, is just one example.

But despite all the statistical tricks that are being invented and applied, the core issue remains unresolved: what is being measured by 'purchasing power' and what is the value of money—other than subjective and individualistic—upon which one could base the calculation?

Along with the statistics related to the figures about the domestic and national product, the price index is one of the most unreliable, most deceiving, and most abused statistical economic numbers. This is the case as the price index provides the basis for a series of other statistical indicators as it serves as a deflator and enters economic growth and productivity figures.

These macroeconomic numbers suffer from the illusion that one could observe the properties of an object—called 'the economy'—and could them measure. Whatever finesse will one applies to their calculation to make these statistics more accurate, it cannot do away with their basic invalidity that results from the impossibility of getting a fixed standard of measurement for value.

Attempts to measure the economy as if it were an object has its origin in government planning. Treating the economy as a whole becomes necessary for socialist central planners and for the economy of a country at war. Price indices and other statistics about macroeconomic variables are needed when some center with decision-making power wants to control the economy. Both 'fathers' of modern national income accounting, John Richard Nicholas Stone (Nobel Prize in economics 1984) and Simon Kuznets (Nobel Prize in economics in 1971) served in war planning offices where they developed and refined the concepts. Stone worked in the British government's War Cabinet Secretariat and Kuznets was Associate Director of the Bureau of Planning and Statistics and Director of Research at the Planning Committee of the U.S. War Production Board.

The results of these planning endeavors are well known; but while socialist-type total economic planning is off the screen even for many devout socialists, central monetary planning by manipulating money, credit, and the exchange rate ranks still high on the public agenda. Central banking is the last refuge for those under the spell of the pretense of knowledge.

Fixing their eyes on the so-called 'price stability' or following the now fashionable inflation targeting schemes, central bankers are not just after a movable target but one that is more symbolic than real. This way, they neglect the inflationary expansion of money and debt.

As with individual prices, the prices of groups of goods and services rise and fall. There are always inflationary and deflationary areas in an economy. When small aggregate price movements occur or when opposing forces are at work, the price index renders no valuable signal. If, however, strong tendencies in one or the other direction of the general price level are underway, and when this turns up in the price index, it is too late for the central banks to catch up.

Price indexes average out the extremes; they are unable to signal the subtler price movements and they leave out relevant items such as asset prices. This way, it is not only the public that is being deceived, the central banks themselves are falling victim to their calculations.

One need not resort to more extreme examples like how to measure today's musical output and compare it in a quality-adjusted form to that of the past. The measurement problem appears also when trying to give a percentage change in the output of software programs or administrative and engineering activities, not to speak of health, legal services, and education. The statisticians may answer that the 'measurement' of output is derived from expenditures. However, money prices measure nothing. Relative prices count as these inform the economic actor about the exchange ratios on the market.

As Ludwig von Mises (Human Action, 1998, p. 218) explained, '(t)he money equivalents as used in acting and in economic calculation are money prices, i.e., exchange ratios between money and other goods and services. The prices are not measured in money; they consist in money. Prices are either prices of the past or expected prices of the future. A price is necessarily a historical fact either of the past of the future. There is nothing in prices which permits one to liken them to the measurement of physical and chemical phenomena'.

Adding up all sales or compounding all assets in an economy eliminates the meaning of prices. This kind of aggregation differs from what a company or a person does when calculating profits or the relative wealth position. When a person adds up the prices of his various assets, he gets a number about his current wealth relative to the price universe he selects as his point of reference. For a company, it is sales, costs, and profits that matter, and for that sound business, one needs accounting. Neither for personal matters nor for business decisions GDP figures are necessary. Kuznets knew of the shortcomings of national income accounting, as his intention was to get a measure of overall well-being that would also include housework and leisure, a project that was doomed from the beginning in the eyes of the U.S. Department of Commerce when he assisted with the design of the national income statistics.

One can determine the weight of the overall output of some certain types of steel, but one cannot, in the same way, come to a reasonable result by measuring in one number the aggregate production of automobiles, of refrigerators, or of personal computers – not to speak about the problems one confronts when one tries to add up the output of teachers, nurses, songwriters or software programmers together with apples and oranges.

A company can count its production in terms of units of model M or T. If the company wants a figure for the total, it must resort to sales. Before sales, one can only enumerate how many units of each specific item category are in stock, and only by assuming that the company's products will catch certain prices, is it possible to calculate the expected monetary amount – but not the 'value' of production.

Mises explained it this way: 'Prices are always money prices, and costs cannot be taken into account in economic calculation if not expressed in terms of money. If one does not resort to terms of money, costs are expressed in complex quantities of diverse goods and services to be expended for the procurement of a product' (Mises, op. cit., p. 39). Likewise, one cannot add up values or valuations. 'One can add up prices expressed in terms of money, but not scales of preference.' (p. 332).

In a private market economy, the aims of economic activity are diverse and represent individual and subjective valuations. For an economy that is to serve multiple private needs, the measuring economic growth makes little sense, if any at all. One may add up nationwide the various monetary prices of the sold goods and services, but besides the aggregation of the monetary values of diverse items – what is the true and reliable informational value of this exercise?

Each good and service has a different value for each user. There is no common standard of value available. This is even more so the case when new products and new kinds of services come to the market. Valuations are not only heterogeneous among persons but also differ for the same person according to the specific circumstances. Human beings have different needs and desires in different situations, and they experience changes in taste. Preferences themselves are experimental devices.

Quality is not an attribute inherent to the things, but it is a valuation, which is imputed to the goods and services by the economic actor. Economic action aims to improve one's condition and what makes up an amelioration is subject to continuous change. Therefore, there is no objective way to measure overall wealth in aggregate form without coarse distortions and without violating the basic principles of economic valuation. Market prices 'are not expressive of equivalence, but of a divergence in the valuation of the two exchanging partners', and the value attached to the unit of supply is subject to the law of diminishing marginal utility (Mises, op. cit., p. 699).

It is the prerequisite of measurement that there must be identifiable objects in the measuring space and that a corresponding fixed standard of measuring unit can be applied. One can measure barrels of oil at the well and determine how much the production has grown or not. Measurement is per definition quantitative. In technical terms, one may measure quality by using technical standards such as that of crude oil, for example, based on its sulfur content, but this measurement is also quantitative. In this case, the measurement shows the usefulness of that good in terms of a criterion that comes from an industrial process. In the 1970s, it was the American economist Paul Samuelson (who was one of the first receivers of the fake Swedish Central Bank "Nobel Prize" in economic 'for his scientific work through which he has developed static and dynamic economic theory and contributed to raising the level of analysis in economic science') who never got tired to present a graph in the various editions of his popular economics textbook that showed that it would be just a matter of a few decades until the Soviet Union would take over the United States in 'production'. Of course, Soviet production figures were a humbug. Serious estimation, based on personal insight into the Soviet economy, come to a fraction of the official statistics (see Yuri Maltsev: https://fee.org/articles/soviet-economic-reforms-an-inside-perspective/).

Another phenomenon as reported by Richard Vedder (Statistical Malfeasance and Interpreting Economic Phenomena, in: The Review of Austrian Economics. Vol. 10, No. 2, 1997, pp. 77-89) refers to the calculated output decline for the U.S. economy in 1946. As later available statistics revealed, this contraction amounted to a fall of 20.6 percent of the gross domestic product. But this decline reflected the 'statistical fiction' that GDP was shrinking when in fact private employment and personal income were rising. The end of the wage-and-price controls meant a higher inflation rate, which in turn increased the recorded GDP price deflator (p. 82) and made the 'real production' statistically shrink. One may only wonder what the government would have done if the statistical information had already been available then.

End the FED

Since its inception, modern central banking has gone through various fashions and has adopted opposing paradigms along the course of its history. The US Federal Reserve System began operating in January 1914 and stood ready to provide the monetary conditions for financing US entry into World War I.

Likewise, the US central bank provided the monetary ammunition for its government to fight in World War II and in the many other military conflicts that were to follow. In Europe, one of the first consequences of World War I was to abandon the gold standard and turning the central banks into the willing tools of governments.

In the early 1920s, the US central bank adopted Irving Fisher's proposal of using the consumer price index as the guide for monetary policy, ushering the economy first into an unsustainable economic boom and then into the Great Depression. In Europe, the Deutsche Reichsbank produced a hyperinflation in the early 1920s, and in the United Kingdom, the Bank of England toiled for decades without success against the economic slump. By the early 1930s, the political supremacy over central banking was complete. Irrespective of the degree of socialism, nationalism, and totalitarianism, the politicization of money and central banking encompassed the central banks from Moscow to Berlin, and from Paris to Washington and Tokyo. Central planning and interventionism had won the day.

After World War II, there was a short period when the so-called Bretton Woods System was firmly in place with the expectation that one held the philosopher's stone for monetary stability in one's hand. Establishing a link between the US dollar to gold and a fixed-exchange-rate system with an adjustable peg for its member countries to the dollar and thereby among themselves, the Bretton Woods System reflected the political power structure with the United States at the center, surrounded by the satellites.

Yet in the 1960s, Keynesianism became the dominant doctrine of central banking. Interest rates had to be low, so the mantra said, to stimulate investment and economic growth. Consequently, the United States government ignored its obligation to limit the dollar emission to the size of its gold stock, and the US central bank put no brakes on a further growth of the money supply. This policy led right into a decade of inflation first and stagflation later.

In West Germany, the 'Bank deutscher Länder' (later called 'Bundesbank') got its seat in Frankfurt and not in the capital city signaling a certain symbolic detachment from politics. The law that created the new German central bank obliged monetary policy to pursue 'price level stability'. Yet in the late 1960s and during the 1970s, inflation and then stagflation hit Germany and other European countries as well. One reason for that was the international monetary system itself, which obliged the member countries to stabilize their exchange rates against the US dollar.

The over-supply of dollars destroyed this system. The Bundesbank, along with other central banks in Europe and Japan, became the 'buyers of the last resort' for the weakening greenback. The world experienced a massive increase in liquidity originating from the US dollar that spilled over to the other major currencies. When the central banks in Europe and Japan bought dollars for their own currencies to stabilize the exchange rate, they expanded their domestic monetary base. After a short liquidity-driven boost, the world economy slipped into the stagflation of the 1970s.

The experience of stagflation led to a turnaround of monetary policy in the late 1970s when the US central bank embarked upon the monetarist experiment. Now, it was the money supply that became the magic word and the most important guideline for central banking. In the 1980s, price inflation rates declined. However, this happened more by accident than by design, because with the onset of the monetarist experiment, the velocity of money circulation — which had been trend-stable for decades — contracted.

Inadvertently, the restrictive monetary policy in place became contractive. In an ironic twist, the major tenet of monetarism — that the velocity of money would be stable or at least trend-stable — no longer held. This happened at that point when the central bankers adopted monetarism as their new credo. The recession of the early 1980s wiped out inflationary expectations. This result came not by design, but by a monetary policy error — an error, however, with beneficial results.

With Alan Greenspan (chairman of the Board of Governors of the Federal Reserve System from 1987 to 2006), the US central bank abandoned monetarism and went on to the next fashion: supply-side economics. Greenspan liked to look at productivity growth as the guideline and the money-supply number became less important. His doctrine said that a central bank can expand the monetary base and have low policy rates when productivity in the economy is rising. This laid the groundwork for the great financial-asset boom of the 1990s. The chairman became the darling of Wall Street, its guru, and the oracle to listen to, and the reliable bail-out guarantor as the man of the last resort for the financial markets.

In Asia, meanwhile, the Japanese central bank produced first an unsustainable economic boom in the 1980s, then instigated the crash of 1989–90, and has tried to re-inflate the economy ever since. In the 1980s, the Japanese central bank saw no need to curb the booming stock and real-estate markets because the price index remained stable, and Japan was seemingly on its way to becoming 'Number One'. The Bank of Japan boosted its monetary base in the 1980s, and after the bust, it lowered its policy rate almost to zero. While the expected recovery did not happen, the Bank of Japan provided a bonanza for financial speculators who practice the yen-carry-trade by borrowing at low-interest rates in Japan and lending at higher interest rates abroad.

Europe introduced a common currency in 1999. The statutes of the European Central Bank (ECB) called for a clear priority of 'price stability' as the guideline for monetary policy. The seat of the European Central Bank is in Frankfurt, Germany, almost equidistant to Brussels, which hosts the executive branch of the European Union, and to Strasbourg, where the European Parliament resides, thus symbolizing that the ECB should be independent and free of political influence.

The autonomy of the ECB has a quasi-constitutional status within the European legal framework. Thus, it remained to be seen what would happen when more serious challenges arise in the euro system. And indeed: instead of risking the departure of a member state in financial trouble, the ECB acted like any other central bank and boosted the money supply according to the central bankers' motto: *après nous le deluge* in the face of the European debt crisis, which began in 2010.

In the United States, Ben Bernanke has been the chairman of the Board of Governors of the US Federal Reserve System from 2006 to 2014. He, too, is an adherent of inflation targeting, yet the US central bank is not explicit about what definite desired rate of inflation (as it is measured by the consumer price index) should be its goal.

The concept of inflation targeting is not new. It has its origins in Irving Fisher's monetary theory. By following this monetary policy concept, the US central bank created the boom of the late 1920s and the great bust. Nevertheless, this theory is now experiencing a revival in Europe and the United States.

The monetary policy concept of inflation targeting suffers from the fundamental problem that a valid price index does not exist. There is no such a thing as a representative basket of goods and services. Fisher's idea was already problematic in the simpler economy of the 1920s; nowadays it is outright obsolete to establish an index that could represent the complex and diverse economy as it exists today. Each individual person has his specific basket of goods and services, and its composition will change for the same individual.

Although a valid price index does not exist, central bankers use this indicator as a guideline to plan a monetary policy that affects the whole economy. Irving Fisher is back, center stage, in the person of Ben Bernanke and his successor Janet Yellen (chairwomen from 2014 to 2018). These two sell their inflation-targeting concept as something new, when in fact it is the rehash of Irving Fisher's theory — a theory that both the facts of history and the economic theory of the Austrian School have discredited.

The record of modern central banking is bleak. Serving as a bailout machine for the financial markets and as a reliable financier of the state, modern central banks by the nature of their origin and existence do not curb the booms (which they could) and do not prevent recessions or depressions (which they would wish to do but cannot). Monetary policy suffers from the same faults as any other centralized economic policy and other forms of interventionism, and like all centralized economic policies and interventionist measures, the monetary policy of active central banks has been failing again and again.

Modern economies are too complex and diverse for central control. The more complex and diverse the economy gets, the more the data will have to be compressed, finally to such a degree that they lose their meaning and become useless at best and misleading at worst as informational tools for decision-making. For monetary policy, which acts like a central-planning agency when it comes to the money supply and the interest rate, the informational quality of the data that central banks use is deteriorating. Aggregates and averages such as the Gross Domestic Product or the inflation rate, productivity growth, or the many other economic indicators that are so popular nowadays with central bankers and the financial press and in econometric studies, hide more than they reveal and are often misleading for decision-making and economic analysis.

Given that there are no constant quantitative relations among the variables, central bankers have no reliable guideline to calibrate their monetary policy measures. One cannot know for sure how monetary impulses transform economic activity and to which degree the monetary streams affect consumer prices or how they will change investment or impact upon asset prices. How the monetary transmission mechanism has worked, shows up in retrospect, and the results are valid only for a specific period.

Research of statistical relations is history. The results provide no certainty about how the transmission mechanism will work in the future. The monetary impulse coming from the monetary base can transform into various degrees of strengths depending on the money multiplier and the velocity of circulation, and from there it can change the components of the real economy. It all depends on the individual human action; and human expectations, plans, and actions change over time, sometimes drastically.

Statistical aggregates per se cause nothing in the economy. What is being measured by the aggregates and averages are the effects of human action, and not their causes. There is no way to know ex-ante whether a specific monetary policy measure affects the so-called price level of final goods — whether the main effect goes into the asset market, or leads to more investment at home, or more imports from abroad. Central bankers do not know whether changes in the money supply and the interest rate will cause a change of credit demand for business investment or a change of credit demand for private and public consumption.

Central bankers sometimes describe their activity as 'more art than science', which is the implicit recognition of their ignorance. The 'art of central banking' is the virtuosity of pretending to know what one does not know. Not only is it not a science; it is not even an art. It is alchemy at best and a gigantic cheat at worst.

When economic systems grow in complexity and diversity, central planning and interventionism become inefficient, and the need arises for more decentralized coordination mechanisms. Modern economies and modern financial markets have become too complex for an active central banking. It is an illusion to believe that more research and better central bankers could improve monetary policy. One needs something else: a monetary system that works without an active central bank.

The world needs a new monetary system. The reform must consist in the de-nationalization of central banking and establishing a private banking system. To deprive the central banks of its power, it suffices to freeze the basic money - the part of the money, which a central bank controls - and to allow a free banking system.

According to this plan, the supply of central bank money – the so-called monetary base – would be fixed at a specific amount. This will limit the range of inflation and contraction of macroeconomic liquidity and thus eliminate a central factor of the major cyclical fluctuations. A complete economic stability, as the politicians once promised, has never been attainable anyway, and it is not even desirable. Even if the volume of the monetary base no longer varies, fluctuations (because of changes in velocity of circulation) would still occur, as it is necessary for a dynamic economy. What is important, however, is to limit the extreme economic swings of boom and bust. Freezing of the basic money supply would be an important step to curtail the possibilities of economic cycles. When there is a fixed amount of central bank money, the commercial banks will cautious in lending and restrain unsound booms. A constant amount of the monetary base combined with a free banking system ties the monetary system to a fixed anchor and makes the economy more stable without impeding the monetary flexibility. Under such a monetary system, macroeconomic liquidity - and thus nominal national income - would still vary within limits because of the elasticity of the monetary multiplier and the velocity of the circulation of money.

The Crisis of 2008

The financial crisis of 2008 did not come from anywhere. Its basis was laid over a long period with the welfare state, the inflation of money and the adoption of the Keynesian economic policy framework as the new orthodoxy. The great American boom since the 1980s was built on monetary expansion, low-interest rates, and a relentless policy of bailouts when the bubbles burst. The result has been the build-up of unsustainable debt burdens. When debt accumulation hit its limit in the private sector and in the banking system, and when markets began 'to freeze', governments jumped in with bailout guarantees and stimulus packages, which only added a fiscal crisis on top of the financial market and economic crisis.

Excessive monetary expansion and the resulting low-interest rates represent the immediate causes of the crisis of 2008. At a deeper level, however, lies the current monetary system. The structure that emerged after the breakdown of the Bretton Woods system in 1971 is cut off from what was left of an anchor. The new monetary schemes have become an engine of debt expansion of the private and the public sector. It is a system devoid of a mechanism that would curb debt expansion in time. The current monetary arrangements allow central banks to make the debt accumulation go on until the final collapse.

The crisis of 2008 and thereafter is as much a financial as an economic crisis and most of all it is a crisis of indebtedness. This excess of debt includes households and governments, and it includes the external balances, the persistent current account deficits of the United States, which, as their counterpart, imply the accumulation of surpluses in China, some other Asian, and of European countries.

What began as a banking crisis and diagnosed as the result of 'too little regulation' has its origin in the notion of central bankers that the problem is 'too little inflation'. The inflationary acts of central banks and governments are at the origin of the troubles that spill over from the financial sector to the real economy. What began as excessive money supply and has produced excessive debt, is now showing up in slow growth and stagnant incomes.

With economic policies, there is often a considerable time lag between the phase when one plants the seeds and the phase when the harvest will come - between cause and effect. In the case of the financial and economic crisis of 2008, the time of planting goes back to the 1960s and 1970s, when the welfare state became the new creed in the Western world, when economic policy adopted Keynesianism, and when the last remnants of the gold standard were removed.

The late 1960s experienced the start of the drastic expansion of the welfare state, and in the early 1970s, the rest of what had remained of a sound monetary system was abandoned. Adopting the Keynesian economic policy model would make the triad complete.

The new consensus encompasses an unhampered expansion of the welfare state, an activist discretionary monetary policy without anchor or definite rules and the economic policy of vulgar Keynesianism with its false promise that government had the tools to lift a country to prosperity and full employment through government spending and easy money.

It did not take long until this kind of policy produced its first disaster: stagflation. Facing the result of the Keynesian politics in the rise of unemployment, economic stagnation, and inflation demand for a new economic policy paradigm arose, and it was found in "monetarism". Monetarism, however, as an economic policy concept, was in some respects an even more simplified version of Keynesianism. Despite its promotion of free markets, there was little true classical economics in the monetarist model. When monetarists declared 'we're all Keynesians now', it meant much more than an ironic twist.

When Reaganomics – the economic policy of President Reagan and his promotion to combine tax cuts and deregulation – came along in the early 1980s, this economic policy failed with its promise to reduce government expenditure. While the American central bank under Paul Volcker brought down the inflation rate and while unemployment fell, government deficits swelled, and the public debt increased to new highs. That was the time when the slogan emerged 'deficits don't matter'.

In this respect, the new economic ideology of 'supply side economics' had become even more Keynesian. Now, the original idea of anti-cyclical public finance was put aside. The governments abandoned the principle that cuts of public expenditure and budget surpluses would be required in good economic times to have the funds to spend when the economy would turn into a recession. The new economic policy consensus says deficits would not matter, and thus that one can ignore the debt levels and neglect the exchange rate of the dollar because central banks were capable of managing the monetary side of the economy.

What was called 'The Great Moderation', and as it was believed by central bankers to be the case, is a macroeconomic constellation, which does not guarantee that the economy is sound. Besides the uncertainties of measuring economic growth and the price index, limiting the theoretical focus only on these two indicators deceives.

The Keynesian-monetarist synthesis that dominated economic policy actions during the decades from the 1980s onwards, stopped paying attention to credit growth and debt accumulation. In the run-up to the crisis of 2008, monetary policy ignored that household liabilities had risen by a factor of 14 since the early 1980s and reached 14 trillion at the outbreak of the current crisis (Data-FRED. https://fred.stlouisfed.org/series/CMDEBT#0)

As long as price inflation seemed under control, the monetary policy concept of the New Keynesians no longer asked what kind of economic growth was happening if macroeconomic statistics registered the expansion of real gross domestic product. What was called 'Great Moderation' and what was experienced as a decades-long boom should better be called a gigantic bubble whose creation and maintenance resulted from the dedicated application of bailout economics by the major central banks of the world.

While a bailout may be beneficial in the individual case and is so for the persons who receive the bailout money, bailouts have systemic consequences: Over time, each new bailout will add to the level of moral hazard and after a series of bailouts, moral hazard will become systemic. What at first is a benign government gift, over time will become a manifest expectation, and bailouts will be nothing less than the rightful claims on government money.

Bailouts produce a moral hazard and this way risk perception will approach diminish. Without the restraint of financial losses, an overexpansion of commercial activities will occur. Bailouts institutionalize perverse risk behavior, and it is not before long that the new aggressive attitude will rule across the board by the business community and by the financial market operators. In fact, bailouts impose a negative selection mechanism where prudence gets punished. With risk perception taken out of business life, the economic expansion means that a growing part of the resulting economic growth exists in unsustainable investments. This, in turn, implies that most of the economic activity that comes as the result of falling risk perception amounts to the squandering of capital. In relation to the point of departure, the economy that appears to be on the path of prosperity is getting poorer. When the bubble pops, the level of prosperity is lower than it was before the false boom. After a decade since the bubble burst, there has not yet been a full recovery, while the new bubble is ready to pop.

***

The so-called 'New Economy' of the 1990s led to stock market prices that exceeded all conventional measures in terms of price-earnings-ratios. Public initial offerings by companies that lacked earnings and sometimes even a product (the only thing they had was a business plan) achieved extreme valuations at the stock market and produced short-term billionaires overnight. Of course, there was hype; there was gullibility, and there was greed involved. Yet these emotions do not fall from the blue sky. In fact, 'irrational exuberance' had a broad basis: liquidity. The same persons who lamented irrationality were the relentless pushers of liquidity.

Flooding the markets with more money provided the basis for the kick-in of the wealth effect due to the rising participation of the population in the stock market through investment funds and 401k accounts. The result was a period of illusionary prosperity. Low-interest rates and ample tax revenues coming from capital appreciation let it even appear for some time as if government debt would disappear.

The financial crisis of 2008 has its origin in excessive lending, which, in turn, is due to a monetary system whose basis is debt.

Due to insufficient domestic savings, the United States has accumulated a net foreign investment position that has reached over eight trillion US dollars. The United States has turned from the world's largest creditor at the end of World War II into the world's largest debtor nation. In addition to its precarious foreign investment position, the US government, when confronted with the outbreak of the financial crisis, has intervened in the private market and taken up positions with financial institutions and major companies close to bankruptcy. At the same time, the US central bank has acted as a lender of the last resort. Along with lowering the Federal Funds Rate, the US central bank has bought up junk papers from the private banking sector and extended its balance sheet with poisonous assets.

The financial situation of the US consumer has become unsustainable. It is illusionary to expect a recovery beginning with consumption. Fiscal expansion and loose monetary policies have achieved extreme proportions. Interest rate policy has touched 'zero bound', and government debt and the foreign debt position of the United States have reached critical levels.

Like in Japan over the past decades, with its ongoing fiscal expansion and loose monetary policy, the positive effect on economic growth of the stimulus packages in the United States has been meager and is petering out.

The current international monetary structure is more a 'non-system' than a system or an order. It does not provide a sound monetary order. Interventionist systems, like the one that is now in existence for monetary matters, drive towards their own dissolution. It seems as if the end stage of the interventionist spiral has come full circle considering that the starting point of the modern interventionist state existed in getting hold of money creation. It is the sovereign authority over money that provides the conditions of the welfare-warfare state and the rise of the modern interventionist state.

The economic and financial crisis of 2008 and its aftermath have exposed the modern monetary system as a mechanism of debt expansion whose inherent dynamics move this system to the limit. The structure of the modern monetary system in its combination with modern populist democracy produces the dynamics which drives it to hyperinflation or bankruptcy. Deflation is the main concern of the monetary authorities' because a falling price level means bankruptcy. Because of the irrational 'fear of deflation', the central bankers work as hard as they can to create debt inflation in order to lift the price level. Yet in as much as they succeed in promoting debt inflation, the final stage will be bankruptcy. Instead of letting the system go the shortcut to deflation and from there to bankruptcy, monetary authorities promote a detour from debt inflation to bankruptcy, and from bankruptcy to deflation. Most of all, however, the modern interventionist policy measures aimed at avoiding any recession and thus prone to prevent a re-positioning of the economy to correct the past errors, produce widening distortions of the capital structures. What one or two decades ago could have been resolved by a short recession does require a much costlier process of adaptation.

Economic policy intervention in the form of bailouts creates a systemic moral hazard that for some time helped to avoid an economic downturn. Yet after that, there will be a collapse much harsher than anything that would have happened earlier it the policymakers had left the economy by itself to adapt.

2008 marks not a crisis of capitalism but a crisis of state interventionism. To get rid of future episodes of this kind, more regulations will not help. On the contrary. Crisis prevention requires the end of the policy of bailouts. If not, the monetary system gets even more perverted. Yet more regulations become necessary – not because markets do not work, but because there are already too many interventions and too many regulations in place. More regulation does not prevent the crises but lays the groundwork for them to happen.

Summary

Fluctuations are part of the economy. Instability by itself is not harmful. Likewise, stability is not always beneficial. Dynamic systems, like a market economy, work on the principle of error and correction. The faster one can correct allocative errors, the better for the system. The individual parts of the economic order must have the freedom to adapt. For the economy, this principle bears the name Laissez-faire. It is therefore important to allow the self-healing powers of the market economy to come to the fore.

At no stage of the cycle do the economic policymakers know which course the economy will take. It is thus impossible to calibrate the measures or even to determine in advance whether the economy needs a stimulant or a sedative. There is no way to know in which direction the economy will move. The forecasting techniques are useless, especially to determine turning points. If everything remains as it is, one does not need a forecast; if one needed a prediction because things change, the prognosis techniques do not work. Policymakers grope in the dark even if they do not admit it.

Instead of economic policy, one needs to apply measures that make the economy more flexible and adaptable. This includes, first, dismantling regulations and reducing the tax burden. Besides the uncertainty already created in the economic process itself, activist economic policy adds another element of uncertainty. The individual economic decision-makers must pay attention to what is changing in the economy and, additionally, what policymakers will do.

Political uncertainty can mean that the economy freezes on a large scale. Economic policymakers then speak of a weak economy. The regret the loss of the spirit of enterprise. These economic policymakers themselves, however, caused the uncertainty and thus the economic paralysis. The rise of uncertainty because of politics was one of the main causes of the Great Depression. Now, a new wave of political hyper-activism is taking place.

VII.

ANARCHO-CAPITALISM

Antony P. Mueller

> *"...we must be able to offer a new liberal programme which appeals to the imagination. We must make the building of a free society once more an intellectual adventure, a deed of courage."*
> F.A. Hayek, The Intellectuals and Socialism (1949)

- The State and its minions
- Voluntary servitude
- The age of the individual
- What is anarchism?
- Concepts
- Is Anarcho-capitalism possible?
- The struggle for liberty
- Death of the gatekeepers
- Toward the new world of freedom
- Sortition (demarchy)
- Agenda
- Outlook

The process of substituting labor through machines enters sectors that have seemed to be exempt from automatization and robotization. The new technologies will transform law, medicine, education, consulting, business administration, and the public service. Job security is a thing of the past. The conventional measures of the welfare state do no longer work. Two kinds of response have emerged to this challenge: either more socialism or more capitalism.

Going on like in the past and more socialism would make things worse. The answer to the challenge is to abolish politics and the state. Selecting the legislators by sortition, the end of the state monopoly on money, and privatizing the system of justice and security, are the main steps to take. In as much as free capitalism would flourish, the costs of living fall, wage rates rise, incomes increase, and the burdens of taxation and bureaucracy fade away. The need to have a permanent job and a steady salary that is so urgent under the present system would vanish.

A libertarian revolution and an anarcho-capitalist order has become possible because the new technologies, with the Internet at its center, undermine the ability of the 'old regime' to maintain its hold over public opinion. Mind control by the modern state confronts the obstacle that the cost to engineer the public opinion outruns its effectiveness. New alternative sources of knowledge compete with the informational privilege of the government. The voice of the government has become one among many.

The necessity of an anarcho-capitalist order is not only a question of the material well-being. If we continue with the present system of governance, the state will grow bigger and bigger and become more totalitarian. In the hands of such a regime, the new technologies turn into deadly weapons against individual freedom.

In order to preserve and expand prosperity and liberty, establishing a libertarian system of governance has become a question of human survival.

Antony P. Mueller

The State and Its Minions

The State is generally considered as a necessity. Even many of those who believe that the State is an evil, regard it is a necessary evil. The State is indispensable, they say, only anarchist would dispute this fact.

Economic theory holds that the State is the provider of public and social goods. The public believes that the State is that organization by which we protect ourselves from ourselves. By subsidizing the supply of certain goods such as education and healthcare the State helps us to consume more of these benefits than we would do individually and with some harmful goods (the 'bads'), the State protects us against the damage that we would inflict upon ourselves if there were easy access to these products. There is a broad consensus that the State is necessary to provide things such as the roads, schools, hospitals, and care for our domestic and external security. Yet to be governed means more than just obtaining the supply of the so-called 'public goods', as Pierre-Joseph Proudhon indicts:

> "To be GOVERNED is to be watched, inspected, spied upon, directed, law-driven, numbered, regulated, enrolled, indoctrinated, preached at, controlled, checked, estimated, valued, censured, commanded, by creatures who have neither the right nor the wisdom nor the virtue to do so. To be GOVERNED is to be at every operation, at every transaction noted, registered, counted, taxed, stamped, measured, numbered, assessed, licensed, authorized, admonished, prevented, forbidden, reformed, corrected, punished. It is, under pretext of public utility, and in the name of the general interest, to be place under contribution, drilled, fleeced, exploited, monopolized, extorted from, squeezed, hoaxed, robbed; then, at the slightest resistance, the first word of complaint, to be repressed, fined, vilified, harassed, hunted down, abused, clubbed, disarmed, bound, choked, imprisoned, judged, condemned, shot, deported, sacrificed, sold, betrayed; and to crown all, mocked, ridiculed, derided, outraged, dishonored. That is government; that is its justice; that is its morality."
>
> (Pierre-Joseph Proudhon: *Idée Générale de la Révolution au XIXe Siècle* (1851) - General Idea of the Revolution in the Nineteenth Century.

More than 150 years late, things have not changed much. In a democracy, the State has not diminished its role but has grown into horrific dimensions as Hans-Hermann Hoppe describes in his "A Short History Of Man":

> "Every detail of private life, property, trade, and contract is regulated...In the name of social, public, or national security, democratic caretakers "protect" us from global warming and cooling, the extinction of

animals and plants and the depletion of natural resources, from husbands and wives, parents and employers, poverty, disease, disaster, ignorance, prejudice, racism, sexism, homophobia and countless other public "enemies" and "dangers." Yet the only task government was ever supposed to assume—of protecting our life and property—it does not perform. To the contrary, the higher the state expenditures on social, public, and national security have risen, the more private property rights have been eroded, the more property has been expropriated, confiscated, destroyed, and depreciated, and the more have people been deprived of the very foundation of all protection: of personal independence, economic strength, and private wealth. The more paper laws have been produced, the more legal uncertainty and moral hazard has been created, and lawlessness has displaced law and order. And while we have become ever more dependent, helpless, impoverished, threatened and insecure, the ruling elite of politicians and plutocrats has become increasingly richer, more corrupt, dangerously armed, and arrogant."

In a democracy, 'we' now are the State ourselves. The State is no longer separated from society, from the family, and from the local community but is in us, the people. "We are the State", the mob exclaims, fired up by the encouragements of the State's own band of cheerleaders. In a democracy, the State is not only necessary, it is we, our own identity.

A deeper analysis, however, reveals, that most of these popular claims are false. The State is not sacred. The State as the people is a fiction.

Along with Franz Oppenheimer in "The State" (1908), Murray Rothbard in his "The Anatomy of the State" (originally published in "Egalitarianism as a Revolt Against Nature and Other Essays" 1974) have thoroughly exploded the common justifications of the State.

As Rothbard points out in his essay, the identification of the people with the State leads to serious errors. Taking the State for the people provides the bases to claim that if "the government has incurred a huge public debt which must be paid by taxing one group for the benefit of another, this reality of burden is obscured by saying 'we owe it to ourselves', if the government conscripts a man, or throws him into jail for dissident opinion, he is 'doing it to himself', and, therefore, nothing untoward has occurred."

Also, in a democracy, the State is not 'we', the government is not 'us'. In a democracy, the "government does not in any accurate sense 'represent' the people".

What then, is the State, asks Rothbard, if the State is not a family or an organ of which we are all part, and his answer is that "the State is that organization in the society which attempts to maintain a monopoly of the use of force and violence in a given territorial area; in particular, it is the only organization in a society that obtains its revenue not by voluntary contribution or payment of services and by the peaceful and voluntary sale of these goods and services to others, the State obtains its revenue by the use of compulsion, that is, by the use and the threat of the jailhouse and the bayonet."

In the footsteps of Joseph Schumpeter (*Capitalism, Socialism, and Democracy*, 1942), Rothbard extends the definition of the State by Max Weber as the "human community that (successfully) claims the monopoly of the legitimate use of physical force within a given territory" (in *"Politik als Beruf"* 1918) by the aspect that the Sate lives on a revenue which is produced in the private sphere for private purposes and must be taken away by political force.

Man is born into this world naked and helpless and of total dependence on care. It takes years for a human being to develop reasoning and to acquire the skills for production. Social association is a necessity in the early life and a requirement when grown up because the social cooperation within the network of the division of labor enhances the individual productivity. The exchange of goods is natural to man. When people exchange goods, they exchange property. Therefore, property rights and the free market exchange form a vital part of human nature.

As Franz Oppenheimer elaborates in '<u>Der Staat</u>' (1908), there are only two means of wealth accumulation: either through the economic mean or by political means. The political means are in the hands of the State. The State is the instrument to plunder the wealth of the private sector. The political instrument to acquire wealth is opposed to the economic way. While the economic method is natural and beneficial to all, the political way is unnatural and detrimental to the general prosperity. By means of the State, a few live at the cost of all. The basis of the political means is not a voluntary exchange but coercion. Not by a social contract comes the State into existence but with conquest and submission.

The State begins with conquest and has gone through a series of stages till our present days. As Oppenheimer recounts human history, the conquering tribe submits the conquered tribe in order to plunder. Yet instead of complete exploitation and elimination, the conquerors opt for a peaceful arrangement with the conquered. The conquerors unite with the conquered under the umbrella of a common State as a nation.

From the stateless society of the huntsmen and gatherers and the nomads and warriors, the State comes into existence with conquest and annihilation. Over time, the conquerors learn to exploit the conquered and use slavery and other forms of bondage instead of annihilation. Instead of getting the honey like a bear, the State acts like a beekeeper. From there emerges the territorial union of conquerors and conquered when the ruling class acts mainly as judicial supervisors and arbitrators for the conquered does finally merge with the people as a nation State. This stage prepares the path for the stateless society of the future, Oppenheimer predicts.

Historical Development Stages of the State
(based on The State by Franz Oppenheimer)

PREHISTORIC STATELESS SOCIETY		
	STATELESS SOCIETY I	Huntsmen and gatherers
	STATELESS SOCIETY II	Herdsmen and Vikings
	STATELESS SOCIETY III	Nomads and warriors
STATE		
	STAGE I	Conquest and annihilation of the conquered
	STAGE II	Conquest and submission of the conquered
	STAGE III	Capitalization and tribute extraction
	STAGE IV	Territorial union
	STAGE V	Rule by arbitration and courts
	STAGE VI	Nation building
POST-HISTORIC STATELESS SOCIETY		
	SELF-GOVERNING SOCIETY	Private law society
	FREEMEN'S CITIZENSHIP	Demise of the state
	ANARCHO-CAPITALISM	Voluntary exchange society

Economic development brings with it that the political means must recede against the economical means. Oppenheimer recognizes that in the political history of humankind there has been a steady ascent of the economic method at the cost of the political scheme. Writing at the beginning of the 20the century, Oppenheimer predicts that the thousands of years of State rule are coming to an end: "The 'state' of the future will be a 'society' guided by self-government", he declares.

So why is the State as an oppressive institution still here with us?

Why do we still have a State, asks Murray Rothbard, when the coercive and exploitive political means run against natural law? The political way is not productive but parasitic, "instead of adding to production, it subtracts from it". Parasitism is the nature of the State, also in its 'democratic' form. The State sucks wealth from the productive sector, it diminished the incentives to produce. The State makes us poor.

In the extension of the definitional approaches by Max Weber, Joseph Schumpeter, and Franz Oppenheimer, Murray Rothbard defines the State as "the systematization of the predatory process over a given territory". While private crime is sporadic and individual parasitism is ephemeral, and can be rejected by the victims, the State "provides a legal, orderly, systematic channel for the predation of private property; it renders certain, secure, and relatively 'peaceful' the lifeline of the parasitic caste in society".

As production comes before consumption, the provision of goods must precede their predation. The State cannot come into existence before the economy. Without the existence of an economy, there can be no 'social contract'. Without a productive basis, the social contract is a myth.

The State still exists. It has at its side the state apparatus and its officialdom. These, however, would not be enough if they were not expanded through State propaganda. Force is the *modus operandi* of the State but ideology provides the State's coherence. Even more so than in earlier times, governments need the consent of the ruled. As the welfare state approaches its economic limit, it becomes more difficult, to use the redistribution as the political means to gain mass loyalty. The group of people that receives net benefits from the State must be a minority. In order to gain the support of the majority, people must be persuaded by an ideology that government is necessary and inevitable, that it is benevolent and beneficial to all. In his *"Anatomy of the State"*, Murray Rothbard identifies the modern intellectuals as the carriers of this task. The intellectuals as the opinion-makers serve as ideological bodyguards of the modern State.

The State and the intellectuals need one another. The State intellectuals are the priestly class of our days. The free market does not sustain many intellectuals. In order to gain a livelihood, they need the funding of the State. A historical alliance exists between the State and its intellectuals. Along with the officialdom, the intellectuals are the other leg how the State maintains its existence as a machinery of exploitation. Along with these allies, the modern secular State has also secured 'science' as its affiliate. While the priesthood decorated the State as holy, science deifies the State as the ultimate ratio. The bodyguards of the modern State are the host of experts that find ample employment in ministries, agencies, commissions, the universities, and at the plethora of national and international institutions.

Rothbard (1974) reveals that the "increasing use of scientific jargon has permitted the State's intellectuals to weave obscurantist apologia for State rule that would have only met with derision by the populace of a simpler age." These experts teach that the robbery by the State helps its victims, that the economy needs politics for its stabilization, and that employment and economic progress is the achievement of government. Under the mantle of science, the State has expanded like never before. It is now 'science' that serves as the apparatus of propaganda to promote the agenda for the expansion of the modern State. Exploitation has become so subtle that hardly anyone notices it anymore

The State protects itself and promotes its power by fear. If one foreign enemy is defeated, the next one is already chosen. Domestic enemies abound not only in a regime like Stalin's Soviet Union but also in the modern 'democracy'. The modern State itself is clad in the cloth of nationhood. The nation now serves as the source of passion, blind obedience, and the rationale of exclusion and condemnation of those individuals who will not succumb. The democratic State needs the nation because it is supposed to represent not the absolute king but the absolutism of the people.

As Hans-Hermann Hoppe (*A Short History of Men*, 2015) points out: "Under democracy the distinction between the rulers and ruled becomes blurred. The illusion even arises that the distinction no longer exists". Democracy transforms the limited wars of the past into the modern total wars where the enemy must be debased and dehumanized in favor of the glory of one's own nation.

The competition of political parties over votes is fundamentally different from competition in a market economy. In a market competition, producer compete as to the sale of their products against payment. In a democracy, politicians compete over votes in an exchange of favors. The apparent benefits that voters expect to receive consist of advantages as the result of coercive redistribution.

Driven by party politics, the democratic State moves inexorably towards its own demise. State bankruptcy looms across the globe. The social-democratic era is over. The capacity of the State to bribe is coming to an end. What to do after the collapse of the modern democratic State? The answer is anarcho-capitalism and the rule of a "*Private Law Society*" (Hoppe). In order to accomplish this change, the pre-condition is the separation between the intellectuals and the State in the same way as the separation of the Church and the State had brought down the old State. It is up to the academics to withdraw their endorsement of the State. The intellectuals have nothing to lose but their chains. The 'march through the institutions' is over. For those who study now, the road to ascendency through State service is closed.

Voluntary Servitude

In his essay on the politics of obedience (*Discours de la Servitude Volontaire*), Etienne La Boétie (1530-1563) asks the central question of political rule: How come that a people, as the majority, lets itself be ruled by a small group, the minority, and sometimes, in the case of an autocrat, falls into the hands of a single person? How is it possible that people permit that to a small group of men tortures, exploits and abuses the majority? Is it not strange, wonders La Boétie, that this dictatorial ruler, as a human, is often physically weak, clownish, feminine, cowardly and of a feeble mind?

Would it not rather be natural that one would obey one's parents as a child but after one has grown-up and gained reason, one would want to be nobody's servant and not the slave of someone else? La Boétie's answer to these questions is that the cause of human servitude cannot be only coercion. No tyrant has so many eyes that he could monitor a whole nation or have so many hands that he could hit the people with so many blows. The answer is obedience. Not coercion explains tyranny but 'voluntary servitude'.

Tyranny can come through elections, by force, or by inheritance. Although the methods differ about how the rulers come into power, the method of dominance is the same. All types of rules, including tyranny, are based on voluntary submission of the people. How did this bondage come about?

One reason is, La Boétie explains, that at some point in history human beings lost their freedom either by external conquest or internal corruption. Thereafter followed one generation after the other that no longer knew about freedom and what it means. Submission had become a habit. Men fell into servitude and became complacent in their condition of captivity. Human nature fell victim to the circumstances, to custom, to upbringing. Systematic state propaganda completed this process of subjection. Over time, the traces of the knowledge of freedom get lost and what has been left is only the experience of servitude as the natural way of human existence.

The second reason for servitude is resignation and diversion. Although servitude makes people uneasy, it also makes people calm in their resignation when other concerns than freedom occupies their mind. The rulers know that and provide the diversions of bread and circus, of gluttony and playfulness. The exhilaration that comes with the diversions that the mass culture delivers extinguishes defiance and the emotional exhaustion keeps the people still in their political resignation.

The third cause of submission is the tyrant's use of religion. People like to believe in miracles and the rulers search the décor that comes with ceremonies that celebrate divinity and holiness. The rulers create a web of taboos and sanctuaries. In tandem with the church service, there is the State service. This way, disobedience of the State becomes a sin, rebellion becomes an act of blasphemy, and tyrannicide becomes deicide.

As the fourth reason of voluntary servitude counts the role of a special class of persons who stand between the ruler and the people. These are the public employees, the state-financed intellectuals, and the rich who profit from the State. These people accept the bribe of the tyrant because they do not know better or because they esteem the benefits that they receive higher than their freedom and righteousness.

In a monarchy, as it was the case at the time when La Boétie lived, the courtiers and the nobility represented this group of the privileged. In the eyes of La Boétie, these persons are deplorable. These are people who have been abandoned by God and humanity, who humiliate themselves before the king and do not oppose the debasing treatment that they receive from their master. While the rest of the population obeys because it must do what told, those who form part of the entourage of the king or of the tyrant "have to think what the king wants them to think". These flatterers must anticipate the wishes of the autocrat and must please him. For them, to obey is not enough, they must adulate the tyrant. "Serving him destroys them, yet they are expected to share his joy, to abandon their tastes for his, to change their nature and constitution". The common people owe only a part of their existence to the tyrant, the sycophants all that they are and what they have.

Tyranny makes everybody suffer, including the tyrant himself. The autocrat can neither give nor receive love. He must not maintain friendship. He is surrounded by cruelty, dishonesty, and injustice.

What to do against this tragedy? How can mankind overcome submission? How can we get out of this scam and leave behind this calamity where everybody must suffer, including the tyrant himself? Let's forget the scholarly, convoluted answers, says La Boétie. The answer is plain. What needs to be done to avoid and to get rid of tyranny is the will and the desire of the individuals to remain free and to get free.

The gift of freedom is humankind's natural possession. It does not require justification or elaboration. All it takes is to reclaim one's freedom. Liberty is not a right but a choice. If it were a right, it could be taken away the same way that it was given. Yet freedom is not a right but a part of human nature. It belongs naturally to the human being. In his youthful optimism, Etienne exclaims: "Be determined to no longer be servants and you will be free." No other feat is required than just stop supporting the tyranny. Remove your support, and the colossus loses its stand and will tumble.

The pursuit of anarchy must not come by fire and rage. The tyrant needs not to be toppled from his throne by another man who becomes the new oppressor after his victory against the old. Throughout history, the consequence of the violent assault against tyranny has been that the leaders of the insurrection emptied the throne only to occupy it themselves. Conspiracies to do away with tyrants, tend to backfire and make matters worse. Insurgence is not the path to freedom.

It is not necessary to confront the tyrant. What needs to be done is removing the foundation of tyranny. Tyranny does not rest on force but on submission. To get rid of tyranny, people must stop their voluntary servitude. It is not the tyrant who puts himself into his position and stays in it but the people who submit to him. It is the people who feed the monster. People must stop to offer sacrifices, devotion, and idolatry, and the tyrant will fall on his own.

In order to end the tyranny of the State, people must stop accepting servitude. They need not take anything away from the tyrant, what they must do is stop yielding. To get out of tyranny, human beings do not need to change the essence of their nature. All one must do is to shed off what hinders individual advancement. When the tyrant does no longer receive obedience and people do no longer obey his orders, the ruler stands naked, without any power and is disarmed of the instruments of his dominance.

Without the support of the people, the tyrant is nothing. He shares the fate of a root that is left without water and nourishment: it turns into a dry, dead piece of wood: "Resolve to serve no more, and you are at once freed. I do not ask that you place your hands upon the tyrant to topple him over, but simply that you support him no longer, then you will behold him, like a great Colossus whose pedestal has been pulled away, fall of his own weight and break to pieces," says La Boétie. Learn anarchy, one may add.

Two centuries after La Boétie, in 1841, David Hume ("Of the First Principles of Government") put forth the same principle of servitude by consent with clarity and distinction:

> *"Nothing appears more surprising to those who consider human affairs with a philosophical eye, than the easiness with which the many are governed by the few; and the implicit submission, with which men resign their own sentiments and passions to those of their rulers. When we enquire by what means this wonder is effected, we shall find, that, as Force is always on the side of the governed, the governors have nothing to support them but opinion. It is therefore, on opinion only that government is founded, and this maxim extends to the most despotic and military governments, as well as to the most free and most popular."*

The story does not end here. While submission and voluntary servitude has been the rule, there will always be a few who feel the yoke of bondage and who will try to shake it off. Such people never will disappear completely from this earth, La Boétie claims: "Even if liberty had entirely perished from the earth, such men would invent it." The desire for freedom cannot be extinguished. Some extraordinary will always rekindle the light of freedom. Although they do not know freedom as a reality, they can imagine it and feel the spirit of liberty. These men, although robbed of their freedom, know that it does exist. Isolated from each other, each of them is lost in his own spiritual world, yet when they get the means to communicate with one another, the end of tyranny has come.

The Age of the Individual

The foremost exponent of the philosophy of anarcho-individualism is Max Stirner (1806-1856). In his "Der Einzige und sein Eigenthum" (Leipzig 1844/45) - "The unique one and his property", he claims that to come to oneself, one must get rid of the host of detrimental external influences that subdue and dissolve the essence of being one as oneself.

It is an obvious lie that man is born free. From birth to death, man forms part not only of society but of a specific society in time and space. For the anarcho-individualist, the human task is not to change society and exchange one power regime for the other. What matters is to liberate oneself from the society, to become oneself as much as one can. Egoism is not anti-social. By pursuing the path of egoism, one contributes - without intent - to a better society. Acting as a rational egoist promotes a better society. The best society is a stateless society composed of rational egoists.

Max Stirner diagnoses that the turn from the 18th to the 19th century marks the beginning of the "political epoch". The rupture came with the French Revolution. The State became the new God. People turned insane in their desires to serve this earthly God; the State cult became the new religion. Serving the State became the highest ideal of all and serving the State the highest honor of all.

Yet the State does not care about the individual, about what is me and what is mine. The State only cares about itself. The individual is nothing to the State; he is random to the State. For the State, the individual is nothing but a contingency. The point is that the State cannot understand the individual because the individual transcends the comprehension of the State. The concepts of the State, the understanding of the State, is too limited to comprehend an individual. Because the State cannot comprehend the individual, the State can do nothing for a man's individuality. The right attitude of the individual to the world is that he will do nothing because of God or because of humanity, but only because of himself.

The death of the old State and the abolition and containment of the monarchy did not liberate the individual. The democratic revolutions provoked the birth of politics and the worship of the State. The idea of the State entered the hearts of the people and aroused a new kind of enthusiasm: the national delirium. Serving the State as the new worldly God became a worship and the new cult. With the victory of classical liberalism, the epoch of the political began. To serve the State and its mystification as the nation became the supreme ideal, the interest of the State became the greatest interest and the civil service (even without being a civil servant) became the highest honor.

This historic fall marks the origin of the horrors of the modern world.

The protagonist of this new world is the politician and the political parties. A politician is a person whose aim is to change the people and the world by means of the State. Domination is the aim of the politician and the State apparatus is the instrument. The bigger and more effective the State, the better the State serves as a tool of suppression and control. The force of the State is universal to the politician - only comparable to God's power. The desire of the politician is the omnipotent State no less than the almightiness of the holy Lord.

Yet in doing so and take the State as his tool, the politician suffers from a great illusion. The State is neither the most comprehensive nor the most effective instrument of control of the individual although the government apparatus is the most visible machine of dominance. Furthermore, in as much as the politician wants to dominate and rule, he himself is under the authority of his own political party. Therefore, being a politician means being unfree. As a member of a political party, the politician must adopt the credo of the party, he must follow the rules of the party and he has to adhere to the party's principles. The truth is that the political party owns the politician. The people know that the politician is a fake because while he pretends to set the rules and to be the master, he himself is the system's deplorable victim.

Politicians do and cannot represent the individual. They have the State in their heads and in their hearts. Politicians do not believe in the individual, they believe in the State. Politicians are possessed by the State, they are "State-believers" and therefore politicians are the enemies of the individual. The politicians evoke the "common good" as their goal. Yet the idea of a "common good" is an illusion. "The common good is not my good", writes Stirner, "The common good cheers, while I suffer- the State shines, while I languish."

Liberalism did not unfetter the individual. "Liberalism" is the application of rational insight to our issues, and thus the aim of liberalism is a "rational order", a "moral conduct", and a "limited liberty". Liberalism opposes anarchy, lawlessness, proper individuality, and in as much as rationality rules, the individual person becomes a subject. Under liberalism, the individual is not his own master. Reason should prevail, says liberalism, also at the cost of the individual and to the detriment of the peculiarities of a person's personality. Instead of an era of freedom, the victory of classical liberalism marks the beginning of the 'epoch of the political'.

Individualist anarchism is the way to overcome the horrors of the modern State. Anarcho-individualism comes into existence as the association of rational egoists. Egoism is different from egotism or brutish selfishness. Rational egoism is not hedonism. The rational egoist is prudent, his mind is balanced. He abhors the immediate gratification that comes with passion and pleasure. The rational egoist is not egotistical and not anti-social. Society as an association of rational egoists requires no ruler. The commercial society exists as voluntary exchange relations. The rational egoist does neither need nor want a ruler. In the same way, as he rejects government, the rational egoist rejects the other rulers that may dominate him such as the greed for money, power, and fame.

Not the individual egoist is egotistical, but the truly egotistical entities are the collectives, such as the nation, the family, the church, and the State. While the egoism of the individual is natural, the egotism of these collectives is artificial. While the egoism of the individual is restrained, the egotism of the collectives is limitless. Collectives may claim altruism, yet their genuine identity is the application of moral terrorism as the way to maintain themselves. While a rational egoist may voluntarily act altruistically under specific circumstances as it serves his wants, a collective, in contrast, will apply moral pressures to force its members to give up their own interests in favor of the so-called common good of the collective. Collectives are brutal egotistical entities, and the coldest, harshest, most brutal of all collectives is the State. The State is that peculiar institution, which systematically combines moral terror with physical force.

There is a permanent conflict between the individual and the collective. The individual and the collective are natural enemies. The individual is a coincidence of the collective. The collective looks only after itself while the individual must take care of his own. The individual's interest is in himself, yet the collective wants all for itself and nothing for the individual. The collective demands self-denial and wants to keep the individual as its subject. Yet the individual wants himself and nothing else than himself.

The power of the collective is the powerlessness of the individual. The humility of the individual is the sovereignty of the collective. The collective rules through the resignation of the individuals. The despondency of the individual provides the courage of the collective to demand the submissiveness of the individual under the authority of the collective. Everything that one, as an individual, can be, one does become not through the collective but against the collective.

Collectives exert moral oppression. Their tools are the false gods of duty, pride, and sacrifice. Yet different from the association of rational egoists, the collective does not give compensation. The pattern of exchange in the collective is not reciprocity but extraction. Of all collectivist entities, the most horrific is the State. The State is the most suppressive and the most dangerous collective and therefore the greatest enemy of the individual because the State is the collective with the most comprehensive access to the application of violence. The modern State is the greatest propagator of modern wretchedness. The modern alienation is not the result of the division of labor but results from the individual's submission under the all-encompassing power of the State.

The State is the great trickster of the modern era. The politicians promise justice, freedom, and equality and in return demand all the power for themselves in the form of getting hold of the State power. By promising all, the State then takes all and makes the individual powerless. For the State, the claim to legality is the claim to violence. Law is created by State power yet a right that is bestowed is not a right and a type of freedom that is not achieved by oneself is not freedom. Justice is an instrument of tyranny and social justice is the tool of absolute tyranny. Equality is the biggest of all State lies. The desire for equality is already fraudulent, claims Max Stirner.

The way out of the captivity under the modern State is the free association of egoists beyond the State. However, under the present system of a comprehensive State, one cannot expect that many people will find their way to themselves. Most people will only become aware of their individuality when the collectivist bondage has ended and when the State is gone.

There will be not freedom as long as there exist a State. Doing away with the State is the great challenge of our time. In a dialectical turn of Hegelian dimension, the abolishment of the State is a political act. Ending the State may be the last and the greatest collective feat, the last and the greatest achievement of politics and it may be the true historical mission of political parties.

Rational egoism as it is promoted by Max Stirner must need be confounded with psychological and ethical egoism. Rational egoism is thoughtful self-interest, while psychological egoism is pathological. Ethical egoism is also off the screen of Stirner's concept of egoism because it would imply a moral obligation, which goes completely against the thrust of the philosophy of Max Stirner.

Types of egoism

```
                    Egoism
         ┌────────────┼────────────┐
   Pschological    Rational      Ethical
   (pathological  (thoughtful    (moral
   self-interest)  self-         obligation)
                   interest)
```

Antony P. Mueller

What Is Anarchism?

> *"Gentlemen, the time is coming when there will be two great classes, Socialists, and Anarchists. The Anarchists want the government to be nothing, and the Socialists want government to be everything."*
> William Graham Sumner (1911)

When we go beyond the mere explication of the concept 'anarchism' as one of Greek origin composed of *'an'* (against) and *'arkhos'* (leader), things get somewhat confused because 'anarchism' is also a political term, and as all political terms it is a polemical concept. In the sense of 'absence of government', the term emerged in France in the 1530s as *'anarchie'* and from the 1660s onwards, it was used as a general expression for the absence of authority and of a state of confusion. With the emergence of philosophers who called themselves explicitly 'anarchist', the term gained its modern meaning in the first half of the 19th century as 'order without power', 'stateless society', and 'direct government'.

Some historians of anarchism will trace back the roots of anarchism to Laozi, the ancient Greeks and the Stoics, while others will locate the origin of anarchism in the decades following the French Revolution. As a concept, too, 'anarchism' is many-layered. Much more than a specific term, anarchism is a generic concept which encompasses a wide range of meanings and many contradictions.

Whatever is the purpose of a classification, a necessary distinction must be made between 'political' and 'philosophical' anarchism. There is little that these two have in common and it may even appear doubtful whether the 'political anarchists' may have a legitimate claim on the title of 'anarchist'. After all, 'political anarchism' means being involved in political action ranging from public agitation to participate in wars (as it happened in the Spanish civil war with the syndicalist anarchists). The representatives of political anarchism such as Pierre-Joseph Proudhon (1809-1865), Mikhail Bakunin (1814-1876), and Peter Kropotkin (1842-1921) took an active part in the political fights of their days and were not less belligerent than their Communist soulmates.

Something else puts the political anarchist also close to their Communist brethren: their demand for economic equality. In this respect, the 'political anarchists' commit the same error as the Communists because they ignore that inequality lies in the nature of man and efforts of making something equal which is naturally unequal requires force and therefore is profoundly anti-anarchistic. More so, by participating in the political battles, the political anarchists betray the anarchist principle of opposing politics. What else is politics than the fight about gaining control of the State apparatus?

Sadly enough, the most widely distributed books about anarchism, such as, for example, Colin Ward's "Anarchism", which appeared in the Oxford series of "very short introductions" (Colin Ward: <u>Anarchism. A Very Short Introduction</u>. Oxford University Press 2004), largely ignore the difference between political and philosophical anarchism and dedicate almost all of their considerations to political anarchism. Ward stands in the tradition of other writers about anarchism such as George Woodcock's 470-page book, <u>Anarchism</u> of 1962, which has enjoyed many reprints as a Penguin paperback and was translated into many languages. Likewise, Peter Marshall's treatise of more than 700 pages called <u>Demanding the Impossible: A History of Anarchism</u> (HarperCollins) of 1992 which enjoys a large readership, does not provide a deep analysis of the philosophical branch of anarchism.

Philosophical anarchism is different from the political anarchism not because it is passive but because it does not choose the political way of bringing about an anarchist order. The philosophical anarchists know that throughout history the forceful replacement of one ruler has only emptied the chair for the next to take the seat of power. The philosophical anarchists also know that dominance does not come from force but by the consent of the dominated. The right way to proceed, therefore, is not confrontation with the State power but removing one's support from the State. The philosophical anarchists follow the insight that it is public opinion that produces voluntary servitude and that submission makes tyranny possible. The task of the philosophical anarchist is enlightenment, not rebellion. The political anarchist's way is more like a mutiny than an uprising.

The path to a free society comes through the change of public opinion. While this way seems long, shortcuts are not an alternative because they lead nowhere and most of the time only bring setbacks in the battle for liberty. Changes of opinion happen in an exponential form. For a long time, it may seem as if there hardly is any progress. Yet as time goes by, the curve gets steeper and finally things change overnight. Philosophical anarchists face only themselves as their foe when they desist and resign.

Different from the political anarchism which emerged in the decades after the French Revolution, philosophical anarchism can be traced back to the pre-Christian era. The time-line of thinkers in this tradition is impressive. Philosophical anarchism can claim the Chinese Laozi (who died in 533 BC) as one of their earliest known representatives of an anti-authoritarian political philosophy ('In governing, don't try to control'), the Greek school of the cynics and the stoics as well as the many elements of anarchistic thinking in Buddhism and Hinduism.

Zeno of Citium, in the footsteps of Diogenes of Sinope, advocated anarchistic forms of society around 300 BC. Zeno's model of a Republic needs no

State structures. In opposition to Plato (ca. 425 BC to 348/347 BC), Zeno opposed the omnipotence of the State, contra its intervention and its regimentation. He argued that man's natural sociability keeps his egoism in check.

Better known than Zeno and Diogenes are the writings of Epicurus (341 BC to 270 BC). Following the atomic materialism of Democritus, the philosophy of Epicurus opposes superstition and divine intervention. As the original thinker of what nowadays is called "epicureanism", he promoted hedonism and for that opposed participation in politics because of its connection to the lust for power and to the desire for fame.

Ancient Rome was the very anti-thesis to anarchism. The stoics Epictetus (50 to 135) and Marcus Aurelius (121-180) are the few thinkers in ancient Rome with some connection to anarchism.

We do not know which philosopher had lived in the commercial realm of Carthage and contributed to anarchist thought. In the three Punic Wars (264 BC to 146 BC), the Roman militarism wiped out Carthage with only a heap of stones left. The Carthaginian commercial empire was one of the economically highest developed communities, a fully commercial commonwealth with strong anarcho-capitalist characteristics. Maybe the Carthaginians had no libertarian or anarchist philosopher because they did not need them as they were already the practitioners of a stateless society.

In the Middle Ages, Meister Eckhart (ca. 1260 – ca. 1328) rose to prominence as a theologian and mystic. His writings had a great influence on the thinking of the communitarian anarchist Gustav Landauer (1870-1919), who in turn inspired the early Zionist kibbutz movement.

Concerning the philosophy of late Middle Ages, one must pay tribute to the great contributions of the Portuguese and Spanish scholastics, particularly the works of Francisco Suárez (1548-1617), with the promotion of concepts such as subjective utility, personal sovereignty, and the justification of tyrannicide.

In the wake of the Reformation, several anarchist movements of Christian character appeared such as Hussites, Adamites and the early Anabaptists. Known as the "Münster Rebellion", the Anabaptists established a short-lived communal sectarian government in 1534 which was crashed down in 1535.

At the beginning of the modern age, the first great master pieces of anti-authoritarian thinking were "The Praise of Folly" (1511) by Erasmus of Rotterdam (1466-1536), followed by "Voluntary Servitude" (written around 1549, published in 1576) by Etienne La Boétie (1530-1563). Both are classics that have not lost any of their relevance.

A milestone in the development of libertarian thinking and anarcho-philosophy came with the publication of *"The Grumbling Hive, or Knaves Turn'd Honest"* in 1705, better known under its later title as *"Fable of the Bees. Private Vices, Publick Benefits"* by **Bernard de Mandeville (1670-1733)**. Without this intellectual breakthrough, this profound transformation of moral values, neither the economic theories of Adam Smith nor the philosophical ideas of David Hume would have come forth, and all of these three have motivated Immanuel Kant (1724-1804) to write his promotion of the world peace of a community of free republics with his *"Toward an Eternal Peace"* (1795).

A proper anarchist literature emerges with William Godwin (1756-1836) who uses the term anarchism with adroit. His *"Enquiry Concerning Political Justice and its Influence on Morals and Happiness"* of 1793 is a classic of anarchist literature. In this work, Godwin denounces the State as the institution that instead of its claim of promoting human progress, restrains the advancement of mankind.

With a grain of salt, one may add to this chronology John Stuart Mill (1805-1873), particularly his *On Liberty* (1859). It is not completely false when some authors name Mill as the founder of what nowadays in American usage is called "liberalism" and elsewhere is known as "social democracy".

The first treatise on individualist anarchism was written by Max Stirner (1806-1856). His *"Der Einzige und sein Eigenthum"* (not quite correctly translated as '*The Ego and its Own*') was published in 1844 (predated to 1845). His philosophy is a radical denouncement of all collectives that terrorize the individual as spooks in the form of abstractions, such as God, the nation, or society.

Individualist anarchism flourished in the 19th century in the United States in the works of such well-known figures as Ralph Waldo Emerson (1803-1882), William Graham Sumner (1840-1910), Benjamin Tucker (1854-1939) and continued to prosper in the 20th century with authors such as Murray Rothbard (1926-1995), Robert Nozick (1938-2002) and many more.

The Austrian School of Economics stands in close connection with the anarchist tradition in the United States. Many libertarian scholars are also Austrian economists such as Murray Rothbard. Austrian economics has its roots in the scholarly contributions of Carl Menger (1840-1921), Eugen von Böhm-Bawerk (1851-1914), Ludwig von Mises (1881-1973), and Friedrich Hayek (1899-1992). This school, in turn, can trace its roots back to the school of Salamanca and the French economists such as Francois Quesnay (1694-1774), Anne Robert Jacques Turgot (1727-1781), Jean-Baptiste Say (1767-1832), and Frédéric Bastiat (1801-1850).

Timeline of modern anarchism

Type	Representative	Major work(s)	Quote
Liberal Anarchism	William Godwin (1756-1836)	*Enquiry concerning Political Justice, and its Influence on General Virtue and Happiness* (1793)	'Government was intended to suppress injustice, but its effect has been to embody and perpetuate it.'
Ego-Anarchism	Max Stirner (1806-1856)	*The Ego and Its Own* (1844)	'What is freedom? To have the will to be responsible for one's self.'
Mutualism	Pierre-Joseph Proudhon (1809-1865)	*What is Property?* (1840)	'Property is theft' 'Property is freedom' 'Anarchy is order'
Socialist Anarchism	Mikhail Bakunin (1814-1876)	*God and the State* (1882)	'Freedom without socialism is privilege and injustice, but socialism without freedom is slavery and brutality.'
Anarcho-Syndicalism	Rudolf Rocker (1873-1958)	*Nationalism and Culture* (1937) *Anarcho-Syndicalism: Theory & Practice* (1947)	'it is the state which creates the nation, and not the nation the state.'

Communist Anarchism	Peter Kropotkin (1842–1921)	*Fields, Factories and Workshops* (1899)	'All things are for all' 'Don't compete!'
Communal Anarchism	Gustav Landauer (1870-1919)	*Revolution* (1907)	'nothing but the rebirth of all peoples out of the spirit of regional community can bring salvation'
Feminist Anarchism	Emma Goldman (1869-1940)	*Anarchism and Other Essays* (1910)	"I demand the independence of woman, her right to support herself; to live for herself; to love whomever she pleases, or as many as she pleases.'
Individualist Anarchism	Benjamin Tucker (1854-1939)	*Individual Liberty*, 1926	'Mind your own business' 'Aggression, invasion, government, are interconvertible'
Anarcho-liberalism (libertarianism)	Murray Rothbard (1826-1995)	*The Ethics of Liberty* (1982)	'Government is a band of thieves writ large'
Anarcho-capitalism	Hans-Hermann Hoppe (1849-)	*Democracy - the God that Failed*	'Democracy has nothing to do with freedom'

***

It does not matter whether one believes in God or in natural selection as long as one sticks to the principle that both, individuality and sociability, are inherent to human nature and therefore no external force is needed for the individual to live and prosper together with other individuals in a community. Anarchism is the freedom from external control beyond that which comes from oneself. Anarchism is anti-state and anti-government, but not anti-social. Because laws are only justified when they are in harmony with human nature, no

State legislation is needed. The laws that are justified by nature need no codification and all other laws are illegitimate.

Anarchism is radical individualism. The theory of anarchism rejects the reality of collectives and adheres to a strict nominalism. Collectives such as the State or the Church are real only insofar as they form part of an individual's belief system.

The common body of anarchism is the pursuit of liberty not in the State and under the State or as the State, but against State and government. Anarchist reject the ancient Roman concept of *libertas* as a republican constitution of a popular government, the Lockean concept of liberty as individual liberty protected by the State or the concept of liberty as *volonté général* by Rousseau or liberty as embodied in the rationality of statehood as in Hegel's philosophy.

Types of Anarchism

```
                        Anarchism
                    /              \
          Political Anarchism    Philosophical anarchism
           /           \            /            \
    Anarcho-    Collectivist   Individualist   Anarcho-
   Syndicalism   Anarchism      anarchism     capitalism
```

The distinction between political and philosophical anarchism is important because it is only partially a separation between politics and theory as it is common also in other areas, such as in economics, for example. As to anarchism, the distinction refers also to the method of how to establish an anarchist society. The way for the political anarchists is political activism, the launch of political parties and the use of direct political exploits. Philosophical anarchists, in contrast, want to bring about the anarchist society through indirect means, through the change of public opinion and by incremental privatizations. The method of the political anarchist is political and confrontational; the method of the philosophical anarchists is persuasive and economic.

Anarcho-syndicalism seeks to establish an anarchist society through the mobilization of the working class. In this sense, this movement is an immediate rival of the Communists who claim to have the same 'revolutionary subject' as their vehicle. It comes as no surprise that the competition between these two groups has been fierce and combative. In the great political battles of the past century, the anarcho-syndicalists were frequently the enemy of both the Communists and the social democrats. In the trenches of the Spanish civil war, the factions of the political anarchism were as much fighting against each other as against the fascists as their common enemy.

Collectivist anarchism shares the Communist ideal of common property but is opposed to the rule of a party. The main representatives of the collectivist anarchism, such as Peter Kropotkin, were rancorous enemies of the Soviet regime as it was established under Vladimir Lenin in 1917. Collectivist anarchism made important contributions to the kibbutzim communities of the Zionist movement during the foundational period of Israel.

The main representatives of philosophical anarchism are individualist anarchism and anarcho-capitalism. The very designation as 'individualist' already prohibits for this line of thinking that one would form political parties or fight together in partisan groups. It would be wrong, however, to classify the individualist anarchist as solitary or anti-social. Not even the most radical of this line of thinking, Max Stirner, called to abandon community and social cooperation. His ideal was an 'association of egoists', where one egoism matches that of the others, and all members profit from social exchange and the division of labor.

Anarcho-capitalism is based on economics. The major difference to the other forms of anarchism is that anarcho-capitalist does promote neither common property nor equality of income and wealth. Anarcho-capitalism demands free markets as extensive and as intensive as possible based on the respect for private property. The theory of anarcho-capitalism holds that under the condition of free capitalism, differences in wealth and income will emerge only temporarily for specific producers and will be wiped-out sooner or later because of technical progress and free market entry. Furthermore, anarcho-capitalism postulates that under the conditions of free competition with low barriers to market entry and market exit, technological progress will happen more rapidly, more frequently, and rather continually so that the disruptive effect of change will be smaller than it is in a more slow-moving society where social and political interests have time to gain power positions and where habit makes people conformist.

For the anarcho-capitalist, freedom and prosperity have their anchor in private property. This way, Hans-Hermann Hoppe explains the Rothbardian ethics:

> "*Everyone is the proper owner of his own physical body as well as of all places and nature-given goods that he occupies and puts to use by means of his body, provided only that no one else has already occupied or used the same places and goods before him. This ownership of "originally appropriated" places*

and goods by a person implies his right to use and transform these places and goods in any way he sees fit, provided only that he does not change thereby uninvitedly the physical integrity of places and goods originally appropriated by another person. In particular, once a place or good has been first appropriated by, in John Locke's phrase, 'mixing one's labor' with it, ownership in such places and goods can be acquired only by means of a voluntary – contractual – transfer of its property title from a previous to a later owner."

A problem shared by all variants of anarchism is the problem that freedom exists in a trilateral field of tension. A look at the dimensions of freedom makes it clear that full liberty is beyond human ability. There will never be complete 'freedom of' or 'freedom to'. The best one can hope to achieve is a high degree of 'freedom from', such as the freedom from tyranny and the freedom from misery.

Dimensions of Freedom

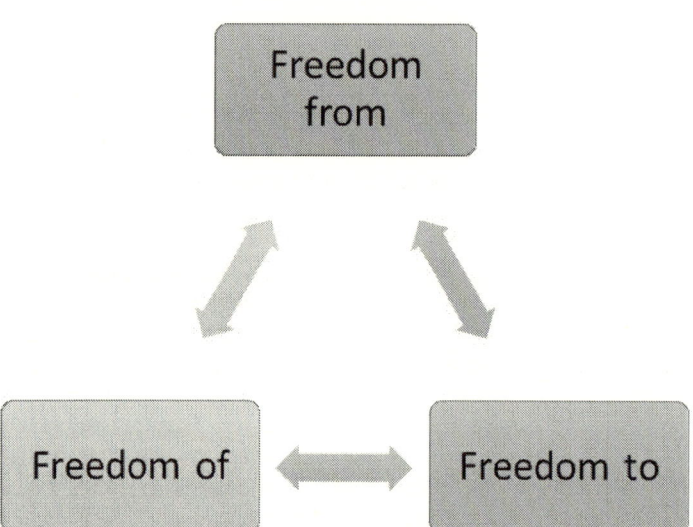

After the disaster of the Spanish Civil War for the political anarchist movement, political anarchism has lost much of its appeal. Even the kibbutzim movement has largely petered out. Fascism, Nazism, and Communism have gone, and with it political anarchism as their main counterpunch. What lives on and has gained more momentum since the beginning of the second half of the 20th century is philosophical anarchism, both as individualist anarchism and as anarcho-capitalism. There is no mutual exclusion between individualist anarchism and anarcho-capitalism. Each line of thinking stresses a somewhat different point. Individualist anarchism focuses primarily on the 'freedom to' - to be one's own personality as one wishes to develop. Both, anarcho-capitalism and individualist anarchism, demand the 'freedom of', such as the freedom of speech and both claim as much 'freedom from' as possible in the sense of freedom from tyranny and economic misery.

***

The books were on the shelf, the knowledge spread, yet the time had not yet come in the past centuries to realize the utopia of a free society. The political means was still too powerful compared to the economic means, as the famous distinction put forward by Franz Oppenheimer says.

In his book about voluntary servitude, Etienne La Boétie lamented that even under the worst suppression by tyranny, there will always be some eminent men who know about freedom, who feel the spirit of liberty but with censorship, difficulties of transport, and the means of communication under State control, these freedom-minded persons have a hard time communicating and remain solitary in their efforts.

In our times, these conditions have changed. The restraints on communication and transport have diminished. All it takes is to maintain and gain back the right of free speech. The right to bear guns as the armament of the people against tyranny is not sufficient without the freedom of speech. These two rights belong together, and it is not a coincidence that they stand side by side as the first and second amendment of the American Constitution.

Today, the main task of the philosophical anarchist is his engagement for free speech because it is the only way how a change of public opinion can come about. Different from the State intellectuals, the philosophical anarchists will not manipulate. Their use of the media is not to indoctrinate the people. It is the creed of the philosophical anarchists that liberty is not a chimera, that it is not something that comes from the outside to the hearts of the men but that it is within everybody, that it is not an attachment to human nature but at the core of his very existence. Free speech is the means to express oneself, to distinguish oneself, to speak about one's wishes and of one's conditions. Free speech means human expression. Without free speech, the essence of being a human gets lost.

The only way to extinguish the human strife for liberty is to suppress free speech. As long as the freedom of expression is with us, the freedom of man is safe. So long as we can speak up freely, the light of liberty will shine, and the message of freedom will spread.

Concepts

The present system of state capitalism has become an obstacle to wealth creation. Under the political system of the modern party-democracy, there is a constant pressure at work to expand government. The rule of the party democracy undermines the free market economy. Interventionism and taxation have become the trademark of the modern State. In order to bring the economy back on the path to prosperity, a fundamental change must be made: not only with the economic order but also with government. Even more, the breakthrough must also encompass the spiritual attitude. The triumph of free capitalism comes with the self-liberation of the individual. Anarcho-capitalism and anarcho-individualism are the two sides of the same coin of a free republic.

The present order is under the full authority of the State. While classical liberalism could still make a distinction between family, society, nation, and state, these distinctions have disappeared in the modern State which has become totalitarian not only in its fascist or socialist shaping. The modern State in its current form as a democracy appears only gentle in its appearance. Behind this façade, this State is as brutal and as violent as any of its predecessors. The modern State has become all-encompassing and subsumes under its authority the nation, government, and the people.

Total State

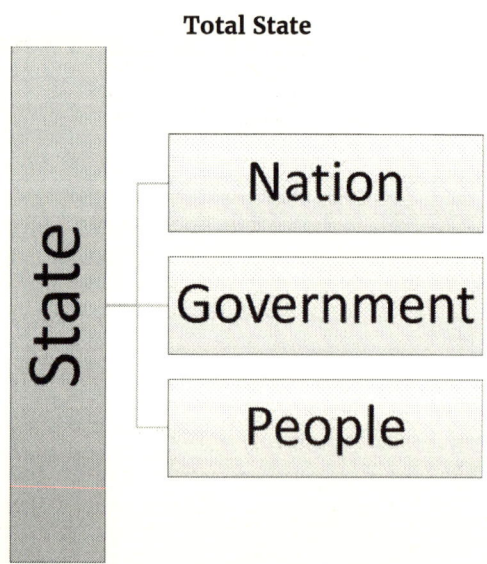

In order to distinguish the present State from a polity of free men, an appropriate term seems to be 'anarcho-republicanism'. Anarcho-republicanism is a polity whose constituent elements are personal ownership, private property, voluntary association, and non-aggression.

Anarcho-republicanism defines a polity based on the voluntary association of free persons for the cooperative attainment of individual aims, a polity that is a republic ("res publica") in its true sense different from state organizations that are hierarchical, dictatorial, and authoritarian.

As to its governance, the anarcho-republic requires an order whose authority is not the State but the people as the term "republic" in the sense of "res publica" - public matters - denotes.

Rule of the res publica

The structure of such a *polity* would comprise a General Assembly composed of members chosen by lot, a Supervisory Board as a special committee as part of the General Assembly and the government, which exerts the executive functions as a private management company under the authority of the General Assembly and the Supervisory Board.

Republic

Republic (res publica)		
General Assembley		Supervisory Board
Laws	State apparatus	Government

While anarcho-individualism denotes the philosophy, libertarianism stands for the political movement aimed at establishing the governance of free persons. Libertarianism stands against all those movements which try to establish an authoritarian or a dictatorial rule. Anarcho-liberalism is the specific political philosophy which promotes a polity based on the voluntary association of free persons for the cooperative attainment of individual aims.

"Demarchy" is a form of governance where the people's representatives are chosen by lottery in contrast to the political systems whose rulers come to power through heritage, force or vote, while "sortition" designates the process through which the representative body of the people is chosen in a lottery in contrast to systems of vote, co-option, and cooptation. Those selected by lot form the members of the General Assembly, which is the representative body of the electorate that form the legislative body of the Republican Polity similar to parliaments or congresses in the modern democracies.

Institutional structure

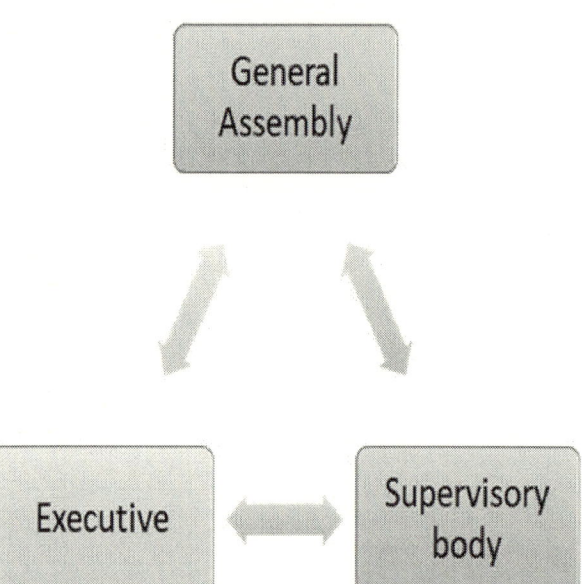

Anarcho-individualism is the guiding philosophy of the model of a free republic. The anarcho-individualist philosophy puts the sovereign individual at the center of the system of values in contrast to all forms of collectivism and hierarchical authoritarian organizations.

The supervisory body is a part of the General Assembly with special assignments of supervision over the private government management agency resembling the old Upper House in Britain or Senates in the original meaning.

In the polity of a free republic, the government is a private government agency that is hired by the General Assembly and supervised by the Supervisory Body to exert executive functions akin to governments in the traditional sense yet without state authority. The judicial management is done by private law agencies that offer services of arbitration similar to current arbitration services and private law agencies that offer services of arbitration similar to current arbitration services. Likewise, policing is assigned to Private police similar to the present forms of non-state law-enforcement bodies. The defense is under the authority of the General Assembly and of the supervision by the Supervisory body, the defense of the community is managed by private companies.

Anarchistic Individualism

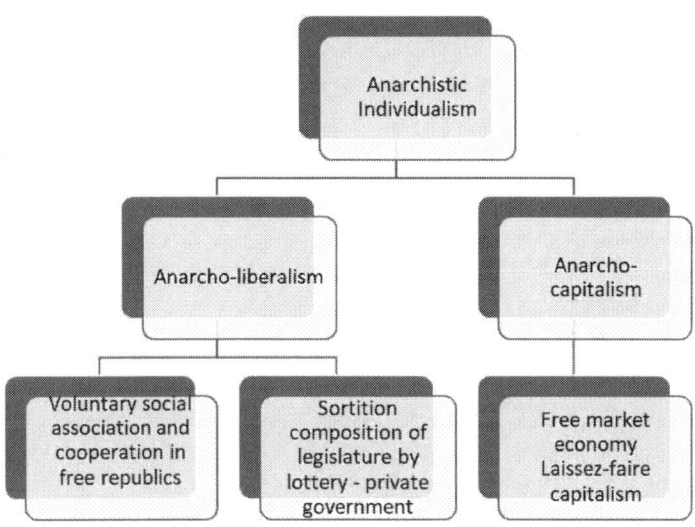

In the context of the polity of a free republic, anarcho-capitalism refers to a free market economy ("Laissez-faire"-capitalism) - an economic order based on private property and free markets in contrast to state capitalism, socialism, communism, and interventionism.

Antony P. Mueller

Is Anarcho-Capitalism Possible?

Even if one agrees that anarcho-capitalism has become a necessity, the question arises whether such a governance is possible. After all, at first sight, insurmountable problems seem to prevent the flourishing of a stateless society. Libertarianism means a private law society. Private businesses in the marketplace provide the traditional functions of the state. An order of anarcho-capitalism substitutes the hierarchical coordination of activities of the state through horizontal cooperation based on voluntary exchange. Although a libertarian order amounts to a revolution as to its consequences, the path to its creation is non-revolutionary. The way to an anarcho-capitalist order is gradual as an on-going process of privatizations. Beginning with the sale of semi-public enterprises and public utilities, privatization will extend step by step to education and health and will also encompass security and the judicial system.

Frequent objections against anarcho-capitalism doubt the possibility to substitute state activity by the private sector. Questions arise such as: 'If there is no state, who would build the roads - who would care for the poor - who would provide for education, health services, security, and justice? If there is no state, who would pay the pensions?' - Such questions are not the result of analysis but of habit. If the supply of socks and underwear were in the hands of the state, people would ask the same questions concerning socks and underwear. If the state takes over an activity, it drives out private supply. This leads to the paradoxical result that government services seem indispensable the more activities the state has under its control.

Not too long ago, many of the activities, which now provides the state, were in private hands. The government did not take over these services because the private sector failed but because the party politicians, in their search for power and its extension, have encroached upon the private sector. Once when the interventionist spiral got started, there was no end: the more the state commands, the mightier politicians and state functionaries become. As the market economy recedes, the easier it gets for the party politicians to bring further activities under their authority.

When the state takes over an economic activity, scarcity does not diminish but grows. Therefore, all major activities of the state - be it education, healthcare or external and domestic security - appear always as being under-funded and in need of expansion. Because of the artificial scarcity, the electorate demands more of these services the more the state provides. No party politicians would dare to deny these wishes. Which political party representative would propose less spending for education, healthcare, and security? The voters do not realize that they are in a trap. They fail to see that beyond the lack of efficiency there is also an oversupply of governmental services.

The limit to an endless expansion of the state in terms of expenditures is the budget constraint. When the state has reached the financial limit, the control mania does not stop but goes on in other areas. When government spending hits its bound and financial restrictions curtail government expenditures, the state turns to the control of those activities that do not require spending money. Consequently, the fastest growing areas of state activities over the past decades have been behavioral sanctions - reaching from what one may eat and drink to what one may say and not say. First, governments regulate what you may take into your mouth, then the state controls what may come out of your mouth.

Under anarcho-capitalism, most of what the state supplies in services could fall to a fraction of the present volume. On a world-wide scale, military spending alone comprises around 1.7 trillion US-dollars annually. The so-called 'public services' would not only become better and cheaper, but it would also turn out that under a free market, the demand for education, healthcare, defense, and domestic security would be much different than it is now. Therefore, to privatize many of the activities, which now are under the authority of state would not only lead to a decrease of the costs per unit of the services but also reduce the volume of supply because a large part of the current supply of so-called 'public goods' is a useless waste. Losing none of the genuine benefits of education, healthcare, and defense, the budgets for these provisions could fall to a fraction of their present size.

If one includes the overblown judicial and public administration apparatus into the reduction of state activity, government spending, which nowadays is close to fifty percent of the gross domestic product in most industrialized countries, could come down to the single digits. Taxes and contributions could fall by ninety percent.

Different from what is presently the dominant belief, to privatize the police functions and the judiciary is not such a big problem. It would mean to extend what is already going on. In the United States of today, for example, private policing, such as by security guards, happens already at a grand scale and comprises more than one million persons. In some countries, including the United States, the number of private police and security already exceeds the number of official policemen. The private provision of judicial services is on the rise. Arbitration courts experience a strong and increasing demand including services for cross-border disputes. These trends will go on because private protection and arbitration is cheaper and better than the public provision. In Brazil, for example, which entertains one of the most expensive judicial systems of the world, currently about eighty million cases are pending without decision, and legal uncertainty has become monstrous.

Antony P. Mueller

The Struggle for Liberty

Some critics of libertarianism ask that if anarcho-capitalism were such a good order, why hasn't it been tried before. The answer to that contention is that there has not yet been a libertarian order because up to now it was impossible to have one. The cause for this is that throughout history, regimes established themselves by force and as soon as a specific person or group of persons had conquered power, they would try to monopolize information to their favor. Bereft of means of communication and under censorship, libertarianism was denied its voice in contrast to the avalanche of theories, opinions, and propaganda that justified and deified the state and government.

Throughout history, information was a monopoly. Most the people could not read or write. Books, pamphlets, and other reading material were beyond the reach of the common man. It was only in the 15th century when a significant change took place with the printing press based on moveable letters. This business innovation lowered the costs of publications. As reading material became accessible, learning to read and to write became a useful skill.

Inventing the modern printing press ended the era of a monopoly of information. Yet this technology was still too limited to bring a full inclusion. What came about was not universality of information but an informational oligopoly. Over the past centuries, a few institutions held the power in their hands. A small group of newspapers, publishing houses, universities and a few relevant TV stations, and film studios have controlled the media and guaranteed the role of a few powerful states and global institutions as the holders of power. This situation is about to change, and the conversion will be as dramatic as that which happened with the shift from the monopolistic age of information to an oligopolistic structure.

Before Johannes Gutenberg invented the printing press with mobile letters in the first half of the 15thcentury, information was a monopoly business. Access to information and its distribution confronted high barriers to entry. For those outside the dominant power structure, it was impossible to overcome these fences. Since technological thresholds restricted the access to and the use of information, it was easy for those in power to control the content and the access to information. Control over information means dominance over people. This constellation established a power system which excluded large parts of the population. When these informational barriers fell, the world began to change like never before.

The first manifestations of the new oligopolistic structure of information was the rise of religious groups outside Catholicism. It is no exaggeration to say that without the modern printing press, neither the Reformation nor the scientific revolution, nor the industrial revolution, could have happened. The modern 'knowledge economy' begins with the printing press because this instrument was essential for the dissemination of knowledge beyond small circles.

The modern age did not yet bring full liberty. The world as it emerged from the fifteenth century onward has remained a world of authoritarian power and control. While the old monopoly structure disappeared, not freedom, but an oligopoly emerged, which allowed censorship and exclusion although in a more limited way than had been the case in the age of the monopoly of information.

It was not only in the religious sphere that an oligopoly supplanted the monopoly, but also in the sphere of politics and science. In almost all its aspects, the modern world presents these oligopolistic structures. For example, there is not much more than about a handful of countries that represent the great powers, as it is institutionalized with the permanent members of the Security Council of the United Nations or the G7. Almost the same oligopolistic structure holds for scientific theories, with dominant ideologies or with the group of prestigious universities. Conflicts did not abate but rose because it had become more difficult to establish a monopoly of information. A fierce struggle among the oligopoly of states, parties, scientific theories, ideologies, and religions characterizes the modern age. Not an era of freedom and peace emerged but a period of atrocious struggles between the members of the various oligopolies with each one striving to become a monopolist.

Now, with the new information technologies, this strife of the members of the oligopoly of becoming the monopolist is falling apart because the new informational landscape has gained a polypolistic structure where not a few participants struggle but many suppliers compete with no one having a chance to dominate the market.

***

With the onset of the industrial revolution, the fight for lower taxes became the main content of the American and the French revolution with the consequent abolishment of the monarchy. Yet doing away with the monarchy did not mean doing away with the state. Libertarian philosophy experienced its first great flourishing at the time of the American Revolution. In continuation of the thoughts and theories of classical liberalism, American pamphleteers popularized liberty and of a state-free economy and prepared the path for the American independence.

Classical liberalism wanted to promote individual liberty and to minimize and to do away with the state as the enemy of individualism and liberty. The political program of the old liberalism called for the lowest level of taxes and wanted to eliminate economic regulations. The aim of liberalism was to set the individual free from the shackles and burdens of the traditional state and its absolutist and authoritarian encroachments. A break-up between the alliance of the throne with the merchants and the church was the intention of liberal movement. Separating these spheres meant to diminish the role of government and of the state-aligned church. Along with promoting peace, an essential part of the liberal project was to reduce the size and power of the state. The main weapon of the liberals in the battle against the state was the fight for lower taxes.

Yet the time was not yet ripe for the full establishment of an anarcho-capitalist order and of the reign of the 'obvious and simple system of natural liberty' as Adam Smith put it. Together with classical liberalism in England, American libertarianism came under the authority of the state as the promoter of what nowadays is called 'liberalism'. This modern liberal - or rather 'social-democratic'- political structure is far removed from the original ideas of classical liberalism and in some respects, it is the opposite. Instead of having less state, liberal democracy comes with more intervention; instead of more individual liberty, the current system has extended its control over the individual.

Even those countries that had gotten rid of the monarchy, suffered from the restoration of the state.

Murray Rothbard ("For a New Liberty. The Libertarian Manifesto p. 12) explains that in the 19th century "*statism and Big Government returned, but this time displaying a preindustrial and pro-general-welfare face. The Old Order returned, but this time the beneficiaries were shuffled a bit; they were not so much the nobility, the feudal landlords, the army, the bureaucracy, and privileged merchants as they were the army, the bureaucracy, the weakened feudal landlord, and especially the privileged manufacturer. Led by Bismarck in Prussia, the New Right fashioned a right-wing collectivism based on war, militarism, protectionism, and the compulsory cartelization of business and industry - a giant network of controls, regulations, subsidies, and privileges which forged a great partnership of Big Government with certain favored elements in big business and industry.*"

Compared to the monarchical rule, things got worse. The new 'democratic' states would not only more spend, tax, and regulate but also become more aggressive. The democratic revolutions gave birth to three poisonous monsters: nationalism, imperialism, and socialism.

In as much as the masses had to be convinced that this new interventionist nationalist state was better for the people than a minimal state and free markets, to manipulate public opinion would now play a central role. With the demise of the churchmen as the main molders of public creed came the rise of the modern intellectual: "*the new breed of professors, Ph.D's, historians, teachers, and technocratic economists, social workers, sociologists, physicians, and engineers*" (Rothbard, op. cit., p. 14). Instead of having of their behavior guided by priests, the gullible public now surrendered to the rule of the 'experts' as the new breed who claimed not to speak in the name of a God but as the disciples of 'science'.

Information was not yet free. Although it was no longer necessary to become a member of the clergy, but in order to gain access to knowledge, one had to pass the state-controlled school and university system. Against this mass of state-controlled information, the voices of liberty had no chance.

Death of the Gatekeepers

The printing press allowed the production and distribution of books and pamphlets and scientific treatises with much lower costs than before. This, in turn, encouraged literacy. But the process of literacy itself, in the form of public education, became a system of control. Access to knowledge has become wider, but it has remained restricted, manipulative, and concentrated. At the entrance to the access of knowledge stood the gatekeepers. Whether it be a school or a university, religious groups or political parties, the oligopolistic structure of power demanded control of the admittance to the realms of knowledge. It is no surprise, for example, that joining a political party is almost like joining a religious group. To climb the ranks of a political party is not much different from making a career in a religious order and both ways are not much different from an intellectual career. Gatekeepers are notorious in excluding unwanted truths and aborting new approaches that defy conventional wisdom.

Now, the ascent of the Internet marks the end of the gatekeepers. Prior to the information revolution, the predominance of oligopolistic structures was ubiquitous, as shown, for example, by the oligopoly of television stations. Now, with the Internet, the multitude of outlets encompasses all the media. The new ways of communication dissolve the old structures. One result of this revolutionary transformation is that informational constraint is over. Access and distribution of information are confronting few barriers as long as the basic liberties still prevail.

This new media revolution has a technical and a sociopolitical side. In the past, technology served as an instrument of exclusion, now it can serve as a means of inclusion. Times of transition are turbulent, and this is also the case with the new media. Much of what now seems dangerous, however, such as the apparent absence of informational filters and of a so-called quality control, will in the future appear as inconsequential as it is now with the Index of forbidden books of the past and the 'Imprimatur' of the Catholic Church.

The current informational revolution with the Internet at its center works in favor of freedom. Unlike in the past, when the media served specific groups to impose their will on the rest of society, the Internet revolution does the opposite. Instead of being instrumental for a limited group in their efforts of maintaining their rule, the Internet will challenge the concentration of power. In this sense, the current revolution is a libertarian revolution. Its first achievement is to dissolute power positions. This process is already in full swing.

Only still a few decades ago, it was costly to spread information. One needed a TV or radio station, for example, or had to launch a magazine or a newspaper. Nowadays, the Internet allows the world-wide storage and the dissemination of ideas at negligent costs. The old barriers are crumbling. Consequently, there is no longer a limitation on the variety of subjects to deal with. Before the information revolution, the providers - whether news channels, academic journals, or booksellers - were forced to focus their supply on the middle of the distribution curve to reach most customers. Because of limited space, the supply was restricted. Nowadays, with almost unlimited storage space, the offer extends to the long tails of the distribution.

With the Internet revolution, the costs of dissemination of new ideas have fallen close to zero. Likewise, access to information has become quasi costless. The consequence is an increase of the mass of information along with its diversification. This phenomenon ranges from music to academic texts. Mass and diversity are the hallmarks of the worldwide web. In the past, there has always been a trade-off between distribution and diversity. To maintain a tabloid with a wide circulation, for example, content had to focus on the most popular themes. Now, free of gatekeepers and with unlimited space, the special topics find a market.

In the past, power was concentrated in the hands of the gatekeepers. The guards decided what was 'correct' and what was 'false', what to publish and what not. The system of gatekeepers included the editors at TV stations and the newspapers, the referees of the scientific journals, and the decision-makers in the ministries of education along with all the other 'authorities' whose task was to take care of the 'truth' - which mostly was nothing but to hide the truths from the public because of the interests of power and because of prejudices.

Now, without the gatekeepers and with an almost limitless space available, diversity is spreading in the new media and it is up to the individual user to judge the content and to decide whether it is worth the access. In the past, the media gatekeepers practiced their power *ex officio* as an authoritarian activity. Claiming this role, the argument was to maintain 'quality standards', but this was a pretext given that the impediment was the limited space that made a screening indispensable. Different from an electronic platform of books, the brick and mortar library buildings have limited space. The modern media remove these restrictions and make the access time more flexible. The new world of information has become a world without major barriers where heterogeneity rules over homogeneity.

Toward the New World of Freedom

The oligopolistic era of modern history is ending. Dominance by the few is coming to an end. When barriers are low and almost nonexistent, supremacy is waning. Nevertheless, the old authorities still seek to maintain and regain their informational privileges. Yet when some governments turn off the Internet or limit access, they undermine their legitimacy and destroy the productivity of their economies. Governments that quit the global information network and shut-off their citizens will push their countries into an economic abyss and will fail to maintain their rule. Closed political systems are able to copy established technologies but have a hard time to develop new technologies.

At the same time when the barriers to the distribution of non-conformist information and opinions fall, the costs to maintain the established institutions are on the rise. Schools and universities, hospitals, and media outlets together with maintaining the welfare-warfare expenditures face an avalanche of costs that will ruin those states which try to go on as in the past. The state as we know it, will disappear. This way or the other: either by voluntary transformation or because of financial collapse. The question is whether the old order will go down with blood and tears or make peacefully way for a new liberty.

The foundations of the new information revolution are firm. Different from the past, this time the fundamentals promote freedom and diversification. The era of authentic liberalism has arrived. While in the past, the media favored authoritarian and totalitarian regimes because both the press and radio and television allowed hierarchical control, the global information network favors free access and distribution on a global scale. This constellation will limit and render the installation and maintenance of totalitarian regimes impossible. Implementing strict controls over the media is difficult. There are many chances that the new epoch in world history will become an era of libertarianism. Libertarianism as a political philosophy does not have, by its very nature, the goal of domination by exclusion as all other political ideologies have. Libertarianism promotes pluralism, diversification, and inclusion. In this sense, the new media, and the Internet are compatible with the libertarian political philosophy. This novelty represents a historical singularity.

Although the risks may seem small that a global totalitarian regime will emerge soon, one must take it into consideration and respond to it with strong voice case in favor of a libertarian revolution. Taking away power from the state is a moral necessity in the face of the prospect that the new technologies would put such an immense arsenal of surveillance and control into the hands of the state that a future totalitarian regime could exert complete control over the individual and produce the uttermost terror. Therefore, to establish an anarcho-capitalist order is a matter of human dignity.

What needs to be done as practical steps to establish a new order of liberty is, first, a change of the system of selection of the representatives through a lottery, called 'demarchy' or sortition.

Sortition (demarchy)

'Sortition' – also called 'demarchy' - is a form of governance that selects the representatives of the people as a random sample from a pool of candidates. Governance by selecting the people's representatives by lottery instead of elections can look back on a venerable history. For Aristotle (384 - 322 BC), to select the people's political representatives by lot instead of voting distinguishes the democracy from oligarchical rule: 'So it is ... democratic to occupy the offices by lot, and for the oligarchy by vote' (Aristotle, Politics, IV, 9, 1294b 7-9). Likewise, for Montesquieu (1689-1755) the lottery procedure corresponds to 'the nature of democracy' ('The spirit of the laws' - 1748).

In the ancient Greek polis, for the 'Great Council of the 500', as well as for judges and for some state officials, selection took place by the lot – as it is still partly the case in Switzerland. In the Republic of Venice, the selection procedure for the government and its members used the lottery in many ways. Until the 17th century, England also practiced the lottery system. Today, modern technology offers the possibility to apply random selection procedures to large populations.

The following advantages of demarchy are evident:
- High degree of popular legitimacy
- Independence of the representatives
- Absence of corruption
- No political parties
- Representation by normal people instead by political power seekers
- Elimination of the costs of the election campaigns
- Reduction of the overall cost of the political apparatus
- Comprehensible laws
- End of the inflation of laws, rules, and regulations
- Minimization of the state (less government spending, lower taxes).

Critics of demarchy claim that a parliament, whose members are selected by chance, has less expertise than an elected parliament, and that this would increase the power of the bureaucracy. The truth, however, is that the specific knowledge that is now present in the assemblies, exists in knowing how to gain and to exert power, and non-political competence is missing. Even more so, the current system of party politics has led to a huge bureaucracy and a massive build-up of the power of the state apparatus. The political parties and the bureaucratic apparatus cooperate to maximize their power which they achieve by having more state, not less.

***

The left-right scheme to denote one's position in the political spectrum is a dangerous device. Limiting the political spectrum to 'left' and 'right' deceives by its simplicity. It leaves a large area open in the center, at the top and at the bottom.

A better distinction than 'left' and 'right' is 'authoritarian' and 'libertarian'.

For the libertarian philosophy, self-ownership is a natural right. It implies the right to be free of aggression by others, including the state. For libertarians, 'freedom' does not mean that one could do as one likes but that each individual as a person owns himself and has a natural right to be free from aggression. Consequently, all legitimate social interaction must be voluntary. The social band that keeps the individuals together is reciprocity, be it in the form of economic exchange, or by friendship, love and sympathy.

The libertarian position is neither left nor right nor centrist. It goes beyond the 'liberal' and the 'conservative' creed as it opposes authoritarianism. Libertarianism also dismisses the distinction between personal and economic freedom because economic freedom is indispensable for personal freedom, and there is no economic freedom without personal freedom.

Sortition (demarchy) in the system of governance

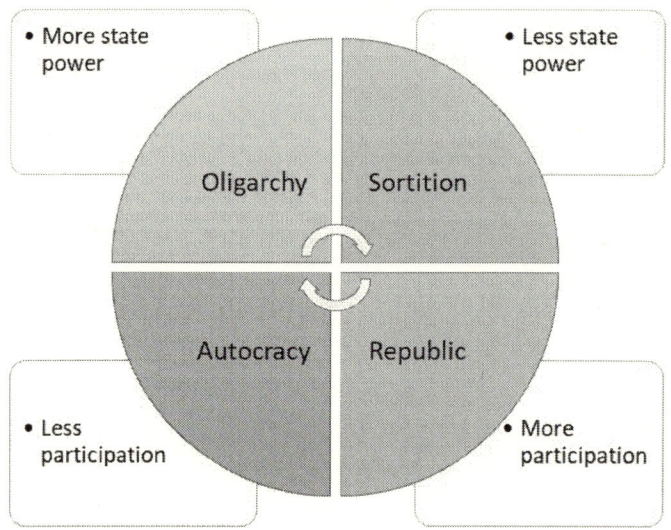

In this scheme, sortition in the upper right corner represents the highest degree of popular participation together with the lowest degree of state power.

In terms of degrees of participation of the people and the extent of state power, '*demarchy*' is the system of governance, which represents the highest level of participation with the least state power (upper right segment).

A system of political party elections is an *oligarchy* and thus, although it allows limited popular participation, has a much higher extent of state power than sortition

Monarchy and *autocracy* have less participation than both oligarchy and sortition.

Autocracy has the least participation combined with the highest degree of state power.

Structure of governance

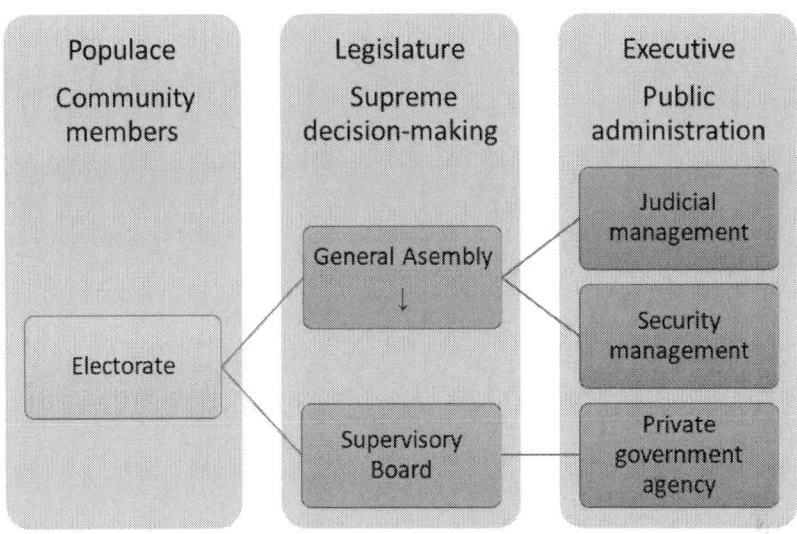

Agenda

The libertarian revolution is a soft revolution without violence. This is and will make the big difference between the anarcho-capitalist order and all other forms of governance. For the libertarian revolution to succeed, one must not 'take power', but conquer the public opinion by persuasion.

Steps on the path to demarchy

A.

- Sortition for the Upper House (Senate) as a second chamber
- Veto of the Upper House against additional public spending and against more taxes and regulations
- Abolishment of the legal tender laws, freeze of the central bank money aggregate

B.

- Transformation of the Upper House into the General Assembly
- Constitution of the Supervisory Body
- Private government management agencies for executive and judicial functions, policing, and defense

I.
Installation of a 'Senate chamber' with members selected by lot
II.
Senate exercises its veto power to halt state, politics, and bureaucracy
III.
Reform of the existing voting system. Establishment of a legislative body in the form of a General Assembly composed of representatives selected by lot
IV.
Reform of the state structure with the addition of a Supervisory Body and an Executive branch to the General Assembly

With the public support to change of the structure of the party democracy in place, the first step would be to complement the present system with an additional chamber. In this chamber - a kind of 'Senate' - members chosen by lot would possess veto rights over the decisions taken by the parliament (Congress) and government (presidency) including the judiciary (Supreme Court). Such a 'fourth power' is the 'voice of the people'. Although it is not yet a government and the lawgiver, the 'Senate' composed by members chosen by lot has the right to stop the encroachments of government and of the state bureaucracy because of the veto power it holds.

The next step would be to create a 'General Assembly' to serve as the prime law-giving body. The Assembly must be large enough to represent the people. For that purpose, it must comprise persons who are selected randomly among the constituency. Establishing the General Assembly requires a reform of the election laws. In order to achieve this, the libertarians must get a majority in the existing parliament (Congress). The final step in the reform of the state structure is to add a supervisory body and an executive branch of the Assembly.

The resulting institutional setting would include three organs: The General Assembly as the representative of the people and the prime law-giver, the Supervisory Body as a special committee to supervise the Executive branch that manages the current affairs of the polity.

The composition of the General Assembly results from a selection by lot according to the principle of 'one citizen one lot'. This legislative assembly must be large enough to provide a *representative sample* of the people. One-fourth of the Assembly should change on a rotating basis, every six months, so that each selected member will have a seat for twenty-four months. The General Assembly is the supreme body for promulgating the laws. It chooses among itself a Supervisory body who will select the government. The Supervisory body can invite, with the consent of the Assembly, qualified persons from outside to serve in the executive branch.

The composition of the General Assembly as the prime legislative body is the result of a random selection in line with the principle of universal suffrage. The General Assembly must be large enough to provide a representative sample of the constituency. Statistically, for example, a number of persons who fit into a large concert hall are adequate to represent a population from five million onwards to several hundred million at an acceptable margin of error and of high confidence, so that also populous countries could have a demarchy although the ideal would be small countries.

One-fourth of the Assembly change on a rotating basis every six month, so that each selected member will have a seat for two years. Every six months one fourth of the size of the Assembly enters while one-fourth leaves after having served for two years in the Assembly.

The Constituency as the body of citizens who have the right to participate in the sortition should be broad. One can leave it open to debate and to the individual situation of a country as to its size and heterogeneity - whether the members of the constituency are the same for general elections or should be more restrictive and only include those persons who register as candidates and who meet specific criteria. Because the demarchy also serves to select the representatives at the level of the individual states of a federation and for municipalities, there is ample room for experimentation with different schemes.

The General Assembly and the Executive

As the service in the General Assembly is for 24 months, each sixth months one-fourth of the members leave, while a new group of the same size enters as the new members of the Assembly. Before the entry of a new group, one fourth of the Assembly would have at this point have served 24 months, one fourth 18 months, one fourth 12 and one fourth and one more fourth would have served six months.

After each new selection, the Assembly exists of four groups with the new members having 24 months to serve, while the group that will leave has six more months to go. In terms of time served, the Assembly comprises four groups after a new selection, with the new group with zero months of service and the longest-serving group with 18 months of membership.

Rotation in Assembly

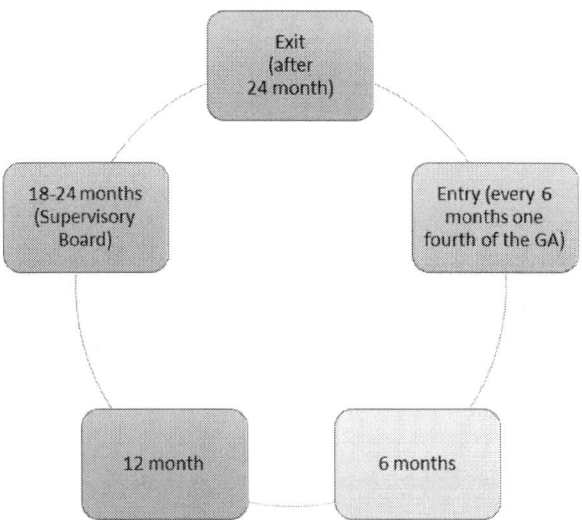

The General Assembly is the supreme body for promulgating the laws. It chooses among itself a Supervisory body that will nominate the government. The Supervisory body exists of the group of the longest-serving members of the General Assembly, that is the group which will leave in six months to return to civil life. The Supervisory body will hire, with the consent of the Assembly, qualified persons from outside to serve as the Executive.

The Supervisory body of the General Assembly oversees and controls the activities of the Executive. The Supervisory body hires a private government management firm to serve as the Executive. As it has been the case with private policing and arbitration, private government management companies will emerge under a libertarian order. These private government companies will offer their services first at the local community and municipal level from which the best firms will expand to the state and the level of unions of states.

Sortition structure

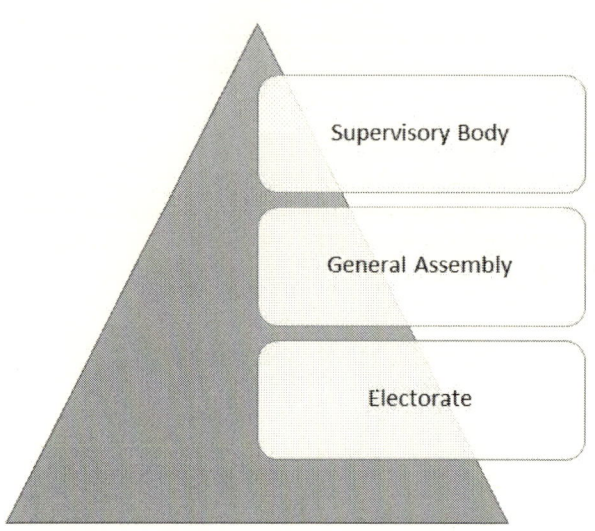

The personnel of these private government management firms will comprise professionals who, different from the governments of the past, will render their service under strict supervision of the Assembly. Private government management companies will employ full-fledged professionals. Their service will be cheaper and better than governments recruited from political parties. Additionally, much less of the personnel will be needed under privatization compared to the public services of nowadays - not only because the firms are private and thus more efficient but also because under a libertarian order the scope of state activities will drastically shrink. Law and order will be maintained at lower costs and with less encroachment on personal liberties.

When a community establishes a chamber, whose members are selected by lot as an addition to the existing structure of government, the 'Senate chamber' should use its veto right to stop all measures that would expand the state and its bureaucracy. After establishing the General Assembly as the prime law-giving body, intermediate measures must follow to reduce the state and its bureaucracy. In the long-run, the task to establish an anarcho-capitalist order requires to remove state money, to stop government spending and to eliminate all taxes and contributions along with eliminating public regulations and public employment, and to privatize the courts, the police force, and defense.

Timeline of the policies

Immediate Measures
- End expansion of money supply
- Stop expansion of government spending
- Halt rise of taxes and contributions
- Halt public regulations
- Stop hiring public employees

Intermediate Measures
- Open financial markets for free banking
- Reduce government spending
- Cut taxes and contributions
- Reduce regulations
- Diminish state employment

Long-term Measures
- Remove state money
- Eradicate government spending
- Eliminate taxes
- Minimize regulations
- Minimize public employment
- Privatize judicial courts
- Privatize police force
- Privatize defence
- Outsource government

SOCIALISM - CAPITALISM

When discussing socialism, the first thing to do is distinguish between 'socialism as a goal' and 'socialism as a method'. Without this difference, one gets easily deceived and, indeed, many people are fooled into believing that to achieve the socialist goal of prosperity for all one must install socialism as a means. By implanting socialism as a method, the opposite of the expected prosperity comes. Instead of prosperity for all, misery and the loss of freedom is the result. The socialist trick their believers into the illusion that because socialism as a goal is so good, socialism as a means is the right way to obtain this goal.

The concept of socialism entails the contradiction between goal and method.

The concept of capitalism does not suffer from this confusion. Capitalism is a means. The goal of capitalism is the production of prosperity, not much different from the socialist ideal, yet be very different means. There are two fundamental ways of capitalism as a means: one is state capitalism, where capitalism is embedded in a state and under the control of government, and the other way is free or anarcho-capitalism where voluntary exchange relations rule.

Socialism's contradiction between method and goal

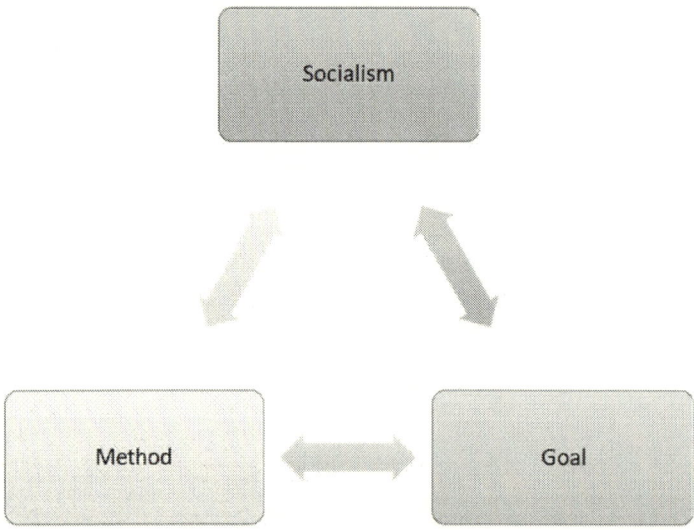

The dispute about capitalism and socialism does not concern the goals, but the means. Which is better to achieve prosperity and freedom? When one puts the problem this way, the answer becomes obvious. Theoretically and historically, socialism has failed on all counts. Therefore, the problem is not socialism versus capitalism, because only fools or fully misguided people would choose socialism. The question is which kind of capitalism is the better method to produce prosperity for all: state capitalism or anarcho-capitalism?

In the past, various forms of state capitalism emerged, most prominently the social market economy since the inception of the second half of the 20th century. The case for anarcho-capitalism comes from the need of doing away with the deficiencies of the present system, which, due to a democracy based on political parties, has produced an excess of government spending which has slowed down economic progress and where the welfare state has not lessened but increased inequality.

Capitalism - methods and goal

```
                    Capitalism
                   /          \
               Method          Goal
              /      \           |
    State capitalism  Anarcho-   Properity
                      capitalism
```

Anarcho-capitalism and electoral democracy are incompatible. To give anarcho-capitalism a chance, the political system must change. The way out of dilemma is demarchy or sortition, a political system where the representatives of the people are selected not by vote but by chance. The polity of a free republic consists in the combination of anarcho-capitalism, demarchy, and private government management.

What is the advantage of anarcho-capitalism over state capitalism? The answer is that anarcho-capitalism generates higher levels of productivity, and that productivity is the source of wealth. Demarchy is necessary to do away with the competition of political parties whose rivalry leads to the appropriation of the state as an instrument of distribution. Private government management is an agency that exerts governmental functions as executive and judicial body without the dominance that comes with the state functions. A free republic must be a polity beyond the state and politics.

Polity of a Free Republic

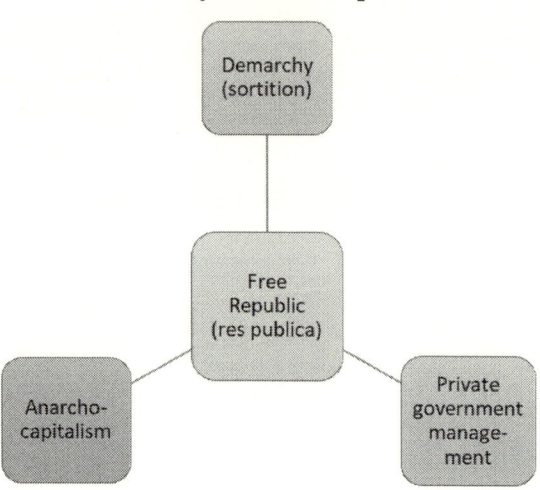

The socialists presume that under a socialist regime the rate of technological progress would be the same as under capitalism. They claim that with the removal of the profit motive one could improve working conditions and have an equal distribution of income. Yet the socialists do not see that the profit motive is the main factor of stimulating technological progress. In a market economy, business can obtain a higher profit rate by way of better productivity, and a higher productivity requires technological progress.

Historically, the evidence shows that technological progress has come with capitalism, and capitalism has come with free enterprise.

The socialists also discard the role of capital and of personal freedom. The socialists see only the accumulated capital but disregard capital accumulation and capital maintenance, i.e. saving. Socialist see the capitalist as an exploiter when in fact his main function if the provision of savings. Likewise, technological progress will not occur in a society where there is no freedom of speech and of private initiative. The meta factors of a capitalist economy are capital accumulation (saving), private initiative (personal freedom) and profit orientation.

Meta factors of a capitalist economy

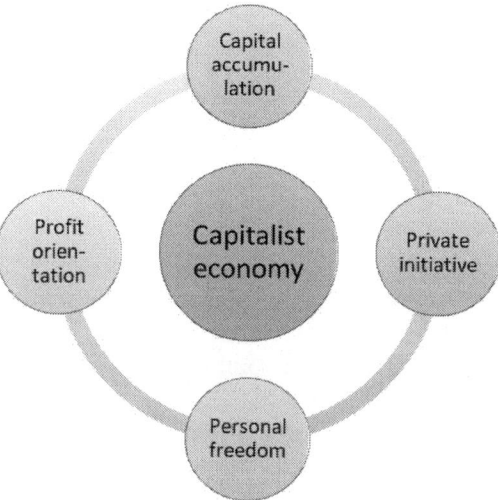

Antony P. Mueller

Summary:
Why capitalism works, and socialism does not

Capitalism is a system in which profits come to those who are best at satisfying the wishes of the customers. 'Better' refers not only to the price but also to the quality, including the appeal of the product to the buyer. In a socialist economy, even a benevolent dictator could not provide the right mix of goods in terms of price and quality because in the socialist system, there are no market prices. Socialism eliminates both: information and incentives. All economic agents, including the planning authority, operate in the dark. A market economy, in contrast, functions like a data processing machine that emits the continuously information about scarcity and excess.

In a market economy, the relative prices of the goods serve as a guide for economic action. The price ratios show how to combine the production factors to best satisfy the needs of the consumers. Relative prices show what consumers want and guide the production process into this direction because this is where the profits emerge. The competition provides the incentives for cost-effectiveness so that consumers receive the goods at the lowest prices based on the best use of the factors of production.

In capitalism, the wishes of the clients regulate the overall structure of the price relations. The preferences of the consumers determine also the value of the investment goods. This so-called 'imputation' means that the value of the final product determines the value of the intermediate goods. Because the consumer determines the value of the final good, the anchor for the value structure of the entire wealth in a market economy is the consumer.

Under capitalism, it is not a planning authority that controls the production structure, but the consumers decide. Production follows the wishes of the consumers. They control the economy because only those entrepreneurs that obey the calls of their clients gain a profit. Businesses must restructure the production according to the changes of the wants, needs, and tastes of the buyers of their products.

Socialists suppose that to implant their rule on the economy all that is necessary is to socialize the private companies, replace the management, and install worker councils, and the new economic order would flourish. The early socialists expected that abundance would follow not least because now the workers would get what before went into the hands of the capitalists as profits. Yet the socialists ignored that the socialization of the means of production was just the beginning. They failed miserably in running the economy.

The planners may know what type of technology a specific production would require, and they can count on the professionalism of the engineers to use their knowledge. The error of socialist economic planning, however, is the to assume that business management could also continue as before after socialist operators take over the capitalist management. While the socialist regime can train administrators and engineers and put the party members in the position of directors, these new leaders cannot decide according to relative scarcities because there is no longer a private property-based entrepreneurial price system available.

Many supporters of socialism suppose that business management is nothing more than a kind of registration or simple bookkeeping. Vladimir Ilyich Lenin (1870-1924), the Soviet revolutionary leader, believed that the knowledge of reading and writing, and some expertise in the use of the four basic arithmetic operations and some training in accounting, would be enough for the conduct of business operations. The socialists then and now ignore the fundamental economic problem, which consists in determining what to produce, for whom, and how.

The socialist planners assume that a plan can stipulate these three tasks and ignore how and from where such a plan should find its standards of valuation. Socialists presume that one could manage a complex economy without capitalists and entrepreneurs. When prices and markets disappear, one loses the orientation about which factors of production are more and which are less scarce along with the loss of knowledge of the costs of the goods used in the production process.

Scarcity makes goods valuable, and relative prices show this in a market economy. By observing the prices, the market participants receive information about scarcity and align their economic decisions to the market signals. Yet when there is no market, information about the relation between the wants for goods and their supply vanishes. The price system informs about scarcity and abundance and makes it possible to decide according to one's own best interests. There is no need for a comprehensive system of information since markets enable to weigh the advantages and disadvantages of economic actions through relative prices because the price system reduces complexity for the individual decision maker to the single number of the price. In a market economy, the economic participants need only partial knowledge to act rationally.

In socialism, however, private ownership of the means of production no longer exists, and thus there is no price system for capital goods. Institutionally, socialism consists in abolishing the market economy and replacing it with a planned economy. Yet beyond the loss of private property, the fundamental problem comes from the consequence that by doing away with private property of the means of production, one wipes-out information. Even if the socialist administration puts price tags on the consumer goods, and the people may privately own consumer goods, there is no economic orientation about the relative scarcity of capital goods. Because the socialist system removes the private ownership of the production goods and eliminates the role of the entrepreneur, there are no markets.

The socialist economy does not serve the consumers. The point of reference for proper management is to execute the commands – the same as in the military. To fulfill plans refers to the respective level in the hierarchy of the command order - not to the consumer. Even if, for example, the central plan should stipulate to produce a certain number of a good, and that the order would go to the respective factories, the question arises how to design and by which combination of the factors of production the manufacturing should take place. Any production faces the problem that there is an almost unlimited number of ways how to produce a good. One can manufacture a commodity with very different raw materials, technologies, and combinations of the production factors and in an endless variety of designs.

Before one can systematically consider the aspects of the technological feasibilities, one must apply economic principles – the calculation of the potential profitability of producing a good. Without costs in relation to sales, a technical evaluation makes no sense. What is technically possible is not economically recommended, and what appears efficient from a technical point of view need not be so in terms of economic expediency. With costs left out of the consideration, socialist production is blind to the risk of producing goods that would cost more than they are worth.

Who determines value? In a market economy, it is the client, and, in the last instance, the consumer. In central planning economy, it is up to the planners to determine the value. This, however, they cannot accomplish because preferences and technologies change, and the complexity of the relationship among the goods exceeds the capacity of anyone's mind or that of a planning committee to grasp.

Socialism suffers from four fundamental defects. Each one of them alone makes socialism already inoperative. Together they multiply the effect.

First, socialism eradicates private property and markets and thus eliminates rational calculation.

Second, socialism allows soft budgets, so there is no mechanism in place to discards inefficient production methods.

Third, abolishing private property and replacing it by the state promotes distorted incentives.

Fourth, the socialist system with its absence of private property and of free markets inhibits economic coordination of the system of division of labor and capital.

Socialism means economic blindness. Information gets lost along with the incentive to act according to the price signals. In capitalism, the motivations of gaining profits and to avoid costs work as an incentive to behave rationally. In a market economy, the prices fulfill the double function to inform and to incentivize the seller and the buyer.

It is no wonder that even a degenerate capitalism produces more prosperity than the best socialism. Therefore, the task ahead cannot be to remove capitalism in favor of socialism but to make capitalism better which means to make it more capitalist.

Outlook

While the 20th century experienced the profound transformation of manufacturing, technology is now revolutionizing the service sector. The professionals - ranging from medical doctors to lawyers, from educators to public administrators - will face tough challenges. The transformation is already on its way. Many apparently secure jobs will be wiped out. Robots and artificial intelligence make complex tasks not only cheaper but also perform better. The new technologies enter the consultants' offices, the legal chambers, the classrooms, and the hospitals. With a click, better diagnoses than humans could deliver show up on the screen in seconds - be it a medical assessment or the analysis of a legal problem. Machines are replacing even sophisticated occupations. What does the future hold for jobs, skills, and wages? What does this mean for the future of capitalism? What kind of economic system is best to meet the challenge?

In the 19th century, one could tell the farm boy to go to the city and learn a trade. In the 20th century, one could say to the young man or girl they should move ahead and go to study. These were all good pieces of advice. Yet in the new millennium, there is nowhere to go upward. The move from agriculture to industry, and from industry to the services, has ended. Now, to go to the university and to get a degree is no longer a guarantee for a well-paid and secure job. Professional positions fall victim to automatization and to the onslaught of artificial intelligence. The sprouts of the ladder are occupied. For one to go up, another one must come down. Upwardly mobile is a feat of the past.

What is the way out? The promise of 'jobs, jobs, jobs' will be in vain. The more the state tries to make jobs available and positions more secure, the more productivity declines, and incomes fall. The new millennium needs a different approach. The answer is to fully embrace technology. The more the new technologies become a complement to human work, productivity will rise. The urgency of having a fixed position as an employed person recedes. The use of one's car as a chauffeur for and renting out one's house or apartment for travelers with are examples of the things to come.

A necessary condition for the surge in productivity is less state and the end of politics. Less state and fewer politics would deliver the citizen from the heavy burden that now confronts him. Productivity would rise as the state fades away. The individual gets liberated from both sides. On the one hand, the burden of taxes and contributions falls. On the other hand, gains of productivity bring down the costs of living.

The current 'all-or-nothing'-trap ('either Yale or jail') would vanish. Now it is so that if one has a professional job, one's material situation is fine. Yet when one loses this position, the fall is enormous. We need a system that avoids this dichotomy. An anarcho-capitalist order would bring down the burden of taxes and of contributions. Free capitalism would open the path to vast productivity gains. Then, the urgency of having a permanent earning position would recede. One could live well even without having a secure job because productivity is so high that also temporary assignments offer a pay that is high enough to maintain a good life. The technology that takes away the jobs is the same that provides the tools which brings down the costs of living and makes leisure time attractive.

Nowadays, there are many professional couples who are both working because one needs two incomes to do well. Many would be glad to have only one breadwinner if they could maintain their living standard. Free capitalism would offer such chances because taxes and contributions would come down to a tenth of the present level and goods would cost less than half of their present prices with income several times higher than today.

Our present economic, political, and judicial system is ill-prepared for the challenge of the future. That was also the case over a hundred years ago at the beginning of the 20th century. Then, many wrong decisions were taken until a system took shape and became accepted that could accommodate the technological changes and the economic transformations. Yet now, new tribulations loom, and they make the dominant 'liberal' - social-democratic - system obsolete.

Resistance will arise - like that which came from the artisans and the home workers at the start of the industrial revolution. The workers feared that with introducing the new machines they would lose their economic existence and be condemned to poverty and misery. Yet they had no chance. And good for them - for because of the industrial revolution, the working class experienced a level of prosperity in the two centuries to come which was unimaginable at the time when the industrial revolution took off.

Protectionism, interventionism, imperialism, communism, and fascism were the many wrong answers in the past. Many believe now that the social-democratic version of capitalism would be the adequate system for the new millennium. Yet this not the case. It is no exaggeration to forecast that when we continue with the social-democratic way, the end would be state-bankruptcy. Serious analyses must conclude that the social security and welfare complex of healthcare, education, pensions, and social assistance have failed. The legal system is in shambles. Likewise, the expectation that the political management of the economy could guarantee employment, economic growth, and financial stability, is illusionary. Trying to maintain, to reform, and to expand the present system will lead to the opposite of the 'liberal' promises.

Without a change of the social security system, healthcare costs alone will absorb more than one fourth of the gross incomes. Pension provisions would require another fourth of the income. In a few decades, the ordinary taxpayer must confront obligatory contributions that exceed half of the income to pay for social security and welfare alone. Besides these contributions, the government would have to require another third of the incomes as taxes to finance defense and the other parts of the state apparatus. Such a burden is impossible to bear. Almost nothing would be left for private use. Before these projections can become a reality, the economy would break down. People would refuse to work, and businesses would stop to invest, the nation would become bankrupt.

Thus, the challenge remains: in the decades to come, young people can no more expect to have a high income just because they get a university diploma. Many job-secure careers in established professions will go away or experience profound transformations. The present horror of unemployment or of not finding the right job comes from being not able to bear the high costs of education, healthcare, housing, public security, and retirement without a high permanent income.

We need a new order. Repairs of the structures in place are not enough. Just as it had made no sense to improve the horse carriage to compete with the automobile, is it a futile effort to improve the current political system and to make the social security system more effective and the economy more efficient.

We need to make a turnaround. Instead of making the present system more social-democratic, we need a libertarian revolution. Instead of making capitalism more socialist, we need a more capitalist capitalism.

A free economy in a free society requires three major institutional changes.

First, the selection of the society's representative body through a process of random selection;

second, a private monetary system to substitute the central banks;

third, the provision of law and security by private suppliers.

In order to establish a state-free society, insight must come first. The legitimacy of a free social order cannot come from the application of force - as it has been the case with all other political systems - but needs as its base the voluntary cooperation of the people to arise as a spontaneous order.

The tentative to establish an 'improved socialism', as it is the aim of the globalist scheme of a world government, would be even more deadly than the socialism of the 20th century. Yet also the milder forms of socialism and fascism, as they are practiced as interventionism, represent no valuable alternative. Likewise, it is pointless to expect that government could manage the economy and provide stability and economic growth so that everybody could have a well-paid secure job.

What we need is a new political and economic order, an order, which does not dilute capitalism with socialism, but a capitalism free of its socialist admixtures. The more the state would retreat from private life, the less the burden of taxes would become. The present schemes of healthcare, education, pensions, legal services, housing, and welfare - not to speak of defense - are not only inefficient but also costly beyond needs. In these areas, the new technologies provide ample alternatives that would lower the costs while making the services better. Doing away with politics would eliminate the silly election campaigns. Sortition would stop the political culture of more government spending.

If we go on with the present system, the state will grow bigger and bigger. With the growing size of the state, governments will become more powerful. Without a halt, the present so-called 'liberal democracy' will transmute into a new totalitarianism.

The great debate is not only about jobs, but even more so how we can maintain human freedom in the face of the new technologies. In the new millennium, the demise of the state is a necessary condition for freedom. If we fail, humanity's fate is an age of slavery. If we succeed, we may welcome a new era of freedom and prosperity. Full employment is a dream of the past. Likewise, it is an empty hope that government could do anything about it. Guaranteed employment would only repeat the errors of socialism. Interventionism and macroeconomic management that should provide employment, growth, and financial stability, do no longer work. Even worse: the more assignments, responsibilities, and rights we assign to the government, the more totalitarian the state will become. With the modern technology at hand, the state of the new millennium would gain all the tools it takes to establish a regime of comprehensive repression with not a trace left of human freedom and dignity.

The hope for the new epoch is not less but more capitalism. The book "Beyond the State and Politics" displays that the instruments of state intervention cannot solve the problems. The more complex society and the economy have become, the more one needs markets as the instrument of coordination and private initiative.

Free capitalism provides the essentials for prosperity and freedom: efficient coordination of individual plans based on voluntary exchange and high productivity.

The coming decades will experience a profound transformation in areas such as law, medicine, education, and public administration - those fields of activity where many of university-educated professionals have found stable and well-paid positions. In the decades to come more of the jobs that seem as secure will disappear or undergo drastic transformations. It is futile to expect that a college degree would be enough to guarantee a well-paid and stable position. A great wave of substitution of machines for labor, which occurred in the 19th century in agriculture, and in the 20th century in manufacturing, will take now place in the service sector including the high-level services.

The current system of managed capitalism is incapable to cope with the challenges of the new era. Not more government is the solution but higher productivity, and to achieve higher productivity we need less state and fewer politics.

To meet the challenge of precarious employment, a drastic reduction in the costs of living will help. This goal requires productivity, and only free capitalism can generate the economic efficiency. We must embrace technological progress in all its forms because this is how productivity will increase. Productivity is not the problem, it is the solution. The problem is the cost of the state and the detrimental effects of the governmental activity.

Along with the concerns of how to get jobs, an even darker danger is lurking. If we do not abolish the state and politics in time, the new technologies will become horrendous instruments of totalitarian control in the hands of the governments. The larger the state and the more powerful the government, the bigger the threat. We must diminish the power of the state and reduce politics to regain and maintain our freedom.

Minimizing and doing away with the state is an urgent mission because otherwise, the modern technology would put terrific instruments of control into the hands of the government. With the new technical devices of supervision and domination, a modern totalitarian state could supersede the terror and suppression of anything in history. The state is not only superfluous and a danger for human liberty but has become a threat to human existence.

Society is a system of coordination. Coordination can be vertical or horizontal: either as a hierarchy of commandos and violent sanctions or voluntary exchange and cooperation. Of all known procedures of coordination, markets work best. There is no other system of production beyond free capitalism that could match pure capitalism's high productivity.

The current political system is not a democracy but is party politics; the economy is not a free market economy but suffers from intervention and state management. To be free and prosperous, this must change.

As the book details, we need a radical reduction of the state and its bureaucracy. The share of the state of around fifty percent of overall production is too high. Public debt is growing and moving the nation toward bankruptcy. The people must bear immense burdens in taxes and contributions. To solve the dilemma, the costs of living must fall. This goal requires productivity, and only free capitalism can generate the economic efficiency.

The point is not having more jobs but to have a system where one need not worry about jobs because the urgency to have one is not so great as it is now. With the massive burden of costs now in place, having a well-paid and stable position is a necessity for gaining a good life. Under a free capitalism, this would change. Productivity would be so high that the costs of living would be low. There will be top jobs available which pay well, but those with a precarious employment situation need not worry because they can also have a good life - including entertainment, which due to the new technologies comes almost for free. Drastic cost reductions would occur in medicine, education, and public administration. Other big cost items, such as transports, would likewise fall in price. Most of all, with the state and politics gone or at least reduced to a minimum, the menace of a suppressive state terror will dissipate.

The organization of politics as a system of competing political parties is an obstacle on the way to the new system. Modern democracy is party politics. Candidates win by false promises. The state expands without delivering better services.

Sortition, the selection of the people's representative by lot, would do away with the wasteful and harmful system of party politics. Choosing the legislative body not by vote but by chance would usher into a new era and mark the move away from oligarchical rule and to an authentic democracy.

Together with privatizing money and of the legal system, ending party politics would open the path to a more prosperous economy with high productivity. There would be no public debt. The burden of contributions and taxes would sink.

With the cost of living down, the risk of unemployment loses its menace. Under an anarcho-capitalist order, temporary or even prolonged unemployment would not be a castigation as it is now. What capitalism is all about is to substitute capital for human labor and to liberate us from the burden of tedious work and from the worries about our next meal and where to lay our head at night.

In order to win the public opinion, libertarianism must present itself as a forward-facing movement whose origins are the rebellions against authoritarianism, dictatorship, and totalitarianism. Libertarians must denounce socialism as old-fashioned, stagnant, and backward-looking. Libertarians must ridicule socialism as the superstition of the modern age. Libertarianism is neither a conservative movement nor is it libertine. The enemy of libertarianism is power. The goal of libertarianism is liberty and its means are peaceful.

Libertarianism as governance and as an anarcho-capitalist economic order stands in the finest intellectual tradition and as such, has been the spearhead of the best that modern age has to offer. Libertarianism represents those elements of modernity that are sound, solid, and ethical. Libertarians must convince public opinion that anarcho-capitalism is a system of governance of the highest standards of intellectual standing and ethics. Anarcho-capitalism is the path to both liberty and prosperity.

The promoters of anarcho-capitalism must nourish the prospect that an anarcho-capitalist order will be a world of plenty. Libertarians must convince the public that under an anarcho-capitalist order, net salaries would rise, first, because there would be much less taxes and contributions to pay and, second, because of the increase in productivity. Beyond that, the purchasing of money would rise because of falling prices. Under an anarcho-capitalist economy, a many-fold increase of wide-spread wealth will happen - and this would only be the beginning.

Anarcho-capitalists must propagate the insight that to produce the so-called public goods is not only inefficient but also useless. Besides being expensive, much of the state-run education and medicine is not only superfluous but prejudicial. The military is needed not because people are bad but because there are states run by psychopaths.

Without taking the power out of the hands of the professional politicians, libertarianism has no chance to become a reality. Therefore, demarchy is a necessary step towards an anarcho-capitalist order. For this to happen, a change of the prevalent ideology must take place. Libertarians must transform public opinion in favor of sortition, the selection of the people's representatives by the lot. For this purpose, the libertarians must refer to the vast number of examples of current and historical examples of the foolishness, idiocy, and brutality of a leadership, which is selected by force and vote. The viciousness, ruthlessness, cruelty, and vindictiveness of these rulers stands in sharp contrast to what leadership under demarchy would be. Most people will see that when normal people are the rulers, the horrors that have come with the political leadership that has come to power by force and vote is a thing of the past. Along with the research and documentation of the past and present behavior of the professional politicians, libertarians should support and extend all forms of ridicule to shed upon the electoral political processes.

As to the theory, advocates of the anarcho-capitalist economic model should not so much stress their allegiance to its historical roots but emphasize that their practitioners march in the frontline of theoretical progress.

Entrepreneurs must abandon their alliance with the state as they have practiced it in the age of corporate capitalism. The state is a mean partner. In the future, besides being malicious, the state will become impotent because of the lack of funds. Reliance on the state is a lost issue. Under state capitalism, individual companies gain special advantages with the help from the state at the cost of the business community. This is not only unethical, but also uneconomical. Businessmen must form a new alliance. Their rightful partner is not the state but the libertarian movement. Instead of throwing money into the mouths of corrupt politicians, the business community would do well for its own future and the prosperity of all if they would fund the libertarian movement.

A wide and fecund field of intellectual projects calls for the endeavors not only of economists and jurists, but also of libertarian historians, political scientists, and sociologists and of the other disciplines, including theology and psychology. Research in these areas needs a new focus: no longer as the praise of the state and of its leaders but, on the contrary, reveal the failure of the state and its leaders.

In this great effort to create a better world and to save humankind from tyranny, everyone has a role to play. The work must begin now because a long way lies ahead of us.

APPENDIX

Anarcho-individualist order – basic concepts
Main types of government failures
Ten fundamental indictments against the State
Principles of economic governance
Principles of anarcho-capitalism
Principles of anarchist individualism

ANARCHO-INDIVIDUALIST ORDER BASIC CONCEPTS

Concept	Definition
Anarcho-republic	A polity based on the voluntary association of free persons for the cooperative attainment of individual aims, a polity that is a republic ("res publica") in its true sense different from state organizations that are hierarchical, dictatorial, and authoritarian
Anarcho-liberalism	The political philosophy which promotes a polity based on the voluntary association of free persons for the cooperative attainment of individual aims
Libertarianism	The political movement aimed at establishing the governance of free persons. Libertarianism stands in contrast to all those movements which try to establish an authoritarian or dictatorial rule
Demarchy	A form of governance where the people's representatives are chosen by lottery in contrast to the political systems whose rulers come to power through heritage, force or vote
Sortition	The process through which the representative body of the people is chosen in a lottery in contrast to systems of vote, co-option, and cooptation
Anarcho-capitalism	Free market economy ("Laissez-faire"-capitalism) - an economic order based on private property and free

	markets in contrast to state capitalism, socialism, communism, and interventionism
Anarcho-individualism	The philosophy that puts the autonomous individual at the center of the system of values in contrast to all forms of collectivism and hierarchical authoritarian organizations
Electorate	Members of the community that form the universe of the sortition similar to the voters in a democracy
General Assembly	The representative body of the electorate that form the legislative body of the Republican Polity similar to parliaments or congresses in the modern democracies
Supervisory Body	A part of the General Assembly with special assignments of supervision over the private government management agency similar to the old Upper House in Britain or Senates in the original meaning
Government management	A private government agency that is hired by the General Assembly and supervised by the Supervisory Body to exert executive functions similar to governments in the traditional sense yet without state authority
Judicial management	Private law agencies that offer services of arbitration similar to current arbitration services
Policing	Private police similar to the present forms of non-state law-enforcement bodies
Defense	Under the authority of the General Assembly and of the supervision by the Supervisory body, the defense of the community is managed by private companies (high-tech)

MAIN TYPES OF GOVERNMENT FAILURES

I.
Knowledge
Government policies suffer from the pretense of knowledge (Friedrich Hayek). In order to perform a successful market intervention, politicians need to know much more than they possibly can. Market knowledge is not centralized, systematic, organized and general, but dispersed, heterogeneous, specific, and individual. Different from a market economy where there are many operators and a constant process of trial and error, the correction of government errors is very limited because of its status as a monopoly and because admitting errors may actually be worse for the reputation of the politician than sticking with a wrong decision - even against one's own insight.

II.
Information asymmetries
While there are also information asymmetries' in the market, for example between the insurer and the insured, or between the seller of a used car and its buyer, the information asymmetry is more profound in the public than in the private sector. While there are, for example, several insurance companies and many car dealers, there is only one government. The representatives of the state as an agency, the politicians, have no skin the game and because they are no stakeholders, they will not make much efforts to investigate and avoid information asymmetries'. On the contrary, politicians are typically eager to provide funds not to those who need them most but to those who are politically most relevant.

III.
Crowding out of the private sector
Government intervention does not eliminate apparent market deficiencies but creates them by crowding out the private supply. If there were not a public dominance in the areas of schooling and social assistance, private supply and private charity would fill the gap as it was the case before government usurped these activities. Crowding-out of the private sector through government policies is constantly at work because politicians can get votes by offering additional public

services although the public administration would not improve but rather deteriorate the issue.

IV.
Time lags

Government policies suffer from long lags between diagnoses and effect. Government notices only those problems for which there is a political pressure. It takes a long time until a problem becomes sufficiently politicized until it finds the attention of the government. After the diagnosis, another lag happens until the authorities have found a consensus on how to tackle the political problem and it takes a further time span until the appropriate political means have found sufficient political support. Only then will the measures get implemented and a further time elapses until the proceedings show some effects. The results of state interventions typically not only deviate from the original intent but actually may produce the opposite result. In every case, the lapse of time between the articulation of a problem and effect is so long that not only the nature of the problem and its context have changed - often fundamentally.

V.
Rent seeking and rent creation

Government intervention invites rent-seeking. Rent seeking is the endeavor of gaining privileges through government policies. Along with existing rents, government policies are induced to create additional rent opportunities in order to gain additional support and votes. This rent creation invites more rent-seeking and leads to a process where the distinction between corruption and decent and legal conduct get blurred. The more a government gives in to rent-seeking and rent creation, the more the country will fall victim to clientelism, corruption, and the misallocation of resources.

VI.

Logrolling and vote trading

The public choice concept of "logrolling" denotes the exchange of favors among the political factions in order to get one's favored project through by supporting the projects of the other group. This conduct leads to the steady expansion of state activity. Through the "quid pro quo," the politicians support pieces of legislation of other factions in exchange for obtaining the political support for one's own piece of legislation. This comportment leads to the well-known phenomenon of "legislative inflation", the avalanche of useless, contradictory and detrimental law production.

VII.
Common good
The so-called "common good" is not a well-defined concept. Similar concepts, such as that of the "public good" which is defined by non-excludability and non-rivalry, misses the point because it is not the good that is "common" or "public" but its provision is deemed as more effective by collective efforts than individuality. However, this is the case with all goods and the market itself is a system of providing private goods through cooperative efforts. Any of the so-called public goods, which the government supplies, the private sector can also deliver, and cheaper and better. A free market economy could not only provide education, health care or old age provision as well as domestic and external security but also better and cheaper.

VIII. Regulatory capture
The term "regulatory capture" denotes a government failure where the regulatory agency does not pursue the original intent of promoting the "public interest" but fall victim to the special interest of those groups, which the agency was set up to regulate. The capture of the regulatory body by private interests means that the agency turns into an instrument to advance the specific interest of the groups that were targeted for regulation. The special interest group may ask for regulation to obtain the state apparatus as the instrument to promote their interests.

IX.
Short-sighted bias
The political time horizon is the next election. In the endeavor that the benefits of political action come quickly to their specific clienteles, the politician will favor short-term project over the long-term even if the former bring only temporary benefits and cost more in the long run than an alternative project where the costs come earlier but larger benefits later.

X. Rational ignorance
It is rational for the individual voter in a mass democracy to remain ignorant about the political issues because the value of the individual's vote is so small that it makes not much difference for the outcome. The rational voter will vote for those candidates who promise most as benefits. Given the small relevance of an individual vote in a mass democracy, the rational voter will not spend much time and effort to investigate whether these promises are realistic or in a collision with his other desires. Thus, the political campaigns do not have information and

enlightenment as the objective but disinformation and confusion. What counts, in the end, to get voted is not the solidity of the program but the enthusiasm a candidate can create with his supporters and how much he can degrade, denounce, and humiliate his opponent. The political election process spreads hatred, division, and the lust for revenge.

Antony P. Mueller

TEN FUNDAMENTAL INDICTMENTS AGAINST THE STATE

The great illusion of the modern time is the belief that a society and the economy would require a State. The State is not a necessary evil but a superfluous evil. That the individual cannot survive without a society and an economy does not mean he could not survive without a State. Anarcho-capitalism and anarcho-individualism are not against the society. The individual is not anti-social when he is anti-state. Not the anarchist is anti-social, but the State.

I

While pretending to protect life, liberty, property, the State has been the supreme enemy of life, liberty, and property. Throughout history, the crimes committed by the State have been boundlessly more than those committed by individuals.

II.

The State is not productive. The origin of the State is parasitism. The social rift is not between the worker and the capitalist but between the parasitic State and those who produce the goods.

III.

The State is the enemy of the prosperity of the people. The State confiscates wealth and punishes productivity. The State misdirects savings and investment.

IV.

Looting is the alimony of the State. The State lets the economy thrive only insofar that it provides the material for the State to plunder.

V.

Aggression is the nature of the State. Its aggression goes likewise against its own subjects as to real or imagined foreign enemies. War is the health of State.

VI.

The State creates its own enemies and thereby justifies its owns existence. Through permanent war and conflict, the State gains the consent of its underlings.

VII.
The State deceives about the legitimacy of its exercise of force and coercion. The State has no authority other than the false authority that comes through violence.

VIII.
The individual is the natural enemy of the State. Therefore, the State will do all it can to annihilate the individual and promote conformism.

IX.
All States fail. The greatest victory of the State carries with it the seed of the decay of the State.

X.
Doing away with the State will open the gate to peace and prosperity. The demise of the State marks the beginning of the triumph of the individual.

Antony P. Mueller

PRINCIPLES OF ECONOMIC GOVERNANCE

1. Production precedes consumption
Before something can be consumed, it must first exist. Consumption goods do not just fall from the sky. They are at the end of a long chain of intertwined production processes. To have more goods for consumption, one must first see that more goods will be produced.

2. Consumption is the final goal of production
Consumption is the objective of all economic activity, and production is its means. Current consumption results from the production process that extends to the past, yet the value of this production structure depends on the current state of valuation by the consumers and the expected future state. Therefore, the consumers are the final de facto owners of the production apparatus in a capitalist economy.

3. Production has costs
Behind every welfare check and behind each research grant lies the tax money of real people. While the taxpayers see that government confiscates part of one's personal income, they do not know to whom this money goes; and while the recipients of government expenditures see the government handing the money to them, they do not know from whom the government has taken away this money. When someone apparently gets something 'for free' from the state to consume, someone else is left with less from what he produced.

4. Value is subjective
Valuation is subjective and varies with the concrete situation and circumstances of an individual. The same physical good has different values to different persons at different times. Utility is subjective, individual, and situational. The value of a good depends on the marginal unit, not on the average or the total. There is no such thing as collective consumption. Even the temperature in the same room feels differently to different persons. The same movie or football match has a different subjective value for each viewer.

5. Productivity determines the wage rate
In a free economy, the marginal output determines the worker's wage rate. In a free labor market, businesses will hire additional workers as long as their marginal productivity exceeds and finally matches the wage rate.

Competition among the firms will drive up the wage rate to the point where it is equal to productivity. The power of labor unions may change the distribution of wages among the different labor groups, but trade unions cannot change the overall wage level, which depends on labor productivity.

6. Expenditure is income and costs

Expenditure is income for the seller but represents costs for the buyer. In macroeconomic terms, spending equals income, and income equals costs. When a government spends it not only creates income but also costs. Grave policy errors are the result when government policies count only the income effect of public expenditures but ignore the cost effect.

7. Money per se is not wealth

The value of money consists in its purchasing power. Money serves as an instrument of exchange. The wealth of a person exists in its access to the goods and services he desires. An economy cannot increase its wealth by simply increasing its stock of money.

8. Labor does not create value

Labor, in combination with the other factors of production, creates products, but the value of the product depends on its utility. Utility depends on the subjective individual valuation. Employment for sake of employment makes no economic sense. What counts is value creation. To be useful, a product must offer benefits for the consumer. The value of a good exists independent from the effort of producing it.

9. Profit is the entrepreneurial reward

In competitive capitalism, economic profit is the extra bonus that those businesses earn that amend allocative errors and that best foresee the future wants of their customers. In a static economy with no change, there would be neither profit nor loss. Economic growth, however, means change, and anticipating changes is the source of economic profits.

10. Economic laws do exist

Economic laws are logical laws. As such they are invulnerable. Legal laws that contradict the fundamental economic laws do not abolish the economic laws but pervert their function. These logical economic laws work like facts. Government can ignore and try to violate the economic laws, but the economic laws will not ignore the ignorant. Those societies fare best where people and government recognize and respect these fundamental economic laws and use them to their advantage.

Antony P. Mueller

PRINCIPLES OF ANARCHO-CAPITALISM

I.
Each man is unique in his personality
(Human uniqueness makes the individual)

II.
Man is an enterprising being
(Human action)

III.
Society is the free association of men
(principle of the division of labor)

IV.
The limit of one person's egoism is the other person's egoism
(checks and balances)

V.
The law of cooperation is reciprocity
(*Do Ut Des*)

VI.
Government exists through consent, not by right
(Government as business management)

VII.
The source of legitimacy is the compatibility of wills
(Freedom)

VIII.
The purpose of private property is free enterprise
(Productive competition)

IX.
There are no rights and no duties other than individual self-preservation
(Scope of existence)

X.
Individual sovereignty is supreme
(Anchor)

Principles of Anarchist Individualism

I.
All I am is my property

II.
Society may limit my freedom but must not curtail my uniqueness

III.
It is better to rely on the egoism of the others than on their compassion

IV.
Society is fate - community is a choice

V.
To use oneself does not mean to be useful

VI.
To amuse oneself is an artform

VII.
I have no duty to anybody and nobody has a duty to me

VIII.
Taking people as they are, is the first step to inner and external peace

IX.
To rule over one's thoughts is the greatest achievement

X.
Not every concept represents an existence

XI.
I am my own truth

XII.
I am the measure of all things

XIII.
The principle of life - any life - is exhaustion

XIV.
My uniqueness is my perfection

XV.
A man of virtue is non-aggressive, self-controlled, superior, cheerful, ironic, open-minded, and benevolent

BIBLIOGRAPHICAL REFERENCES

Achen, Christopher H. and Larry M. Bartels: Democracy for Realists: Why Elections Do Not Produce Responsive Government (Princeton Studies in Political Behavior) Princeton University Press 2017

Antonopoulos, Andreas M.: The Internet of Money. Merkle Bloom LLC. 2016

Applebaum, Anne: Gulag. A History. Anchor Books. 2004

Applebaum, Anne: Red Famine: Stalin's War on the Ukraine. Doubleday. 2017

Ashford, Nigel and Stephen Davis (eds.): A Dictionary of Conservative and Libertarian Thought (Routledge Revivals). Routledge. 2012

Bagus, Philipp: In Defense of Deflation (Financial and Monetary Policy Studies). Springer 2014

Bagus, Phillipp and Andreas Marquart: Blind Robbery!: How the Fed, Banks and Government Steal Our Money. FinanzBuch Verlag. 2016

Baldwin, Richard: The Great Convergence: Information Technology and the New Globalization. Belknap Press. 2016

Banerjee, Abhijit, and Esther Duflo: Poor Economics: A Radical Rethinking of the Way to Fight Global Poverty. Public Affairs. 2012

Barnett, Anthony: The Athenian Option: Radical Reform for the House of Lords (Sortition and Public Policy Book 5). Imprint Academic. 2017

Barrat, James: Our Final Invention: Artificial Intelligence and the End of the Human Era. St Martin's Griffin. 2015

Belke, Ansgar and Thorsten Polleit: Monetary Economics in Globalised Financial Markets. Springer. 2009

Belloc, Hilaire: The Servile State. T. N. Foulis 1912

Benda, Julien: The Treason of the Intellectuals. Routledge. 2006

Benson, Bruce L: The Enterprise of Law: Justice Without the State. Independent Institute. 2011

Birner, Jack and Pierre Garrouste (eds): Markets, Information and Communication: Austrian Perspectives on the Internet Economy (Routledge Foundations of the Market Economy). Routledge. 2003

Block, Walter: Defending the Undefendable. Ludwig von Mises Institute. 2008

Block, Walter: The Privatization of Roads and Highways: Human and Economic Factors. CreateSpace Independent Publishing Platform. 2012

Block, Walter: Toward a Libertarian Society. Ludwig von Mises Institute. 2014

Boaz, David (ed.). The Libertarian Reader: Classic & Contemporary Writings from Lao-Tzu to Milton Friedman. Simon & Schuster 2015

Boaz, David: The Libertarian Mind. A Manifesto for Freedom. Simon & Schuster. 2015

Boehm-Bawerk, Eugen von: Karl Marx and the Close of His System: A Criticism (Classic Reprint). Forgotten Books. 2012

Boehm-Bawerk, Eugen von: Positive Theory of Capital. Ludwig von Mises Institute. 2007

Bostroum, Nick: Superintelligence: Paths, Dangers, Strategies. Oxford University Press 2016

Boetie, Etienne de la: The Politics of Obedience: The Discourse of Voluntary Servitude. With an Introduction by Murray Rothbard. Ludwig von Mises Insitute. 2015

Boettke, Peter J.: Living Economics: Yesterday, Today, and Tomorrow (Independent Studies in Political Economy). Independent Institute. 2012

Boettke, Peter J.: Calculation and Coordination: Essays on Socialism and Transitional Political Economy (Routledge Foundations of the Market Economy). Routledge 2001

Boettke, Peter J.: The Oxford Handbook of Austrian Economics (Oxford Handbooks). Oxford University Press. 2015

Boettke, Peter J.: The Political Economy of Soviet Socialism: the Formative Years, 1918-1928. 1990th Edition. Springer 1990

Boldrin, Michele and David K. Levine. Against Intellectual Monopoly. Cambridge University Press. 2010

Bourdieu, Pierre: On the State: Lectures at the College de France, 1989 - 1992. Polity 2015

Bouricius, Terry: (S)election: Sortition, the democratic alternative (Fomite Interrogations: A Series of Tracts for Our Time) (Volume 6). Fomite Publishers 2017

Boyes, William J.: Managerial Economics: Markets and the Firm (Upper Level Economics Titles). South-Western College Publications. 2011

Brafman, Ori and Rod A. Becksstrom: The Starfish and the Spider: The Unstoppable Power of Leaderless Organizations. Portfolio. 2008

Brafman, Ori and Rod A. Becksstrom: The Starfish and the Spider: The Unstoppable Power of Leaderless Organizations. Portfolio. 2008

Brackins, Daniel Alexander: Private Property, the Law, and the State. CreateSpace Independent Publishing Platform. 2017

Braun, Eduard: Finance behind the Veil of Money. CreateSpace Independent Publishing Platform. 2016

Brennan, Jason: Against Democracy. Princeton University Press. 2016

Brick, Howard: Transcending Capitalism: Visions of a New Society in Modern American Thought. Cornell University Press. 2016

Brynjolfsson, Eric and Andrew McAfee: The Second Machine Age: Work, Progress, and Prosperity in a Time of Brilliant Technologies. W. W. Norton & Company. 2016

Buchanan, James and Richard Wagner: Democracy in Deficit. The Legacy of Lord Keynes. Emerald Group Publishing. 1977

Burnheim, John: The Demarchy Manifesto. For Better Public Policy (Societas). Imprint Academic 2016

Burnheim, John: Is Democracy Possible? The Alternative to Electoral Politics. University of California Press. 1985

Burnheim, John: The Demarchy Manifesto: For Better Public Policy (Societas). Imprint Academic. 2016

Bylund, Per L.: The Problem of Production: A new theory of the firm. Routledge 2015

Cachanosky, Nicolas: Monetary Equilibrium and Nominal Income Targeting (Routledge International Studies in Money and Banking). Routledge. 2018

Caplan, Bryan: The Case against Education: Why the Education System Is a Waste of Time and Money. Princeton University Press. 2018

Caplan, Bryan: The Myth of the Rational Voter: Why Democracies Choose Bad Policies. Princeton University Press. 2008

Chafuen, Alejandro A.: Faith and Liberty: The Economic Thought of the Late Scholastics (Studies in Ethics and Economics). Lexington Books. 2003

Christinsen, Clayton M.: The Innovator's Dilemma: When New Technologies Cause Great Firms to Fail (Management of Innovation and Change). Harvard Business Review Press. 2016

Clark, Gregory: A Farewell to Alms: A Brief Economic History of the World (The Princeton Economic History of the Western World). Princeton University Press. 2009

Cogan, John F.: The High Cost of Good Intentions: A History of U.S. Federal Entitlement Programs. Princeton University Press. 2017

Conquest, Robert: The Great Terror: A Reassessment 40th anniversary Edition. Oxford University Press. 2007

Conquest, Robert: The Harvest of Sorrow: Soviet Collectivization and the Terror-Famine. Oxford University Press; Reprint edition. 1987

Cowen, Tyler and Alex Tabarrok: Modern Principles of Economics. Worth Publishers. 2014

Cowen, Tyler: Average Is Over: Powering America Beyond the Age of the Great Stagnation. Plume. 2014

Cowen, Tyler: The Great Stagnation: How America Ate All the Low-Hanging Fruit of Modern History, Got Sick, and Will (Eventually) Feel Better. Dutton 2011

Coyne, Christopher J. and Abigail R. Hall: Tyranny Comes Home: The Domestic Fate of U.S. Militarism. Stanford University Press. 2018

Cwick, Paul F.: An Investigation of Inverted Yield Curves and Economic Downturns. Ludwig von Mises Institute.

Dahlen, Michael: Ending Big Government: The Essential Case for Capitalism and Freedom. Mill City Press. 2016

Dalrymple, Theodore: Nothing but Wickedness: The Origins of the Decline of Our Culture. Gibson Square Books. 2018

Davidson, James Dale and William Rees-Mogg: The Sovereign Individual: Mastering the Transition to the Information Age. Touchstone. 1999

Delannoi, Gil and Oliver Dowlen (eds.): Sortition: Theory and Practice (Sortition and Public Policy). Imprint Academic. 2010

Deneen, Patrick J.: Why Liberalism Failed (Politics and Culture). Yale University Press. 2018

Diamandis, Peter H. and Steven Kotler: Abundance: The Future Is Better Than You Think. Free Press. Reprint edition. 2014

Di Iorio, Francesco: Cognitive Autonomy and Methodological Individualism: The Interpretative Foundations of Social Life (Studies in Applied Philosophy, Epistemology and Rational Ethics). Springer 2015

Dilorenzo Thomas J.: How Capitalism Saved America: The Untold History of Our Country, from the Pilgrims to the Present. Crown Forum. 2005

Dilorenzo, Thomas: The Problem with Socialism. Regnery Publishing. 2016

Doherty, Brian: Radicals for Capitalism: A Freewheeling History of the Modern American Libertarian Movement. Public Affairs. 2008

Dorn, James A. (ed.): Monetary Alternatives: Rethinking Government Fiat Money. Cato Institute 2017

Dorn, James A., Steve H. Hanke and Alan A. Sir Walters (eds.); The Revolution in Development Economics. Cato Institute. 1998

Dowlen, Oliver: The Political Potential of Sortition: A study of the random selection of citizens for public office (Sortition and Public Policy). Imprint Academic 2009

Drochon, Hugo: Nietzsche's Great Politics. Princeton University Press. 2016

Drucker, Peter: Innovation and Entrepreneurship. HarperBusiness. 2006

Easterbrook, Gregg: It's Better Than It Looks: Reasons for Optimism in an Age of Fear. PublicAffairs. 2018

Easterly, William R.: The Elusive Quest for Growth: Economists' Adventures and Misadventures in the Tropics. The MIT Press. 2002

Easterly, William: The White Man's Burden: Why the West's Efforts to Aid the Rest Have Done So Much Ill and So Little Good. Penguin. 2007

Easterly, William R.: The Tyranny of Experts: Economists, Dictators, and the Forgotten Rights of the Poor. Basic Books. 2015

Ebeling, Richard and Jacob G. Hornberger: The Failure of America's Foreign Wars. Future of Freedom Foundation. 1996

Ebeling, Richard M.: Monetary Central Planning and the State. The Future of Freedom Foundation. 2015

Emerson, Ralph Waldo: The Essential Writings of Ralph Waldo Emerson (Modern Library Classics). Modern Library. 2000

Eire, N. N. Carlos: Reformations: The Early Modern World, 1450-1650. Yale University Press. 2016

Eucken, Walter: The Foundations of Economics: History and Theory in the Analysis of Economic Reality. Springer. 2011

Eusepi, Guiseppe and Richard E. Wagner: Public Debt: An Illusion of Democratic Political Economy (New Thinking in Political Economy series). Edward Elgar Publications. 2017

Erhard, Ludwig: Prosperity Through Competition. Praeger. 1958

Ertel, Wolfgang: Introduction to Artificial Intelligence (Undergraduate Topics in Computer Science). Springer 2018

Evans, Anthony J.: Markets for Managers: A Managerial Economics Primer (The Wiley Finance Series). Wiley. 2014

Evans, Michelle and Augusto Zimmermann(eds.): Global Perspectives on Subsidiarity (Ius Gentium: Comparative Perspectives on Law and Justice). Springer 2014

Evans, Stanton M.: Stalin's Secret Agents: The Subversion of Roosevelt's Government. Threshold Editions. 2013

Ebeling, Richard: Austrian Economics and Public Policy. Restoring Freedom and Prosperity. The Future of Freedom Foundation. 2016

Ferguson, Niall: The Square and the Tower: Networks and Power, from the Freemasons to Facebook. Penguin Press. 2018

Ferguson, Niall: Civilization: The West and the Rest. Penguin Books. 2012

Fareed, Zakaria: The Future of Freedom: Illiberal Democracy at Home and Abroad (Revised Edition). W. W. Norton & Company. 2007

Feyerabend, Paul: Against Method. Verso. 2010

Folsom, Burton W.: The Myth of the Robber Barons: A New Look at the Rise of Big Business in America. Young America Foundation. 1991

Ford, Martin: The Rise of the Robots: Technology and the Threat of a Jobless Future. Basic Book. Reprint edition. 2015

Foss, Nikolai J. and Peter Klein (eds.): Entrepreneurship and the Firm: Austrian Perspectives on Economic Organization. Edward Elgar Publishing. 2002

Frank, Malcolm, Paul Roehrig, Ben Pring: What To Do When Machines Do Everything: How to Get Ahead in a World of AI, Algorithms, Bots, and Big Data. Wiley 2017

Friedman, David D.: The Machinery of Freedom: Guide to Radical Capitalism. CreateSpace Independent Publishing Platform; 3rd edition. 2015

Friedman, Milton and Anna Jacobson Schwartz: A Monetary History of the United States, 1867-1960. Princeton University Press. 1971

Friedman, Milton: Capitalism and Freedom. Fortieth Anniversary Edition. University of Chicago Press. 2002

Fukuyama, Francis: The Origins of Political Order: From Prehuman Times to the French Revolution. Farrar, Straus and Giroux. 2012

Garrison, Roger: Time and Money: The Macroeconomics of Capital Structure (Routledge Foundations of the Market Economy) New Edition. Routledge 2007

Gatto, John Taylor: The Underground History of American Education, Volume I: An Intimate Investigation Into the Prison of Modern Schooling. Valor Academy 2017

Guerin, Daniel (ed.): No Gods No Masters: An Anthology of Anarchism. AK Press 2005

Giddens, Anthony: The Third Way: The Renewal of Social Democracy. Polity Press. 1999

Giddens, Anthony: Capitalism and Modern Social Theory: An Analysis of the Writings of Marx, Durkheim and Max Weber. Cambridge University Press. 1973

Goodwin, Barbara: Justice by Lottery (Sortition and Public Policy). Imprint Academic 2005

Gordon, Robert J. : The Rise and Fall of American Growth: The U.S. Standard of Living since the Civil War (The Princeton Economic History of the Western World). Princeton University Press 2017

Gordon, David: An Austro-Libertarian View: Current Affairs, Foreign Policy, American History, European History (Essays by David Gordon). 3 vols. The Ludwig von Mises Institute. 2017

Granovetter, Marc: Society and Economy: Framework and Principles. Belknap Press: An Imprint of Harvard University Press. 2017

Grant, James: The Forgotten Depression: 1921: The Crash That Cured Itself. Simon & Schuster. 2014

Halberstam, Davin: The Best and the Brightest. Modern Library. 2002

Harford, Tim: Fifty Inventions that Shaped the Modern Economy. Riverhead Books. 2017

Harris, Fred and Alan Curtis (eds.): Healing Our Divided Society: Investing in America Fifty Years after the Kerner Report. Temple University Press. 2018

Haskel, Jonathan and Stian Westlake: Capitalism without Capital: The Rise of the Intangible. Princeton University Press. 2017

Hathaway, Oona A. and Scott J. Shapiro: The Internationalists: How a Radical Plan to Outlaw War Remade the World. Simon & Schuster. 2017

Hayek, Friedrich A. von: Individualism and Economic Order. University of Chicago Press. 1996

Hayek, Friedrich A. von: The Constitution of Liberty: The Definitive Edition (The Collected Works of F. A. Hayek). University of Chicago Press. 2011

Hayek, Friedrich A. von: The Road to Serfdom: Text and Documents -The Definitive Edition (The Collected Works of F. A. Hayek, Volume 2). University of Chicago Press. 2007

Hayek, Friedrich A.: Denationalisation of Money. The Argument Refined. CreateSpace Independent Publishing Platform. 2014

Hazlitt, Henry: Economics in One Lesson: The Shortest and Surest Way to Understand Basic Economics. Crown Business. 1988

Hazlitt, Henry: The Failure of the New Economics. Martino Fine Books. 2016

Heidegger, Martin: The Question Concerning Technology, and Other Essays (Harper Perennial Modern Thought). Harper Perennial Modern Classics; Reissue edition. 2013

Hennig, Brett: The End of Politicians: Time for a Real Democracy. Unbound Digital. 2017

Herbener, Jeffrey M. : Pure Time-Preference Theory of Interest. Ludwig von Mises Institute. 2011

Heyne, Paul L., Peter J. Boettke, and David L. Prychito: The Economic Way of Thinking. Pearson Series in Economics. 2013

Hicks, Stephen, R. C.: Explaining Postmodernism: Skepticism and Socialism from Rousseau to Foucault (Expanded Edition). Ockham's Razor Publishers. 2011

Higgs, Robert: Against Leviathan: Government Power and a Free Society (Independent Studies in Political Economy). Independent Institute. 2004

Higgs, Robert: Crisis and Leviathan: Critical Episodes in the Growth of American Government, 25th Anniversary Edition (Independent Studies in Political Economy). Independent Institute; Anniversary edition. 2013

Higgs, Robert: Depression, War, and Cold War: Studies in Political Economy. Oxford University Press. 2006

Higgs, Robert: Taking a Stand: Reflections on Life, Liberty, and the Economy. Independent Institute. 2015

Hirschman, Albert O.: The Passions and the Interests. Political Arguments before its Triumph (Princeton Classics). Princeton University. 2013

Hirschmann, Albert O.: Exit, Voice, and Loyalty: Responses to Decline in Firms, Organizations, and States. Harvard University Press 1970

Holcombe, Randall G.: Advanced Introduction to Public Choice (Elgar Advanced Introductions series). Edward Elgar Publishers. 2016

Holcombe, Randall G.: Advanced Introduction to the Austrian School of Economics (Elgar Advanced Introductions series). Edgar Elgar Publishers. 2014

Holcombe, Randall G.: Producing Prosperity: An Inquiry into the Operation of the Market Process (Routledge Foundations of the Market Economy). Routledge 2015

Holcombe, Randall G.: Entrepreneurship and Economic Progress (Routledge Foundations of the Market Economy). Routledge 2006

Hoppe, Hans-Hermann: A Short History of Man: Progress and Decline. Ludwig von Mises Institute 2015

Hoppe, Hans-Hermann: A Theory of Socialism and Capitalism. Ludwig von Mises Institute. 2003

Hoppe, Hans-Hermann: Democracy. The God that Failed: Economics and Politics of Monarchy, Democracy and Natural Order (Perspectives on Democratic Practice. Routledge. 2001

Hoppe, Hans-Hermann: The Economics and Ethics of Private Property: Studies in Political Economy and Philosophy, 2nd Edition. Ludwig von Mises Institute. 2010

Hoppe, Hans-Herman: The Myth of National Defense: Essays on the Theory and History of Security Production. Ludwig von Mises Institute. 2003

Horwitz, Steve: Hayek's Modern Family: Classical Liberalism and the Evolution of Social Institutions. Palgrave Macmillan. 2015

Howden, David and Joseph T. Salerno (eds.): The Fed at One Hundred: A Critical View on the Federal Reserve System. Springer. 2014

Huebert, Jacob H.: Libertarianism Today. Praeger 2010

Huerta de Soto, Jesus: Money, Bank Credit, and Economic Cycles. Ludwig von Mises Institute. 2012

Hülsmann, Jörg Guido and Stephan Kinsella (eds.): Property, Freedom, and Society: Essays in Honor of Hans-Hermann Hoppe (LvMI). Ludwig von Mises Institute 2011

Hülsmann, Jörg Guido: The Ethics of Money Production. Ludwig von Mises Institute. 2008

Humboldt, Wilhelm von: The Sphere and Duties of Government (The Limits of State Action). Martino Fine Books. 2014

Illich, Ivan: Deschooling Society (Open Forum S). Marion Boyars Publishers Ltd; New edition edition. 2000

Illich, Ivan: Limits to Medicine: Medical Nemesis, the Expropriation of Health. Marion Boyars Publishers Ltd; Revised ed. Edition. 2000

Infantino, Lorenzo: Individualism in Modern Thought: From Adam Smith to Hayek (Routledge Studies in Social and Political Thought). Routledge 2014

Irwin, Douglas A.: Against the Tide. An Intellectual History of Free Trade. Princeton University Press. 1996

Joshi, Vijay: India's Long Road: The Search for Prosperity. Oxford University Press. 2017

Juma, Calestous: Innovation and Its Enemies: Why People Resist New Technologies. Oxford University Press. 2016

Kant, Imanuel and H.S. Reiss (ed). Kant: Political Writings (Cambridge Texts in the History of Political Thought). Cambridge University Press. 1991

Kealey, Terence: The Case Against Public Science. Cato Unbound. August 2013

Kealey, Terence: The Economic Laws of Scientific Research. Palgrave Macmillan. 1996

Kengor, Paul: The Politically Incorrect Guide to Communism (The Politically Incorrect Guides). Regnery Publishing 2017

Kenny, Charles: Getting Better: Why Global Development Is Succeeding - And How We Can Improve the World Even More. Basic Books. 2012

Keynes, John Maynard: The General Theory of Employment, Interest and Money: With the Economic Consequences of the Peace (Classics of World Literature). Wordworth Editions 2017

Kinsella, Stephan: Against Intellectual Property. Ludwig von Mises Institute. 2015

Kirzner, Israel: Competition and Entrepreneurship (The Collected Works of Israel M. Kirzner). Liberty Fund. 2013

Knight, Frank: Risk, Uncertainty and Profit. Martino Fine Books. 2014

Kocka, Jürgen: Capitalism. A Short History. Princeton University Press. 2017

Kroeber, Arthur A.: China's Economy: What Everyone Needs to Know. Oxford University Press. 2016

Kuehnelt-Leddihn: Eric Ritter von: Liberty or Equality: The Challenge of Our Times. The Ludwig von Mises Institute. 2014

Kuehnelt-Leddihn: Eric Ritter von: Menace of the Herd or Procrustes at Large. Ludwig von Mises Institute. 2012

Kurer, Oskar: John Stuart Mill (Routledge Revivals): The Politics of Progress. Routledge 2018

Kurer, Oskar: The Political Foundations of Development Policies. UPA Publishers 1996

Kurlansky, Mark: Nonviolence: The History of a Dangerous Idea (Modern Library Chronicles). Modern Library 2008

Kurzweil, Ray: The Singularity Is Near: When Humans Transcend Biology. Penguin Books. 2006

Lavoie, Don: Rivalry and Central Planning. The Socialist Calculation Debate Reconsidered (Advanced Studies in Political Economy). Mercatus Center at George Mason University. 2015

Leeson, Peter: Anarchy Unbound: Why Self-Governance Works Better Than You Think (Cambridge Studies in Economics, Choice, and Society). Cambridge University Press. 2014

Leonard, Thomas C.: Illiberal Reformers: Race, Eugenics, and American Economics in the Progressive Era. Princeton University Press. 2017

Legutko, Ryszard: The Demon in Democracy: Totalitarian Temptations in Free Societies. Encounter Books. 2016

Lenin, Vladimir Ilich: State and Revolution. Martino Fine Books. 2011

Leoni, Bruno: Freedom and the Law. Liberty Fund. 1991

Lerch, Hubert: An Introduction to Political Philosophy. CreateSpace Independent Publishing Platform. 2011

Levin, Mark R.: Rediscovering Americanism: And the Tyranny of Progressivism. Threshold Editions. 2017

Levitsky, Steven and Daniel Zieblatt: How Democracies Die. Crown 2018

Lewis, Hunter: Economics in Three Lessons and One Hundred Economics Laws: Two Works in One Volume. Axios Press. 2017

Lewis, Hunter: Where Keynes Went Wrong: And Why World Governments Keep Creating Inflation, Bubbles, and Busts. Axios Press. 2009

Lilla, Mark: The Once and Future Liberal: After Identity Politics. Harper. 2017

Lindsay, Brink: The Age of Abundance: How Prosperity Transformed America's Politics and Culture. Harper Business Reprint edition. 2008

Lingle, Christopher: The Rise and Decline of the Asian Century: False Starts on the Path to the Global Millennium. Bookworld Services. 1998

Lingle, Christopher: The Rise and Decline of the Asian Century: False Starts on the Path to the Global Millennium. Bookworld Services. 1998

Machaj, Mateusz: Money, Interest, and the Structure of Production: Resolving Some Puzzles in the Theory of Capital (Capitalist Thought: Studies in Philosophy, Politics, and Economics). Lexington Books. 2017

Mallaby, Sebastian: The Man Who Knew: The Life and Times of Alan Greenspan. Penguin Books. 2017

Maltsev, Yuri: Requiem for Marx. CreateSpace Independent Publishing Platform. 1993

Maltsev, Yuri: Mass Murder and Public Slavery: The Soviet Experience. The Independent Review 2017

Mandeville, Bernard: The Fable of the Bees and Other Writings (Hackett Classics). Hacket Publishing Company. 1997

Marx, Karl: Das Kapital: A Critique of Political Economy. CreateSpace Independent Publishing Platform. 2011

Marx, Karl and Friedrich Engels: The Communist Manifesto. International Publishers Co; New edition. 2014

McCaffrey, Matthew: The Economic Theory of Costs: Foundations and New Directions (Routledge Frontiers of Political Economy). Routledge 2017

McCloskey, Deirdre: The Bourgeois Virtues: Ethics for an Age of Commerce. University of Chicago Press. 2007

McGroarty, Emmett, Jane Robbins, and Erin Tuttle: Deconstructing the Administrative State. Liberty Hill Publishing. 2017

McLuhan, Marshall: The Gutenberg Galaxy. University of Toronto Press, Scholarly Publishing Division. 2011

Menger, Carl: Principles of Economics. CreateSpace Independent Publishing Platform. 2007

Mencken, H. L.: Notes on Democracy. CreateSpace Independent Publishing Platform. 2013

Mesquita, Bruce Bueno de and Alistair Smith: The Dictator's Handbook: Why Bad Behavior is Almost Always Good Politics. PublicAffairs. 2012

Mierzejewski, Alfred C.: Ludwig Erhard: A Biography. University of North Carolina Press. 2014

Mill, John Stuart: On Liberty, Utilitarianism and Other Essays (Oxford World's Classics). Cambridge University Press. 2015

Miller, Tom: China's Asian Dream: Empire Building along the New Silk Road. Zed Books. 2017

Mises, Ludwig von: Human Action. The Scholar's Edition. Ludwig von Mises Institute. 2010

Mises, Ludwig von: Liberalism. Liberty Fund. 2005

Mises, Ludwig von: Economic Calculation in the Socialist Commonwealth. Ludwig von Mises Institute. 2012

Mises, Ludwig von: Interventionism: An Economic Analysis (Lib Works Ludwig Von Mises PB). Liberty Fund. 2011

Mokyr, Joel: A Culture of Growth: The Origins of the Modern Economy (Graz Schumpeter Lectures). Princeton University Press 2016

Mokyr, Joel: Gift of Athena: Historical Origins of the Knowledge Economy. Princeton University Press 2014

Mokyr, Joel: The Lever of Riches: Technological Creativity and Economic Progress. Oxford University Press. 1992

Molyneux, Stefan: Practical Anarchy. The Freedom of the Future. CreateSpace Independent Publishing Platform. 2017

Mueller, Antony P.: Bubble or New Era? Monetary Aspects of the New Economy. In: Birner, Jack and Pierre Garrouste (eds): Markets, Information and Communication: Austrian Perspectives on the Internet Economy (Routledge Foundations of the Market Economy). Routledge. 2003, pp. 249-261

Muller, Jerry Z.: The Tyranny of Metrics. Princeton University Press. 2018

Muller, Jerry Z.: The Mind and the Market: Capitalism in Western Thought. Anchor. 2003

Murphy, Robert: The Politically Incorrect Guide to the Great Depression and the New Deal (The Politically Incorrect Guides). Regnery Publishing. 2009

Murphy, Robert: Choice: Cooperation, Enterprise, and Human Action. Independent Institute. 2015

Molinari, Gustave de: The Production of Security. Edited by Richard Ebeling with an Introduction by Murray Rothbard. Create Space. 2009

Murray, Charles: In Our Hands: A Plan to Replace the Welfare State. AEI Press. 2016

Murray, Charles: By the People: Rebuilding Liberty Without Permission. Crown Forum. 2015

Murray, Charles: Losing Ground: American Social Policy, 1950-1980. Basic Books. 2015

Nietzsche, Friedrich: The Will to Power. Independently published. 2017

Niskanen, William A.: Reaganomics: An Insider's Account of the Policies and the People. Oxford University Press. 1988

Norberg, Johan: Ten Reasons to Look Forward to the Future. Oneworld Publication. 2017

North, Douglas C. and Robert Paul Thomas: The Rise of the Western World: A New Economic History. Cambridge University Press. 1976

North, Douglass C.: Institutions, Institutional Change and Economic Performance (Political Economy of Institutions and Decisions) Cambridge University Press. 1990

North, Gary: Mises on Money. Ludwig von Mises Institute. 2012

Novak, Michael and Paul Adams: Social Justice Isn't What You Think It Is. Encounter Books. 2015

Nozick, Robert: Anarchy, State, and Utopia. Basic Books Reprint. 2013

O'Driscoll, Gerald P. and Maria Rizzo: The Economics of Time and Ignorance. Routledge Foundations of the Market Economy. Routledge 1996

OECD (Organization for Economic Cooperation and Development: The Sources of Economic Growth in OECD Countries. OECD 2003

Oliver, Michael J.: The New Libertarianism: Anarcho-Capitalism. CreateSpace. 2013

Olson, Mancur: The Logic of Collective Action. Public Goods and the Theory of Groups. Second printing with new preface and appendix (Harvard Economic Studies). Harvard University Press. 1971

Oppenheimer, Franz: The State: Its History and Development Viewed Sociologically. (Classic Reprint). Forgotten Books. 2012

O'Rourke, P. J.: Parliament of Whores: A Lone Humorist Attempts to Explain the Entire U.S. Government. Grove Press. 2003

O'Rourke, P. J.: Eat the Rich: A Treatise on Economics. Atlantic Monthly Press. 1999

Ortega y Gasset, José: The Revolt of the Masses. W. W. Norten & Company. 1994

Ostrom, Elinor: Governing the Commons: The Evolution of Institutions for Collective Action (Canto Classics). Cambridge University Press; Reissue edition. 2015

Ostrowski, James: Progressivism: A Primer on the Idea Destroying America. Cazenovia Books. 2014

Palmer, Tom: Realizing Freedom: Libertarian Theory, History, and Practice. Cato Institute. 2014

Palmer, Tom G, Virginia Prostel, Brink Lindsey, and Tyler Cowen: Libertarianism. Past and Prospects (Cato Unbound Book 32007). Cato Institute. 2007

Parijs, Philippe Van and Yannick Vanderborght: Basic Income: A Radical Proposal for a Free Society and a Sane Economy. Harvard University Press. 2017

Paul, Ron: End the Fed. Grand Central Publishing. 2010

Paul, Ron: Revolution. A Manifesto. Grand Central Publishing. 2009

Pesek, William: Japanization: What the World Can Learn from Japan's Lost Decades. Wiley 2014

Phelps, Edmund: Mass Flourishing. How Grassroots Innovation Creates Jobs, Challenge, and Change. Princeton University Press. 2015

Pilling, David: The Growth Delusion: Wealth, Poverty, and the Well-Being of Nations. Tim Duggan Books. 2018

Pinker, Steven: Enlightenment Now: The Case for Reason, Science, Humanism, and Progress. Viking 2018

Pinker, Steven: The Better Angels of Our Nature: Why Violence Has Declined. Penguin Books. 2012

Postrel, Virginia: The Future and Its Enemies: The Growing Conflict Over Creativity, Enterprise. Free Press. 2011

Powell, Benjamin: Out of Poverty: Sweatshops in the Global Economy (Cambridge Studies in Economics, Choice, and Society). Cambridge University Press. 2014

Powell, Jim: FDR's Folly: How Roosevelt and His New Deal Prolonged the Great Depression. Crown Forum. 2004

Powell, James and Paul Johnson: The Triumph of Liberty: A 2,000 Year History Told Through the Lives of Freedom's Greatest Champions. Free Press. 2000

Qui, Insula: Capitalism Works. Independently published. 2018

Rachels, Chase and Christopher Chase Rachels: A Spontaneous Order: The Capitalist Case for a Stateless Society. CreateSpace Independent Publishing Platform. 2015

Raico, Ralph: Classical Liberalism and the Austrian School. CreateSpace Independent Publishing Platform. 2012

Raico, Ralph: Great Wars and Great Leaders: A Libertarian Rebuttal. Ludwig von Mises Institute. 2015

Ratner-Rosenhagen, Jennifer: American Nietzsche: A History of an Icon and His Ideas. University of Chicago Press; Reprint edition. 2012

Rawls, John: Justice as Fairness: A Restatement. Belknap Press: An Imprint of Harvard University Press. 2001

Rand, Ayn: Capitalism. The Unknown Ideal. Signet; Reissue edition. 1986

Reed, Lawrence R.: Great Myth of the Great Depression. Foundation for Economic Education. 2015

Reisman, George: Capitalism. A Treatise on Economics. TJS Books 1996

Reisman, George: The Government Against the Economy. Jameson Books. 1985

Reybrouck, David van: Against Elections. The Case for Democracy. Random House U.K. 2017

Reynolds, Morgan O.: Making America Poorer: The Cost of Labor Law. Cato Institute. 1987

Richman, Sheldon: America's Counter-Revolution: The Constitution Revisited. Grifien & Lash. 2016

Ridley, Matt: The Rational Optimist: How Prosperity Evolves. Harper Perennial. 2011

Rifkin, Jeremy: The Zero Marginal Cost Society: The Internet of Things, the Collaborative Commons, and the Eclipse of Capitalism. St. Martin's Griffin; Reprint edition. 2015

Ritenour, Shawn (ed.): The Mises Reader Unabridged. Ludwig von Mises Institute. 2016

Roberts, Paul Craig: The Tyranny of Good Intentions: How Prosecutors and Law Enforcement Are Trampling the Constitution in the Name of Justice. Crown. 2008

Rockwell, Llewellyn, H. Jr.: Against the State. An Anarcho-Capitalist Manifesto. Rockwell Communication. 2014

Rosenberg, Nathan and L. E. Birdzell: How the West Grew Rich: The Economic Transformation Of The Industrial World. Basic Books. 1987

Rosling, Hans, Anna Rosling Rönnlund, Ola Rosling: Factfulness: Ten Reasons We're Wrong About the World--and Why Things Are Better Than You Think. Flatiron Books 2018

Rothbard, Murray N.: Anatomy of the State. Bhpublishing. 2014

Rothbard, Murray N.: For a New Liberty. The Libertarian Manifesto. CreateSpace Independent Publishing Platform. 2006

Rothbard, Murray N.: What Has Government Done to Our Money? Ludwig von Mises Institute. 2015

Rothbard, Murray N.: Man, Economy, and State with Power and Market, Scholar's Edition. Ludwig von Mises Institute. 2011

Rothbard, Murray N.: America's Great Depression. Ludwig von Mises Institute. 2000

Rummel, Rudy J.: Death by Government: Genocide and Mass Murder Since 1900. Routledge 1997

Rummel, Rudy J.: The Blue Book of Freedom: Ending Famine, Poverty, Democide, and War. Cumberland House Publishing. 2007

Salerno, Joseph T.: Money: Sound and Unsound. Ludwig von Mises Institute. 2015

Say, Jean-Baptiste: A Treatise on Political Economy: Or the Production, Distribution and Consumption of Wealth. CreateSpace Independent Publishing Platform. 2013

Schiff, Peter: How an Economy Grows and Why It Crashes. Wiley. 2010

Schmitt, Carl: The Leviathan in the State Theory of Thomas Hobbes: Meaning and Failure of a Political Symbol (Heritage of Sociology). University of Chicago Press Ed Edition. 2008

Schmitt, Carl: The Concept of the Political: Expanded Edition Enlarged Edition with a Commentary by Leo Strauss. The University of Chicago Press. 2007

Schoolland, Ken: The Adventures of Jonathan Gullible. A Free Market Odyssey. Liberty Publishing. 2011

Schumpeter, Joseph A.: Business Cycles: A Theoretical, Historical, and Statistical Analysis of the Capitalist Process (2 Vols.). Martino Fine Books. 2017

Schumpeter, Joseph A.: Can Capitalism Survive?: Creative Destruction and the Future of the Global Economy. Harper Perennial Modern Classics. 2009

Schumpeter, Joseph A.: Capitalism, Socialism, and Democracy: Third Edition. Harper Perennial Modern Classics. 2008

Schumpeter, Joseph A.: Essays: On Entrepreneurs, Innovations, Business Cycles and the Evolution of Capitalism. Routledge 1989

Schumpeter, Joseph A.: Theory of Economic Development (Social Science Classics Series). Routledge 1981

Schwab, Klaus and Nicholas Davis, Satya Nadella: Shaping the Fourth Industrial Revolution. World Economic Forum. 2018

Scruton, Roger: Fools, Frauds and Firebrands: Thinkers of the New Left. Bloomsbury Continuum. 2017

Selgin, George: Financial Stability without Central Banks. London Publishing Partnership. 2018

Selgin, George: Money: Free and Unfree. Cato Institute. 2017

Selgin, George: Less Than Zero. The Case for a Falling Price Level in a Growing Economy. CreateSpace Independent Publishing Platform. 2014

Selgin, George: The Theory of Free Banking. Rowman & Littlefield Publisher. 1988

Sen, Amartya: Development as Freedom. Anchor. 2000

Sévillia, Jean: Le terrorisme intellectuel (French Edition). Tempus Perrain. 2017

Shaffer, Butler: Boundaries of Order: Private Property as a Social System. CreateSpace Independent Publishing Platform. 2009

Shaffer, Buttler: The Wizards of Ozymandias: Reflections on the Decline and Fall. CreateSpace Independent Publishing Platform. 2012

Shlae, Amity: The Forgotten Man: A New History of the Great Depression Harper Perennial. 2008

Simon, Julian Lincoln: The Ultimate Resource 2. Princeton University Press. 1998

Sintomer, Yves: Das demokratische Experiment: Geschichte des Losverfahrens in der Politik von Athen bis heute (German Edition). Springer 2016

Smiley, Gene: Rethinking the Great Depression (American Ways). Ivan R. Dee Publisher. 2003

Smith, Adam: The Theory of Moral Sentiments. Digireads.com. 2010

Smith, Adam: The Wealth of Nations (Bantam Classics). Bantam Classics; Annotated edition. 2003

Snyder, Timothy: On Tyranny: Twenty Lessons from the Twentieth Century. Tim Duggan Books. 2017

Sombart, Werner: The Quintessence Of Capitalism: A Study Of The History And Psychology Of The Modern Business Man. Scholar Select. Andesite Press. 2017

Solzhenitsyn, Aleksandr: The Gulag Archipelago. The Harvill Press. 2003

Soto, Hernando de: The Mystery of Capital: Why Capitalism Triumphs in the West and Fails Everywhere Else. Basic Books. 2003

Sowell, Thomas: Basic Economics. Basic Books. 2014

Sowell, Thomas: Economic Facts and Fallacies. Basic Books. 2011

Sowell, Thomas: The Quest for Cosmic Justice. Free Press 2002

Spencer, Herbert: Social Statics: Or, The Conditions Essential to Human Happiness Specified and the First of them Developed. Nabu Press. 2011

Srinivasa, Bhu: Americana: A 400-Year History of American Capitalism. Penguin Press. 2017

Steil, Ben: The Marshall Plan: Dawn of the Cold War. Simon & Schuster. 2018

Steil, Ben: The Battle of Bretton Woods: John Maynard Keynes, Harry Dexter White, and the Making of a New World Order (Council on Foreign Relations Books). Princeton University Press. 2014

Stirner, Max: The Ego and His Own: The Case of the Individual Against Authority (Dover Books on Western Philosophy). Dover Publications. 2005

Stone, Peter: Lotteries in Public Life: A Reader (Sortition and Public Policy). Imprint Academic. 2012

Stringham, Edward Peter: Private Governance: Creating Order in Economic and Social Life. Oxford University Press. 2015

Susskind, Richard and Daniel Susskind: The Future of the Professions: How Technology Will Transform the Work of Human Experts. Oxford University Press. Reprint edition. 2017

Suvorov, Viktor: Icebreaker. Who Started the Second World War? PL UK Publishing. 2012

Taleb, Nassim Nicholas: Skin in the Game: Hidden Asymmetries in Daily Life. Random House 2018

Taylor, Frederick: The Downfall of Money: Germany's Hyperinflation and the Destruction of the Middle Class. Bloomsbury Press. 2015

Taylor, Mark Zachary: The Politics of Innovation: Why Some Countries Are Better Than Others at Science and Technology. Oxford University Press. 2016

Thiel, Peter: Zero to One: Notes on Startups, or How to Build the Future. Currency Publishers. 2014

Thornton, Mark: The Bastiat Collection. Ludwig von Mises Institute. 2017

Thornton, Mark: The Economics of Prohibition. Ludwig von Mises Institute. 2014

Tilly, Charles: Coercion, Capital and European States, A.D. 990 – 1992. Wiley-Blackwell. 1992

Tirole, Jean: Economics for the Common Good. Princeton University Press. 2017

Tooley, Hunt: The Great War: Western Front and Home Front. Palgrave 2015

Tucker, Jeffrey: A Beautiful Anarchy: How to Create Your Own Civilization in the Digital Age. Laissez Faire Books. 2012

Vance, Laurence M.: War, Empire, and the Military: Essays on the Follies of War and U.S. Foreign Policy. Vance Publications. 2014

Vedder, Richard: Going Broke By Degree: Why College Cost. AEI Press. 2004

Veryser, Harry C.: It Didn't Have to be This Way: Why Boom and Bust Is Unncessary – and How the Austrian School of Economics Breaks the Cycle (Culture of Enterprise).ISI Books.2013

Volcker, Paul and Toyoo Gyohten. Changing Fortunes. Crown. 1992

Walsh, Michael: The Devil's Pleasure Palace: The Cult of Critical Theory and the Subversion of the West. Encounter Books. 2017

White, Lawrence: The Clash of Economic Ideas: The Great Policy Debates and Experiments of the Last Hundred Years. Cambridge University Press. 2012

White, Lawrence: The Theory of Monetary Institutions. Wiley-Blackwell. 1999

White, Lawrence: Competition and Currency: Essays on Free Banking and Money. New York University Press. 1992

Wisniewski, Jakub: The Economics of Law, Order, and Action: The Logic of Public Goods (Routledge Advances in Heterodox Economics). Routledge. 2018

Williams, Walter E.: American Contempt for Liberty (Hoover Institution Press Publication). Hoover Institution Press 2015 Williams, Walter E.: Race & Economics: How Much Can Be Blamed on Discrimination?. Hoover Institution Press. 2011

Wolfram, Gary: A Capitalist Manifesto: Understanding The Market Economy And Defending Liberty. Dunlap Goddard. 2013

Woods, Thomas E.: Meltdown: A Free-Market Look at Why the Stock Market Collapsed, the Economy Tanked, and Government Bailouts Will Make Things Worse. Regnery 2009

Yergin, Daniel and Joseph Stanislaw: The Commanding Heights: The Battle for the World Economy. Free Press. 2002

Zelmanovitz, Leonidas: The Ontology and Function of Money: The Philosophical Fundamentals of Monetary Institutions (Capitalist Thought: Studies in Philosophy, Politics, and Economics). Lexington Books 2015

Appendix

Anarcho-Capitalism: An Annotated Bibliography
by Hans-Hermann Hoppe

Here is the essential reading on anarcho-capitalism, which might also be called the natural order, private-property anarchy, ordered anarchy, radical capitalism, the private-law society, or society without a state. This is not intended to be a comprehensive list. Indeed, only English-language works currently in print or forthcoming are included. Please note that suggestions are welcome, especially for Section IV: Congenial Writings.

I. Murray N. Rothbard and Austro-Libertarianism

At the top of any reading list on anarcho-capitalism must be the name Murray N. Rothbard. There would be no anarcho-capitalist movement to speak of without Rothbard. His work has inspired and defined the thinking even of such libertarians such as R. Nozick, for instance, who have significantly deviated from Rothbard, whether methodologically or substantively. Rothbard's entire work is relevant to the subject of anarcho-capitalism, but centrally important are:

The Ethics of Liberty, the most comprehensive presentation and defense of a libertarian law code yet written. Grounded in the tradition of natural law and in its style of axiomatic-deductive reasoning, Rothbard explains the concepts of human rights, self-ownership, original appropriation, contract, aggression, and punishment. He demonstrates the moral unjustifiability of the state, and offers smashing refutations of prominent limited-statist libertarians such as L. v. Mises, F. A. Hayek, I. Berlin, and R. Nozick.

In For A New Liberty Rothbard applies abstract libertarian principles to solve current welfare-state problems. How would a stateless society provide for goods such as education, money, streets, police, courts, national defense, social security, environmental protection, etc.? Here are the answers.

Power and Market is the most comprehensive theoretical analysis of the inefficiencies and counterproductive effects of every conceivable form of government interference with the market, from price controls, compulsory cartels, anti-trust laws, licenses, tariffs, child labor laws, patents, to any form of taxation (including Henry George's proposed "single tax" on ground land).

Egalitarianism As a Revolt Against Nature is a marvelous collection of Rothbard essays on philosophical, economic, and historical aspects of libertarianism, ranging from war and revolution to kids' and women's liberation. Rothbard shows his intellectual debt both to Ludwig von Mises and Austrian economics (praxeology) and to Lysander Spooner and Benjamin Tucker and individualist-anarchist political philosophy. This collection is the best single introduction to Rothbard and his libertarian research program.

The four-volume <u>Conceived in Liberty</u> is a comprehensive narrative history of colonial America and the role of libertarian ideas and movements. Rothbard's magisterial two-volume **An Austrian Perspective on the History of Economic Thought** traces the development of libertarian economic and philosophical thought throughout intellectual history. <u>The Irrepressible Rothbard</u> contains delightful libertarian commentary on political, social, and cultural issues, written during the last decade of Rothbard's life.

Justin Raimondo has written an insightful biography: **Murray N. Rothbard: An Enemy of the State**.

The Austro-libertarian tradition inaugurated by Rothbard is continued by <u>Hans-Hermann Hoppe</u>. In <u>Democracy — The God That Failed</u> Hoppe compares monarchy favorably to democracy, but criticizes both as ethically and economically inefficient, and advocates a natural order with competitive security and insurance suppliers. He revises fundamental orthodox historical interpretations, and reconsiders central questions of libertarian strategy. <u>The Economics and Ethics of Private Property</u> includes Hoppe's axiomatic defense of the principle of self-ownership and original appropriation: anyone arguing against these principles is involved in a performative or practical contradiction.

<u>The Myth of National Defense</u> is a collection of essays by an international assembly of social scientists concerning the relationship between State and war and the possibility of non-statist property defense: by militias, mercenaries, guerrillas, protection-insurance agencies, etc.

II. Alternative Approaches to Anarcho-Capitalism

The following authors come to similar conclusions but reach them in different ways and varying styles. While Rothbard and Hoppe are natural-rightsers of sorts and praxeologists, there exist also utilitarian, deontic, empiricist, historicist, positivist, and plain eclectic defenders of anarcho-capitalism.

Randy E. Barnett's <u>The Structure of Liberty</u> is an outstanding discussion of the requirements of a liberal-libertarian society from the viewpoint of a lawyer and legal theorist. Heavily influenced by F.A. Hayek, Barnett uses the term "polycentric constitutional order" for anarcho-capitalism.

Bruce L. Benson's <u>The Enterprise of Law</u> is the most comprehensive empirical-historical study of anarcho-capitalism. Benson provides abundant empirical evidence for the efficient operation of market-produced law and order. Benson's sequel <u>To Serve and Protect</u> is likewise to be recommended.

David D. Friedman's <u>The Machinery of Freedom</u> presents the utilitarian case for anarcho-capitalism: brief, easy to read, and with many applications from education to property protection.

Anthony de Jasay favors a deontic approach to ethics. His writing — in <u>The State</u>, in <u>Choice, Contract, Consent</u>, and the excellent essay collection <u>Against Politics</u> — is theoretical, with a neo-classical, game-theoretic flavor. Brilliant critic of public choice and constitutional economics — and the notion of minarchism.

Morris and Linda Tannehill's The Market for Liberty has a distinctly Randian flavor. However, the authors employ Ayn Rand's pro-state argument in support of the opposite, anarchistic conclusion. Outstanding yet much neglected analysis of the operation of competing security producers (insurers, arbitrators, etc.).

III. Precursors of Modern Anarcho-Capitalism

The contemporary anarcho-capitalist intellectual movement has a few outstanding 19th and early-20th century precursors. Even when sometimes deficient — the issue of ground land ownership in the tradition of Herbert Spencer and the theory of money and interest in the Spooner-Tucker tradition — the following titles remain indispensable and largely unsurpassed. (This listing is chronological and systematic, rather than alphabetical.)

Gustave de Molinari's pathbreaking 1849 article The Production of Security is probably the single most important contribution to the modern theory of anarcho-capitalism. Molinari argues that monopoly is bad for consumers, and that this also holds in the case of a monopoly of protection. Demands competition in the area of security production as for every other line of production.

Herbert Spencer's Social Statics is an outstanding philosophical discussion of natural rights in the tradition of John Locke. Spencer defends the right to ignore the state. Also highly recommended are his Principles of Ethics.

Auberon Herbert is a student of Spencer. In The Right and Wrong of Compulsion by the State, Herbert develops the Spencerian idea of equal freedom to its logically consistent anarcho-capitalist end. Herbert is the father of Voluntaryism.

Lysander Spooner is a 19th-century American lawyer and legal theorist. No one who has read "No Treason," included in **The Lysander Spooner Reader**, will ever see government with the same eyes. Spooner makes mincemeat of the idea of a social contract.

A concise history of individualist-anarchist thought and the related movement in 19th-century America, with particular attention to Spooner and Benjamin Tucker, is James J. Martin's Men Against the State.

Franz Oppenheimer is a left-anarchist German sociologist. In The State he distinguishes between the economic (peaceful and productive) and the political (coercive and parasitic) means of wealth acquisition, and explains the state as instrument of domination and exploitation.

Albert J. Nock is influenced by Franz Oppenheimer. In Our Enemy, the State he explains the anti-social, predatory nature of the state, and draws a sharp distinction between government as voluntarily acknowledged authority and the State. Nock in turn influenced Frank Chodorov, who would influence young Murray Rothbard. In his Fugitive Essays, a collection of pro-market, anti-state political and economic commentary, Chodorov attacks taxation as robbery.

IV. Congenial Writings

While not directly concerned with the subject of anarcho-capitalism and written by less-than-radical libertarian or even non-libertarian authors, the following are invaluable for a profound understanding of liberty, natural order, and the state.

John V. Denson's <u>The Costs of War</u> is a collection of essays by a distinguished group of libertarian and paleo-conservative scholars from various disciplines. Exposes the aggressive nature of the state. Possibly the most powerful anti-war book ever. Also to be recommended is Denson's collection <u>Reassessing the Presidency</u> on the growth of state power.

David Gordon's <u>Secession, State, and Liberty</u> is a collection of essays by contemporary philosophers, economists, and historians in defense of the right to secession.

<u>Friedrich A. Hayek</u>, <u>Law, Legislation, and Liberty</u>, Vol. I, is an important study on the "spontaneous" evolution of law, and the distinction of law versus legislation and between private and public law.

Bertrand de Jouvenel, <u>On Power</u>, is an outstanding account of the growth of state power, with many important insights concerning the role of the aristocracy as defender of liberty and mass democracy as a promoter of state power. Related, and likewise to be recommended is his <u>Sovereignty</u>.

Etienne de la Botie, <u>The Politics of Obedience</u>, is the classic 16th-century inquiry into the source of government power. La Botie shows that the state's power rests exclusively on public "opinion." By implication, every state can be made to crumble — instantly and without any violence — simply by virtue of a change in public opinion.

Bruno Leoni, <u>Freedom and the Law</u>, is an earlier and in some regards superior treatment of topics similar to those discussed by Hayek. Leoni portrays Roman law as something discovered by independent judges rather than enacted or legislated by central authority — and thus akin to English common law.

Robert Nisbet, <u>The Quest for Community</u> (formerly published under the more descriptive title Community and Power) explains the protective function of intermediate social institutions, and the tendency of the state to weaken and destroy these institutions in order to gain total control over the isolated individual.

<u>The Journal of Libertarian Studies. An Interdisciplinary Quarterly Review</u>, founded by Murray N. Rothbard and now edited by Hans-Hermann Hoppe, is an indispensable resource for any serious student of anarcho-capitalism and libertarian scholarship

The following JLS articles are most directly concerned with anarcho-capitalism.

Anderson, Terry, and P.J. Hill, <u>The American Experiment in Anarcho-Capitalism</u>, 3, 1.

Barnett, Randy E., <u>Whither Anarchy? Has Robert Nozick Justified the State?</u>, 1,1.

—, Toward a Theory of Legal Naturalism, 2, 2.

Benson, Bruce L., Enforcement of Private Property Rights in Primitive Societies, 9,1.

—, Customary Law with Private Means of Resolving Disputes and Dispensing Justice, 9,2.

—, Reciprocal Exchange as the Basis for Recognition of Law, 10, 1.

—, Restitution in Theory and Practice, 12, 1.

Block, Walter, Free Market Transportation: Denationalizing the Roads, 3, 2.

—, Hayek's Road to Serfdom, 12, 2.

Childs, Roy A. Jr., The Invisible Hand Strikes Back, 1,1.

Cuzan, Alfred G., Do We Ever Really Get Out Of Anarchy?, 3, 2.

Davidson, James D., Note on Anarchy, State, and Utopia, 1, 4.

Eshelman, Larry, Might versus Right, 12, 1.

Evers, Williamson M., Toward a Reformulation of the Law of Contracts, 1, 1.

—, The Law of Omissions and Neglect of Children, 2, 1.

Ferrara, Peter J., Retribution and Restitution: A Synthesis, 6, 2.

Fielding, Karl T., The Role of Personal Justice in Anarcho-Capitalism, 2, 3.

Grinder, Walter E., and John Hagel, III, Toward a Theory of State Capitalism, 1, 1.

Hart, David M., Gustave de Molinari and the Anti-Statist Liberal Tradition, 3 parts, 5, 3 to 6, 1.

Hoppe, Hans-Hermann, Fallacies of Public Goods Theory and the Production of Security, 9, 1.

—, Marxist and Austrian Class Analysis, 9, 2.

—, The Private Production of Defense, 14, 1.

Kinsella, N. Stephan, Punishment and Proportionality, 12, 1.

—, New Rationalist Directions in Libertarian Rights Theory, 12, 2.

—, Inalienability and Punishment, 14, 1.

Liggio, Leonard P., Charles Dunoyer and French Classical Liberalism, 1, 3.

Mack, Eric, Voluntaryism: The Political Thought of Auberon Herbert, 2, 4.

McElroy, Wendy, The Culture of Individualist Anarchism in Late 19th-Century America, 5, 3.

McGee, Robert W., Secession Reconsidered, 11, 1.

Osterfeld, David, Internal Inconsistencies in Arguments for Government: Nozick, Rand, Hospers, 4, 3.

—, Anarchism and the Public Goods Issue: Law, Courts, and the Police, 9, 1.

Paul, Jeffrey, Nozick, Anarchism, and Procedural Rights, 1, 4.

Peden, Joseph R., Property Rights in Celtic Irish Law, 1, 2.

Peterson, Steven A., Moral Development and Critiques of Anarchism, 8, 2.

Raico, Ralph, Classical Liberal Exploitation Theory, 1, 3.

Rothbard, Murray N., Robert Nozick and the Immaculate Conception of the State, 1, 1.

——, Concepts of the Role of Intellectuals in Social Change Toward Laissez Faire, 9, 2.

——, Nations by Consent: Decomposing the Nation-State, 11, 1.

Sanders, John T., The Free Market Model versus Government: A Reply to Nozick, 1, 1.

Smith, George H., Justice Entrepreneurship in a Free Market, 3, 4 (with comments by Steven Strasnick, Robert Formani and Randy Barnett and a reply by Smith, in the same issue).

Sneed, John D., Order without Law: Where will Anarchists Keep the Madmen?, 1, 2.

Stringham, Edward, Market Chosen Law, 14, 1.

Tinsley, Patrick, Private Police: A Note, 14,1.

Watner, Carl, The Proprietary Theory of Justice in the Libertarian Tradition, 6, 3—4.

Source:
https://www.lewrockwell.com/2001/12/hans-hermann-hoppe/anarcho-capitalism-2/

***

ABOUT THE AUTHOR

German-born Antony Peter Mueller is a professor of economics currently at the federal university UFS in Brazil.
Over his academic career, Antony P. Mueller held positions and did research at universities in Europe, the United States, where he was a Fulbright scholar, and Latin America.
His publications cover macroeconomics, monetary policy, sovereign risk analysis, social and economic policy issues, and economic and monetary integration.
Antony P. Mueller is a senior fellow of the American Institute of Economic Research (AIER), an associate scholar of the Ludwig von Mises Institute, USA, and a member by merit of the Brazilian Mises Institute (IMB).
He obtained his doctorate in economics summa cum laude from the University of Erlangen-Nuremberg, Germany.

Websites:
http://www.continentaleconomics.com/
http://capitalstudies.org/
Amazon author's page
https://www.amazon.com/-/e/B07BHF4RG8
CONTACT: antonymueller@gmx.com

Made in the USA
Middletown, DE
16 August 2020